THE PERSPECTIVE DRAWING GUIDE

SIMPLE TECHNIQUES FOR MASTERING EVERY ANGLE

SPENCER NUGENT

THE PERSPECTIVE DRAWING GUIDE:
SIMPLE TECHNIQUES FOR MASTERING EVERY ANGLE

SPENCER NUGENT

Editor: Kelly Reed
Project manager: Lisa Brazieal
Marketing coordinator: Katie Walker
Copyeditor: Joan Dixon
Interior layout: Hespenheide Design
Cover design: Aren Straiger
Cover images: Spencer Nugent

ISBN: 978-1-68198-903-7
1st Edition (1st printing, November 2022)
© 2023 Spencer Nugent

All images © Spencer Nugent unless otherwise noted.

Rocky Nook Inc.
1010 B Street, Suite 350
San Rafael, CA 94901
USA

www.rockynook.com

Distributed in the UK and Europe by Publishers Group UK
Distributed in the U.S. and all other territories by Ingram Publisher Services

Library of Congress Control Number: 2022937201

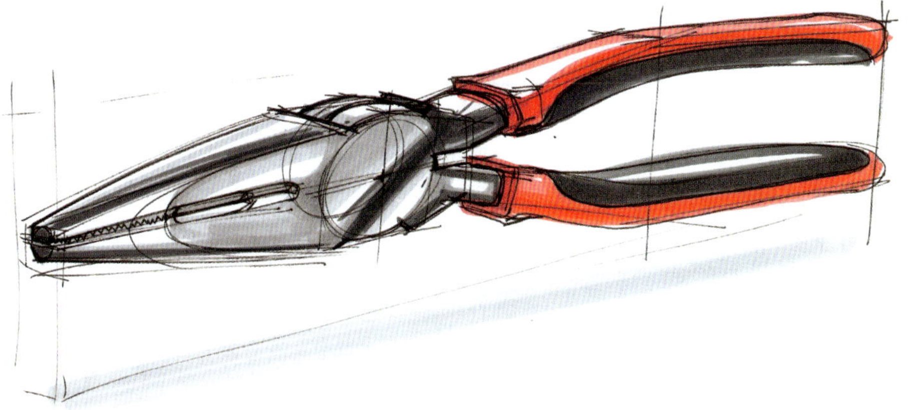

TABLE OF CONTENTS

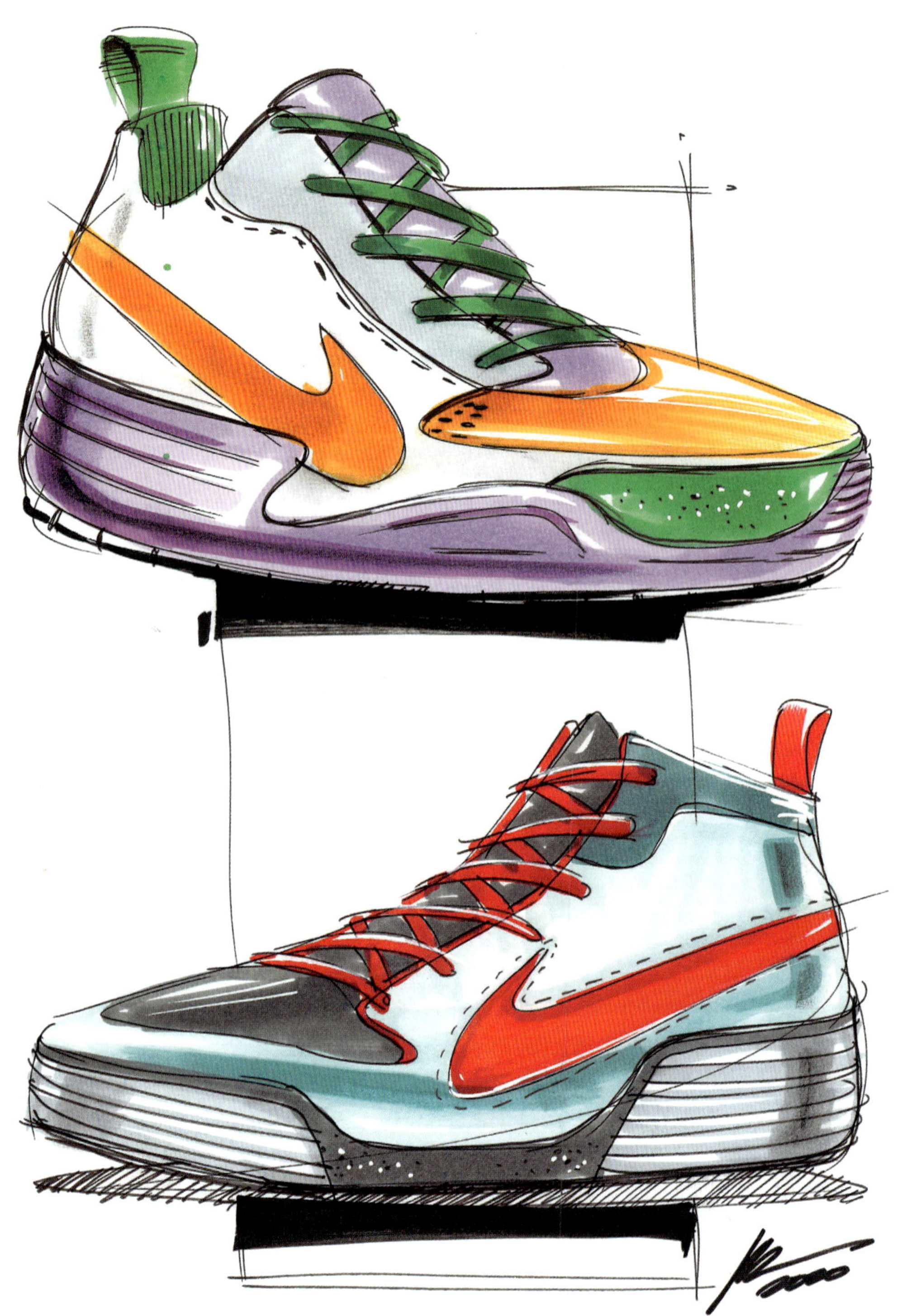

INTRODUCTION

"Passion is the process."

If you want to get good at something, you must commit to doing a little bit of it every day and must come to terms with initially being bad at it. Accepting that you will not be good right away is the first step, because it opens you up to the possibility of learning.

As a product designer, for example, I have to draw objects in perspective daily to capture ideas and explain concepts to clients and other designers. Communicating visually is almost a magical superpower in my field. Yet, drawing is a skill that took me many years to become comfortable with.

My father was a hobby artist, and daily while growing up I would see him paint and draw a variety of subjects on the veranda of our home in Jamaica. I was always inspired by his dedication and consistent practice at the craft of drawing and painting, but it wasn't until college that I realized I could turn my creativity and interest in visual communication into a career path that would be rewarding, satisfying, and ultimately transformative in my life.

I actually started studying math, computer science, and physics. As I transitioned into studying industrial design, I found myself feeling anxious and sometimes confused at drawing as a practice. Up until that point, I had mostly just doodled crude visualizations in my notes to help me understand complex concepts. Suddenly, I had to learn how to see things so that I could draw those things. If I couldn't figure out how to communicate design concepts, how could I be a successful industrial designer?

One of my professors assured the class that talent is only 10% of what's needed. He was right. Although I did have some natural ability to draw, it wasn't until I consistently practiced and observed that I saw the improvement I so desired. It turns out that you can learn a lot by simply being more attentive and aware. Drawing started to click for me when I was able to see the simplicity within the complexity of objects all around me. I started becoming more observant of the world, learning from the way light worked, how objects in the distance looked and felt from my perspective, and how more complex objects were built up from simple forms and shapes.

It Takes Time

It takes time to learn to draw well, to progress from the simple to the complex. I now teach design students, and I field many questions that show they have a desire to improve at a pace that is often faster than reality itself. My advice to them—and you—is don't rush the process. It takes time to level up and be more confident and competent at drawing and visualizing concepts in perspective.

One of the best things you can do is have a desire and passion to be better. Developing a daily habit around sketching is critical to improving your skill. This book, the culmination of my passion for visual communication and perspective drawing, will provide tips to help you and explanations of how to observe the world around you, so you can better draw objects that feel realistic, whether they're loose, sketchy, or tight in appearance.

You don't need the most expensive, fancy tools or a complete art studio to start drawing objects. You don't need a digital drawing tablet with the latest apps. Your most important tools are the ability to understand the nature of what you see and the willingness to practice drawing what you observe so that you can draw from imagination.

Be prepared to be a little frustrated, but I promise you with consistent effort and application, you will see improvement in your skill and ability.

When you start drawing, the process can be frustrating because your brain and motor function are trying to connect with your cognitive ability and imagination. All these parts of yourself are trying to communicate and make sense of what you ultimately want. It's okay for the process to feel this way. It was frustrating for me too. Every artist I've spoken to has had these moments of difficulty in connecting concepts to execution.

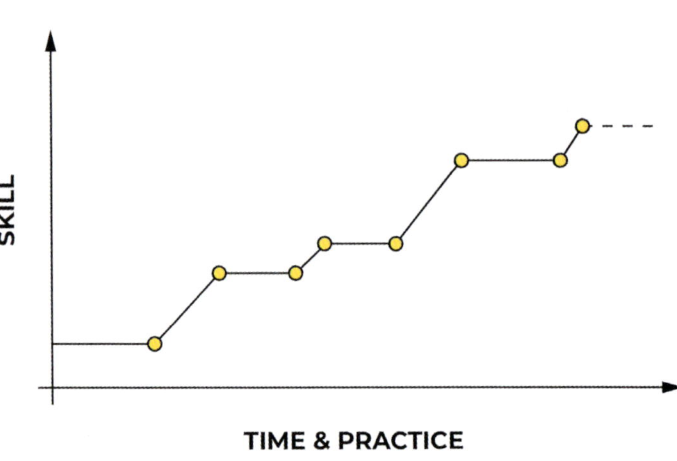

Developing your skill set may feel a bit flat and plateaued at times. Push through these times and be consistent. If you do, ultimately you will get to a point where everything just "clicks." You may feel a rush of excitement as your skills improve because you're able to connect ideas and concepts and to execute on the level you hadn't before.

Inevitably, however, you will hit another plateau when it feels like you're not getting better. Do not give up! Push through these times. Give yourself some grace and understand that improvement and learning take time. It's an honor to share a bit of my experience and knowledge and explain concepts in a way that makes sense to me. I hope you find this approach to be understandable and that it gives you the tools and perspective (no pun intended) to be a better artist, illustrator, or designer.

A Little Bit Every Day

If you truly want to be great, you have to commit to doing a little bit every day. Be a little bit better at the things you're passionate about. If you take the concepts and activities in this book seriously and apply yourself to connecting with them, you'll have a greater understanding of how to tackle complex objects and quickly sketch ideas with a depth and perspective reality to them.

Your drawings may not be perfect, but you can be perfectly passionate about the process.

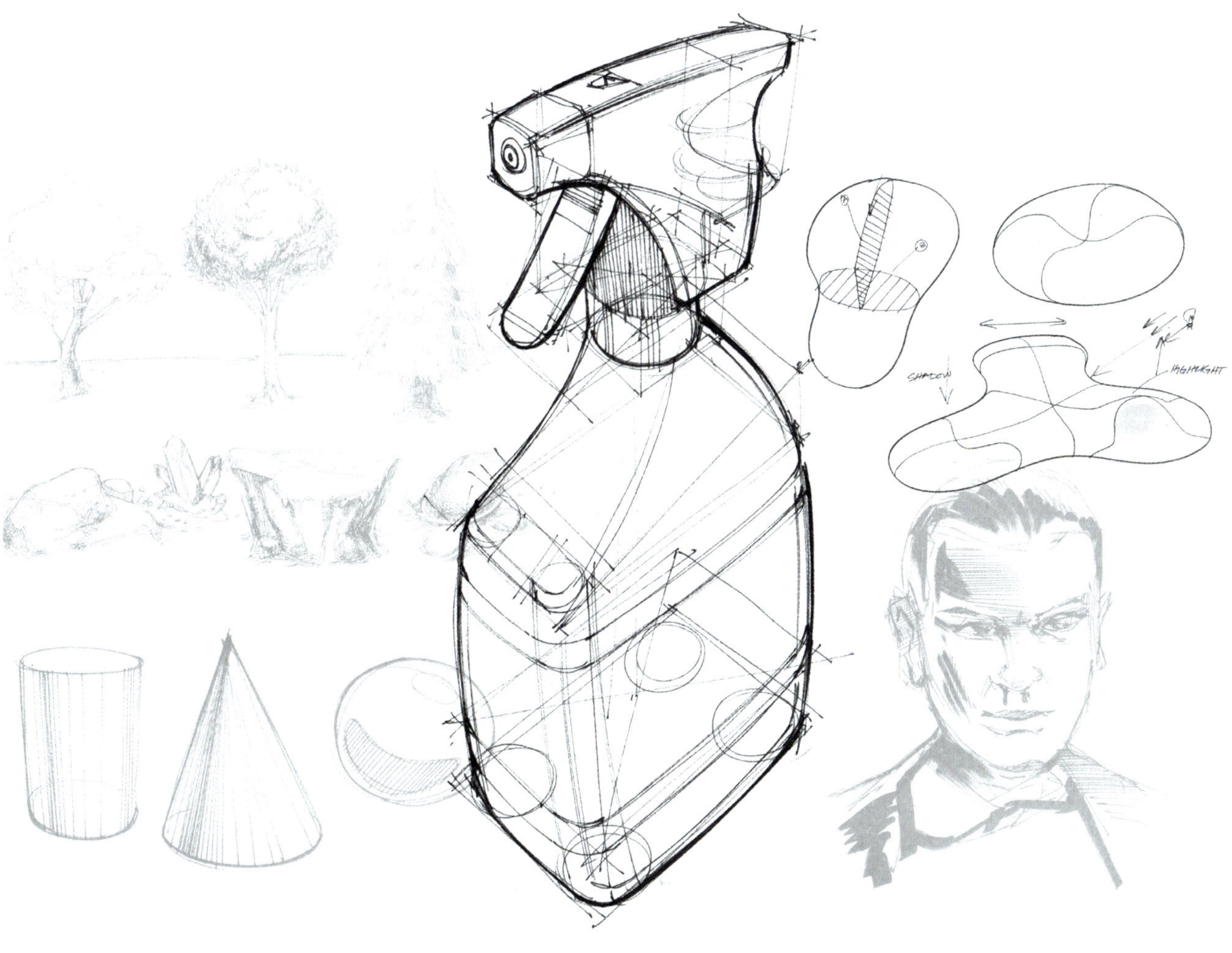

CHAPTER 1

ALL ABOUT LINES

I think a lot about lines. For a line-focused artist, lines are fundamental to creating quick sketches that communicate objects and ideas effectively. Lines, however, are merely concepts and do not exist in real life. I have never observed a no zero-thickness object bounding another object. A line is merely a concept that represents the limits of what you can see of an object in view. Understanding this idea will help you, as the artist, decide where to put a line in your drawing and how thick or thin to make the line while sketching objects.

Line Weight

Lines in drawings have key characteristics that make them more or less suited for one part of a drawing or another. *Line weight* refers to how thick or thin a line is in a drawing, and you can use lines that vary in line weight to communicate different aspects of a drawing. For example, bolder lines work well on the outline of a drawing, while thinner lines are better for general construction of an object or scene. You might use a line with thickness between those two extremes for overlaps or internal details on an object or in a scene. Lines can also vary in thickness along their length. These expressive lines can add attitude or gesture to a sketch.

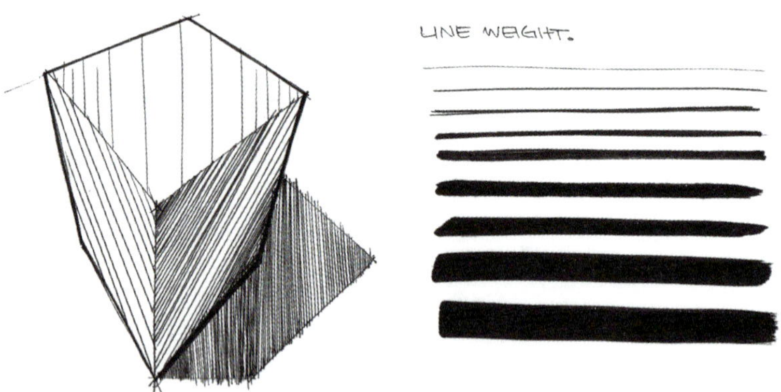

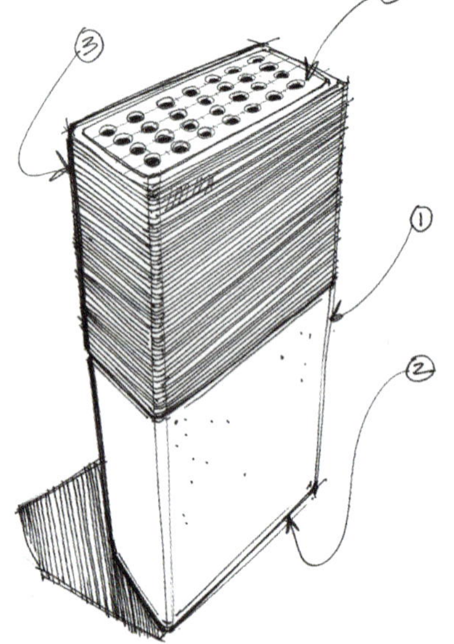

When drawing objects and ideas, it's important to have good, clean line quality. At the core of any drawing exercise is the idea of communication. Drawing is just another language we use to express concepts. The need for a specific type of line or line quality may vary depending on your target audience and the message you are conveying. Another artist or designer may be able to appreciate a rough thumbnail sketch with much of the line work being gestural, while a client or someone not used to sketches may struggle to interpret the intent of your drawing and its contents.

I once had a design meeting with a client where the client was fixated on a white line used in a rendering. The review meeting was somewhat derailed by their fixation on the sketch and this white line and shapes that were being used to communicate reflectivity. As designers, my team and I saw no problem with the drawing's approach, however. This experience was a good lesson: Not everything you intend may be interpreted in the way you want. Be mindful that lines, though conceptual, can sometimes be confusing

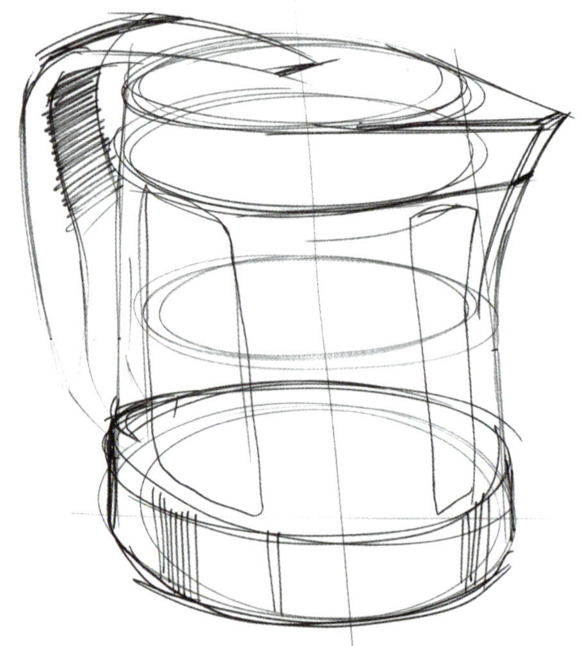

when used in ways that may be distracting to someone not comfortable or used to using lines the way you do when drawing.

Having good, appropriate line quality suited for the type of drawing and audience will ensure that the message isn't lost or misunderstood in your sketch's rough or unkempt presentation, but rather it will shine through and communicate with clarity and intention. Clarity is tantamount when drawing objects, and having viewers understand your work is the objective, especially when you're drawing something from your imagination that people may not be familiar with. As an industrial designer, I prioritize communicating with clarity when drawing.

Loose vs. Sloppy vs. Tight

Loose, *sloppy*, and *tight* are terms that you may see used during discussions of drawing. *Loose* refers to a confident yet expressive stroke quality in your line work. A *sloppy* line is one that is executed with little concern for precision or purpose and feels unconsidered and carefree. Sloppy lines tend to tend to be hesitant and rough and may involve multiple attempts at the same line, which results in a "hairy" outcome. Sometimes rough and sloppy lines can be useful when quickly working on an idea or visualization of an object; however, this is merely a stop on the way to creating a clearer drawing with an overlay.

A *tight* line is one in which the execution of the line, although precise, is also rigid and stiff. A tight line can be clear but also lack personality. Tight lines are often found where too much attention was paid to the precision of a drawing and the

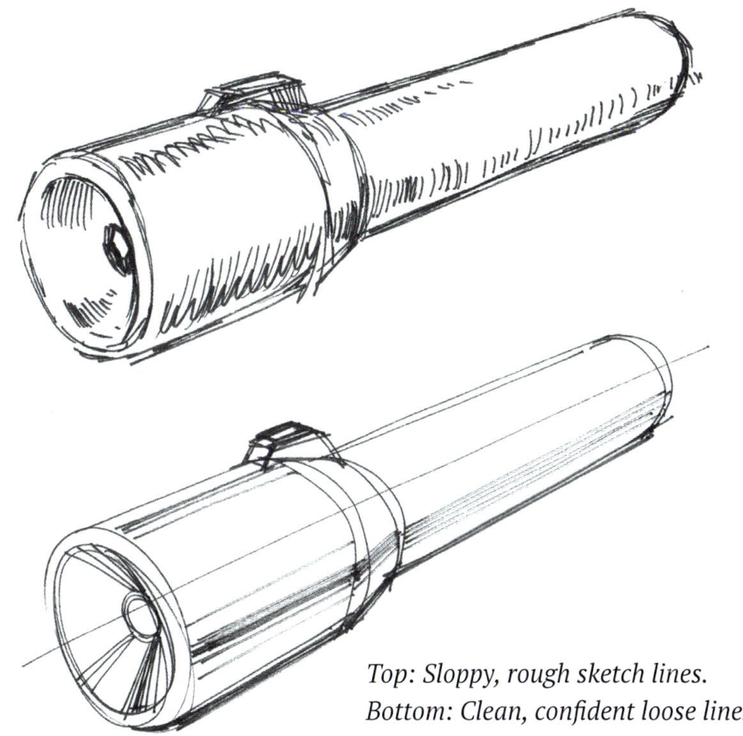

Top: Sloppy, rough sketch lines.
Bottom: Clean, confident loose lines.

emotive quality was sacrificed to provide clarity. When you're creating an overlay, for example, tracing the underlying drawing often can eliminate some of the gestural and emotive quality of the underlying sketch, because you're focusing too closely on the precision of the resulting overlay drawing. Finding the right blend of looseness and tightness in lines can help your drawing communicate objects clearly, while at the same time be interesting and engaging in appearance.

There is certainly a place for personality and expression in lines and both these qualities form the foundation of style when drawing and expressing a concept, form, or object. By virtue of your individuality, personality, and technique, style will be a natural outgrowth when you draw with your skills and tools.

Line Types

You'll use a variety of line types when drawing objects, and each has a different purpose in communication.

Construction Lines

Construction lines are the lines you use to build objects and form when you may not immediately know how to draw the subject in a final, crisp, and defined way. Because of the nature of construction lines, they can give a sense of an idea or object being in progress or unfinished. At times, this may be appropriate for the intent or audience for the drawing. For a product designer in a design review, for example, a sketch that looks unfinished can communicate the state of the project as well as pliability in the process.

As a matter of preference and circumstance, construction lines may be hidden in appearance or lighter in value or contrast in line weight. To achieve this, you could apply less pressure with a pencil or use a light gray marker, for example. If you prefer, however, construction lines, can be deliberate. They also can serve as a record of your thinking along the way when drawing and may be useful in keeping track of your idea generation and object creation.

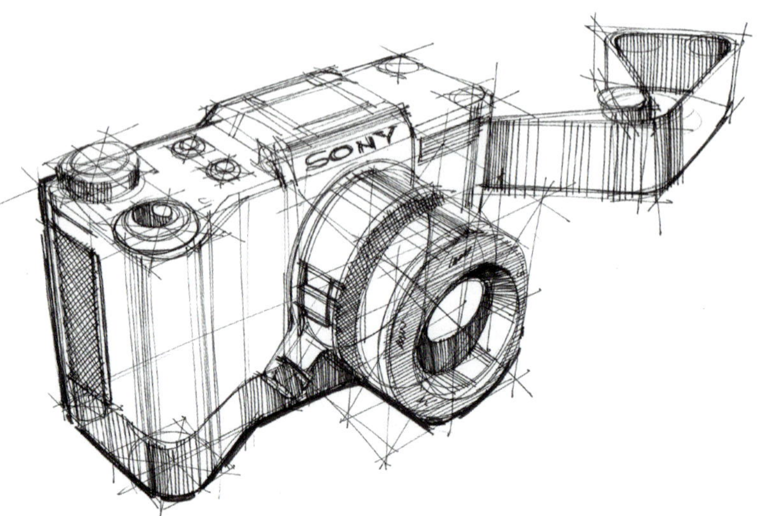

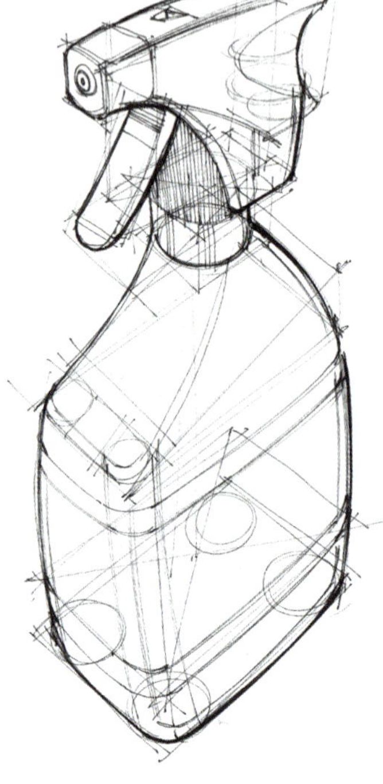

Implied Lines

Implied lines are perceptual lines and are often invisible in a drawing. Implied lines are formed when the viewer visually connects disparate lines across a gap; the line is implied as the eye traces continuity from one part of an object to another. In other words, despite a visual break in a line, it continues, in effect, across an area of a drawing. In music, some of the most interesting songs contain purposeful breaks in patterns and continuity, making the composition more engaging overall. A purposeful break in a drawing can be just as interesting visually.

This technique and application of lines can be useful when trying to show materiality,

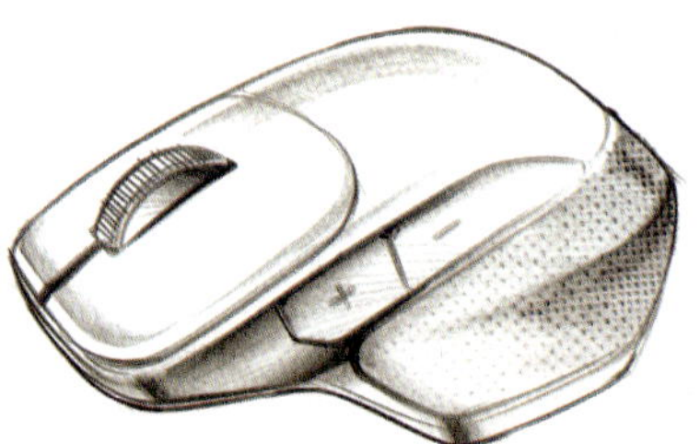

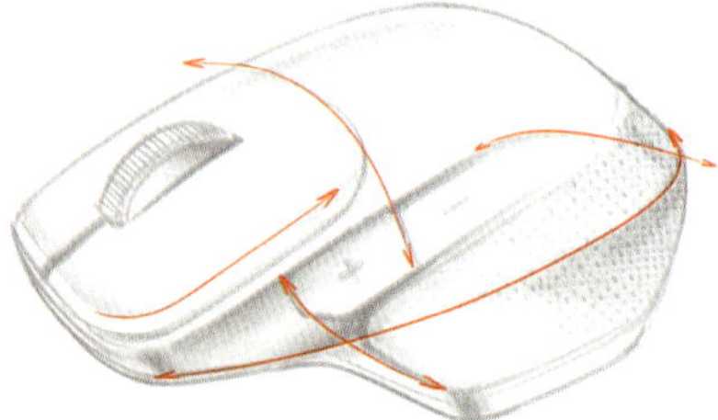

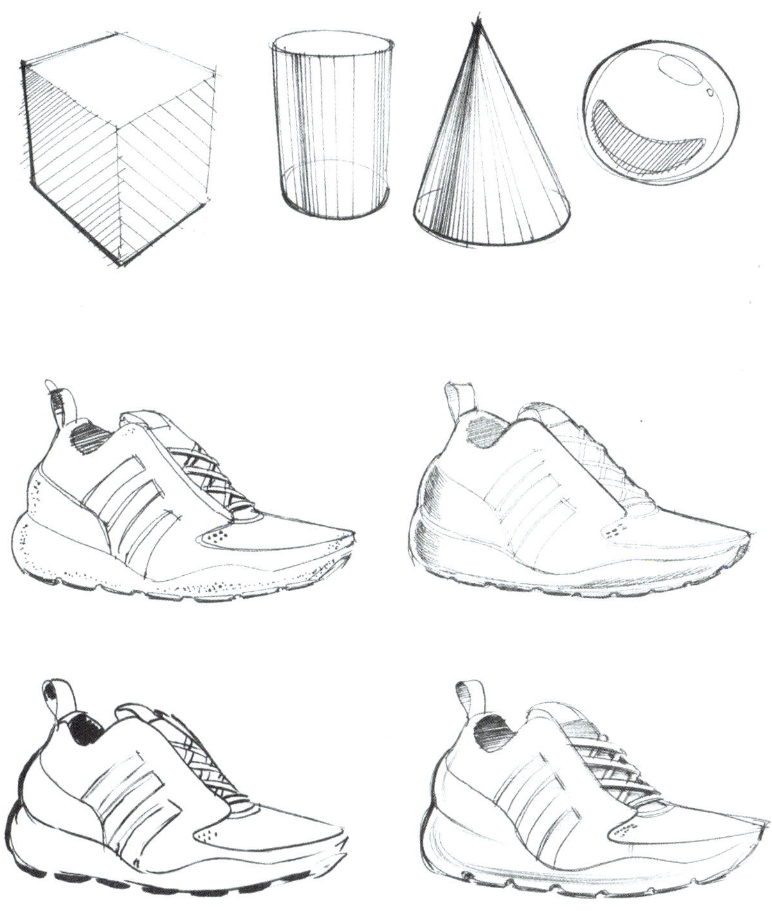

Clockwise: Examples of outlines using felt pen, gel pen, brush pen, and ballpoint pen.

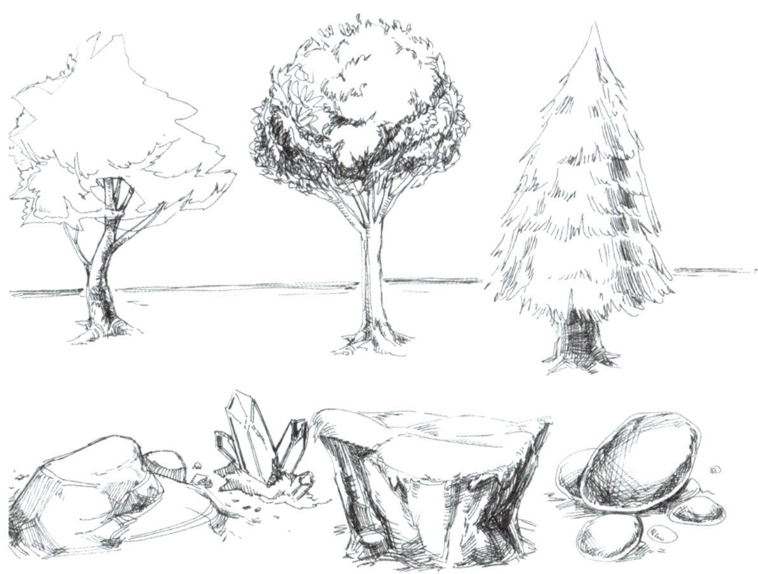

as transitions, or to lighten a drawing when using a pen that created whole lines, such as a felt or gel ink pen. Where working with a pen has limitations, intentionally breaking a line can lend to the materiality of the object while sketching. Breaking a line as well as being intentionally imprecise in execution can also lend itself to further communicating the nature of a material or object.

Outlines

Outlines are the outermost line that defines the silhouette of an object or form. Outlines define the shape of an object in view. Outlines are the boundary of what may be observed of an object as it obscures the view of what may be behind it. Outlines also delineate between the space inside the object as opposed to the space outside the object. As such, outlines are usually the boldest, consciously drawn lines in a drawing of an object.

Texture Lines

Texture lines are the lines that make up the expression of texture in a visual manner. They simulate materials or textures in real life through the use of repeating patterns, directions, length, intensity, and even color. Texture lines usually follow the shape and contour of a three-dimensional form when drawn. When you're working quickly, texture lines can be a great way to add extra dimension to a line drawing or texturally complement color that may be added to the drawing. The length of texture lines, as well as their direction and expression, can all complement the extra depth being expressed. Check out the chapter on texture for more information about texture lines and how textures are conveyed.

Gesture lines

Gesture lines have an inherent imprecision that is emotional and expressive. Gesture lines tend to be visually varied, free-flowing lines that evoke emotion, movement, or other qualities you wish to convey. Lines that are gestural may be an interpretation of such adjectives as *fast*, *slow*, *heavy*, or *light* when drawn. Gesture lines may vary in thickness not only across the entirety of the stroke, but also within the entirety of the stroke itself. Using a brush pen, soft pencil, or even charcoal can be a great way to create gesture lines. I tend to use a brush pen or a soft colored pencil when drawing gesturally.

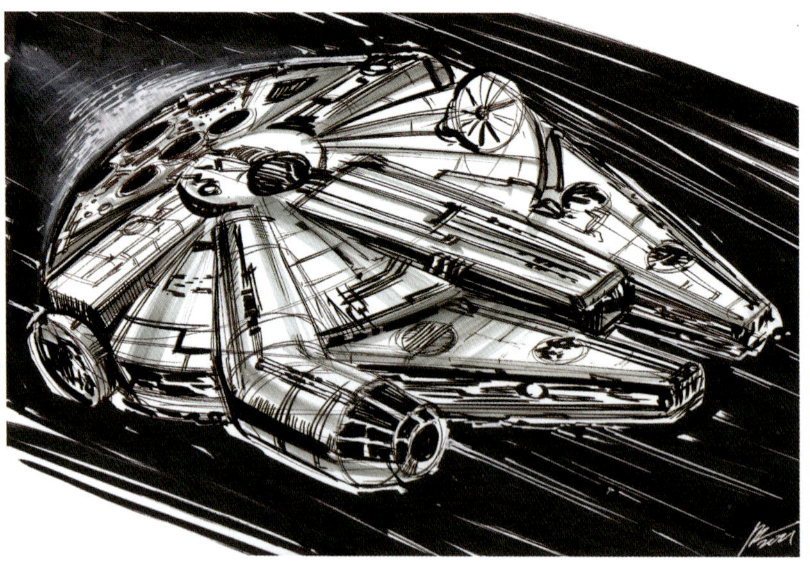

Contour Lines

Contour lines traverse the surfaces of a drawn object to show what an orthogonal axial slice of the object looks like while contained within the object or form itself. Think of the contour line as a slice of the form itself drawn within the form and

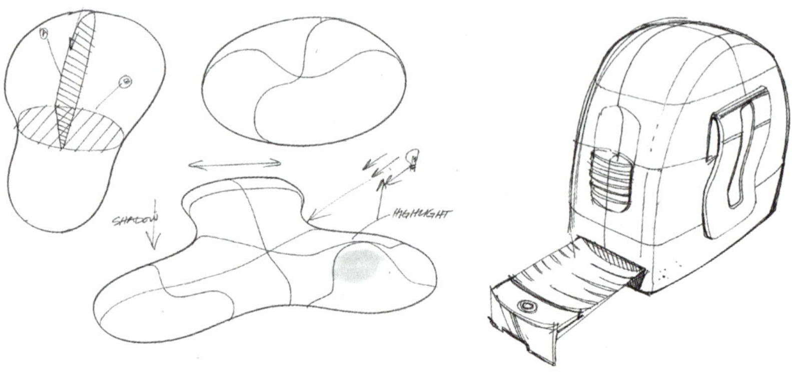

observed by the viewer. Contour lines serve as a useful shorthand for communicating the three-dimensionality of a form. If you start with a silhouette or outline of a form as a two-dimensional shape, contour lines can be used by drawing a transverse line that brings depth to the shape without requiring additional shading or coloring to communicate the depth in the form or object. Contour lines are a great and efficient way to work quickly and lightly in communicating the three-dimensionality of a form or object.

How to Get Good Lines

Now that you have a sense of the weight and type of lines you need, how can you improve your skill at drawing them? Concentrating on a few basic skills will help.

Grip

As discussed in Chapter 3, "Getting Started," how you hold your drawing tool impacts the quality of the lines you create. A loose, yet confident grip about halfway up the barrel of your drawing tool will give you better results than holding it close to the tip with a writing-oriented grip. This is a good starting point for being in the right place to draw confidently. This type of grip may feel unusual or foreign at first; however, it does allow you to have good visibility while drawing. Being able to see where you want to start and stop a line increases your odds for successful, confident sketches and drawings. It's a bit like life: You need to know where you are and where you're going to increase the odds for success. Don't hesitate to experiment with refining your grip. Finding the grip that works best for your drawing style is in part an exercise in trial and error; it took me years to find mine.

Speed and Flow

"Draw quickly!" one of my college professor would exhort, while pushing us students to move through copious amounts of ideas. Drawing quickly leaves less time to second-guess yourself and allows for a more instinctual or emotive expression in your lines. Your drawing doesn't need to be perfect, just finished when you've gotten to the objective you set for yourself. Good ways to get faster and more confident in your line work are to complete daily warm-up exercises and to sketch something in perspective every day.

The quicker you draw, the less likely you are to exhibit doubt or hesitation in your sketch lines, as there is less time for a mistake with each line. It may feel uncomfortable to sketch a bit faster than you might be accustomed to; however, with some effort, drawing in this fashion may feel more natural.

Ergonomics and Stance

Your relative position to the drawing surface can affect not only the accuracy of your perspective and measurements, but also the quality of your lines. Avoid positioning yourself in a way that creates a distorted point of view while sketching. Sketching while you are slouched or at an acute angle relative to the paper or drawing medium means you will be unable to accurately view and execute the drawing of a particular object. If you draw while maintaining an extreme relative point of view, what you draw will be distorted as well.

Drawing with your elbow and shoulder as pivot points reduces the likelihood for the sort of errors in your lines that appear when you draw with your wrist. In addition, you can draw longer, more flowing and expressive lines this way. Being able to extend your arm fully while drawing results in cleaner and more confident lines with less error in the stroke. Sometimes it will be necessary to draw with your wrist rather than using your shoulder and elbow as pivots. When you're working on a small, detailed area of a drawing or a very small concept sketch or thumbnail, drawing with your wrist may help you maintain a higher degree of control. Still, having a fluid and confident stroke is essential to creating a fluid and confident sketch of an object or design.

Material and Object Breaks

Because of the way light works, when two materials or objects are juxtaposed next to each other, a slight small shadow is cast at the point of contact. No two objects are perfectly divided and maintain perfect contact and as such, even the minuscule gap between the objects or the division is enough to cast a tiny shadow and pick up a highlight at the point of separation.

A double line, even slight in appearance, is a good way to convey the three-dimensionality of an object and its divisions, even at a small scale. Using a double line when drawing is a subtle yet effective detail when drawing objects and their components. The line that is closest in proximity to the light source should have the heavier line weight of the two, because of the shadow cast by the edge. If you were to zoom in for a very detailed look at what is happening with the edges, you would be able to see a slight shadow being cast by the edge closest to the light source, and this is why that edge would have a heavier line weight when you draw it. That heavier line weight is not only visually interesting but also packs with it inherent information about the nature of the edges.

Similarly, if an edge is slightly rounded, you could use a double line instead of single lines on the edges of the form break to show roundness. Combined with a contour line to show the slight filleted rounding of the edges, these simple line combinations can also be used to show a detail that would normally require some level of visual rendering with color or shading.

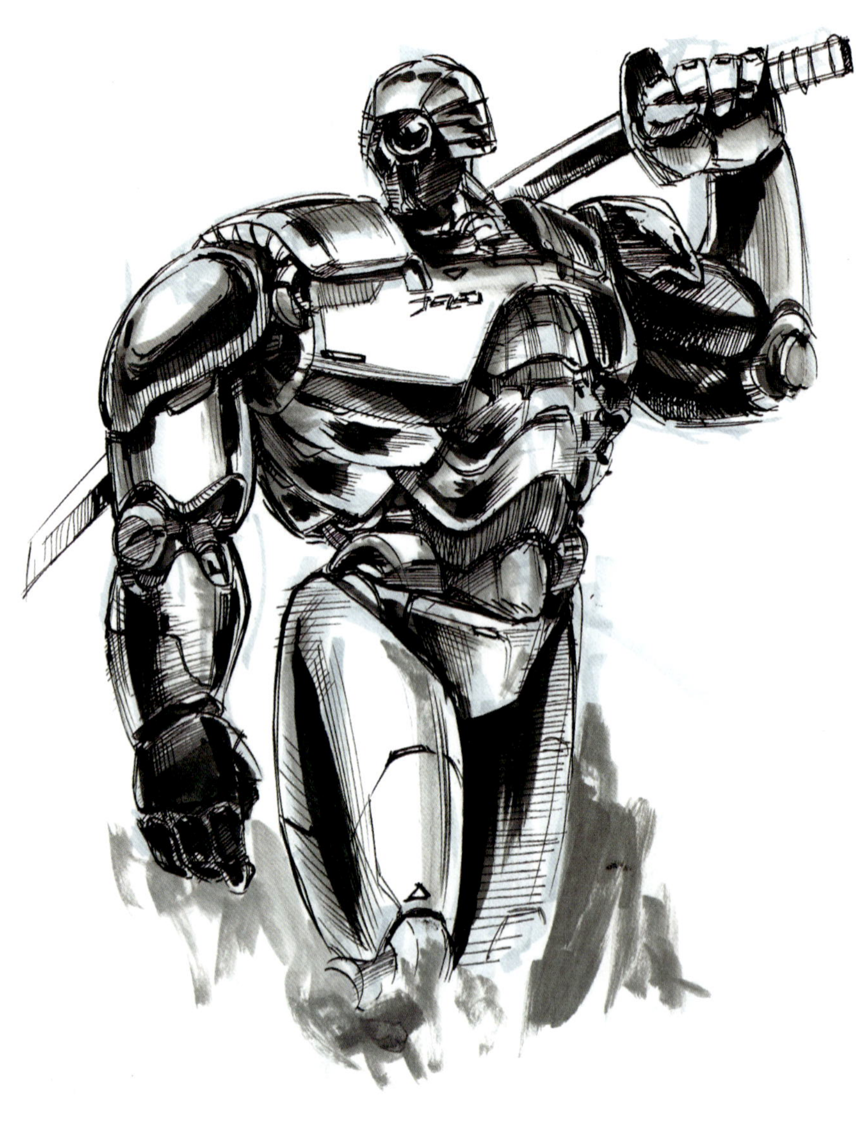

Mentality and Follow Through

Your frame of mind and attitude can have a positive or negative effect on how well your lines show up while drawing. Early in my design education, I spent an internship designing cars at General Motors. I was terrified, stressed, and concerned about my ability to keep up with the other interns. I felt as though I was totally out of my depth, as I had not attended an educational institution focused on car design. I worked hard all summer, despite my self-doubts. Although I did "good work" and completed the full program successfully, I often could not do my *best* work because I was so stressed. I could see it in my lines, color, shading, and rendering. I still regret that today because I missed a growth opportunity due to my own self-doubt. My state of mind compromised my ability to grow and learn and to put out my best work.

Relaxing and having a mindset of success while drawing will prime you to do your best with your lines and your work in general.

Much like conversation, there is an approach to drawing lines that does depend on the confidence you exude. A confident person understands words, sentences, and concepts and how to use them to their advantage in a persuasive conversation. Lines are not much removed from conversation, as drawing is visual communication. The more confident your lines and presentation, the more persuasive the presentation of your work will be, and the more people will trust in the idea or object being visualized.

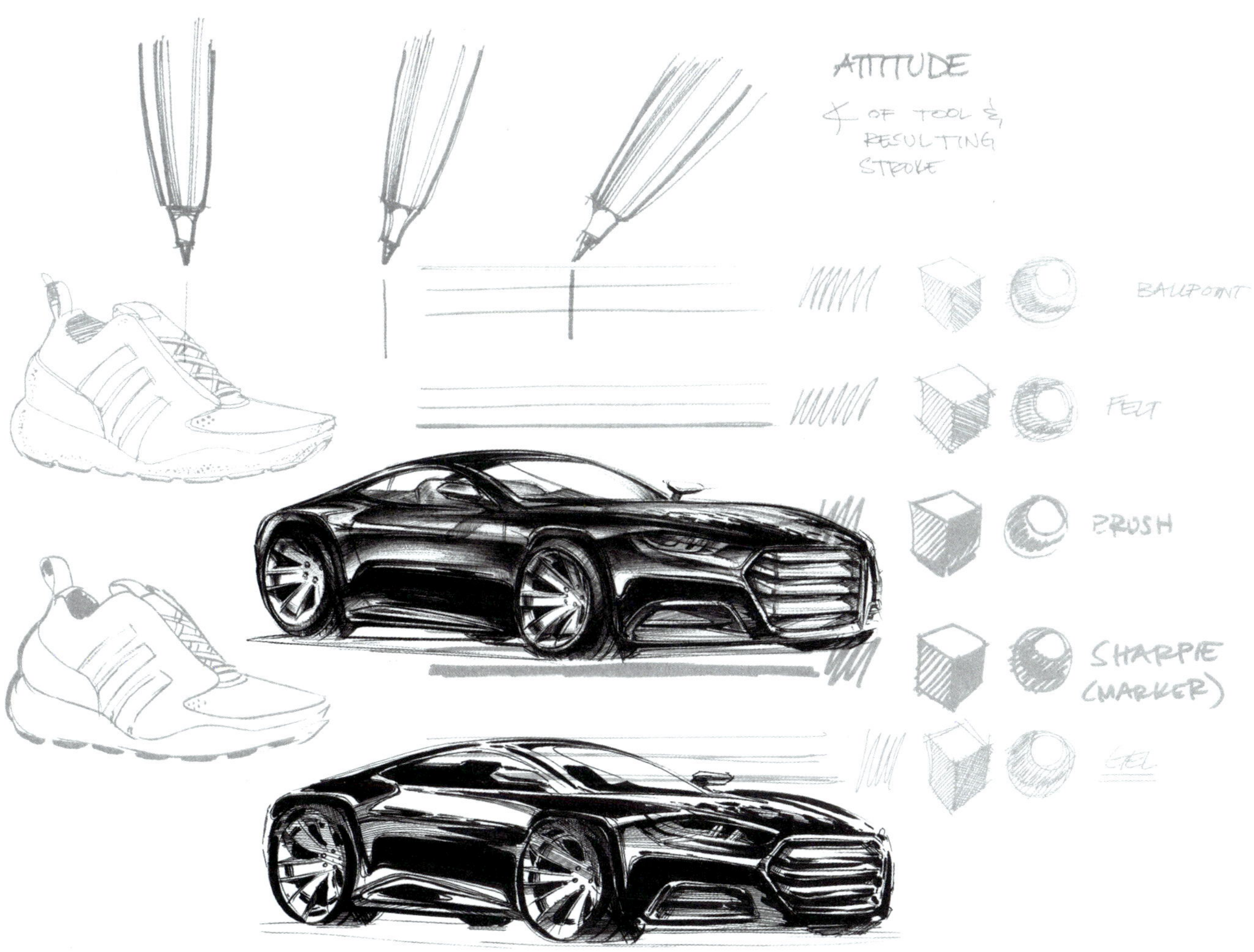

— CHAPTER 2 —

YOUR DRAWING TOOLKIT

Choosing your materials when learning to draw can be intimidating. Which pen is the best one? What pencil should I use? How do I choose the right paper? These questions can be answered with some trial and error, as well as by paying attention to how you feel while using the materials and how successful your drawing turns out. Budget limitations may also be a consideration when selecting your own tools, and each choice comes with caveats and trade-offs. For example, some markers are cheap but not refillable, while others are expensive and refillable or come as a system with accessories to expand their functionality. (We'll go over markers in more detail in Chapter 9, "Color.")

For much of this text, I recommend sticking to a simple set of drawing materials: pens, pencils, and design markers along with paper suitable for each medium. Simplifying your toolset can help you focus on learning how to master these tools before moving to another medium.

Additionally, narrowing your focus to tools that are simple and convenient means that you can draw wherever you go and at a moment's notice.

Pens (Reservoir)

Pens are a fun and effective way to quickly jot down thoughts, express ideas, or create elaborate illustrations with eye-popping detail and expression. Pens can be very challenging to use when sketching but can be very enjoyable at the same time.

I've always enjoyed challenges and the satisfaction of learning. I tell my students and anyone else learning to draw today, "If you want to be good at drawing, use a pen that never forgives and never forgets." Use a pen that is unforgiving, and you will push yourself closer to being more excellent in your drawing craft. Over the last 20 years, I've learned drawing with pens challenges your ability to think before you act, as well as react in unpleasant circumstances. This means using a pen that is capable of producing a whole, consistent line when drawing. Of course, pencils are an option, but I find that using a pen that doesn't allow much room for mistakes primes your cognitive processes, prompting you to consider what you want to draw before committing to the drawing. If you make a poor stroke, you must be able to think about what you can do to adapt your drawing to the misplaced stroke. (Warming up by drawing on scrap paper first is always a good idea.)

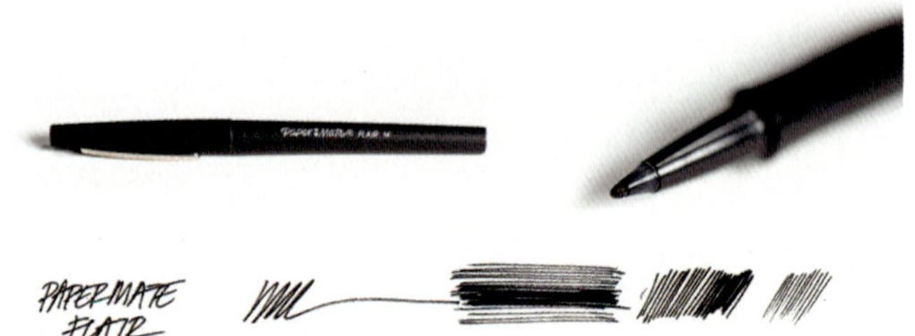

The confidence you develop when drawing with pens will translate to drawing in other mediums, such as pencils, markers, and even digital drawing tablets. If you want to be good, impose a constraint on yourself like drawing with pens, learn to work with your mistakes, and be more thoughtful and creative with each stroke.

With time, you will develop an ability to create drawing with striking texture, light, and shadow using only a pen of your choice. Your speed and ability to think quickly and conceptualize ideas will increase drastically. It won't be easy, but it is a worthwhile challenge in pushing yourself and your drawing abilities.

Pen Types

Different pens and pen tips will give your sketch different appearances. Below are examples of the same sketch done with a ballpoint (top) and felt with marker (bottom). Ballpoint pens allow for more flexibility and subtle shading because they respond to pressure and repetition for buildup, while felt-tip pens require you to think a bit differently about how you might

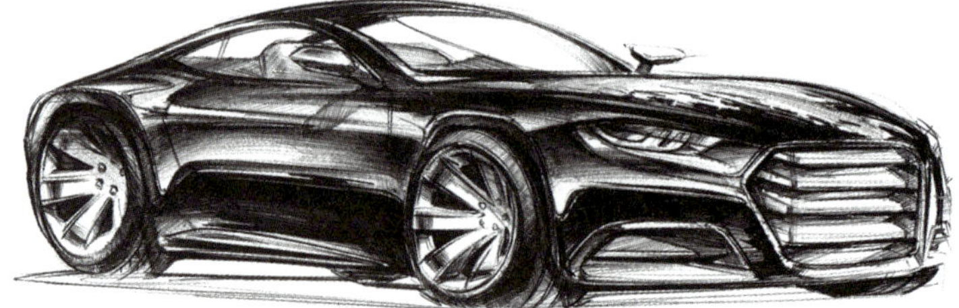

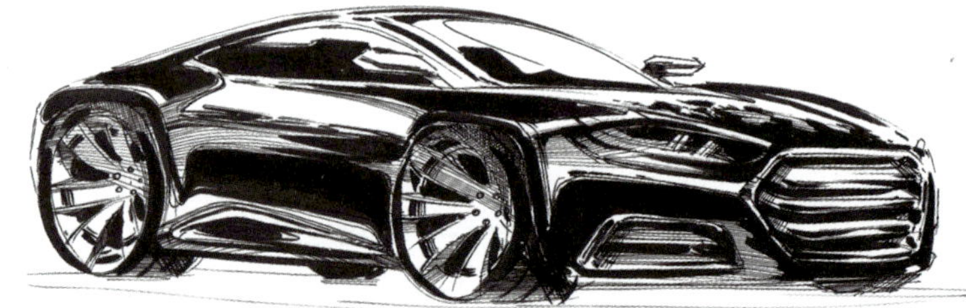

show subtle shading, gradation, and texture. Felt-tip pens are great for quick drawings consisting of whole lines, for instance. Some felt-tip pens can even produce expressive lines that are gestural if you modify your pen grip, drawing speed, and/or pen pressure. The pen you choose as a tool often will dictate how you approach sketching an object.

Brush pens have a tip made of individual fibers in a solid flexible nib that mimics a brush you might paint or ink with. Because brush pens have a flexible nib, pen pressure and line control are a bit more difficult when you're trying to create a consistent line thickness. When you want to sketch objects in perspective or create rich textures on an object, however, brush pens can produce very expressive lines of varied line weight. Give them a try when you are feeling confident enough to mix things up and see how they slot into your workflow and drawing approach.

Pens Have Different Inks

The ink in a pen usually consists of pigment and a solvent. Much like markers, pens have different solvents, pigments, and bases, and this affects their price. In addition, some pen inks will be more lightfast (resistant to fading) than others. The appearance of black from pen to pen may also differ, appearing more red-black, blue-black, or neutral black in color.

For example, ballpoint pens feature an ink that is a paste compound mixed with an alcohol-based solvent. Felt-tip pens feature water-based or alcohol-based solvents with some glycols added.

Understanding the chemical makeup of your ink is much less important than taking some time to test your inks and how they lay down on paper and intermix with other drawing media. If you want to paint over sketched pen lines, for example, conduct a few tests with various pens and the medium you plan to paint on to see which combination works the best.

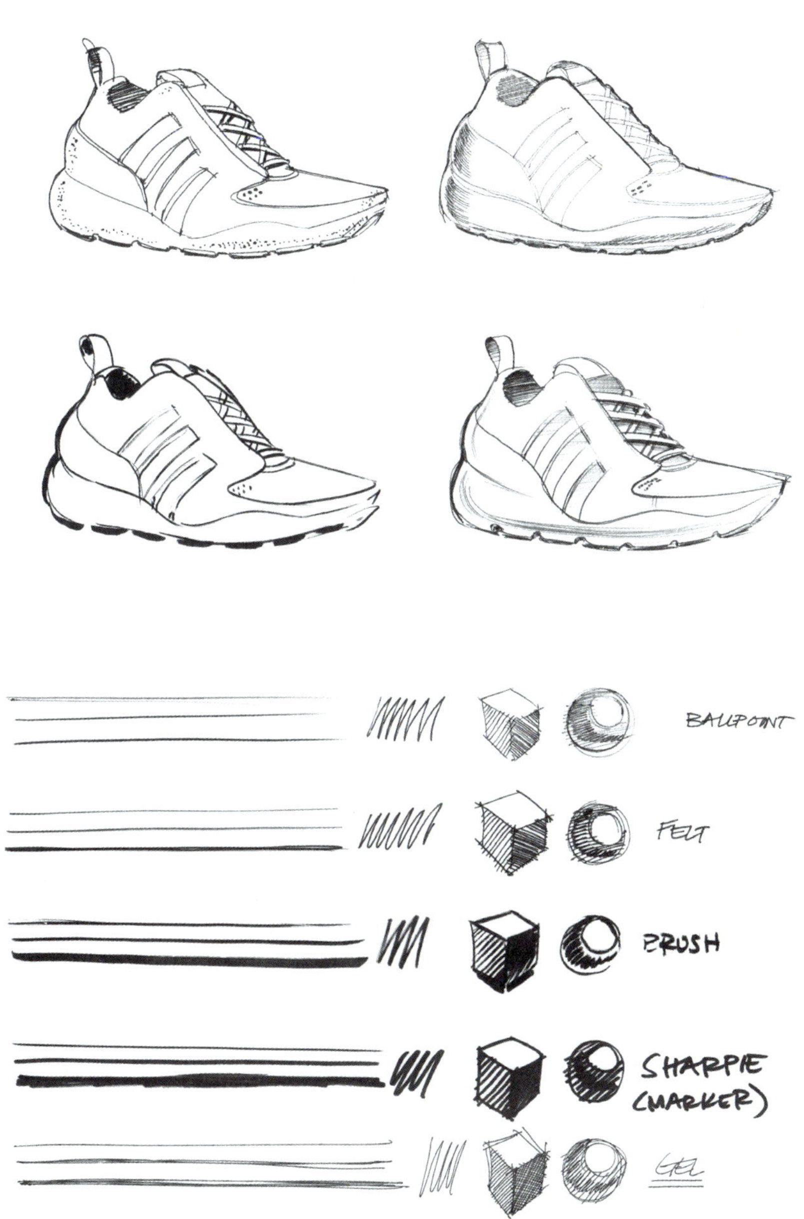

Fountain Pens

Recently, I started using fountain pens as another drawing medium. They're a great way to add a different feel and look to your line work. Fountain pens are responsive to pressure when drawing, so the lines you draw have an inherent expressive quality to them. Be prepared, however: Getting used to recharging the pen's nib with ink as you use it does take some time.

Fountain pens are fairly simple in construction, and some manufacturers sell the pen shaft separately from the nibs, enabling you to customize your drawing experience to your liking. Whether you prefer a shaft with the larger diameter or something nimbler and thinner, you can likely find a shaft that will work for you.

The nib you choose for your pen can change the line you produce. If you want a very delicate stroked line, for example, look for finer point nibs. If you need to fill large areas, look for a nib with a large, flat, somewhat chiseled surface area. These work well for blocking in things like shadows and reflections, as well as drawing.

One thing about fountain pens that may be stressful or frustrating is that you do need to pay attention to maintaining the nibs of your pen. Although you can find a variety of soaps and cleansers to refresh your nibs, I find isopropyl alcohol to be sufficient for cleaning more often than not.

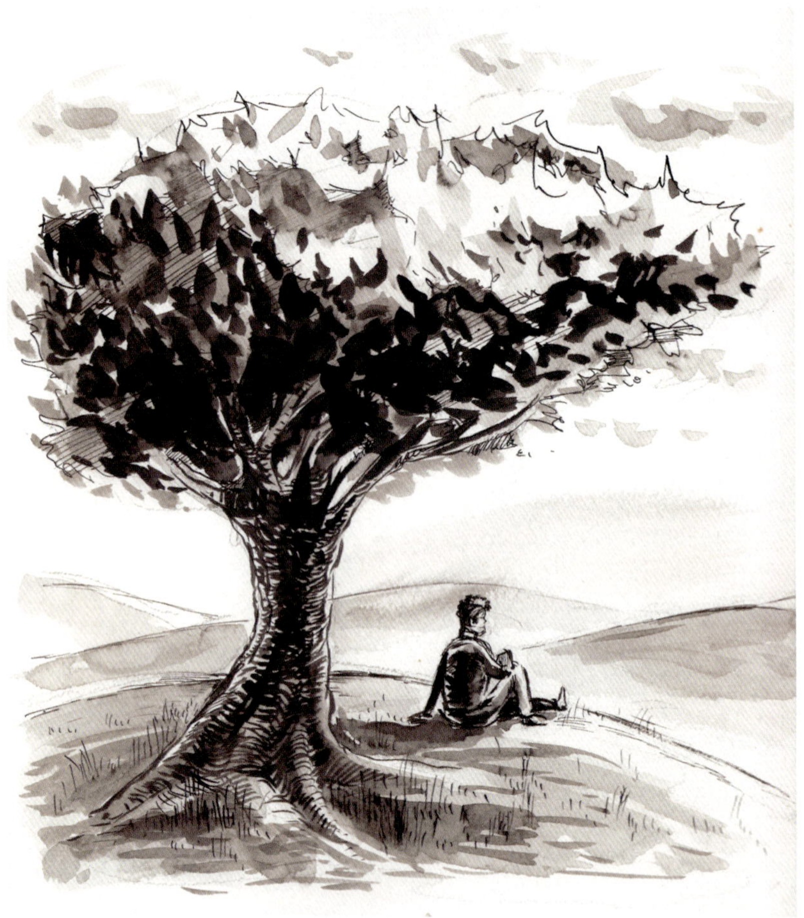

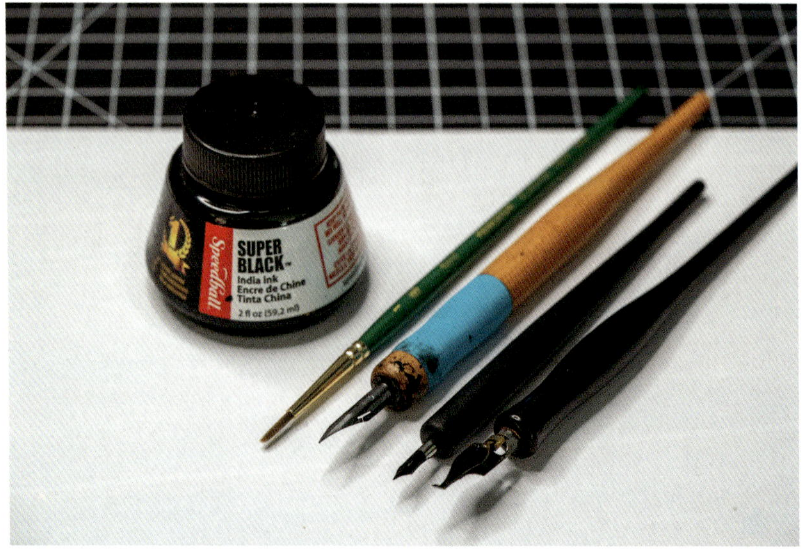

Because fountain pens do not come with any specific ink, you may want to experiment a bit. For example, some inks are dyes that you dip your pen in and then draw with. Lately, I've taken to using India ink when creating illustrations. Along with using your fountain pen to draw lines, you can brush or paint with diluted ink to create halftones in a sketch or drawing. You can even find and source inks of different pigments to use in your fountain pens.

If you're looking to mix up your drawing toolset and try something different, give fountain pens a look!

Pencils

Fantastic and versatile tools, pencils operate in a fundamentally different way than pens. A pencil deposits material from its internal core—whether that's made of wax, graphite, or other pigment-containing material—onto your paper as you draw. Drawing with a pencil literally dulls its tip as you move it across the paper. A pen, on the other hand, simply deposits ink onto the paper without affecting the quality of the nib or tip of the pen. Because pencils progressively get duller as you work, rotating your pencil in your hand after each stroke can help keep it "sharper" for a longer time with a crisp edge produced by the execution of the previous stroke. This trick works for only so long, however, before the pencil becomes dull.

How do you reduce the likelihood of having pencil strokes in your sketching that appear dull and unrefined? One option is to work with a sizable batch of mechanically sharpened pencils. When a pencil gets dull, simply select another that has a fresh tip. Or invest in an electric pencil sharpener with an auto-stop feature. The auto-stop feature will prevent you from grinding away wastefully once your pencil comes to a sharp point. You can also sharpen both ends of the pencil to further expand the number of available sharp tips. You may not want to burn a candle at both ends but sharpening a pencil at both ends works just fine.

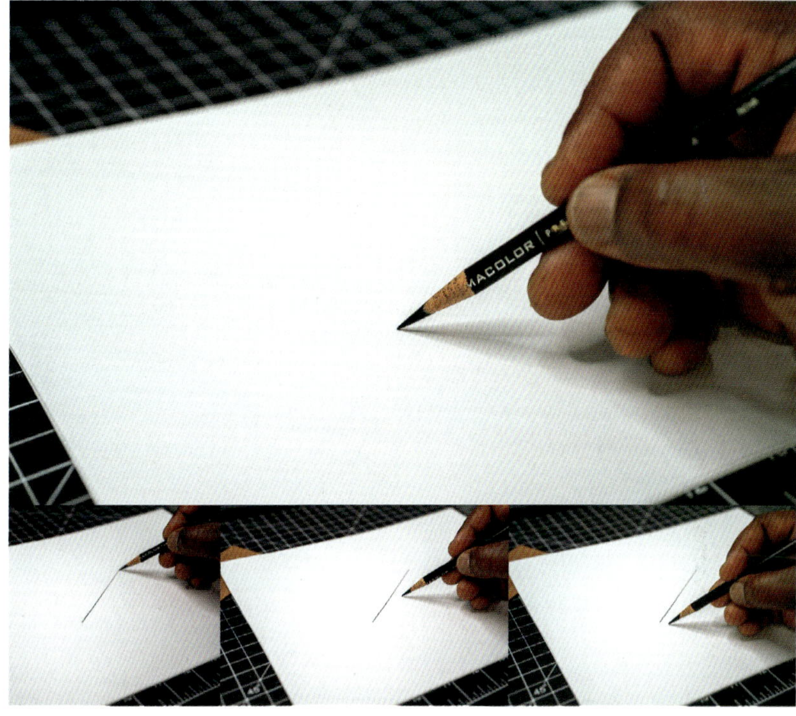

A dull tip isn't necessarily a bad thing, however. If the subject in your drawing requires a softer look and feel in texture or shading, having a more rounded tip can help with blending, shading, and toning as you draw.

By varying the pressure of your pencil on the paper, you can vary the line weight, contrast, and value as you draw. Pressing lightly will result in a thinner and lighter line, whereas pressing more heavily on paper will generate a thicker and bolder line with more contrast and sometimes more definition. In addition, paper with a heavier texture will result in pencil lines that have a bit more texture and variation to them than the pencils would exhibit with a smoother paper texture.

Speaking of pressure, be mindful of the temptation to lean into more hesitant and uncertain strokes when working with pencils. The hesitation can show up as hairy, rough, and sloppy line work, rather than demonstrating the confidence you will develop when learning to draw with pencils.

If you sharpen your pencil to reveal a bit of extra lead along its side, you can use it with a tilted grip for shading or creating stokes that work very well for showing depth in three dimensions. This grip and shading technique works particularly well with two-dimensional sketches that need a bit of oomph and three-dimensionality as expressed with shadow cores or highlights.

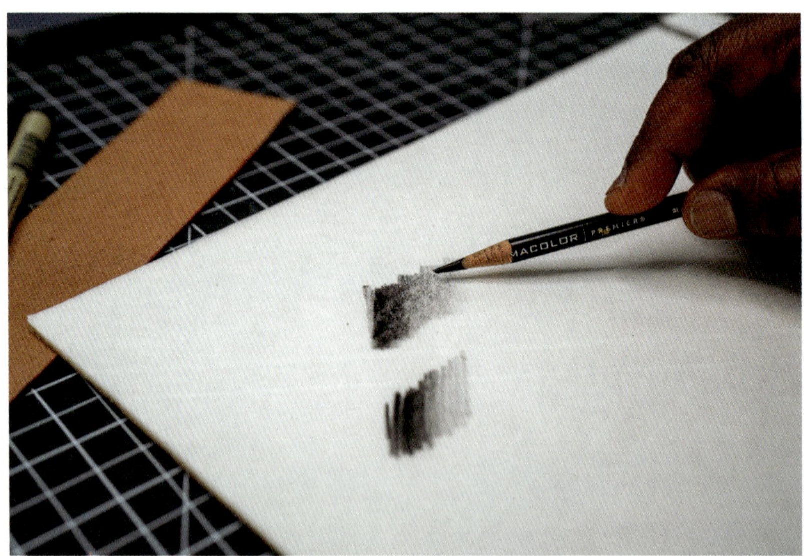

The type of lead (core) in a pencil also affects how it behaves. One brand of colored pencil, for example, may have a hard waxy lead, while another brand may have a softer, more pressure-responsive lead. Generally, I work with colored pencils as opposed to graphite pencils. With colored pencils, I find that a Prismacolor Premier black or indigo blue works well for general sketching. The color is less important, however, than figuring out what pencil type works best with your drawing style. Finding a good pencil will take some effort and potentially some trial and error, purchasing various options.

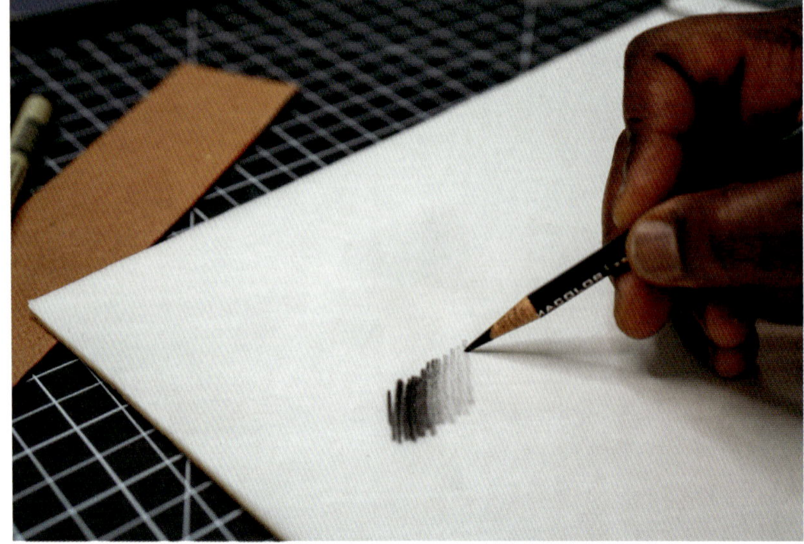

Markers

I quite enjoy drawing with markers. Markers generally come in three ink types: alcohol-based, xylene-based, and water-based. Most of my experience is with alcohol-based markers. Marker ink is translucent, and subsequent, layered strokes can build up its intensity. Each stroke covers the next and "wakes up" the ink below for blending and deeper saturation, whether you work with disparate colors or analogous colors.

Marker inks may also react differently with different types of paper. Although they tend to be more expensive than regular bond paper, a variety of papers are made specifically for use with markers. Marker paper has a coating on the back to prevent bleed-through of the marker ink onto the papers or work surface below your drawing. This coating also prevents overuse of your markers because it makes for a less absorbent paper. Instead of acting like a dry sponge with water, marker paper takes in less ink than an uncoated paper would. Colors are also more vibrant and saturated on marker paper than they appear on other papers. In addition, marker paper can help with lightfastness. If you enjoy drawing with a marker, I suggest investing in some marker paper for your drawings.

Another item to consider when using markers, or any sort of coloring medium, is how the ink or medium may affect the lines of your drawing. For example, some pens use ink types that do not work well with the application of marker on top of the inked lines. Be sure to thoroughly test the interplay of your pens and markers before you commit to coloring your drawing. If you miss this step, you may open yourself up for a lot of heartache during your coloring process.

Paper

Is the most expensive paper the best paper? Not necessarily. I tend to err on the side of affordable when it comes to paper for general sketching. I often find myself doing multiple quick sketches of the same object or idea before committing to a final presentation. In such cases, working with a material that is cheap (or recyclable) means that I can produce multiple ideas for the same cost as I could using a more expensive, higher quality paper. You should be able to achieve results similar to most of the drawing samples in this book using run-of-the-mill printing paper or a pad of marker paper. A ream of printer paper should be more than enough for ample sketching practice and exploration.

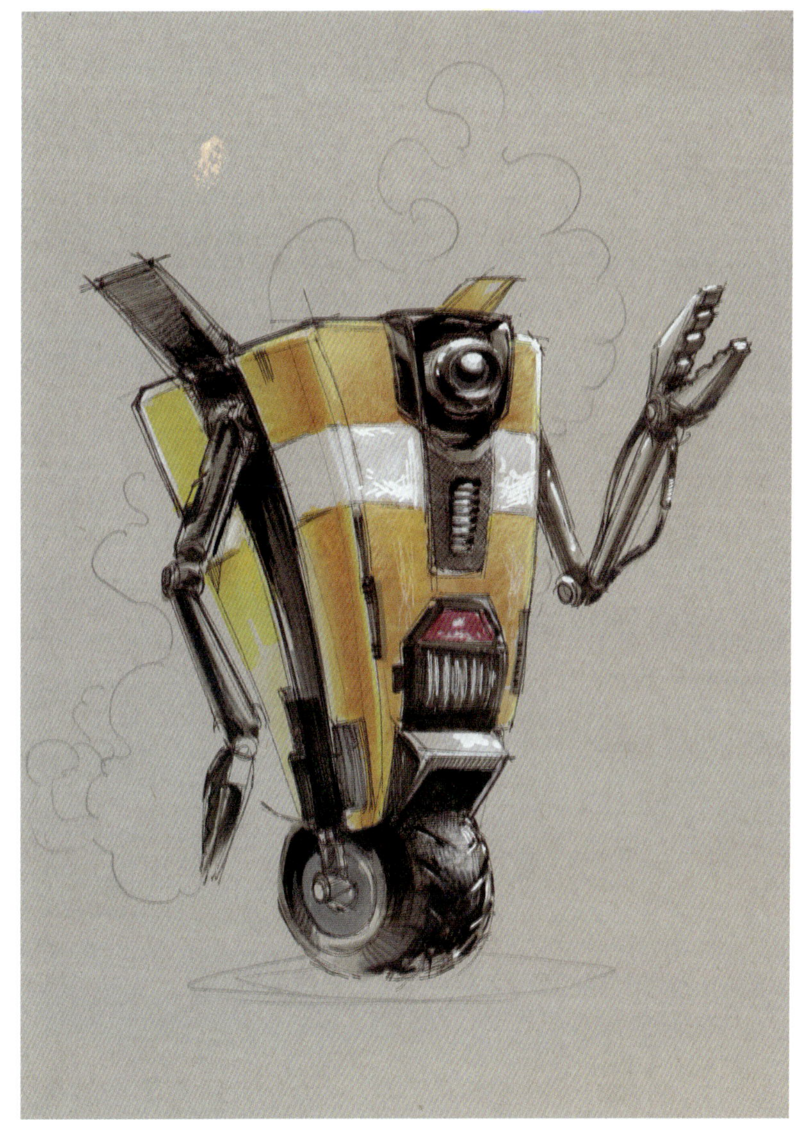

For pencil sketching and more refined sketches, a slightly textured, coated paper works well, such as any higher quality marker paper. For other media, a thicker or heavier paper is a good choice. Thicker paper holds up well for paint, for example, or it may feature a texture that enhances pastel and chalk work. Toned paper can also be a fun varietal option when drawing. A toned paper makes for quick, rich drawings because of the mid-tone of the paper and the ability to draw with lighter colored media and darker media for a unique effect.

Paint

Sometimes paint is useful, even when you're drawing quickly. Specifically, gouache or opaque paint is useful for creating highlights on surfaces that have divisions and for shape breaks where two parts meet to produce a highlight. Rather than having to worry about accidentally coloring in the area that should be highlighted, you can add a highlight after the fact with a little paint and a fine brush.

Alternatively, paint pens provide the benefits of being able to draw an opaque white (or other color) line, while also being transportable and somewhat contained. Compared to packing up an entire paint setup to travel, a paint pen is very convenient. Paint pens are not all the same nor use the same type of pigment, however. Test and try each tool to see how it feels and to discover your preferences. At time of writing, I find that Posca paint pens perform consistently and reliably well.

Of course, you can use other types of paint when illustrating or drawing. Watercolor is a great option for adding a painterly effect to drawings, backgrounds, and other elements. Be mindful, however, that because of the water involved in this paint process, your paper may warp or become eroded as you work. Overall, I find using colored pencils and markers less time consuming than painting.

There Is No Magic Pen

Despite the multitude of tools available for drawing, there is no magic pen! I learned this back in college, and it has stuck with me for decades. The pen is less important than the *process and practice* you put into learning how to draw better.

After you develop skills with a tool of your choice, don't be afraid to expand your range. Try another tool while leveraging the experience and techniques you learned while using your main tool. For example, starting with a felt-tip pen that produces a whole line helps you build confidence that you can later applied to drawing with pencils or even a digital tablet.

In your drawing practice, you may find that you gravitate toward one tool or another. This is totally fine! I like to think of it a bit like a having a clutch hitter on a baseball team or that go-to player on a basketball team. Having confidence in that player and knowing that they will carry out the play helps build confidence for the entire team. Pick a tool, master it, and then think of ways to extend those skills to other tools or activities related to drawing.

Remember, ultimately it is practice and time spent drawing that will make you better. It matters less what you use to draw and more *how much* you draw. As a matter of principle, I try to complete one drawing every day. This way I establish some discipline around daily practice and maintaining skills, even as life presents its challenges and pressures on time. Decide now: Commit to working hard and consistently at your practice of drawing, and the results will come

Basic Drawing Set

Now that you know a little bit about a variety of tools, you may be wondering what you need to work through the book's exercises. The following list of recommendations is by no means a comprehensive toolset, but it is enough to get you started exploring the exercises and building confidence as you learn to draw in perspective and represent objects in three-dimensional space.

- 3 Cool or warm gray markers
- 3 Color markers (6 if you want to expand)
- Colored pencil
- Inking Pen (white pen optional)
- Ruler
- Printer paper
- Marker paper

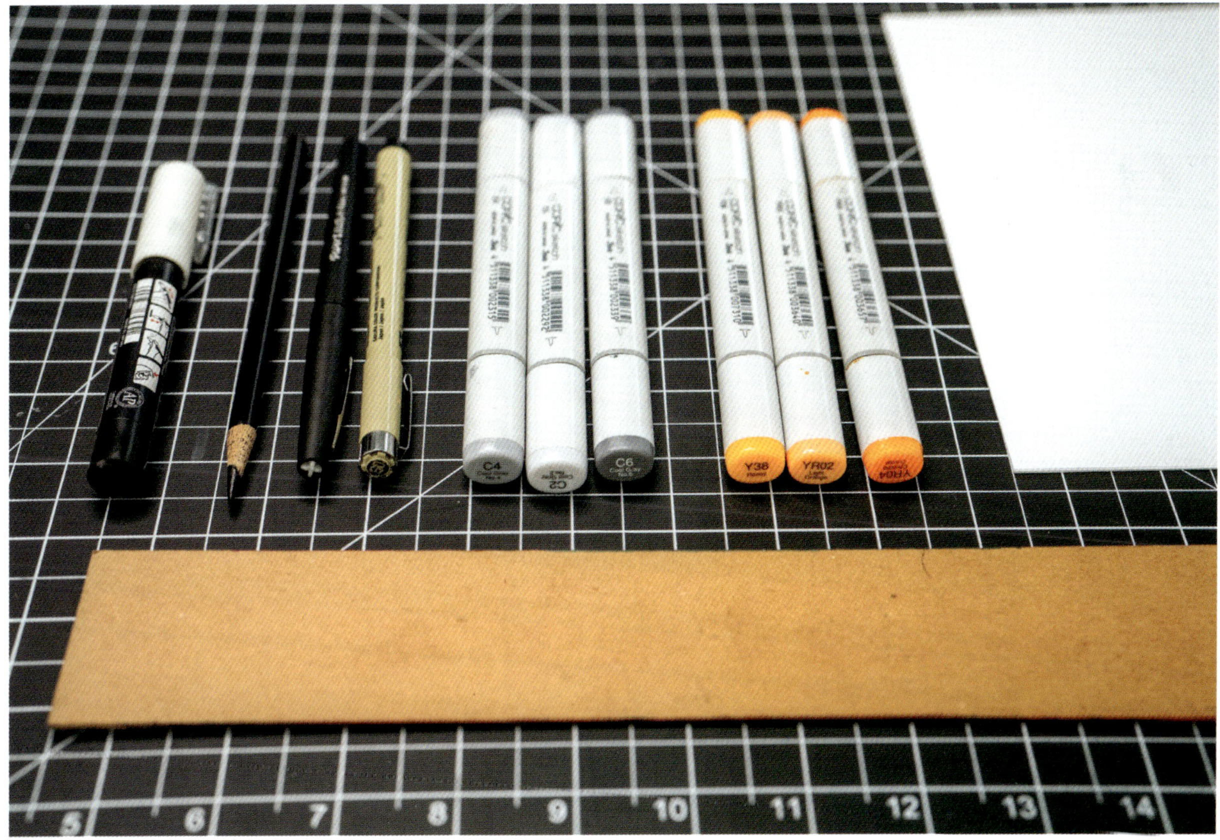

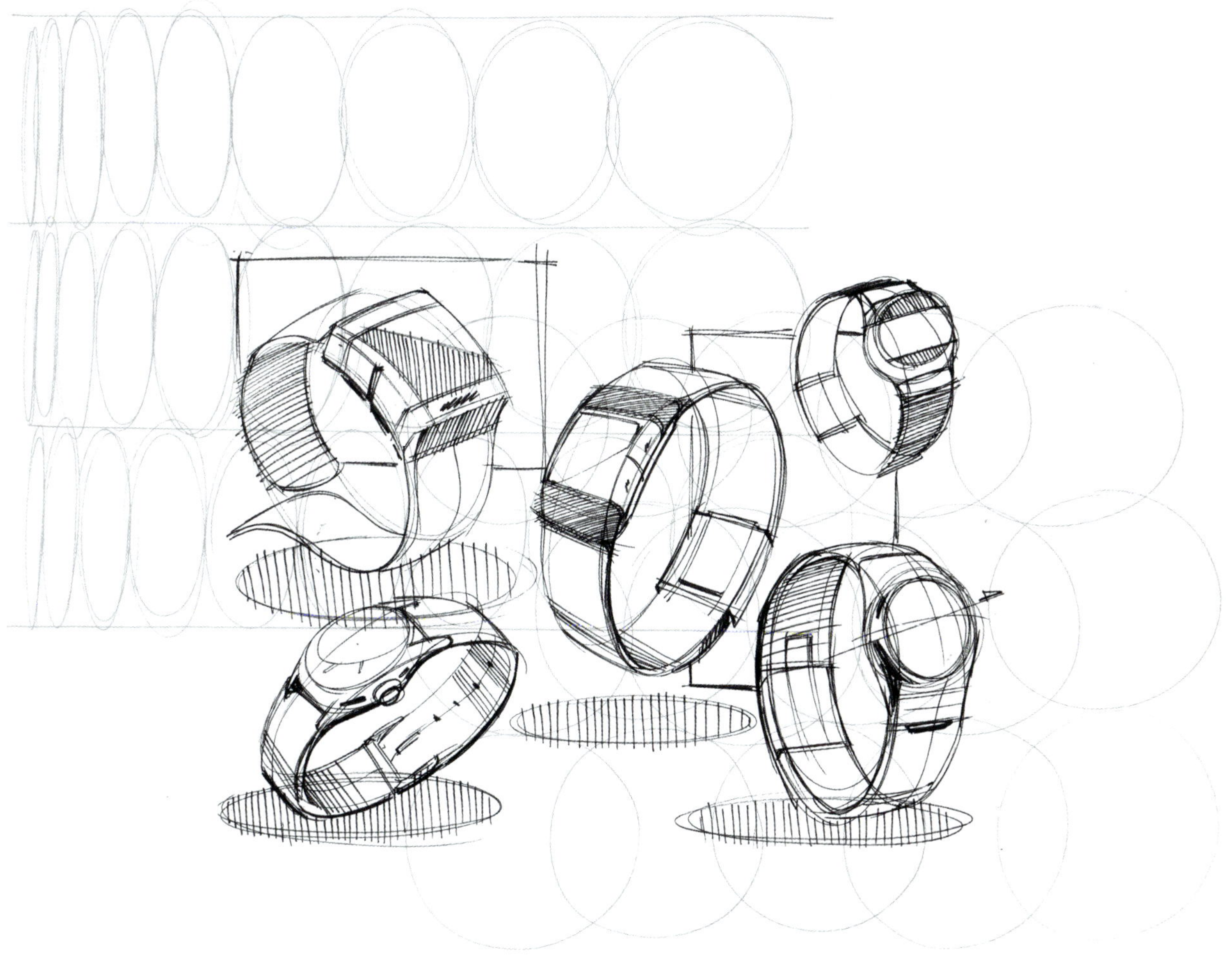

CHAPTER 3

GETTING STARTED

Being in the right mindset to draw is super important. Not only will it make a noticeable difference in how you approach your work, but the right mood will also affect your work's quality and creativity. If you're feeling stressed, anxious, or frustrated, try to find a way to relax a bit before picking up your pen, pencil, or brush. I've found that walking away from my work can be one of the best ways to open my creativity. Take a minute to do something radically different to release your creative energy. When you feel more ready to draw, ease into it with some warmups.

Warming Up

Warming up is critical to performance. Champion marathon runners with years of experience still stretch and prepare before races. The most impressive body builders still perform warmups using lighter weights and basic moves. Drawing is no different: Warming up primes your brain, eyes, and muscles to help you create your best work. I like to think of it a bit like priming the circuit connecting your eyes to your brain and to your muscles. A bit of practice with a few simple exercises every day will go a long way in developing your drawing skills and the quality of your work.

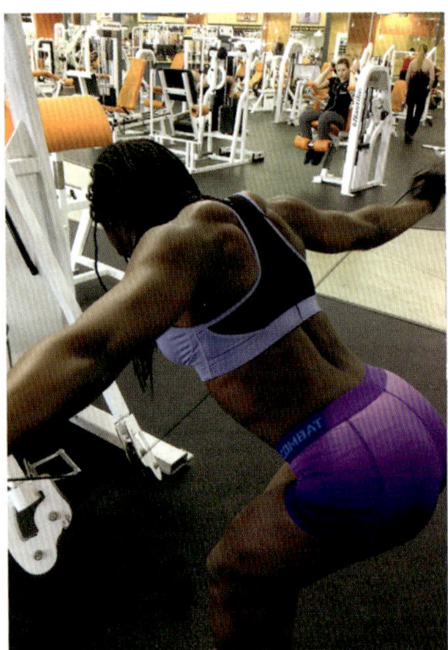
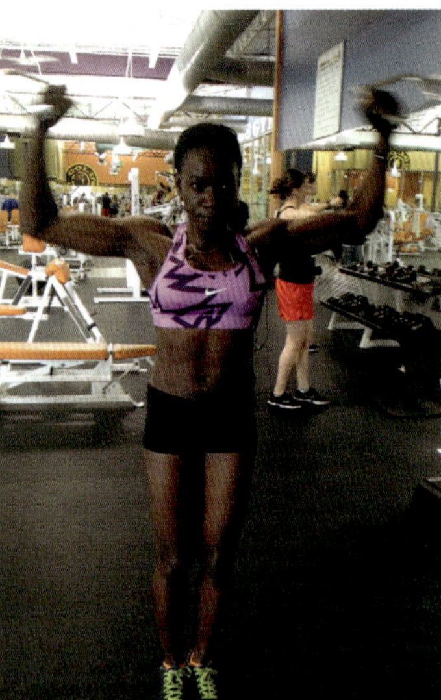

Holding Your Drawing Tool

Try to hold your drawing tool loosely but confidently at about halfway up the barrel. If that grip position feels uncomfortable, move your fingers down the pen or pencil until you feel more comfortable with your grip. Remember to relax, too. Tension in your grip will show through in your drawing. Finding the right balance of position and grip strength can be tricky but well worth it. Pay attention to the way your pen or pencil grip feels during your warm-up exercises and the quality of the lines you create.

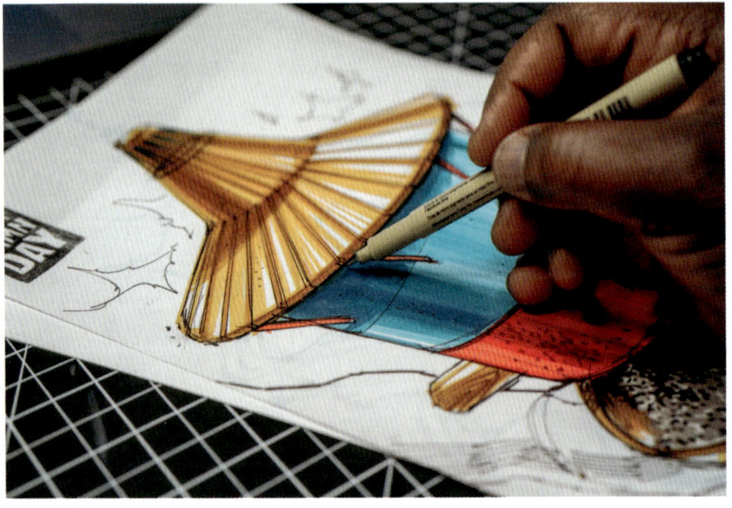

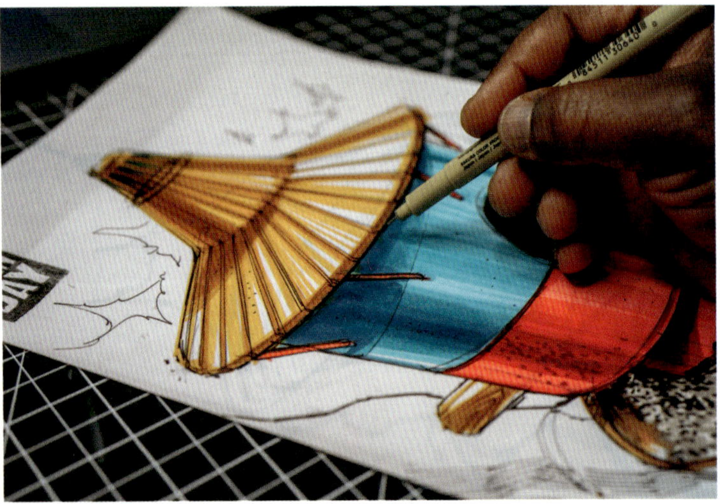

Drawing with Your Shoulder

Draw with your shoulder, using your shoulder and elbow as pivot points for your arm, to create straight and fluid lines. When you are drawing with your full arm this way, you'll be able to create more expressive and gestural strokes that are exciting and full of energy—rather than the wiggles that result from drawing with your wrist. You'll also be able to move your pen or pencil with consistency and confidence for longer distances over your drawing surface. Following through with your drawing stroke is also easier when you draw with your shoulder. It may feel unnatural at first, especially if you are used to small scribbles and doodles but give it a try!

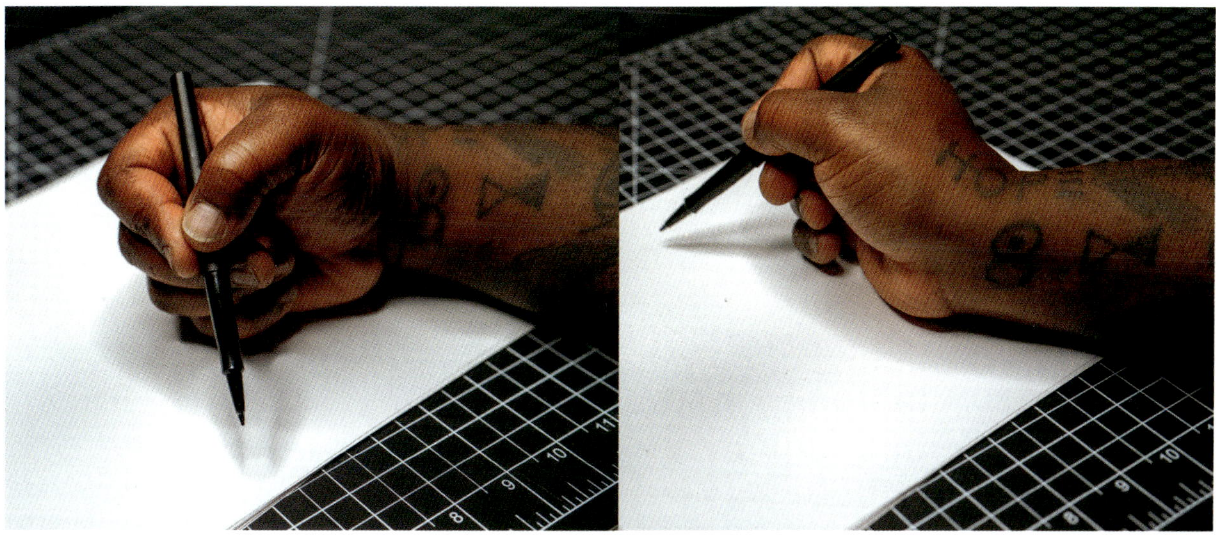

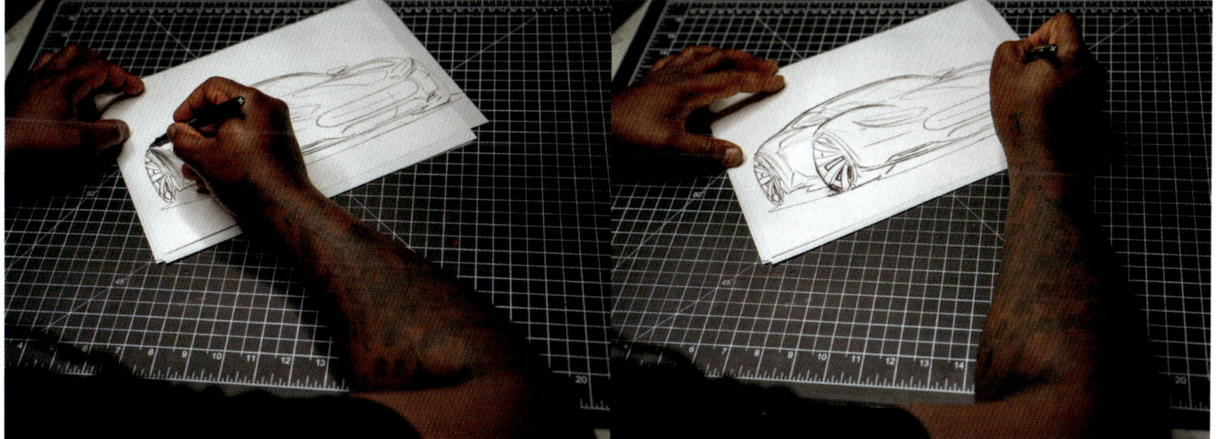

Exercise 1: Lines

Draw a series of parallel lines as straight as possible.

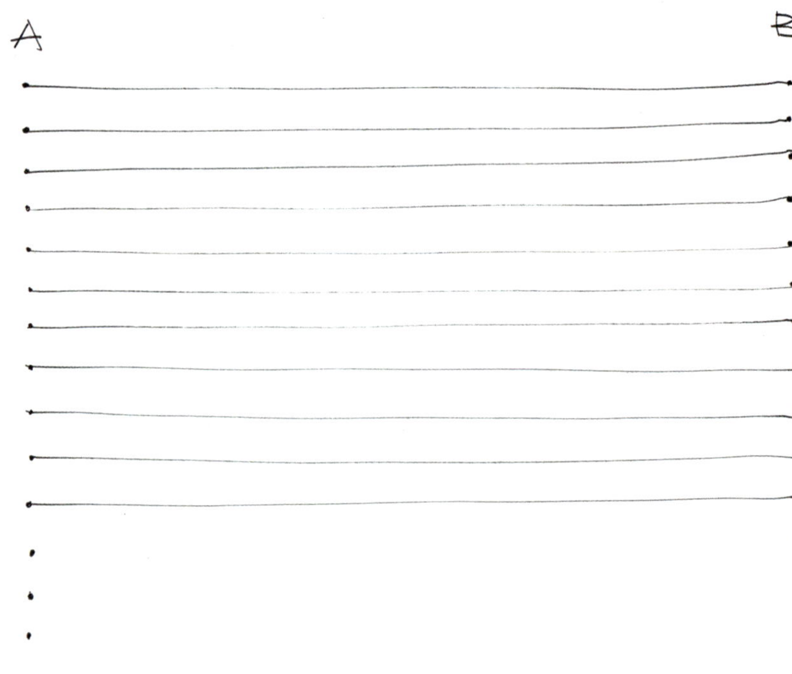

While this exercise may sound simple, it can be quite challenging. To begin, mark a series of corresponding points on opposite edges of your paper, then orient your paper to draw horizontal lines between them. I prefer to use the longer dimension of the page for this exercise; the movement is more challenging and primes me to draw larger than I may be comfortable with.

Focus on where you're going, not where you are as you draw the line. Think of the exercise like life. Focusing on the end goal is very important and following through on your stroke will help you increase your accuracy.

Remember to draw with your shoulder and elbow as pivots. Try to lock your wrist so you won't wiggle as you go. No need to be tense, just try to minimize movement in your wrist. Draw quickly. The slower you draw, the more opportunity there will be for error along your stroke's path. Practice a few pages per day of this exercise to improve your fluidity in drawing.

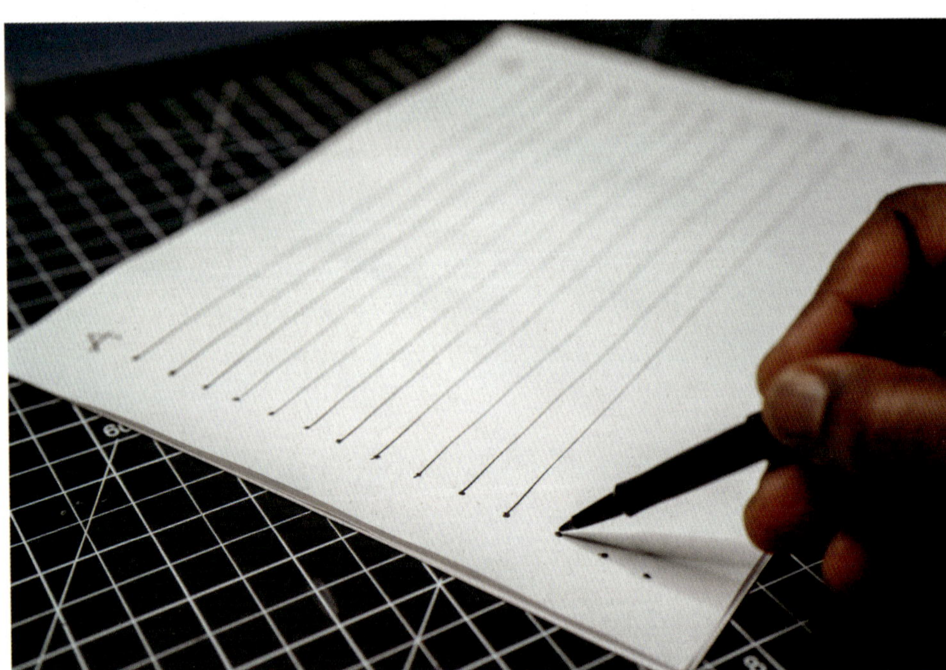

Exercise 2: Circles

Draw a series of circles

When you draw each circle, hover over the sheet of paper and draw the circle in the air before actually making contact with your pen. Called *ghosting*, this technique gives you a bit of practice before you commit to the final lines for your circles.

Stay loose and relax, then commit to the final circle. Aim for circles of about 2 to 3 inches (50 to 75 mm) in diameter. Remember to draw quickly and fluidly for the best results. For efficiency, I usually practice my circles over my pages of line exercises.

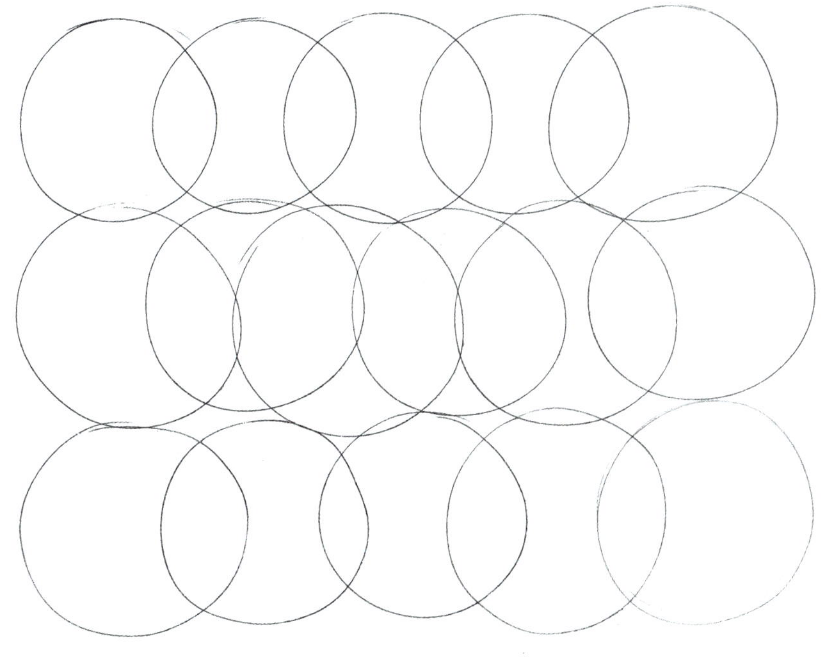

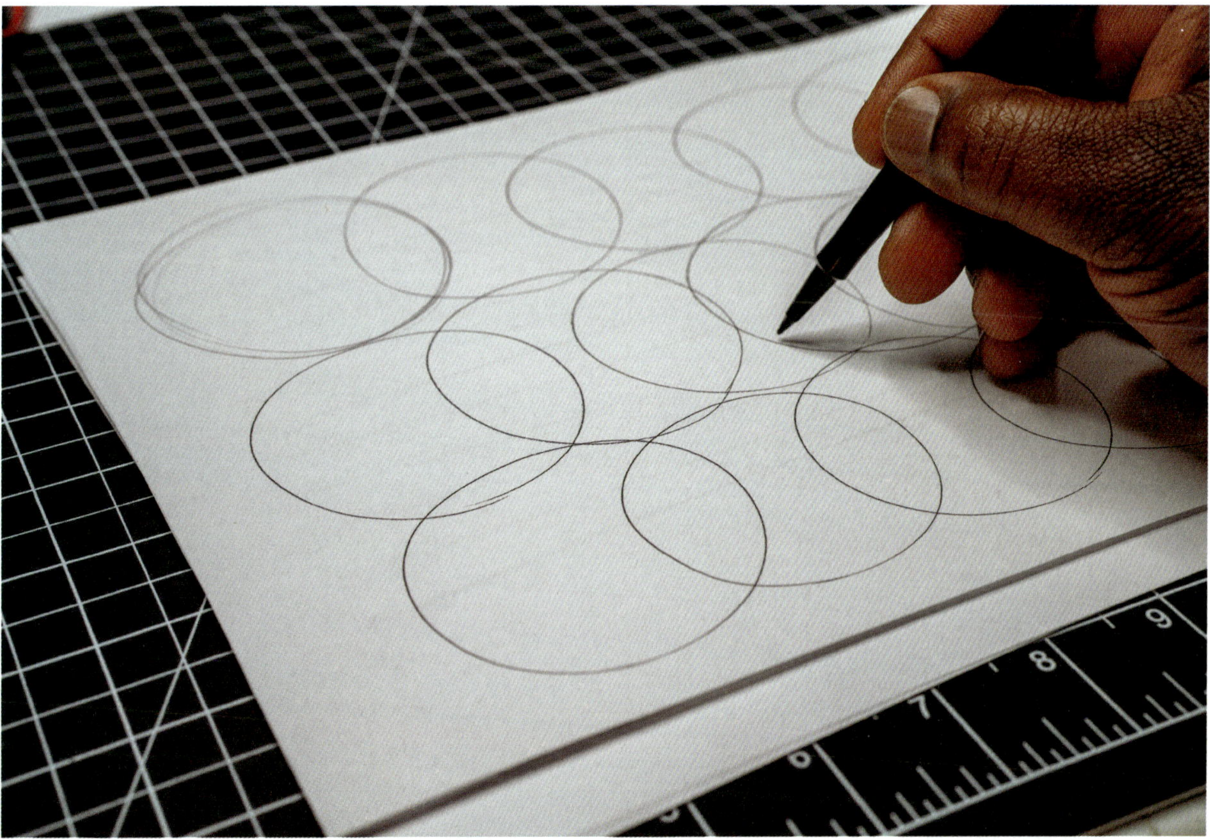

Exercise 3: Ellipses

Draw a series of ellipses.

Just like drawing circles, when I draw an ellipse, I try to hover over the sheet of paper before making contact.

To set up the exercise, draw a series of parallel lines about 2 to 3 inches apart. Rotate your page to a comfortable angle, and then draw a series of ellipses that increase in *degree* (get wider in the shorter dimension). Think of the degree of an ellipse as the angle at which you view the circular rim of your favorite coffee mug. Depending on the angle relative to your eyes, the rim may appear narrow or wide to you. (You'll learn more about this in Chapter 5, "Learning to See in Three Dimensions," and Chapter 6, "Drawing with Depth in 3D.") Draw big: Aim for about 2 to 3 inches (50 to 75 mm) wide at the longest dimension.

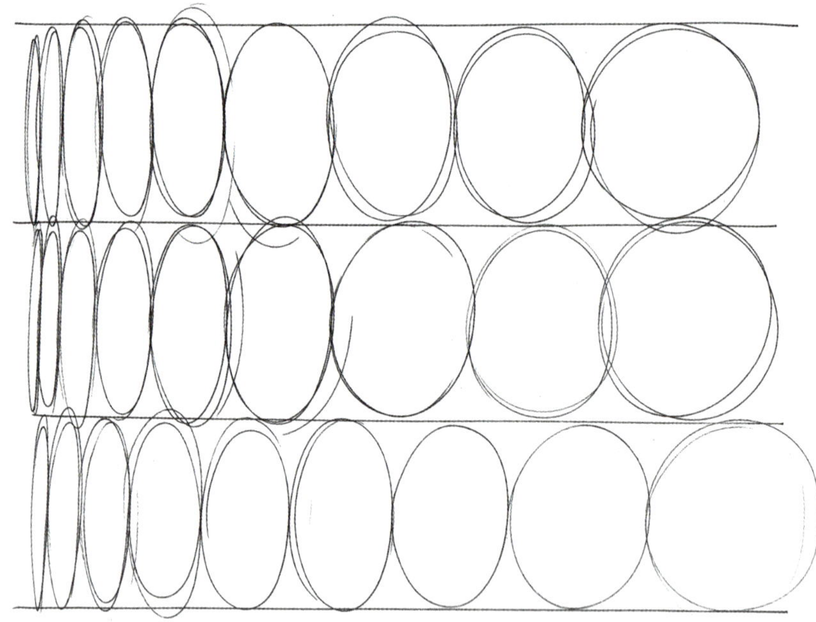

Stay loose and relaxed; hover and ghost in your ellipses before committing to the final shape. Remember to draw quickly and fluidly for the best results.

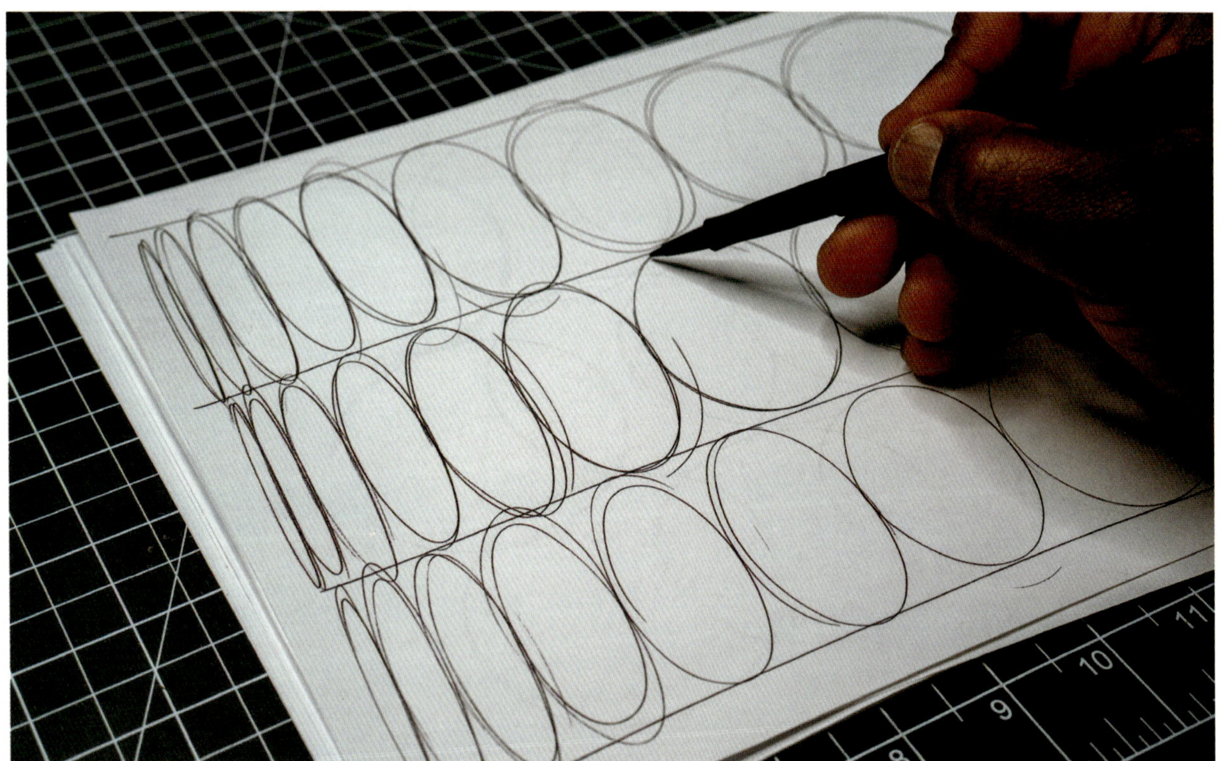

Get Moving and Keep Moving

There is no one right way to warm up. Some artists, designers, and illustrators choose to warm up by creating a sketch of an object or scene rather than performing repetitive mechanical movements. If that works better for you, fine! I prefer these exercises; they're simple and don't require me to come up with some new idea to draw just to practice. Figure out what feels right for you and do that. The most important thing is to maintain regular practice and rigor around drawing.

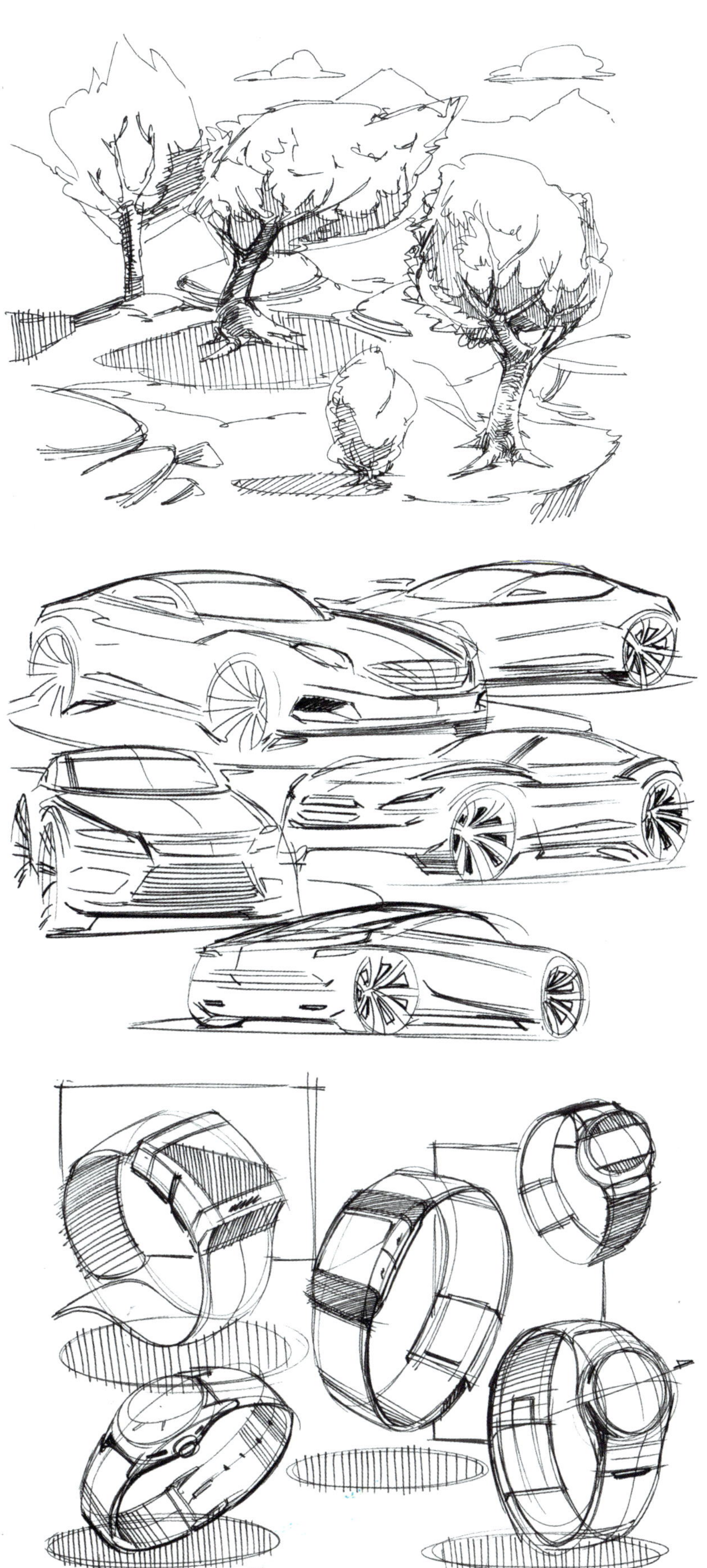

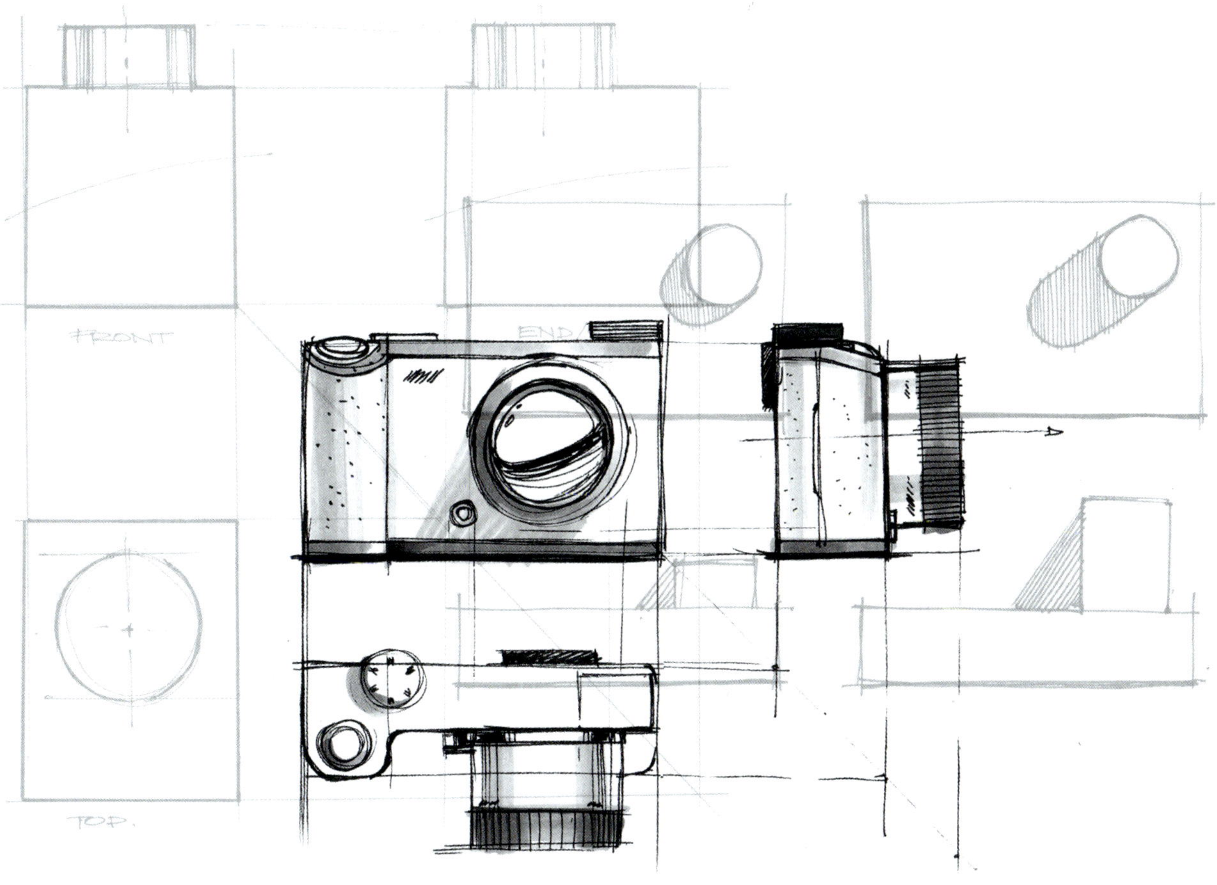

CHAPTER 4

LEARNING TO SEE IN 2D

Drawing in two dimensions can be an easier, more efficient way to think about the general geometry or shape of an object. Two-dimensional (2D) drawing simplifies the potential complexity of having to think about the overall three-dimensional (3D) perspective of an object while at the same time thinking about the visualization of that object. Working quickly is paramount for designers and starting in 2D is the quickest way to ideate.

Imagine drawing a simple box. In our 3D world, the box has six sides to look at, and each side has a profile or shape that together make up the object. Drawing each side of the box would present six views of that box and effectively describe what the object is without your having to draw the entire object in a perspective view.

Now, the sides of a box may not be all that interesting to contemplate, but they can help you think about which sides of a more complex object to observe and subsequently draw in two dimensions. You don't need to see all six sides to know a box is a box; a front, top, and side view effectively communicate its box-ness. Likewise, drawing these same three views is generally enough to describe any object you are visualizing and communicate relevant details about it in your 2D rendering.

Drawing in two dimensions is also a great way to make sure that the dimensions related to the object being visualized are consistent between views. By projecting or drawing lines from one view to another, you can carry dimensions across the drawing. Drawing in this fashion matters, because to correctly show enough information about an object in a proportional and measured manner, accurate and consistent dimensioning is necessary.

Two-Dimension Sketch Demonstration

Sometimes the easiest way to understand a process is to try it.

1. In your mind, visualize a camera with a lens, and draw a simple outline of one view. Alternatively, you may use a camera as reference for drawing each view. You can start with the front, top, or side view, but for this demonstration I will start by drawing the front view.

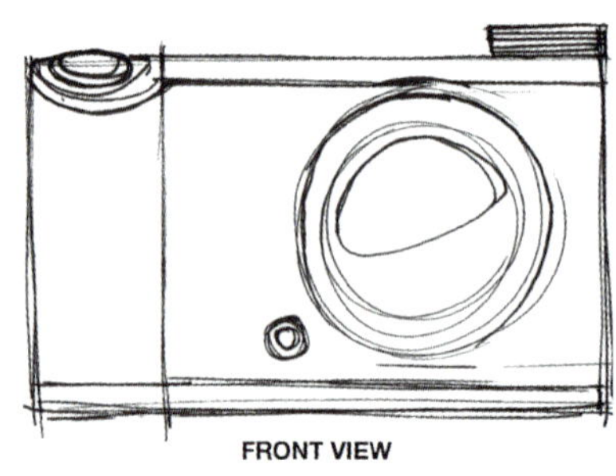

2. From the silhouette and details of the camera, project lines to the right of the front view to create an end view. Note the location of details on your first view, and make sure that you carry the details across to the right in the end view. Estimate the depth of the camera, lens, and grip and draw those in. If needed, a very light rough sketch in pencil or marker may be completed first as a guide.

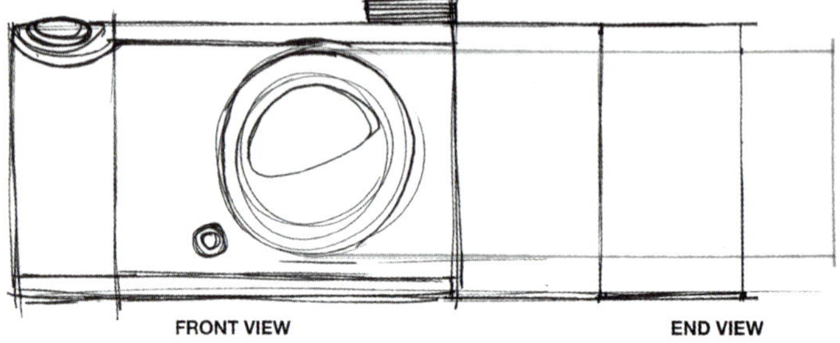

3. Add details to the end view to mirror the details from the front view. Here, you can see the grip, battery door, viewfinder, lens, and flash have been shown in the end view.

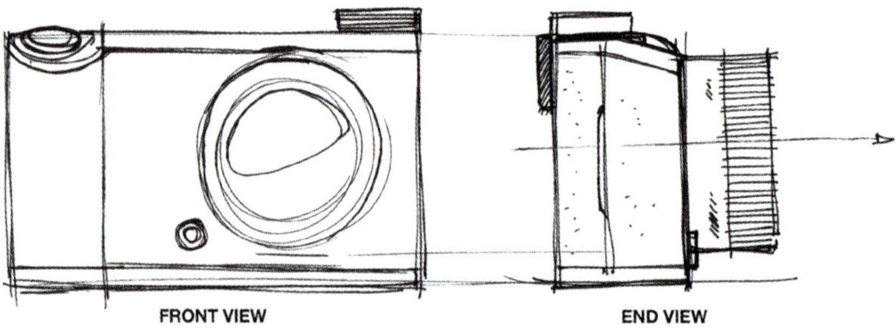

4. Starting at the lower right corner of the front view sketch, project a line downward at approximately a 45° angle and extend far enough to be directly below the end view. From the end-view, project lines downward vertically to intersect this new diagonal line. These lines will be your measurements for the top view, which you will place below your front view.

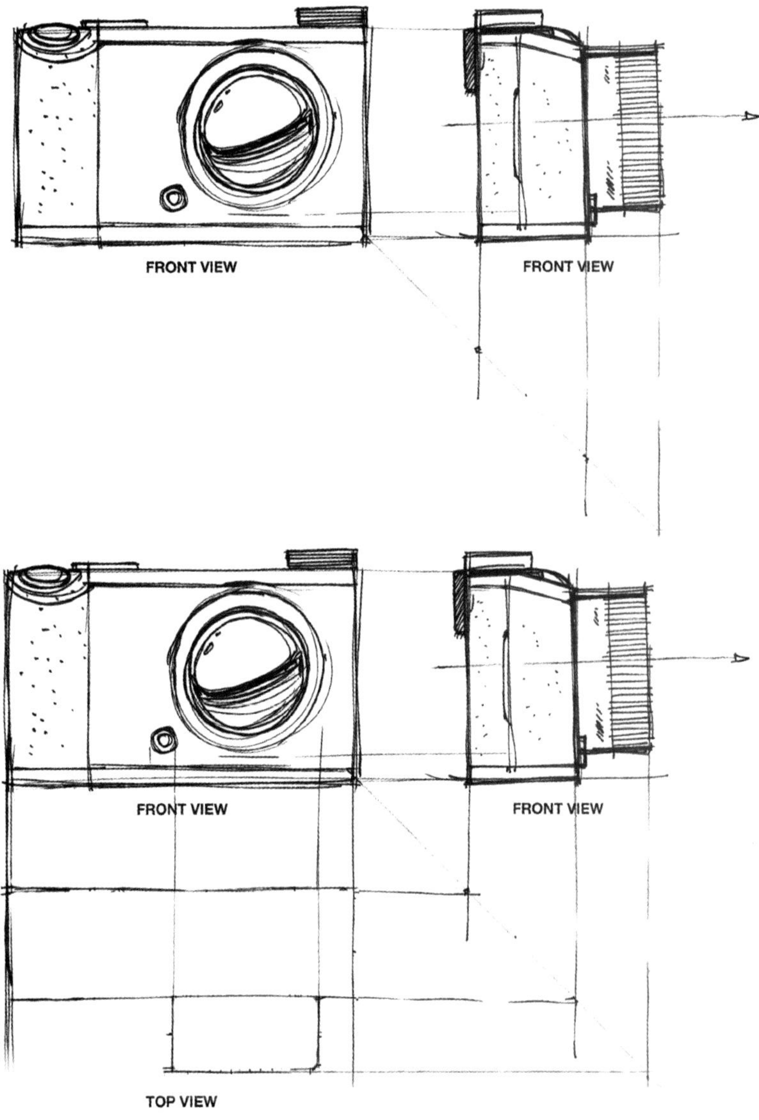

5. To complete the transfer of dimensions, project lines to the left from the intersection points along the diagonal line drawn in step 4. Be sure to extend the lines far enough to be placed below the front view.

   Next, project lines downward from the front view to intersect the lines underneath the front view. At this point you should have a measured representation of the outline of the area for your top view as represented by your box.

6. Carry over any additional details from each view using a similar technique and flow. Remember to capture details along the way as you project lines and draw in shaped.

   At this point, I have sketched in and proportionally measured details such as the adjustment knobs, lens, flash and viewfinder as they would appear from the top view.

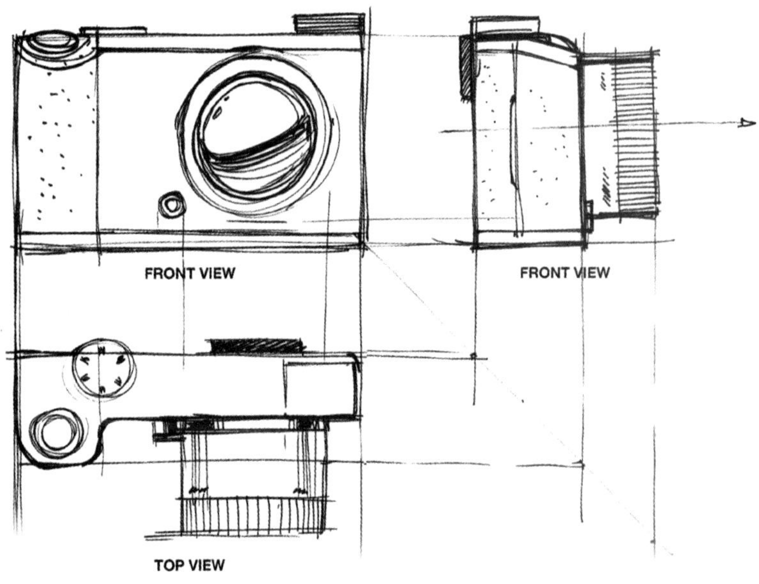

7. I finish up by cleaning up line-work with a repeated pen stroke on outlines of shapes and adding a bit of gray marker for a subtle hint of depth. More on this technique ahead in the next section, "Drawing with Depth in 2D."

Eventually, with enough practice, you'll be able to rotate the object in your mind and visualize each view as you draw. Mastering this skill is key to being able to draw any object you want in perspective, whether simple or complex.

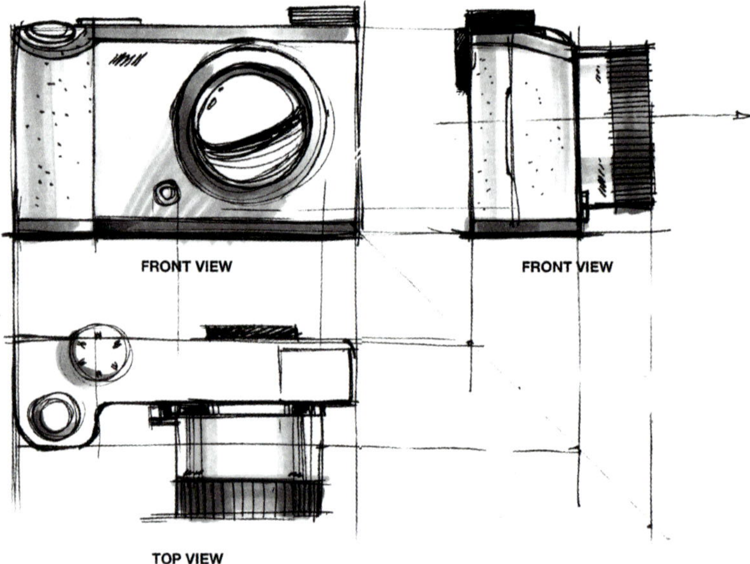

Drawing with Depth in 2D

While 2D drawings may contain lots of visual information about a concept, they also tend to be a bit flat sometimes. The illusion of depth, shadows, and color can enhance the appearance of your drawing, and they're easier to add than you might expect.

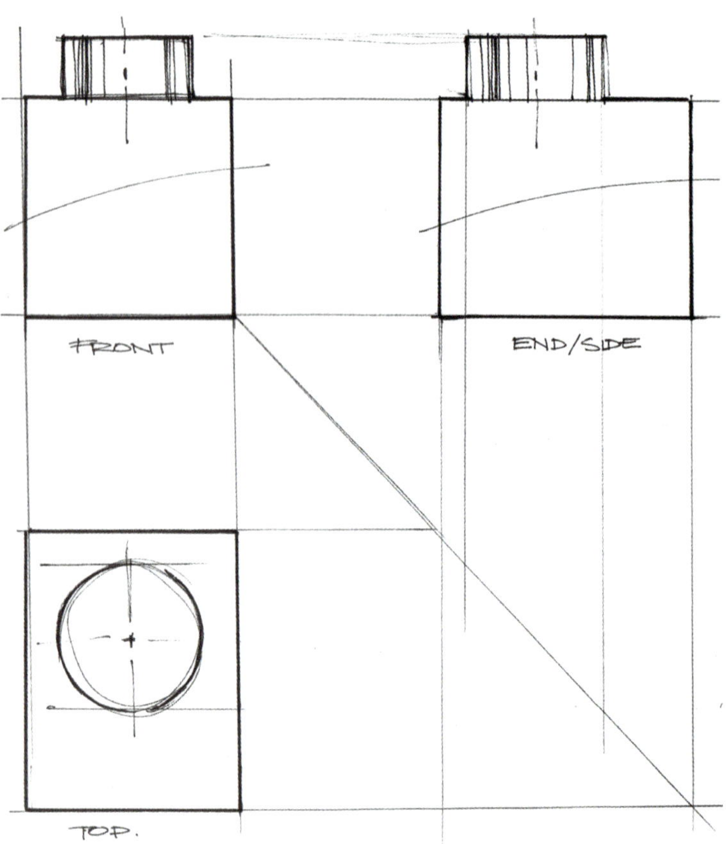

To add depth, think of each element in your drawing as having some volume and depth, then maintain that idea of depth and lighting as you sketch. The simplest way to do this is using scale. If, for example, you're drawing two of the same object, you can scale one object dimensionally and proportionally to be larger than the other to create the illusion of depth without having to go through the trouble of setting up a full perspective drawing scene. Remember, an object that is closer to you and has depth will cast a shadow on the surface or area nearby, so include one in your work.

Let's look at a simple example: a three-view setup of a simple cylinder that is mated (intersected) with a cuboid. In 2D views it might look something like this illustration.

Because the cylinder protrudes from the cuboid and the 2D view is from a point of view above the object, you could add a shadow to show that the cylinder has depth, even though it appears as just a circle from above. Drawing this cast shadow in the top-down 2D view adds information in a way that gives the view more dimension. Someone viewing your drawing can even infer how tall the object is from the length or direction of its shadow.

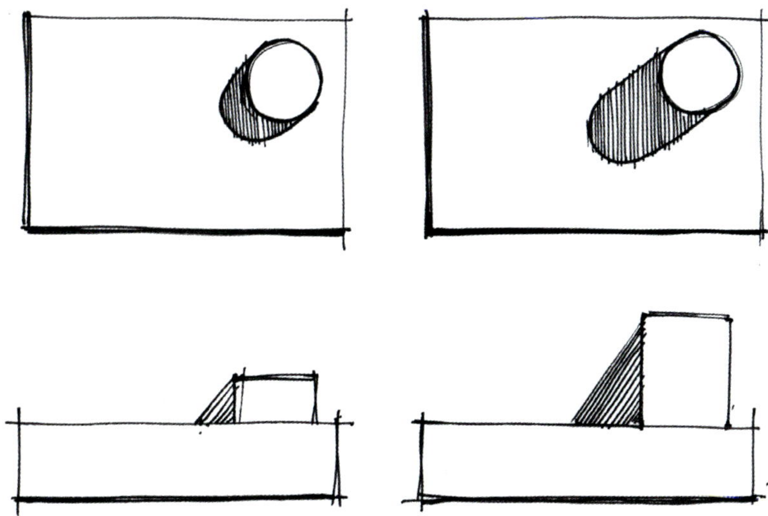

When simulating depth in a scene with multiple objects, consider their positioning. For example, if two objects overlap and are drawn in a 2D view, line weight and a cast shadow work well to communicate a sense of depth. When one object is above the other and lit from the front, a cast shadow creates a sense of depth and placement. As with the cylinder example, the size or intensity of the shadow in your 2D drawing can communicate relative placement in a 3D space.

Color is another way to communicate perspective when drawing in 2D. Try an experiment: Look outside and compare the saturation of the colors you see close to you with those in the distance. The more distant colors will appear less saturated. This effect is called *atmospheric perspective*, and you can mimic it in 2D drawing by placing more saturated colors on the object you wish to bring to the foreground. The viewer's brain will connect conceptually what is observed in real life with the symbolic placement of color in your drawing and infer depth in your scene. We will discuss this concept further later in Chapter 9, "Color."

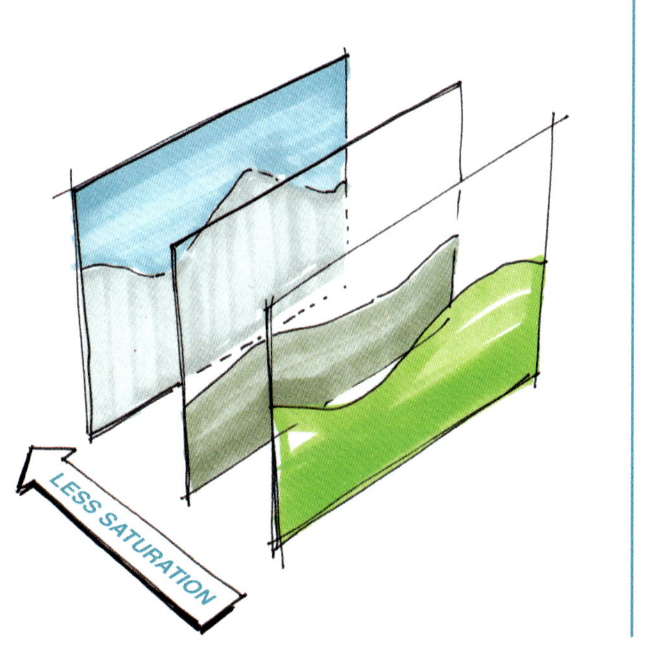

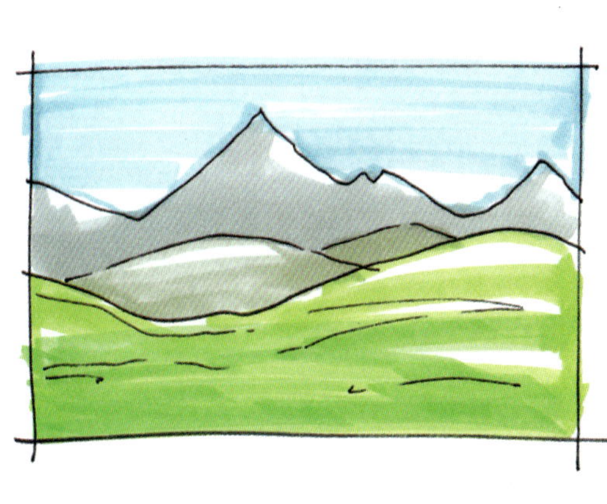

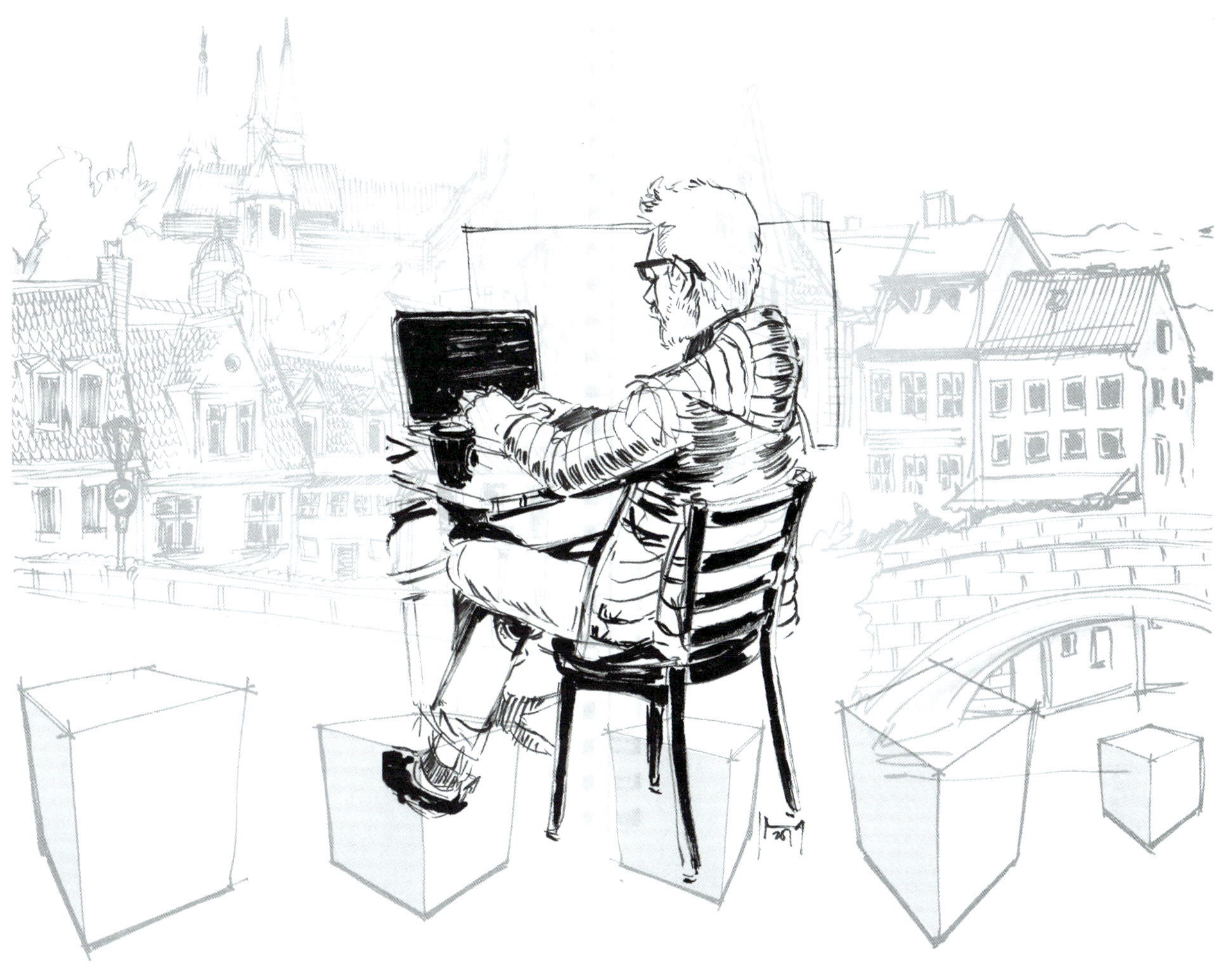

CHAPTER 5

LEARNING TO SEE IN THREE DIMENSIONS

Whether you're drawing objects you observe or objects from your imagination, the ability to see the world in three dimensions is an essential tool in your artistic skillset. Yes, we all perceive depth and scale instinctively (otherwise we'd be stumbling, bumping, and dropping our way through the day), but as artists we need to turn a more critical eye to how things look in the world around us.

So much can be learned about seeing the world in three dimensions simply by paying attention. In real life, objects are more than just the simple shapes or silhouettes of a 2D drawing. Objects have dimensions in three directions that are orthogonal to each other: length, height, and width. Those same three directions (represented by the x, y, and z axes in mathematics) can describe the relative positions of objects in a space. Because of this, depth and scale are observable characteristics of three-dimensional space and the objects found within that space. Honing your observational skills can help you make the leap into giving objects from your imagination a three-dimensional appearance in your drawings.

Some of the simplest 3D objects—the cube, cone, sphere, cylinder, pyramid, and torus—are called *primitives* or reference objects. In various combinations, these primitives form the basis of more complex objects in the three-dimensional world we live in. Learning to see the simple objects within the complex will help you build your observational skills—and your perspective drawings.

Observing the World Around You

You can learn much by taking a moment to observe objects in the environment around you, as well as the environment itself. Suppose, for example, you're standing in the middle of a street. The buildings, people, cars, and trees you see seem to diminish in size, presence, and even color saturation as they are located further away from you, the observer. The progression of scale as objects recede into the distance is a consistent characteristic of observed three-dimensional space and perspective. Remember this detail: One of the most effective ways to communicate depth in a drawing is the progressive reduction in size and detail of objects relative in distance to the viewer.

Your view from the middle of the street is an example of *one-point perspective*. One-point perspective is the view in which there seems to be one point to which all objects scale, diminish, or vanish. Another name for this conceptual point off in the distance is the *vanishing point*. One-point perspective has one vanishing point along the *horizon line*. The horizon is where

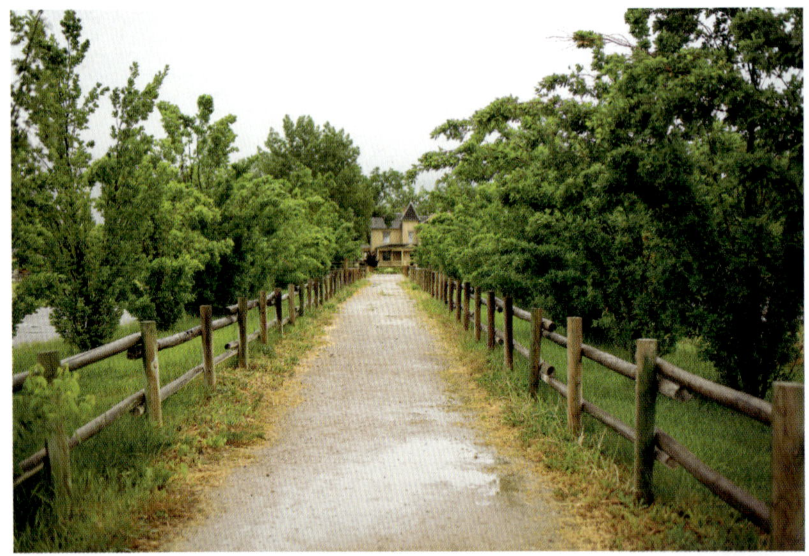

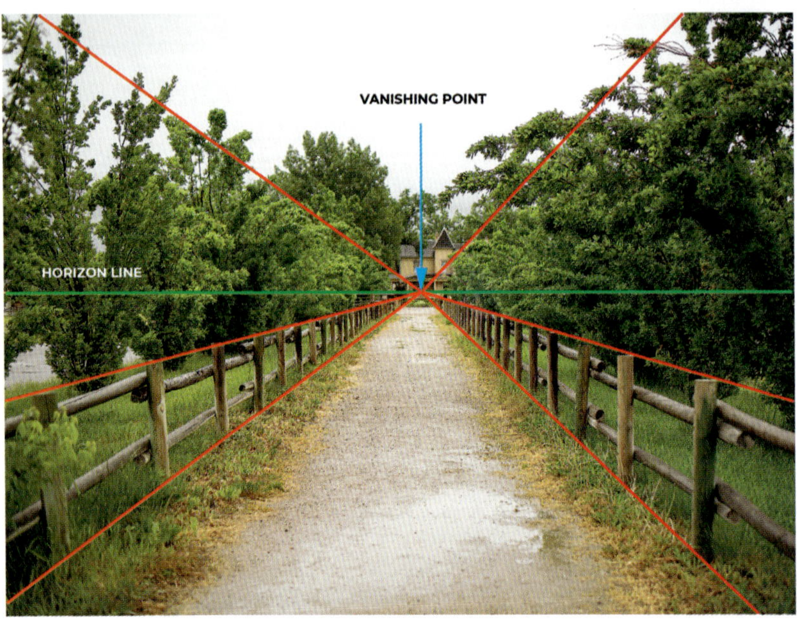

everything visible diminishes in size and seems to taper off to being effectively out of sight and indistinguishable from the sky or the Earth itself.

Standing in the middle of a road is not the only way (nor, perhaps, the safest) to observe perspective at work in the world around you. A simple object like a box will show the effects of perspective at a glance if you observe carefully.

Notice that the edges of the box, although parallel and an equal distance apart in real life, appear to get closer together on the long side of the box, just like in the road scene. (Chapter 6, "Drawing with Depth in 3D," will explain the two-point or three-point perspective theories behind why this happens.)

The visual effect of tapering edges and reduced size at a distance is even more noticeable with larger box-like objects. Look for examples in your own immediate area, such as a table, and observe the change in apparent scale of lines and edges closest to you, as compared to lines and edges further away from you. A building or structure outside will show tapering sides much more prominently, because of the relative scale of the structure to you, the viewer.

Curvilinear shapes, such as tubes, are also a good means of observing perspective in action. Perspective affects how you perceive the relative sizes of the ends of the tube and how the shapes appear long with a general tapering along the length of the tube toward the end that is farthest away. When viewed dead-on, the end of the tube will appear circular. Change the angle relative to your eye, and the end of the tube will now appear oval. These oval shapes in perspective are called *ellipses*. Simply put, ellipses and ovals are circles viewed at an angle in perspective or three-dimensional space.

Ellipses are a somewhat tricky to understand but important part of drawing correct perspective of objects. Take some time to make observations about what you see related to how a cylindrical object—a straw, a Pringles can, your coffee mug—is placed relative to your eyes. View the cylindrical object from a variety of points of view and see how the object changes in appearance.

As objects in three-dimensional space recede into the distance, you can make a few other observations about their appearance and

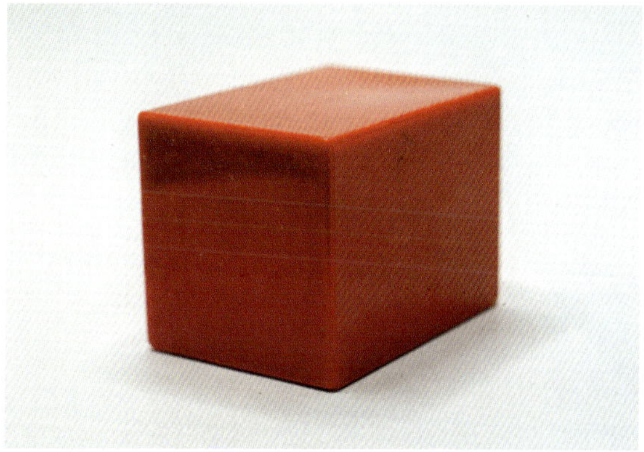

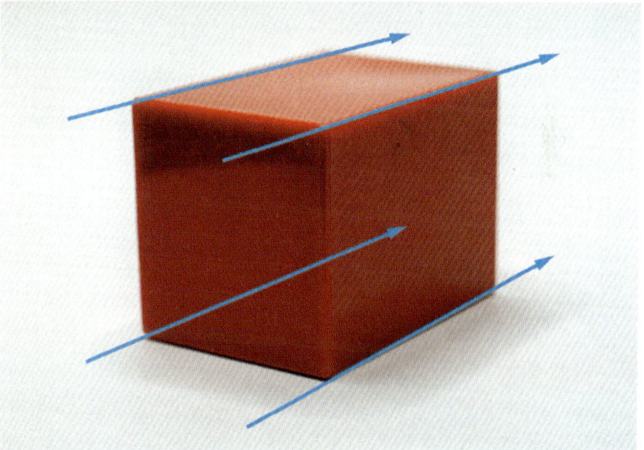

Edges appear to converge when an object is viewed in perspective.

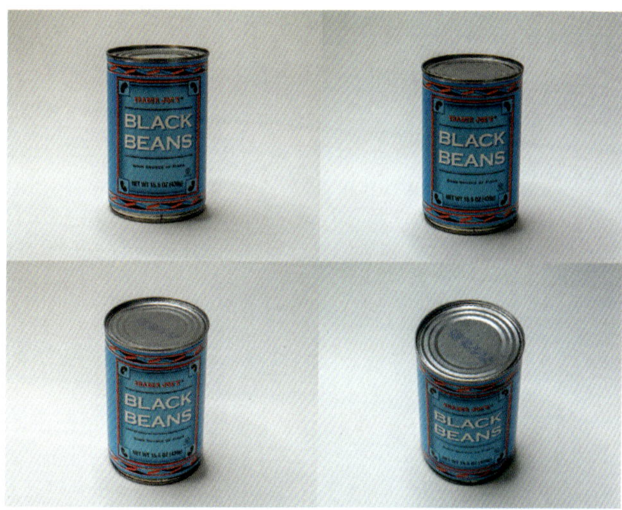

Can viewed at varying points of view. Ellipses are narrow or wide depending on view.

placement. The keys to look for are color and detail, relative scale, point of view, and contrast.

Color and Detail

As mentioned in chapter 4, the further away an object is from you, the less intense and saturated its colors will seem. This is due to *atmospheric diffusion*: As light is dispersed in the atmosphere, color becomes fuzzier and more desaturated. Combined with the focal length of your eyes' lenses, atmospheric diffusion also is why you cannot see minute details of faraway objects. In a three-dimensional view, objects viewed at distance will show less detail than objects viewed up close. Distant objects mainly appear as silhouettes and shapes, although associations from your memory may help you fill in such unobservable details as texture, pattern, or distinct parts. We'll discuss color and atmospheric perspective a bit more in Chapter 9, "Color."

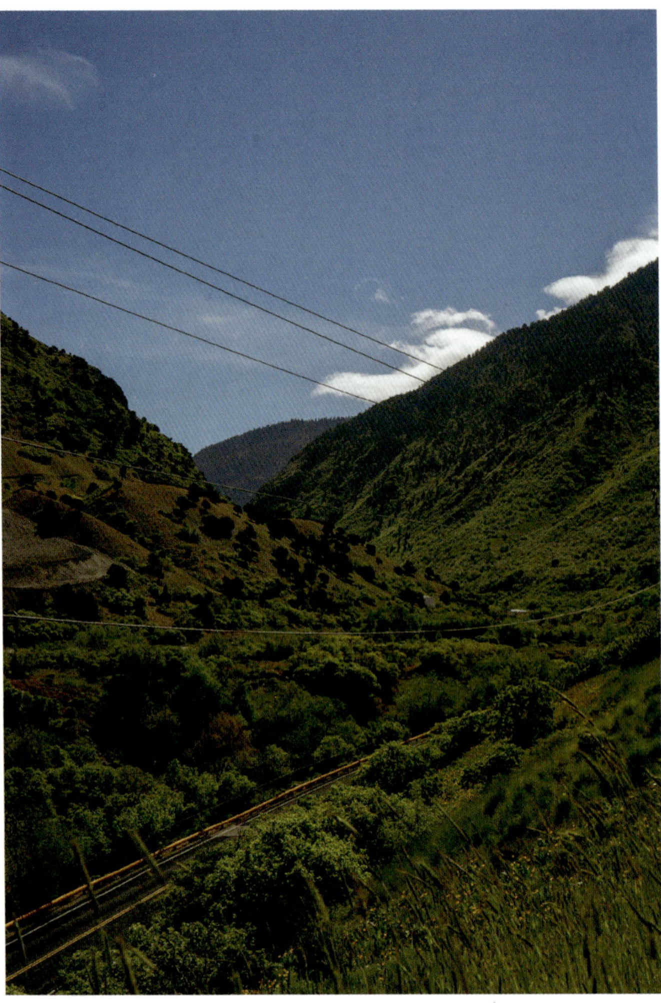

Notice the color fade off as objects recede to the horizon.

Relative Scale

Relative scale is another way we observe perspective in real life. *Relative scale* is how we create associations by comparison in scale and placement of the object in reference to another object in view. Consider, for example, these sketched primitive boxes.

If you cover all but one of the boxes with your hands, there is no way to tell how big the remaining box is compared to anything else. Without another object nearby, the box could be as large as a house or as small as a game die. Adding an object that is relatable and familiar may help the viewer interpret what size the box actually is. A simple silhouette of a human is a great way to show relative scale. What other objects might be familiar and useful in creating a sense of scale while drawing?

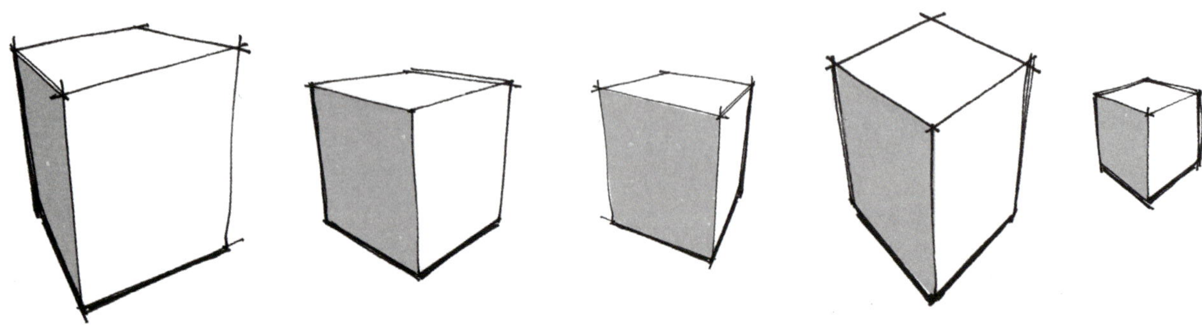

Point of View

Point of view refers to the relative position of you, the observer, to the object or scene. If an object is below your eye level, you will see more of the top of the object. If the object is above you relative to your eye level, you will see more of the bottom of the object. Point of view can also be used to suggest scale in a less definitive, yet relatable way. Something that is above you tends to be perceived as large, and objects that are located and viewed below eye level tend to be perceived as being smaller. An object at eye level also has a distinct and relatable scale that is implicit in its placement. For example, a building may be at eye level and rise a bit above eye level while receding and tapering toward its respective vanishing points.

Contrast

Visual contrast and changes in value are other clues you can observe to learn about 3D perspective. Whenever a surface changes direction, you will see a difference in the value or tone of the surface. While sitting in a room, look at the walls around you. Visually follow one wall to its closest corner. You will likely notice that there is a difference in value between the walls as they change direction. This is due to the relative position of the walls to the light source in the room, whether it be a window, lamps, or overhead light. What observations do you notice in your environment with space, depth, and contrast?

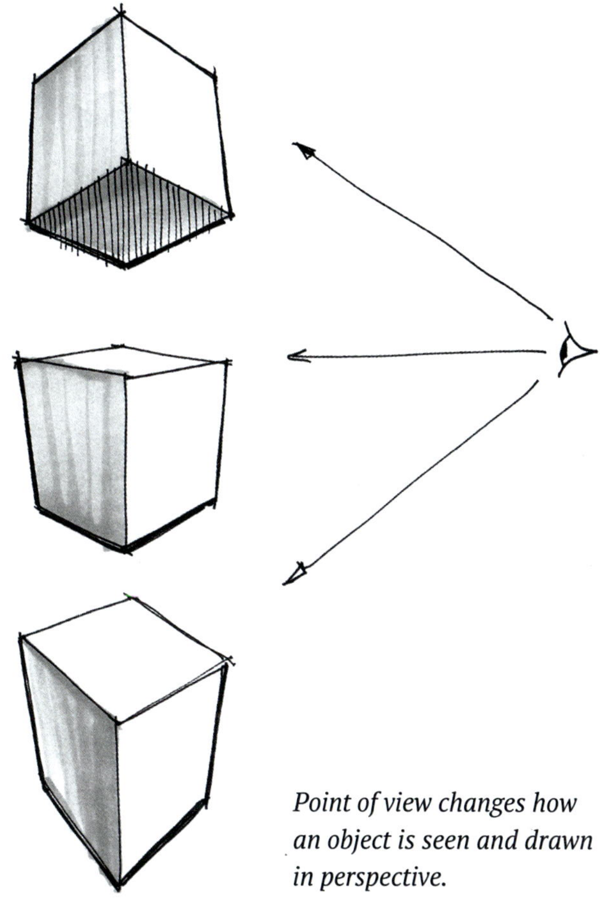

Point of view changes how an object is seen and drawn in perspective.

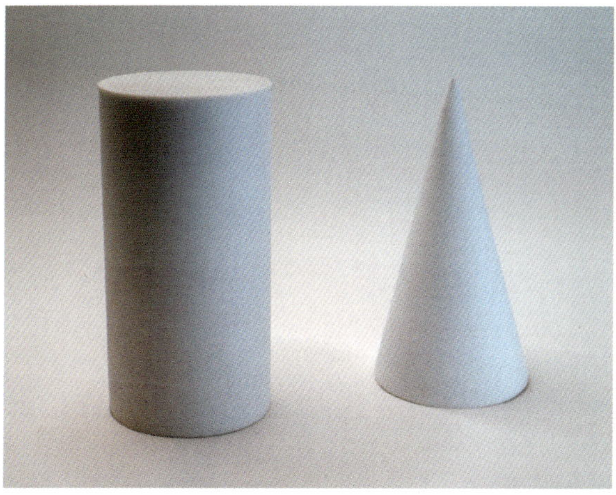

Rounded objects behave similarly. As a cylinder or sphere curves in form and, therefore, changes direction relative to the light in the environment, it will have a core shadow along its surface. The theory behind this effect is mathematically involved and somewhat complex, so for now, just pay close attention to the way light helps you see the three dimensionality of objects in your environment.

The intensity of contrast is not as important as noticing that there is a difference in value. Value changes give us a sense of the relative space and placement of objects in your environment. Value at times may also give a sense of depth relative to where you may be in relation to the object in view. We will discuss contrast further when diving a bit deeper into light, shadow, and reflections and how these elements communicate three-dimensional forms. (See Chapter 7, "Light and Shadow")

Draw from Observation to Draw from Imagination

One of the most effective ways to observe reality and solidify your understanding of three-dimensional space is by drawing from observation. *Drawing from observation* means looking at an object or scene in real life and interpreting what you see in a two-dimensional medium such as pen, pencil, and paper. When I left corporate employment, I decided to take some time to focus on drawing from observation. I would go to my local coffee shop and draw everything I could see that was interesting and even pushed myself to try different subject matter, as well. The experience was a fantastic exercise in speed, depth perception, and translation from reality to what I could capture in a brief timeframe.

By drawing from observation, you learn to capture what you see with the tools you may have. Although there are means of measuring proportion when drawing from observation, the exercise is less about precision and more about perception for me. Observing and drawing how one object stacks up to another when considering the progression of scale in a room, for example, requires you to compare placement and details about each object to establish their relative scale and visual presence on paper. Observational drawing will help you build a visual vocabulary of symbolic ways to represent reality that you can draw from when sketching objects in imagined settings. Much like with language, we must practice and learn the vocabulary of drawing by observing and connecting concepts mentally.

While commuting to work by public transit in San Francisco, I wanted to make the best use of my travel time. Armed with my sketchbook and a pen, I would draw people on the train from observation as well as dipping into imagined objects and

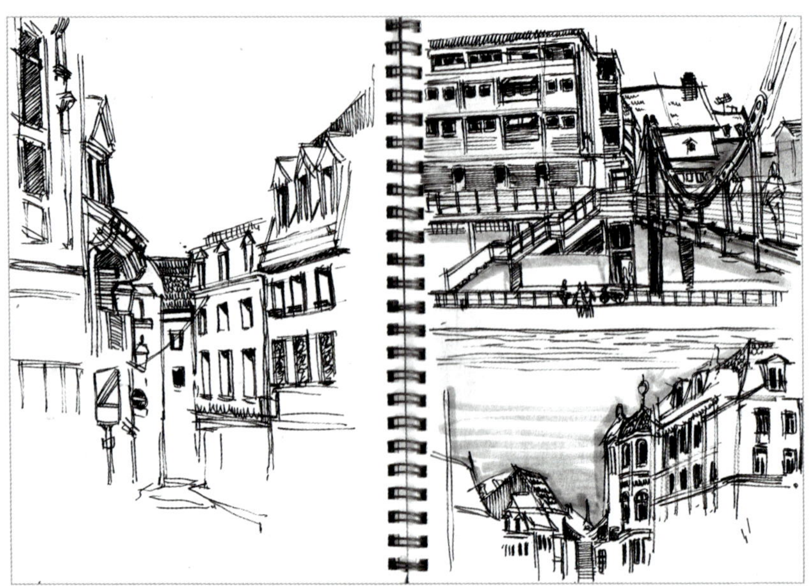

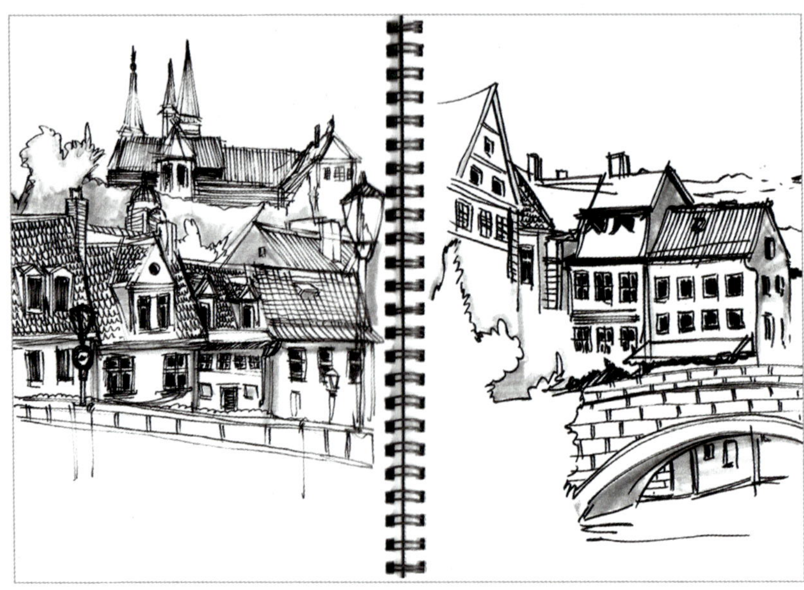

Practice drawing from observation wherever you go.

enhancements to the people in view. Drawing from my imagination became much easier the more I practiced this way, as I was able to pull from an established visual vocabulary of objects and scenarios that I had previously drawn from reality.

Likewise, drawing from photo references can be a convenient and appealing avenue for practice—if you know the difference between the reality captured by photography and reality itself. Lenses that have different focal

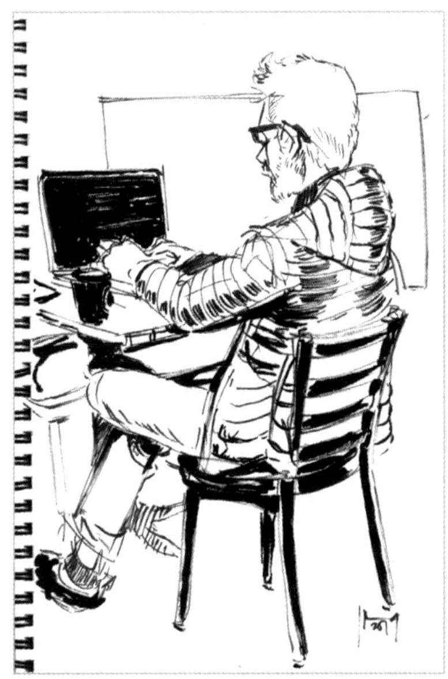

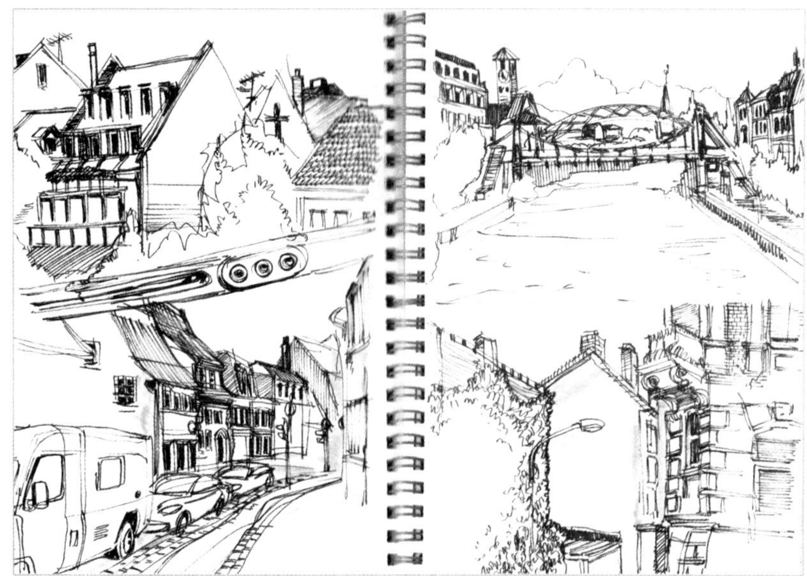

lengths than the human eye may capture photos with distortions that skew or flatten the three-dimensional appearance of real objects. Spotting these distortions takes a keen eye and a familiarity with such differences as how much the linear sides of an object may taper at various focal lengths. Drawing is about communication. If you want to communicate objects in a natural-looking perspective, it's important you learn to see things as they are in real life.

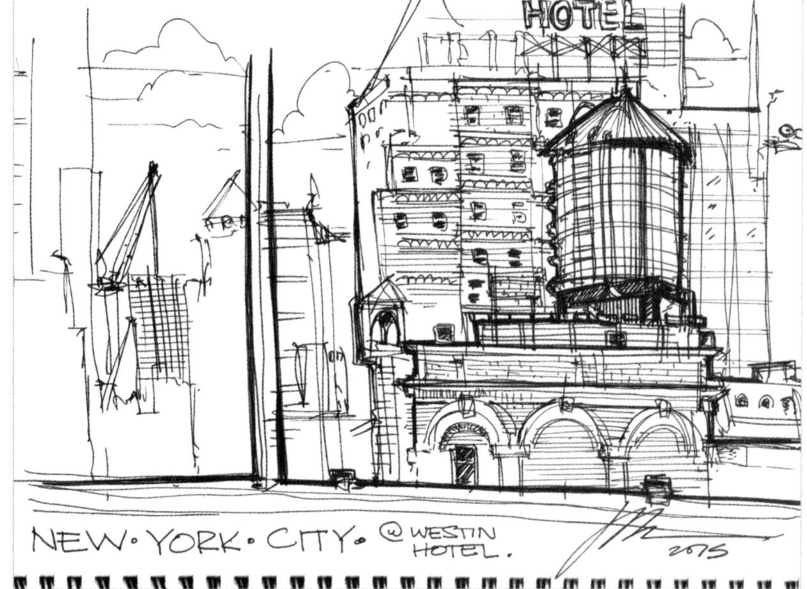

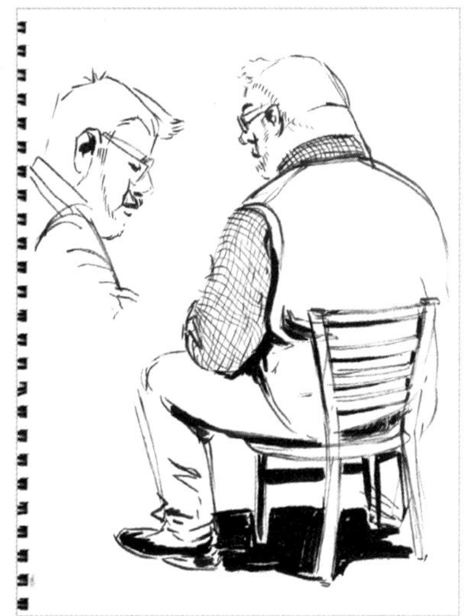

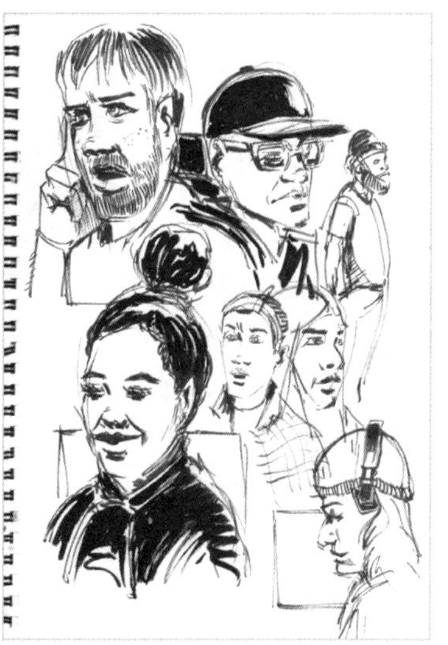

Find Inspiration in Other Artists' Work

I'm glad you're reading this book! Finding inspiration in the work of other artists, illustrators, or designers and watching their approach to drawing objects in perspective and three dimensions is a fantastic way to learn techniques for tackling tough perspective problems.

I spent a long time avoiding using other artists' work as a means of learning and looking back I realize that was very stubborn on my part. At the time, I had concerns about being authentic to my own self as an artist and not wanting to "copy" the work of others. The truth is no matter how much you try, even when mimicking the work of another artist, the result will be yours. Your perspective, point of view, and approach to drawing will make the work your own. Of course, if referencing the work of another artist, illustrator, or designer, be sure to give credit where credit is due!

You can learn much from those who have gone before and done the work to figure out perspective drawing, and you may find new or interesting techniques that work for you, too.

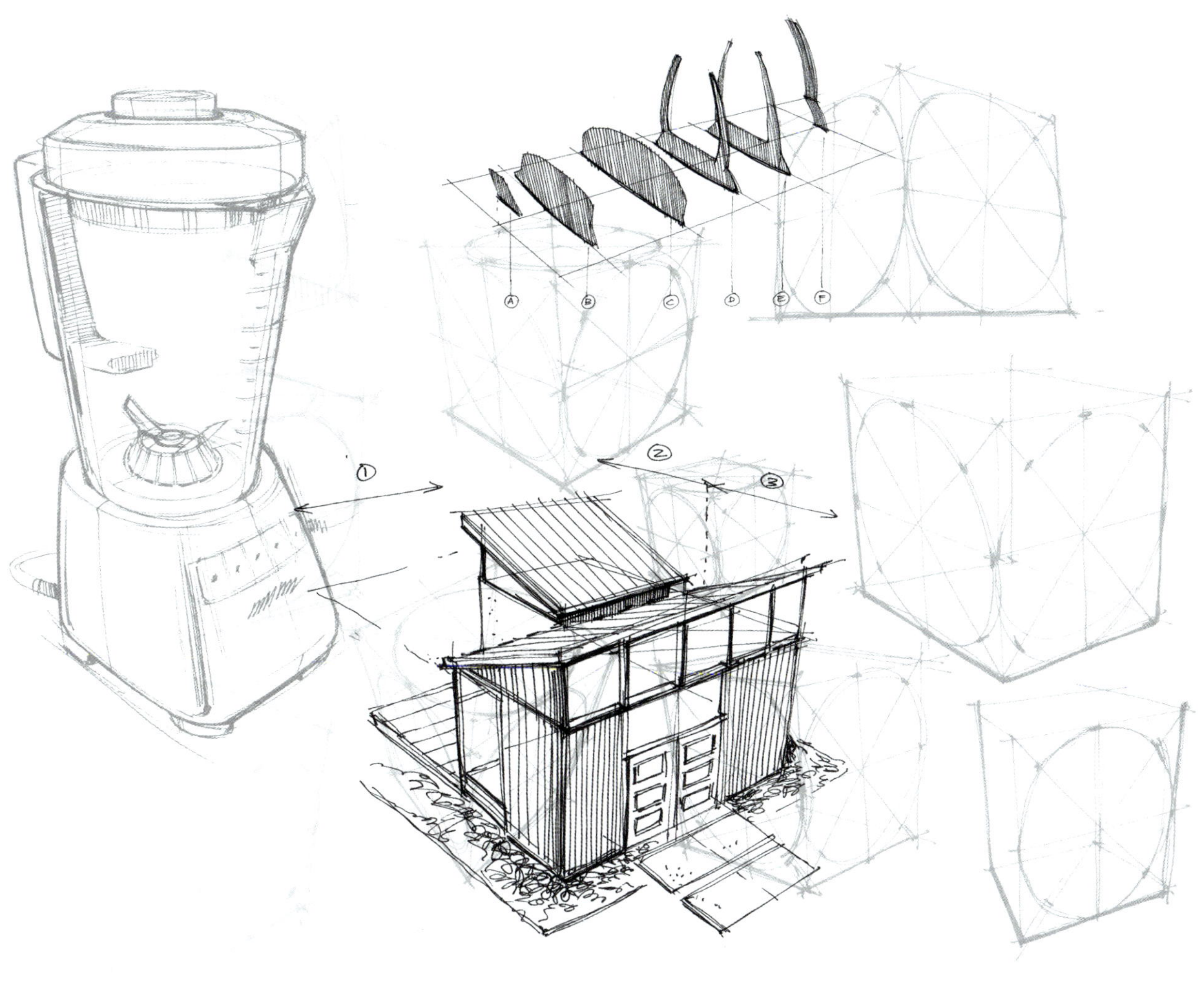

CHAPTER 6

DRAWING WITH DEPTH IN 3D

Creating a *measured perspective* drawing involves projecting lines, proportional calculations, and using geometric tricks to create a precise and accurate representation of reality. *Estimated perspective* drawings, on the other hand, use measurements based on what the artist feels and knows, rather than precise geometric calculations. Although learning measured perspective can be useful, this book focuses on estimated, or *perceptual*, perspective. With this style, honing your observational skills (as discussed in Chapter 5, "Learning to See in Three Dimensions") is very important to sharpening your perspective drawing skills. Still, a quick look at measured perspective drawing can help give you a better understanding of foreshortening and what to expect when estimating perspective while drawing.

Likewise, when drawing from your imagination, a good understanding of the real-world principles of proportion, placement, and perspective can help you conceptualize anything!

Vocabulary of Perspective

An understanding of the key principles starts with learning the vocabulary of perspective drawing. Here are a few definitions before we dive into drawing.

- **Horizon Line.** The horizon line is where sky and Earth meet. If you were standing in an open field with a clear view, it would be where both the sky and the grassy field seem to touch. The horizon line is where you will find or place vanishing points when drawing.
- **Vanishing Point.** Vanishing points are points where lines that are receding to the distance seem to converge on the horizon line. A drawing may have one, two, three, or more vanishing points. Additionally, if an object is rotated off-axis relative to another that is resting on a ground plane, there may be auxiliary vanishing points that describe the shape and taper of the object.
- **Ground Plane.** The ground plane is the plane, or surface, on which the objects in the scene rest. Another way to think of the ground plane is the surface of the Earth or the floor that an object may be resting on or relative in position to.
- **Point of View.** Point of view is the relative position of you, the viewer, to the object you're drawing. From an eye-level point of view, the top of an object may appear flat. From slightly below or above eye level, the top or bottom of an object may be visible, relative to your position.

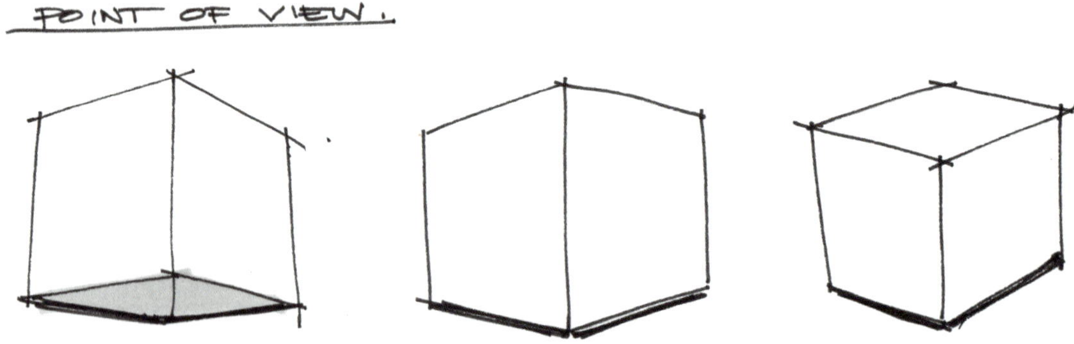

- **Eye Level.** Eye level refers to an imaginary line that extends from your eyes out to the front and sides of your head.
- **Picture Plane.** The picture plane is an imaginary plane that is a 2D representation of the planar view of the object being observed or imagined. Picture plane comes in handy when thinking about different types of perspective. In one-point perspective, the plane of an object is coplanar with the picture plane. In two-point perspective, the leading edge of an object is coplanar with the picture plane. In three-point perspective, the leading top corner of the object or bounding box is coincident with the picture plane.

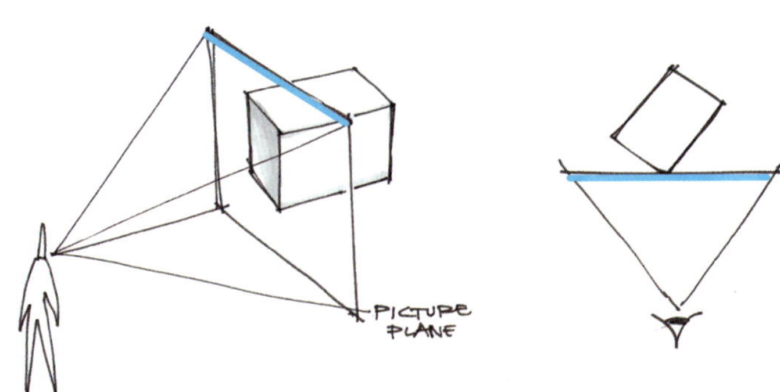

Left: Diagram of virtual picture plane as viewed by an observer.
Right: Diagram of picture plane as viewed from above by an observer.

- **Taper.** Taper refers to the visual effect of parallel sides of a rectilinear object appearing to converge toward a vanishing point. It may also refer to the difference in distance of a leading edge as compared to the receding edge of a rectilinear object. For organic forms and shapes, taper may refer to the apparent scaling in proportion as the form recedes away from you, the viewer.
- **Progression of Scale.** Progression of scale is the visually observed effect of a sequential reduction in apparent size of objects as they recede away from view. Think of the light poles or fence posts along a road; they diminish in size the further away from the viewer they are. This progression of scale establishes a sense of place and proportion of objects in each scene.

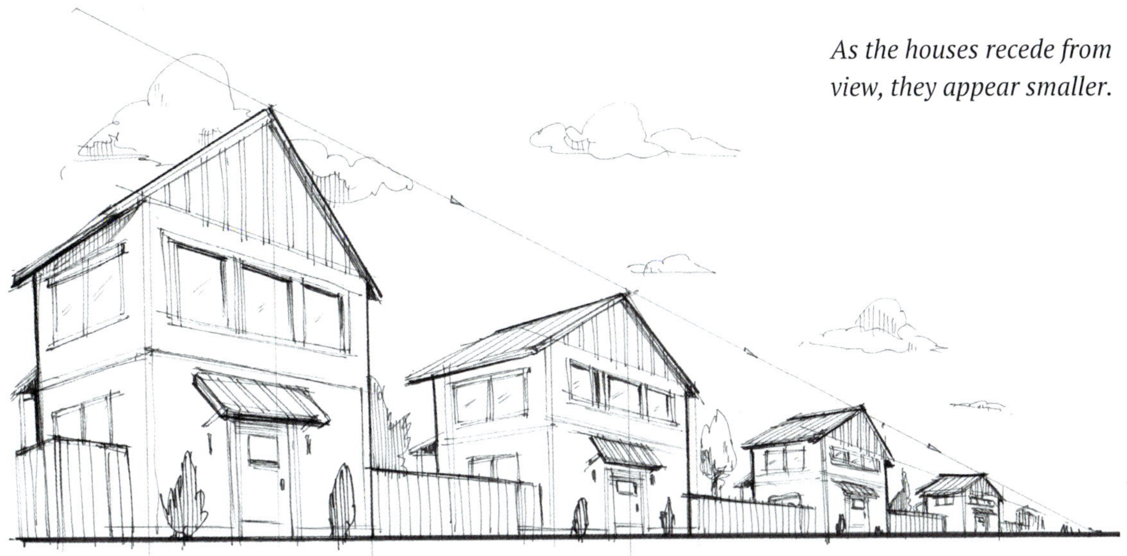

As the houses recede from view, they appear smaller.

Perspective is simply the way we geometrically represent three-dimensional reality on paper in a two-dimensional medium. Perspective drawing uses principles based on observed geometric effect related to how we see the world around us. It is merely a proxy for what we see, and in most cases, unless precise measurement and execution is taken, the resultant drawings will be representative and not literal in nature.

To learn about one-point perspective, two-point perspective and three-point perspective, let's start with a simple primitive shape — a cube. A cube is a great way to analyze perspective because of its simple geometry and presentation as an object. In fact, a cube is also a great way to evaluate three-dimensional geometry related to objects in our everyday space and lives. Do you notice any cubes in your vicinity? Maybe there's an appliance, piece of furniture, or some other object that is made up of cubes that you see around you.

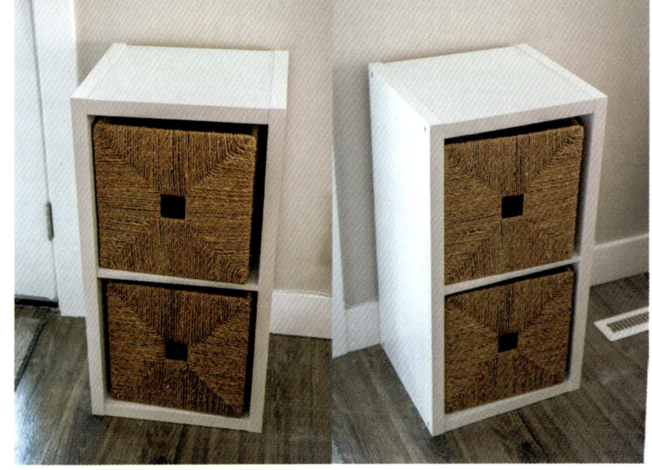

If you closely observe a cube, you'll notice a few things. A cube has six faces that are 90° or orthogonal to each other. Each of the edges of the cube is at 90° to each other as well. Because the faces of a cube are square, the length of each edge of a cube is equal to the other edges that make up the cube, and the surface area of each face is equal as well.

One-Point Perspective

To start, let's examine how one-point perspective works and how apply it for your drawings.

As mentioned in chapter 5, Learning to See in Three Dimensions, one-point perspective can be easily observed by looking down the hallway, down a straight road, or even while sitting against the wall in a square room. Observing straight lines in each of the scenarios will reveal a taper and progression of scale.

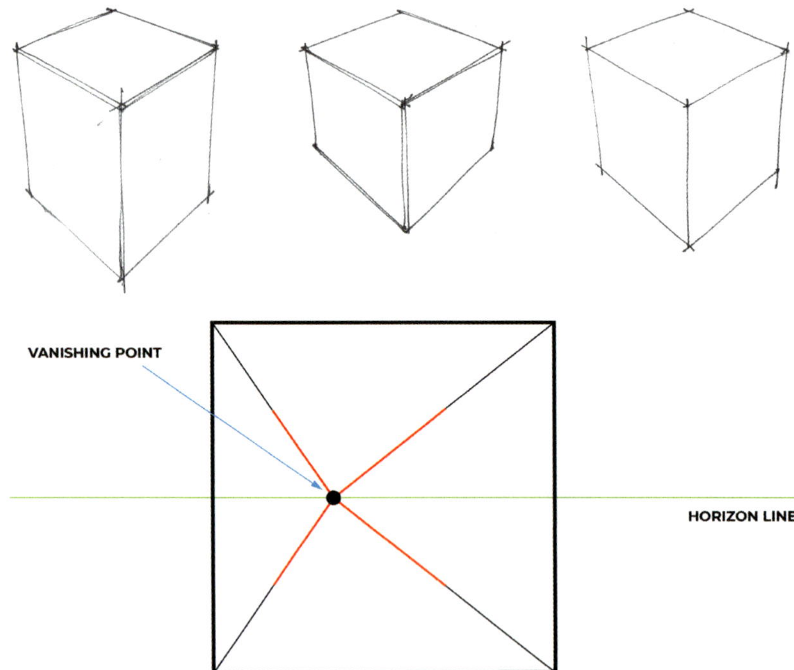

I've created a small prop cube to show what one point perspective looks like with a smaller object.

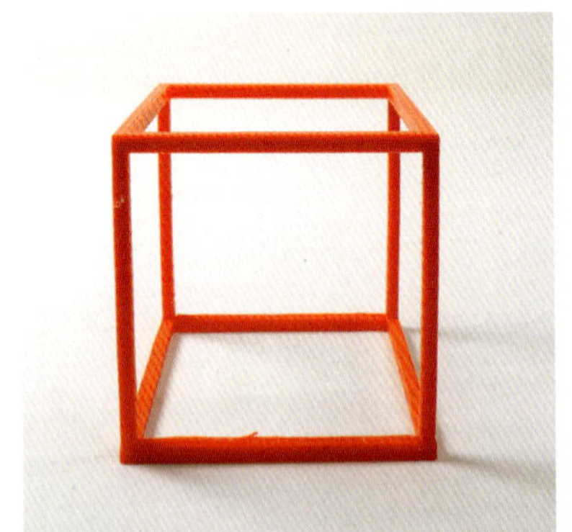

To draw a simple one-point perspective object, start with one square face. Draw a square face in a two-dimensional view. Since we're drawing a cube, measure or estimate the length of each edge of the leading face and transfer that measurement two lines that are drawn parallel to each other. Connect each tick mark or points on these parallel lines to create a new Square. Voila!

This process creates a parallel projection of a cube. That sounds like a technical term, but it basically means that all sides of the cube are parallel to each other. Because distances appear shorter in perspective, will need to create the effect of shortening these distances.

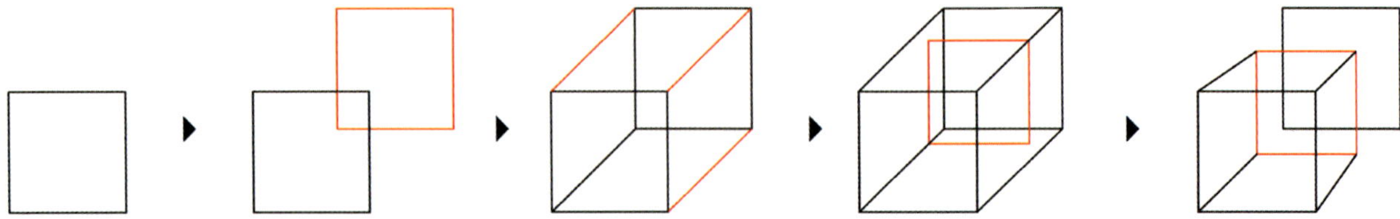

While there is a technical means of measuring the distance on the receiving edges, simply eyeball an estimate a slightly shorter side. Additionally, offset the square size to be a bit smaller. This will create the fact of edges that converge to a vanishing point somewhere on paper.

Exercise

Practice drawing several one-point perspective cubes using this technique in this fashion. As a bonus, compare your cube to another cube to get used to differences with distances that are shortened in perspective.

Two-Point Perspective

Often times when looking at a home or structure that is larger than you, the viewer, but not as large as a skyscraper, you will see that home or structure in two-point perspective. A home is simply a cube that has been scaled, transformed, or combined with other forms to create the overall object of the home. Thus, understanding how a cube looks in two-point perspective is fundamental to being able to draw structures like a home, or other items in our vicinity. The main difference between two-point perspective and one-point perspective is that there is a leading edge as opposed to a leading face that is parallel to you, the viewer. I've created a small prop cube to show what two-point perspective looks like with a smaller object.

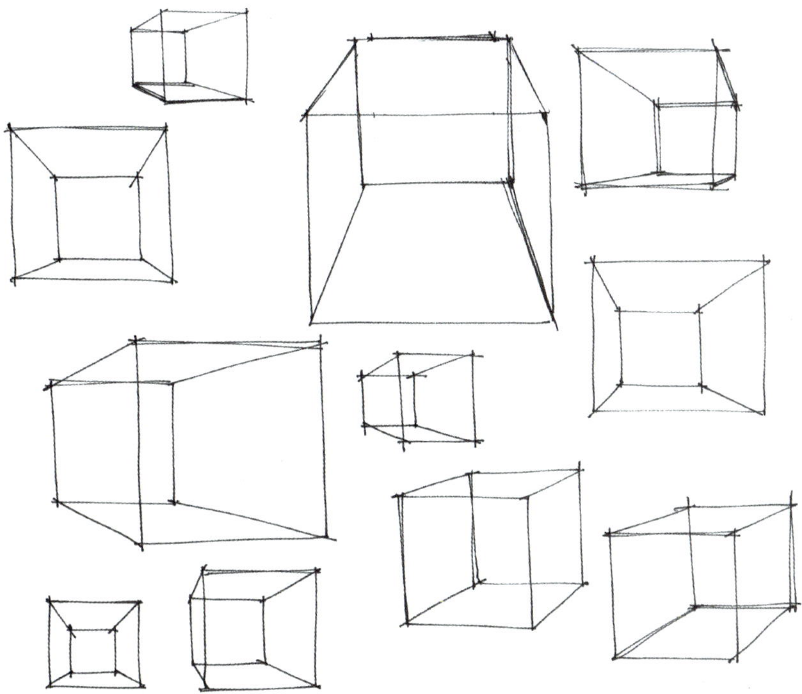

Example of two-point perspective sketch exercises.

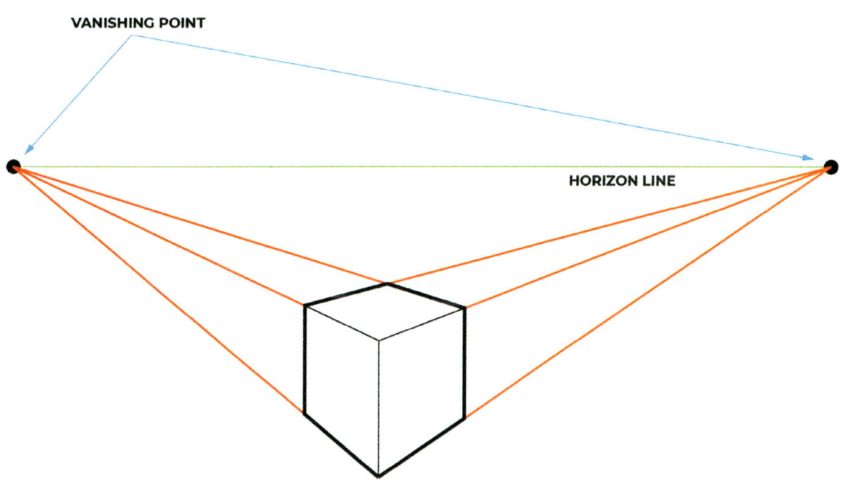

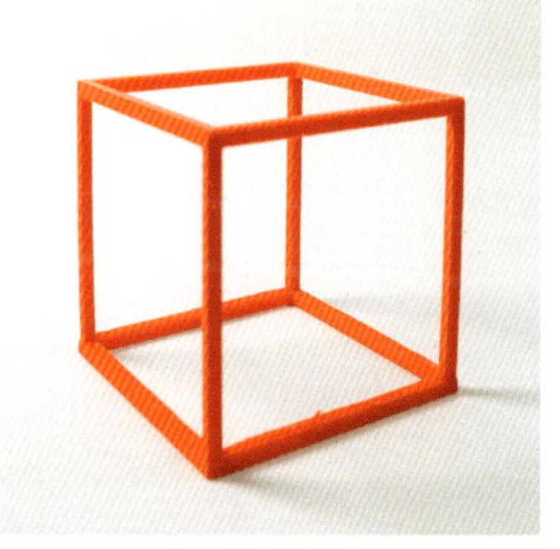

For two-point perspective, let's start by drawing a cube by viewing the cube with a leading edge. The leading edge is the closest edge to you, the viewer, and will create the effect of perspective. Take a look at this photo as reference for the cube you're about to draw.

If we ignore the tapering of sides of the cube, the cube is effectively presented as three connected diamond shapes. Let's start by making the shapes equal in overall size. Remember a cube has equal sides, and since all lines are parallel, we can simply duplicate the measurement of the leading edge along the receiving edges and sides of the cube.

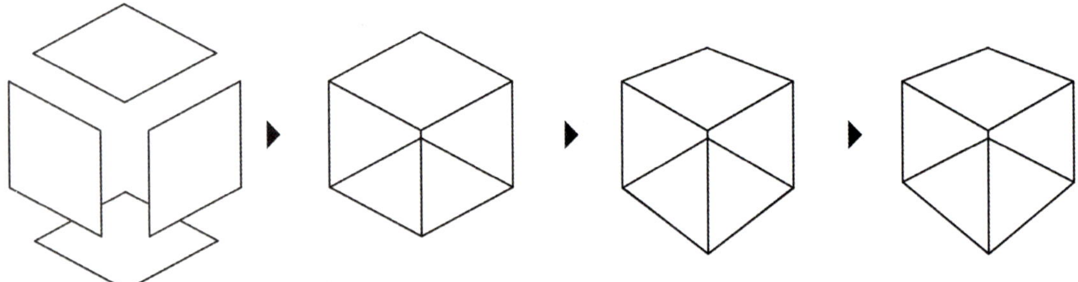

In two-point perspective, vertical lines are parallel to each other. So, we won't mess with the angle of those lines at all. However, to create effective perspective, we will need to adjust the height of the outermost left and right edges as well as the topmost corner of the top diamond.

Mentally lowering the position of the top corner as illustrated will create a feeling of perspective. Additionally, moving each of the lower most corners of the cube slightly up vertically will also create a taper that creates the feeling of perspective for the sides of the cube.

Since distances are reduced as objects move away from us in perspective, a slight adjustment needs to be made to the position of the bottom left and right edges is viewed. Mentally move or redraw these edges to adjust the shape of your cube.

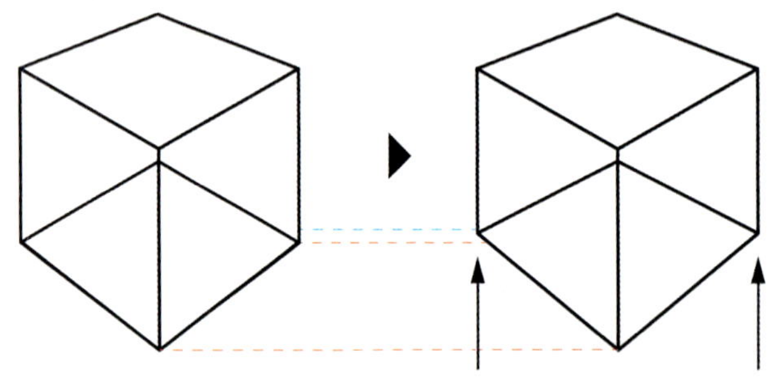
Shifted Corners

Much like the one-point perspective example, figuring out the proportional difference between your leading edge and receding edges is a matter of observing a box or cube in your vicinity. With enough practice you'll get accustomed to what feels right perceptually when drawing a cube.

Exercise

Practice drawing several two-point perspective cubes using this technique in this fashion. As a bonus, compare your cube to another cube to get used to differences with distances that are shortened in perspective.

Example of a two-point perspective sketch exercise.

Three-Point Perspective

Three-point perspective is similar to two-point perspective with the difference that rather than an edge being closer to you, the viewer, a corner of the cube is closest to you. This causes an apparent convergence of all edges of the cube to one of three vanishing points.

Three-point perspective in real life looks something like this at small scale. I've intentionally switched my camera lens and position to emphasize the taper in the sides of my prop cube.

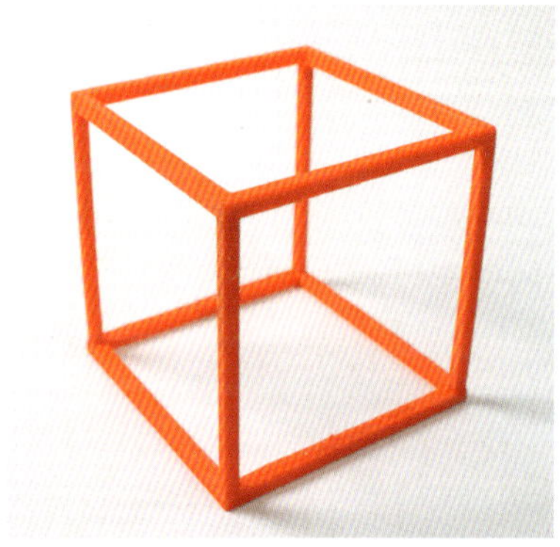

To create a three-point perspective cube, follow the steps outlined in the two-point perspective example. But rather than moving the outermost edges in toward the leading edge, move the lower left and right corners of the left and right diamond shapes inward to create a converging effect.

Granted, your leading edge (the edge closest to you) may not be always vertical as it was in the two-point perspective example, but this serves as a reasonable shortcut to creating the effect of three-point perspective.

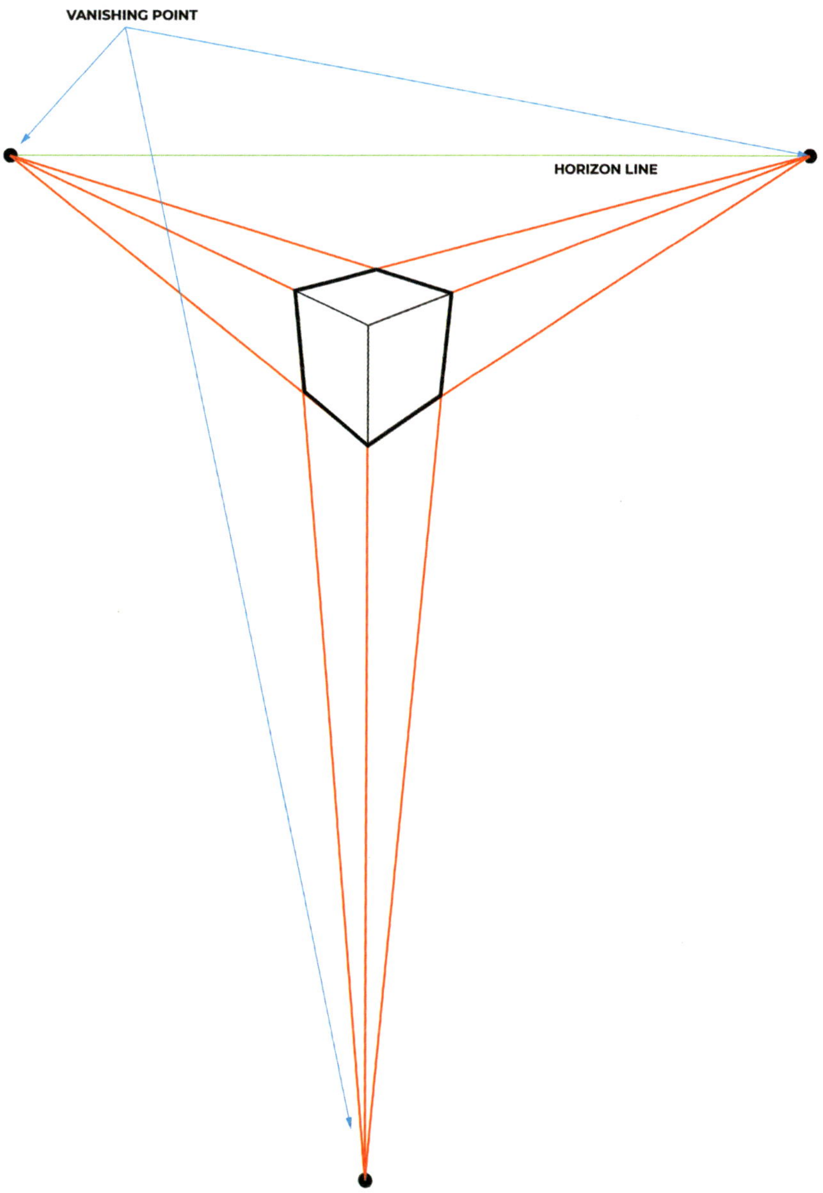

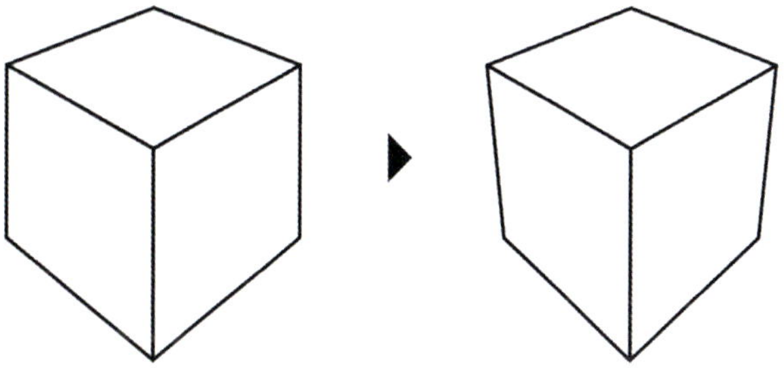

Three-point perspective adds a slight angling of vertical lines converging downward or upward to a third vanishing point.

Exercise

Practice drawing several three-point perspective cubes using this technique. As a bonus, compare your cube to another cube to get used to differences with distances that are shortened in perspective.

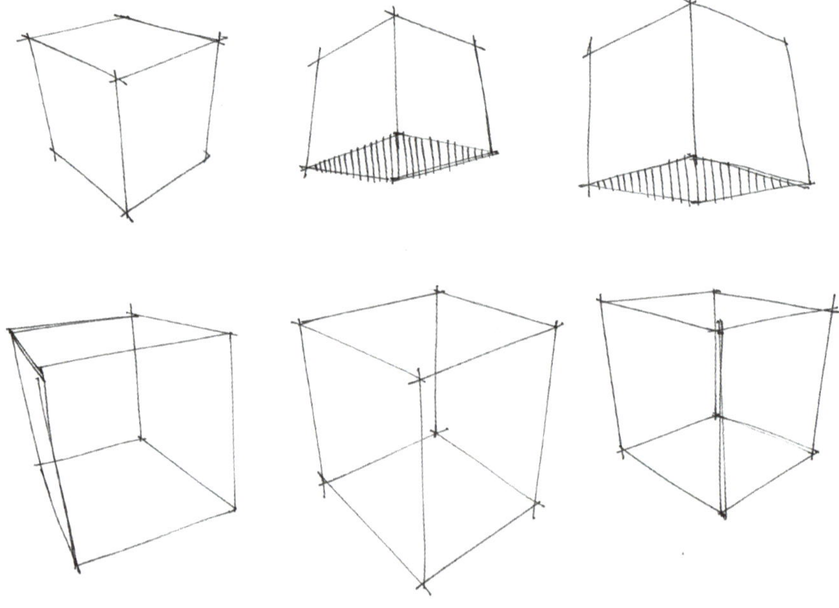

Fanning Lines

"Fanning" lines is another great way to practice drawing cubes in perspective. The idea behind drawing lines this way relates to practicing how lines in perspective converge to some vanishing point in whatever perspective setup you choose.

To fan your lines, start by drawing one line of a reasonably short length. A good way to think about the length of the line is to think about how long you might draw the edge of a cube you might want to draw. There is no set length to the line, however, but rather pay attention to the angle at which you drew the line. Imagine that this line extends off to a point and would meet at that point off in the distance, perhaps even off the page. Draw another line that perceptually would meet at the first point, intersecting your first line. Draw a third line that would also meet at this virtual point.

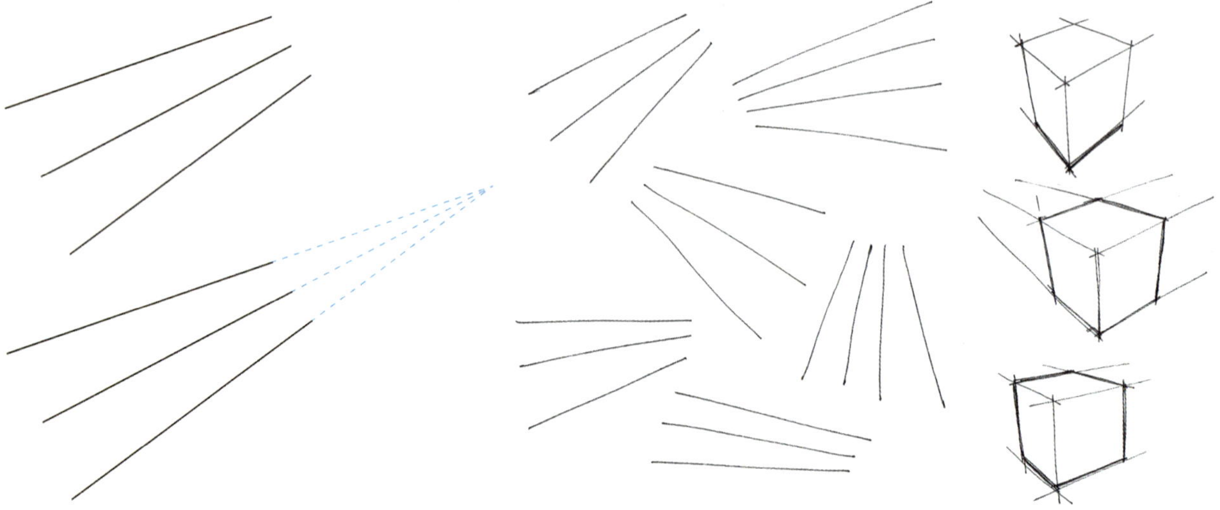

A good follow-up to this exercise is to check where these lines might actually converge by extending these lines with a ruler or by drawing freehand with your elbow and shoulder as discussed in Chapter 3, "Getting Started." If your lines all reasonably meet at this point, your drawing should be reasonably accurate.

A Quick Note on Distortion

Sometimes perspective can feel too distorted, extreme, or forced. A good rule of thumb is to maintain an angle of 90° or greater for the bottom corner of the cube you are drawing or virtually visualizing. There are exceptions to the rules, however, but generally the angle here should be around 90°. If the angle is less than 90°, your perspective drawing may begin to feel distorted and making estimates and calculations in the following sections may prove difficult.

This will take practice, but to see why this is the case, pay attention to cube-like objects in your environment and observe what the bottom corner looks like. In fact, if you do have a small enough cube-like object, you can rotate the cube and observe this to be true.

Drawing Objects at Angles or Rotated in Perspective

Learning perspective drawing is as much observation as it is learning by practice. When objects are rotated in perspective, I try to think about the invisible path of the object as it rotates. Usually, this path is circular or curved in some fashion relative to a central axis or point to the object that is rotated. If I can understand this geometric concept, then it makes it easier to place the object in three-dimensional space at off orthogonal positions.

In this photo, you'll see two cubes placed on top of each other. Notice the cube on top appears to be in one-point perspective while the cube on the bottom appears to be in two-point perspective. Each of these vanishing points exist along a virtual horizon line off in the distance.

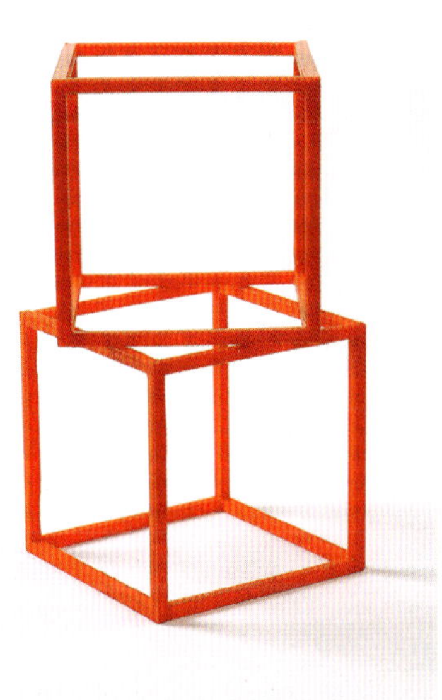

Most importantly when drawing objects that are rotated in perspective in this fashion, to consider whether the face of the object, edge of the object or corner of the object is closest to you, the viewer. This will tell you which type of perspective to use. Because the face of the uppermost cube is parallel to my vantage point, the cube appears to be in one-point perspective. Because the cube on the bottom is slightly rotated, it appears to be in two-point perspective relative to me, the viewer.

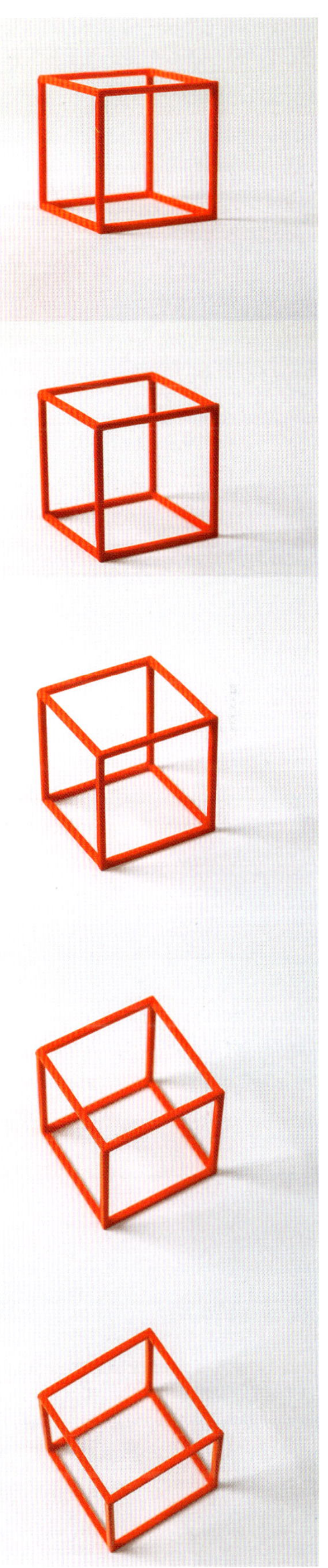

Similarly, a cube rotated and placed next to a more orthogonally oriented cube will show that there are additional vanishing points to which the lines converge.

Now that we have observed cubes in real life, it's important to understand how to draw a face at an angle that is not 90° relative to the other faces of the object. When a face is not at 90° to other faces of a cube or object, the sides of the face taper towards an auxiliary vanishing point, which is a point directly above or below the left or right vanishing point in a perspective set up.

A good way to observe auxiliary vanishing points is by looking at a simple structure with an angled roof like a house or shed. Notice that the edges of the roof structure appear to converge toward some point.

With enough practice, you should be able to comfortably draw a cube in perspective at any angle. Next, we will take a look at why this skill is important and how to use a cube as a basic unit when drawing objects in perspective.

Multiplying a cube is one of the most useful activities you can learn when drawing in three-dimensional space. Think of a cube as a basic unit of measurement when drawing with proportion in mind in perspective.

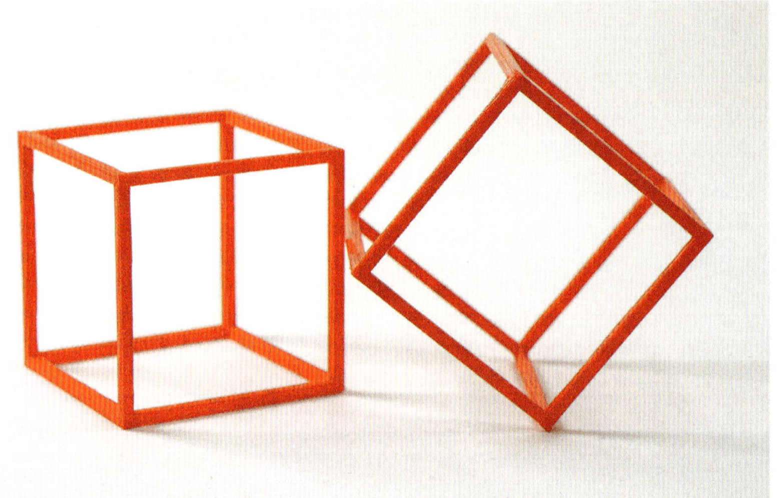

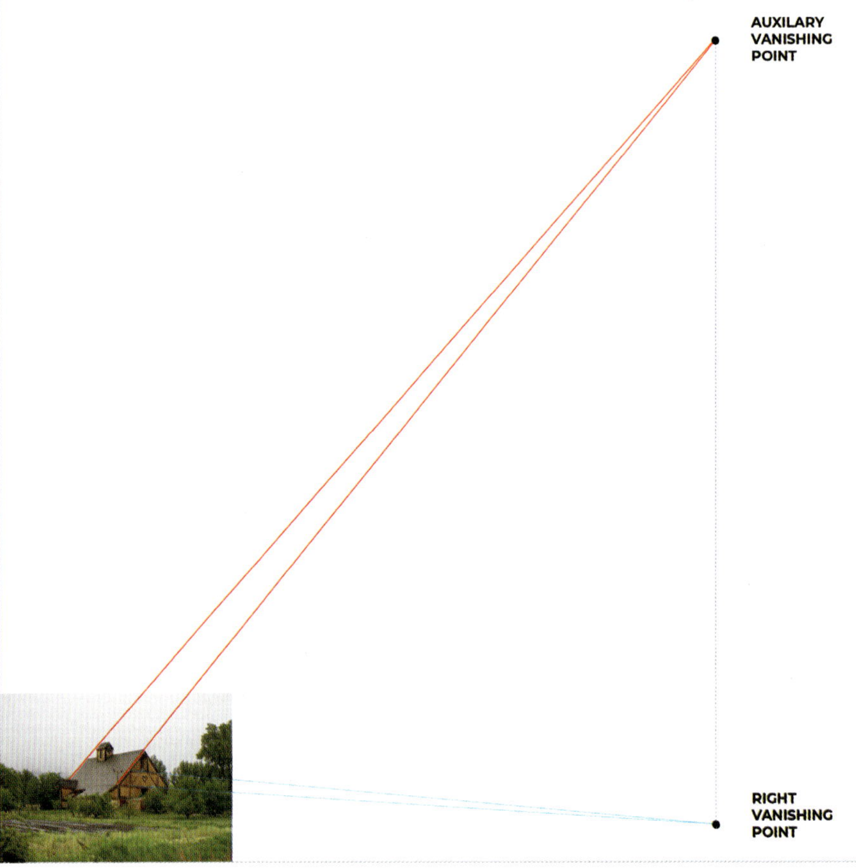

Dividing and Multiplying a Cube

Because a cube is a fundamental three-dimensional form, you can use it as a means of proportionally measuring in three dimensions. For example, if you can draw a cube, you can draw a cylinder that is the same height as the cube, or a sphere contained in the cube or a pyramid with the same size base as the cube. You can also subdivide that cube or use multiples of it to help you create more complex objects. A cuboid is a multiple of a base cube, on which operations have been carried out. We'll talk about operations a little bit later in the chapter; for now, consider that the cuboid may be made of two or six or eight cubes arranged in a specific fashion. Multiplying square faces or any rectilinear face in perspective is a useful skill in estimating distances. You will use the skill in Chapter 8, "Reflections," so it is important to understand how it works.

The first step to multiplying faces is finding their midpoints. In a two-dimensional drawing of a square or rectangle, you can divide the rectangle or square equally from corner to corner to find the midpoint of the shape. Extending out to the right or left from the midpoint to intersect a vertical side of the shape will help you find the midpoint of the vertical side. (Of course, you could measure the midpoint, but you may not always have a ruler at your disposal.)

With the midpoint of the vertical side identified, you can now proceed to multiply the shape. Extend the baseline of the square or rectangle to the right or left depending on which side you would like to multiply the shape. I'm extended the square baseline to the right in the example. Draw a line from the opposite top corner of the shape relative to the midpoint that you found using the midpoint on the vertical side of the shape. Extend this line so that it intersects the base line you extended. This intersection point should be the same length as the relative side of the square or rectangle that is on the baseline.

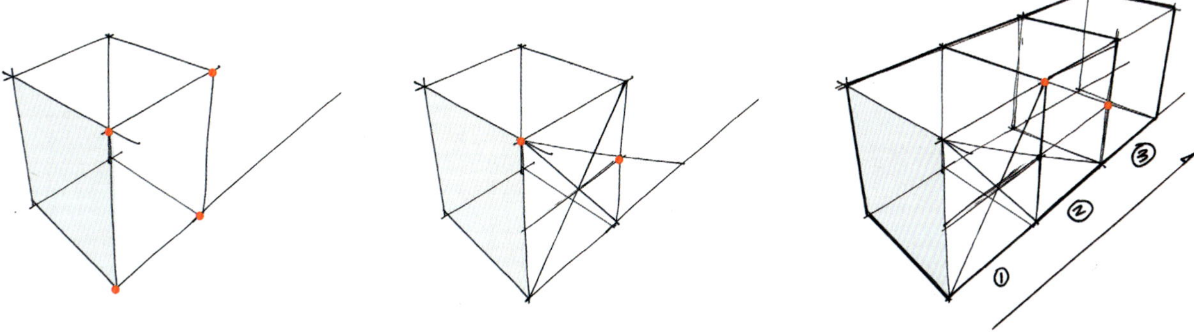

Now that you've duplicated the base side of the square or rectangle, you can extend upward as well as extend the topmost edge of the square or rectangle to intersect and complete a duplicate shape.

You can also use this technique in perspective to multiply a square face on a cube. Follow the steps outlined above for a two-dimensional square, but rather than working in two dimensions, extend the baseline of the square face consistent with the perspective setup you chose. This will work with one-, two-, or three-point perspective, just remember that lines in perspective taper toward the vanishing points as they recede away from view. In addition, unlike working in two dimensions, you must locate the center of the square by drawing from corner to corner. Distances cannot be measured accurately with a ruler in perspective like they can in a two-dimensional drawing.

As you divide the side of the square into equal parts and extend the line to the baseline, continue to mimic the two-dimensional multiplication of the cube in perspective by extending a line upward from the intersection point at the extension of the base of the cube. Complete the shape of the cube by extending the topmost edge and face of the cube and projecting from the intersections toward the vanishing points. You can apply this process in any direction you would like to multiply the cube.

You may be wondering, "Why multiply a cube?" Being able to draw a proportionately accurate cube is a good way to establish a base unit of proportion when drawing in perspective. Many shapes can be described as multiples of a cube. A rectangular house is simply several cubes joined together to create the building's final shape.

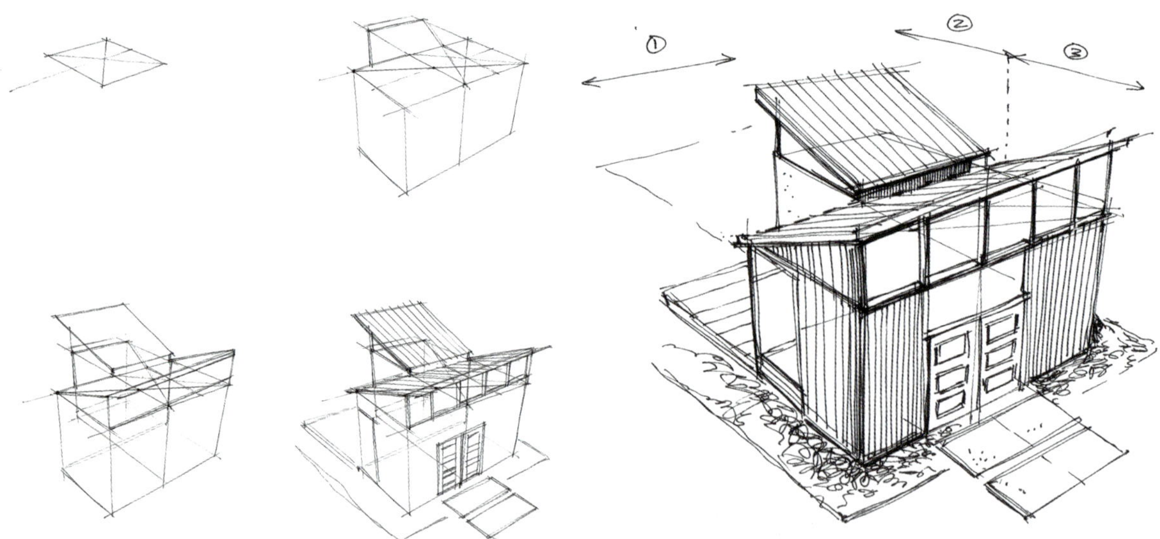

A train engine could be described as several cubes progressively connected after multiplying the cubes in a perspective scene. Each wheel on the locomotive contained in the square is also multiplied and repeated along the length of the engine. While these construction lines aren't always shown, understanding the underlying structure of this approach to drawing in perspective can help make drawing complex objects much easier to understand.

Planes

Planes are two-dimensional shapes drawn in three dimensions; they lack a third dimension, be it depth, height, or length. At their simplest, planes are useful for drawing such shapes as ellipses and triangles in three dimensions. As long as a shape can be bound by a box, you should be able to translate that shape into a 3D perspective view.

Circles in Perspective on Planes

Circles in perspective are an important aspect of drawing. For example, parts of an object may have a curve made up of many circles of differing radii. As you may remember, a circle in perspective is also called an ellipse.

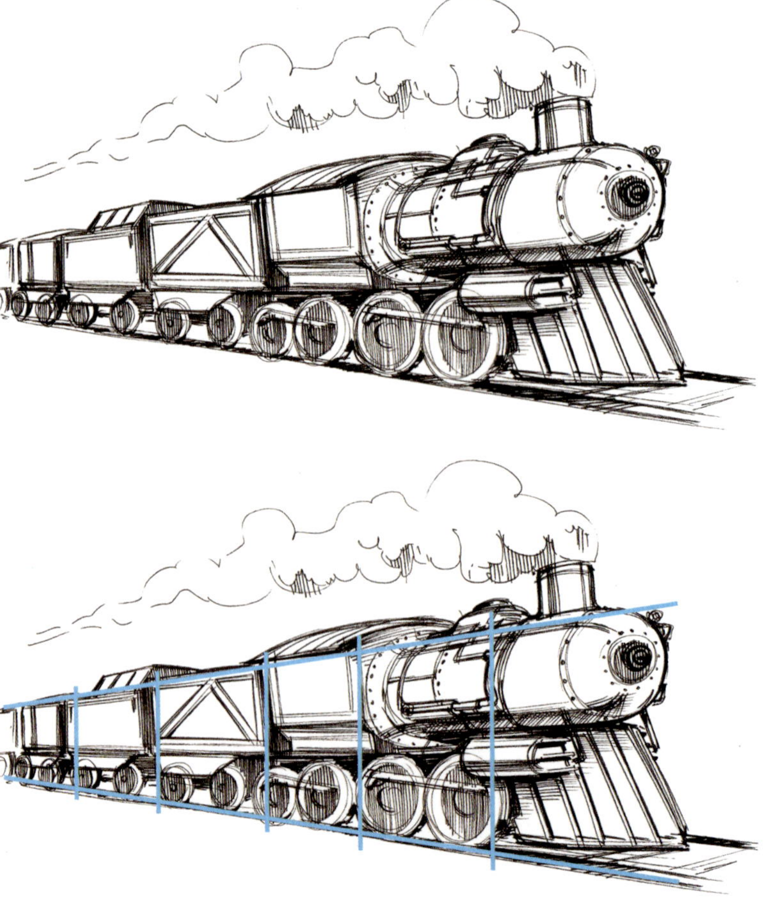

To draw a circle in perspective, start by drawing a circle in two dimensions. Next, inscribe the circle in a square box. Divide the circle into eight equal parts top to bottom and diagonally. Take note of tangency and intersection points. You can translate this relationship to an accurately constructed square in perspective by dividing the square similarly into eight parts. The circle should intersect the diagonals at roughly one-third of the way in from each corner. This is not a precise measurement, but rather an estimation that is consistent.

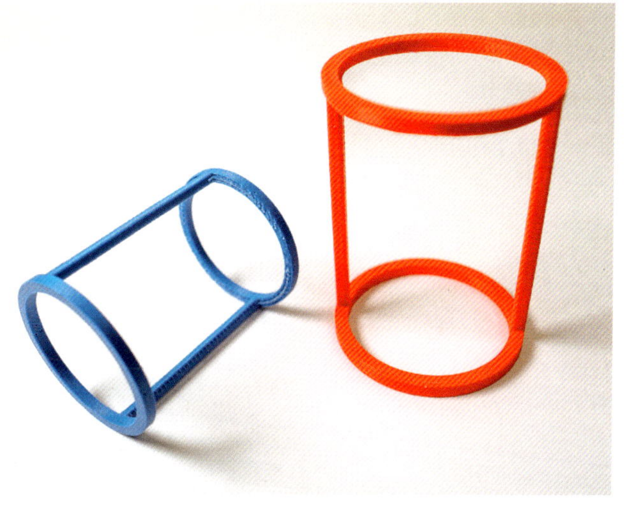

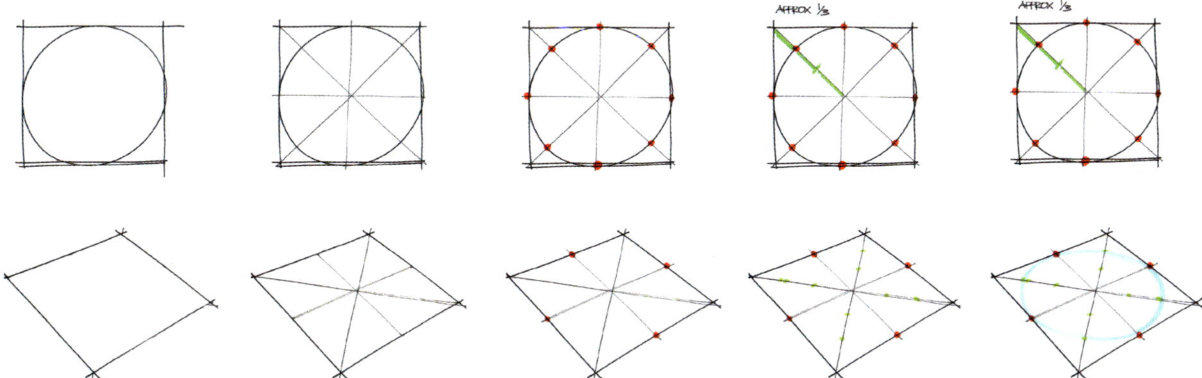

Ellipse Tips

An ellipse in perspective has a few key properties. By drawing a square in perspective and dividing it corner to corner and top to bottom, you can also create eight points to be used in drawing a reasonably accurate ellipse.

Paying attention to these will help improve your drawings. For example, an ellipse is asymmetrically non-uniform in dimension relative to its center and as such possesses a major and minor axis.

Example of ellipses in action.

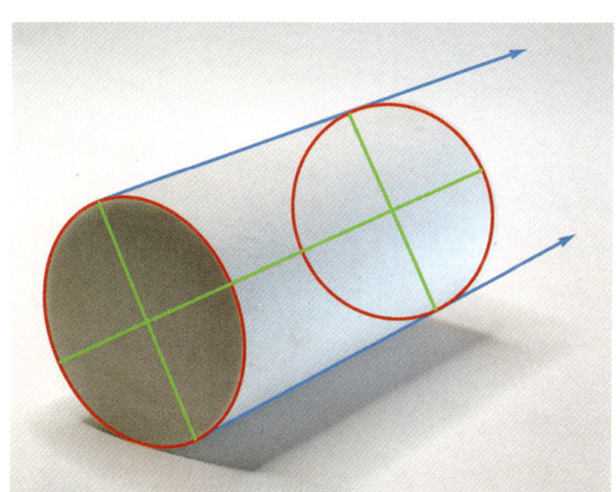

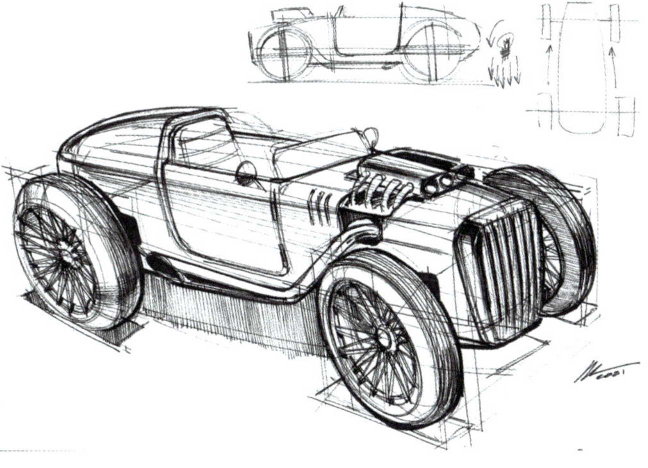

The major and minor axis of an ellipse are always at 90° to each other. Additionally, in perspective, the minor axis of the ellipse is always positioned toward the vanishing point. You can usually tell if an ellipse is "off" by how it's rotated relative to the vanishing point.

If you're ever in doubt about the placement of your ellipse, check the minor axis and major axis. Make sure that the axes are 90° to each other and that the minor axis points toward the vanishing point in your scene. With estimated perspective, you'll need keen observation skills, as you may not have used vanishing points in a more structured perspective setup. The more practice you have drawing ellipses, the more natural this will feel. Practice by constructing ellipses and observing how their minor axes point toward vanishing points.

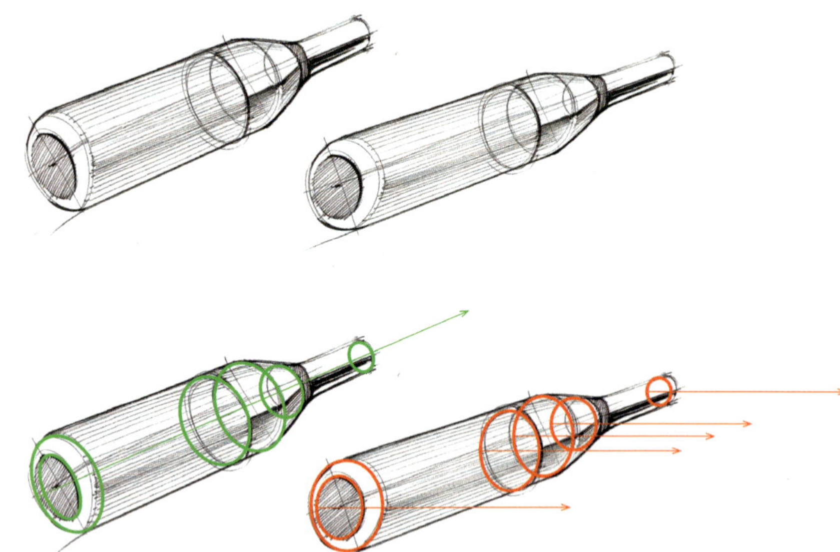

Left: Correct ellipse orientation. Right: Ellipses drawn incorrectly.

Exercise

Draw several cubes with square faces in perspective. Divide each face as described in the "Circles and Other Shapes in Perspective on Planes" section and draw ellipses on each face. Observe the major and minor axis of the ellipses on each face. See what observations you can make in the process.

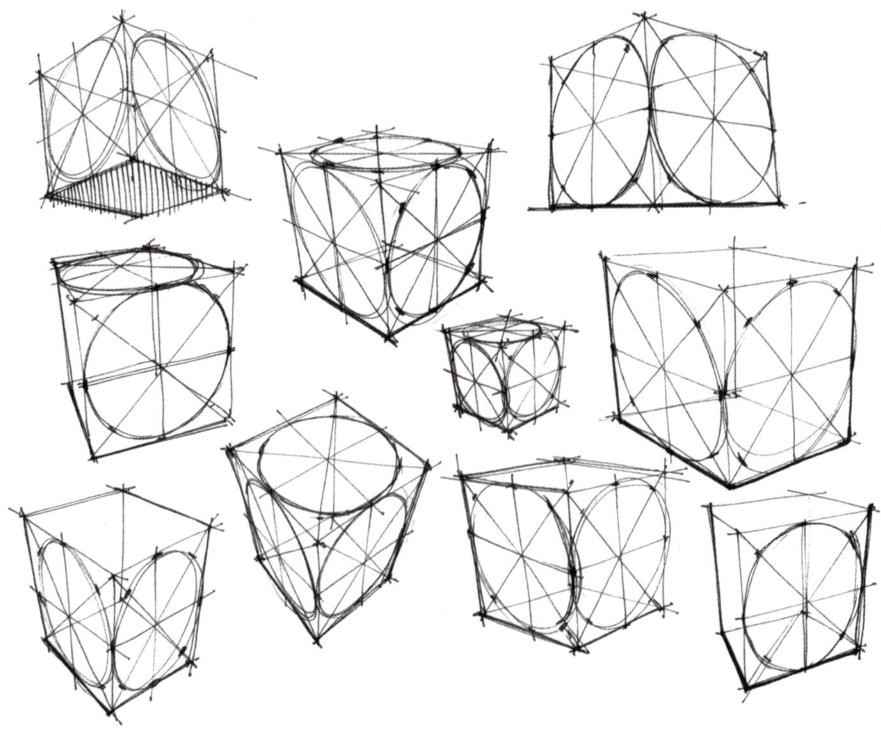

Other Shapes

The technique used to construct an ellipse in perspective may work with other shapes, but there is an alternative method that involves the use of a grid. As long as you can encapsulate your shape in a rectilinear box, you can divide that box and transfer points in perspective.

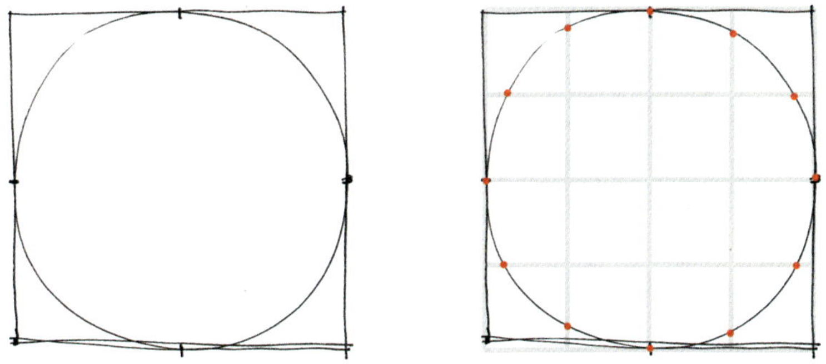

Alternatively, if a grid is constructed with nine equal parts, this 2D drawing can be translated to a 3D plane to make the shape a part of a three-dimensional scene. With the intersection of the circle with the grid lines, translating a circle into perspective is fairly simple.

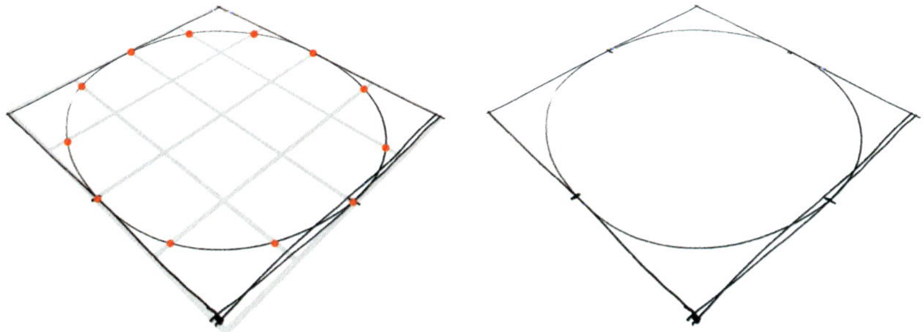

Drawing a square in perspective and dividing the square into nine equal parts and translating the approximate position of the intersection in perspective will provide enough information to draw an accurate ellipse.

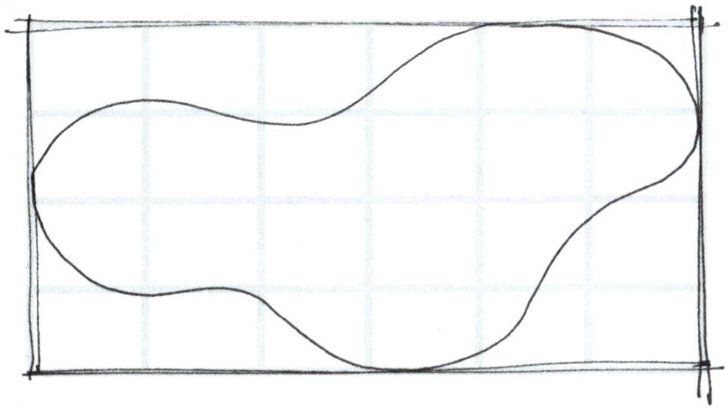

Degree and Placement of an Ellipse

Upon completing the practice exercise, you may have noticed that ellipses appear narrower or wider depending on their relative position to vanishing points in your scene and the field of view. Again, whereas you may not be using vanishing points in normal drawing, the ellipses you draw may be bound by a virtual square face.

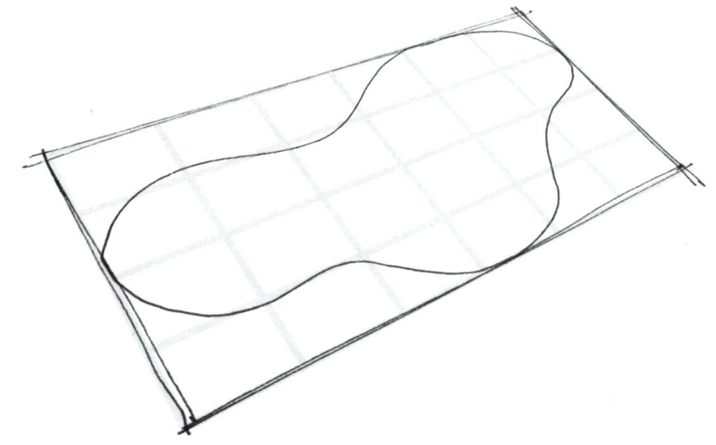

This visual quality of ellipses being narrower or wider is called the *degree* of an ellipse. As you remember from Chapter 3, "Getting Started," you can think of the degree of an ellipse as the angle at which you view the circular rim of a coffee mug or glass. Depending on the angle relative to your eyes, the rim may appear narrow or wide to you. View the top of your glass at eye level, and its top appears to be a straight line. As you move the glass up or down relative to your eye level, the top or bottom of the glass now appears wider. You're observing the degree of an ellipse in real life.

Now, let's give you a superpower: Imagine a laser line projecting outward from your eyes (careful, don't melt your glass). The degree of an ellipse is effectively the relative angle between that laser line and the circle you're observing in perspective. A 5° ellipse means that there is a 5° relationship between the current circle view and the perspective at eye level. Similarly, a 75° ellipse means that there is a 75° relationship between the current view and perspective at eye level.

When viewed left to right, an ellipse can also have a progressively increasing degree. For example, hold your glass 90° to its original orientation and move it left to right. Notice that you can see more or less of the circular rim of the glass depending on how you hold it. The angular relationship in this instance is now related to the center of your field of view (about the center of your nose).

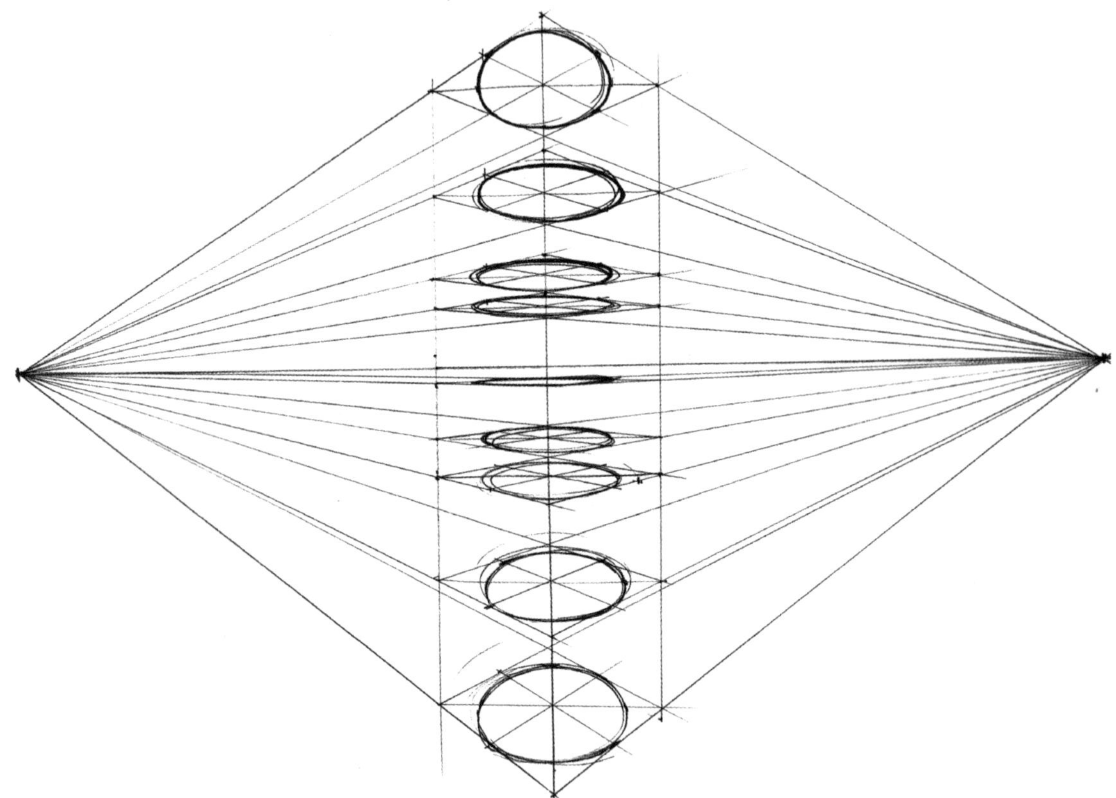

Although these concepts may sound complex, paying keen attention when observing real objects will help you associate the theory with what you see in reality. Then, when drawing ellipses, focus on the major and minor axis:

- Make sure that the minor axis points toward the corresponding vanishing point.
- Imagine what the bounding square in perspective for the ellipse might look like as this will tell you what degree of ellipse you should be drawing.

Exercise

Find a cylindrical object and move it around relative to your eye level within your field of view. What observations can you make?

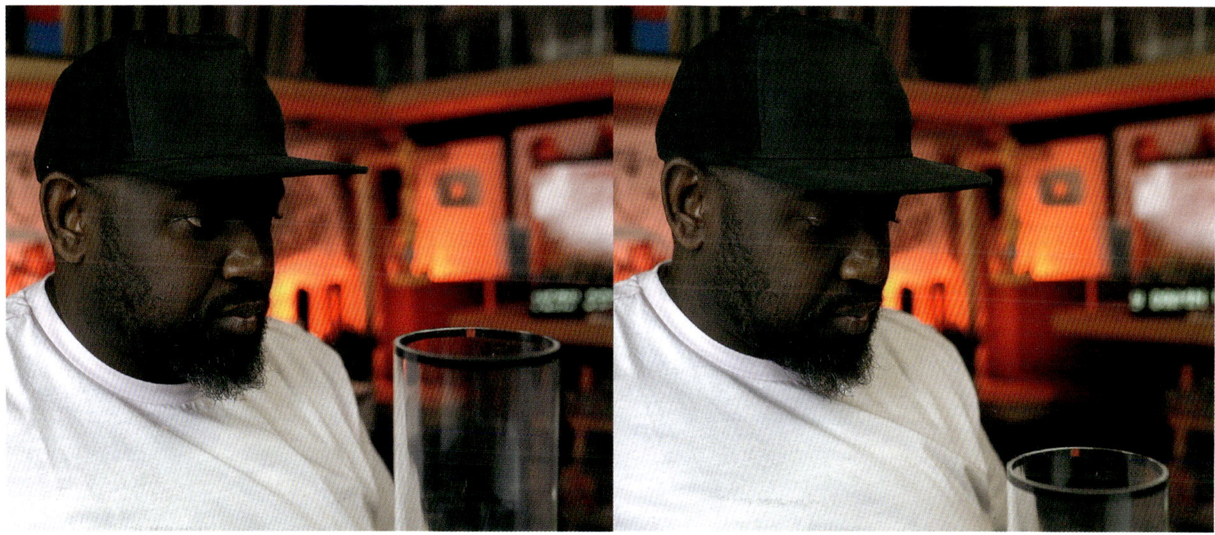

Offsetting Shapes to Create Form

Offsetting shapes in perspective is a means of communicating three-dimensionality using comparative depth and size with shapes. For example, offsetting two ellipses that differ in size and position creates an effect known as a *chamfer*. Depending on the relative position of the shapes, the viewer will interpret visual effect as either pushing in or out of the form. Contour lines can help reinforce the expression of depth when offsetting shapes to create form. Adding shading to the offsets can quickly communicate and reinforce the nature of the three dimensionality of the offset, as well.

Offsetting two squares and connecting those squares also creates a chamfer. You can then round the corners of that chamfer to create smoother shapes. We will discuss surface transitions in the section

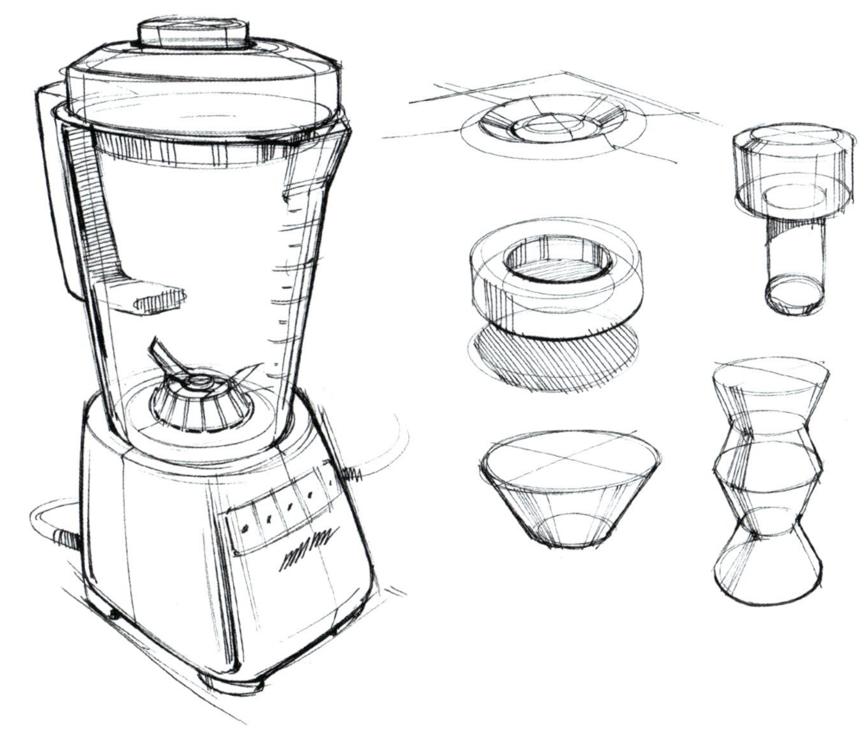

dealing with understanding how to draw more complex objects in Chapter 12, "Tackling Complex Objects." For now, practice drawing shapes and offsetting those shapes. The figure shows a few examples of shapes offset and the resultant effect.

Other 3D Forms with Planes

Planes are a useful way of building 3D forms that are organic or curvy in nature as well as drawing shapes that are more structured. Think about a sliced loaf of bread: All together the slices make up the entirety of the bread loaf. Each slice is a bit of the bread on a plane in three dimensions. Even if you removed a few slices from the loaf, the gaps wouldn't be enough to hide the fact that the object is a loaf of bread.

You could still trace the outside of each slice and see that it is indeed a loaf of bread. You could even take away a few more slices of the bread; the object would still clearly look like a loaf of bread, albeit missing a few more slices.

Drawing with planes is much like using enough slices of the bread to figure out the three-dimensional shape being drawn. When drawing an organic or curved object in three dimensions, think of it a bit like the loaf of bread. Which slices of the object are essential so you can draw a more complete, recognizable view of it?

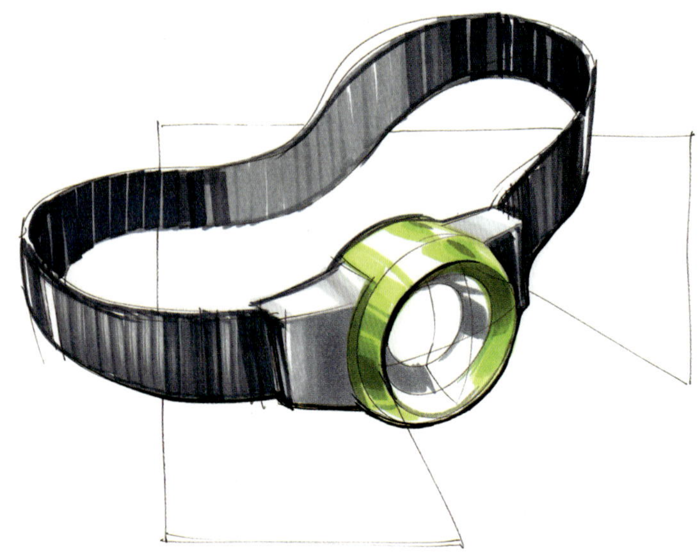

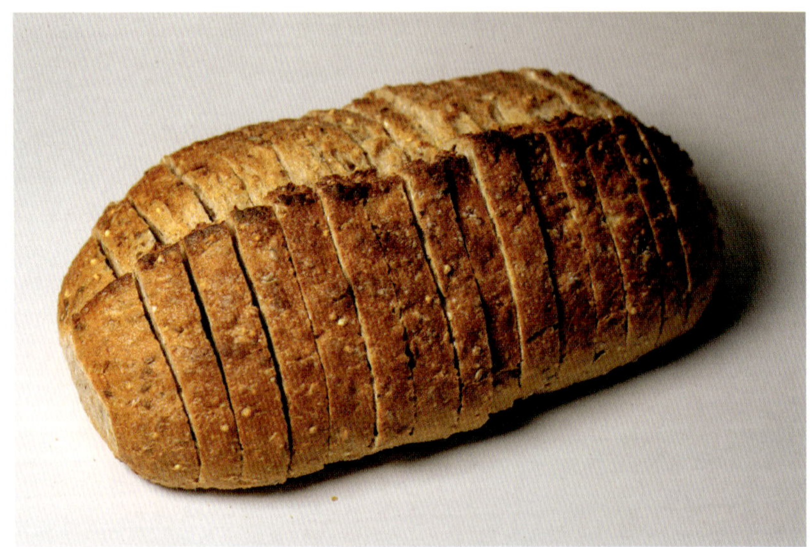

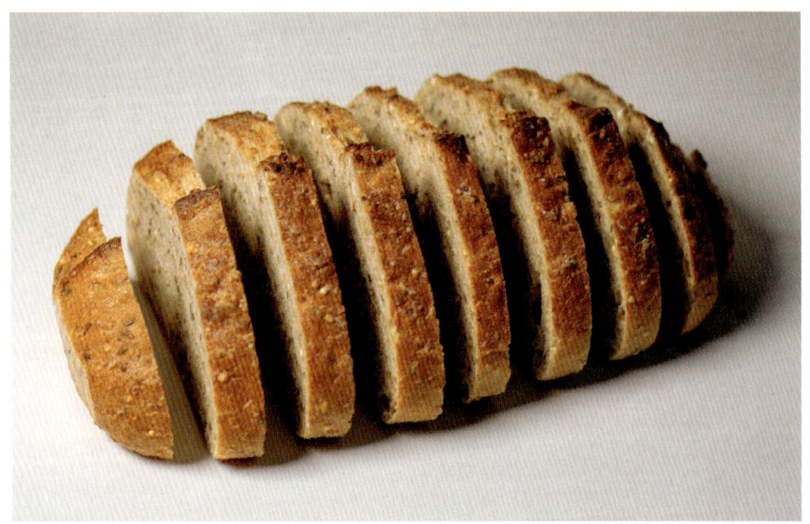

Top: Whole loaf of bread. Bottom: Loaf with slices removed.

Remember, too, that you used planes to define the overall shape of your box when you drew boxes in one-point, two-point, and three-point perspective. When using planes to draw organic shapes, the difference is that you may define the planes not only on the outside the object but also between the object's faces to show transitional form.

Drawing with Planes Demonstration: Computer Mouse

Let's draw a computer mouse in perspective using planes positioned in a three-dimensional space. Much like for two-dimensional drawing, you can observe the mouse in three distinct views: top, side or end, and front. Understanding these views is the beginning of understanding planes on which you can draw the views in perspective.

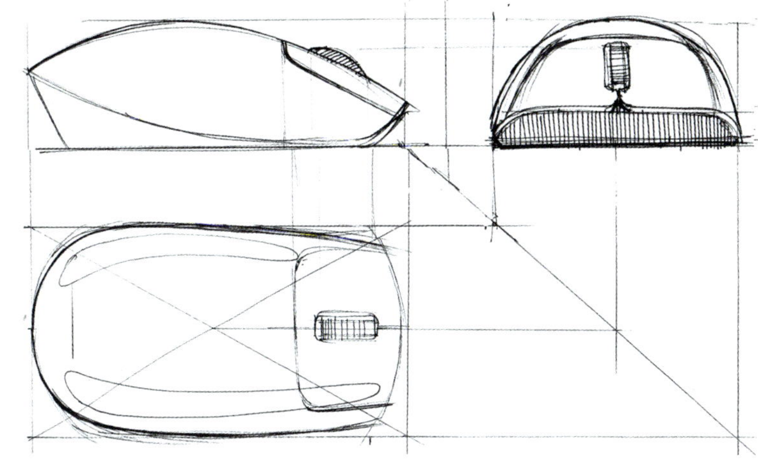

1. Starting with the three-view setup, it is fairly straightforward to pull points that reference relative distance and proportion from the views and, therefore, translate into perspective. For example, we discussed multiplying squares and rectangles into dimensions and in perspective. The mouse is essentially a two-square proportion, so multiplying a single square in perspective is enough to create a proportional plan as a base for the mouse in perspective.

2. Draw a plane representing the base of the mouse, including the center of the mouse in both axial directions. These planes should be orthogonal to each other and look something like the image included here.

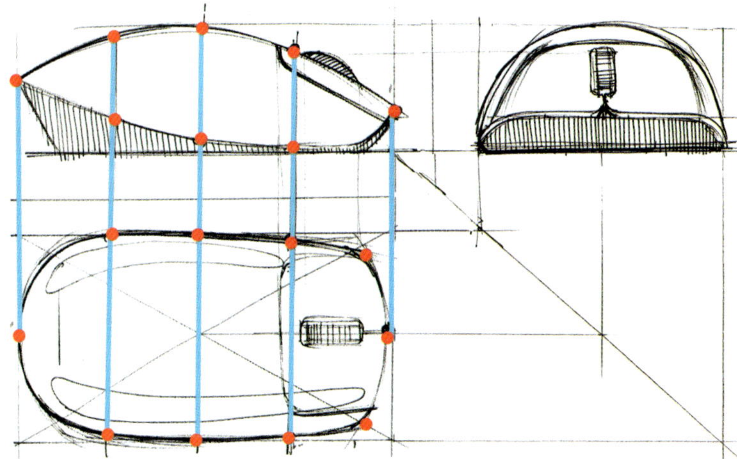

3. If the mouse were a loaf of bread, what slices would be most essential in communicating the overall shape of the mouse? If necessary, reference the 2D drawing of the mouse to help you determine the size of each slice of the mouse.

4. Sketch each two-dimensional view on each plane of the mouse. Although you could precisely transfer the 2D sketch of each view of the mouse onto each plane, I find the process tedious and largely unimportant when drawing the complete 3D view of the mouse. Estimate

measurements and perspective and do your best to translate the sketch of each view onto each three-dimensional plane.

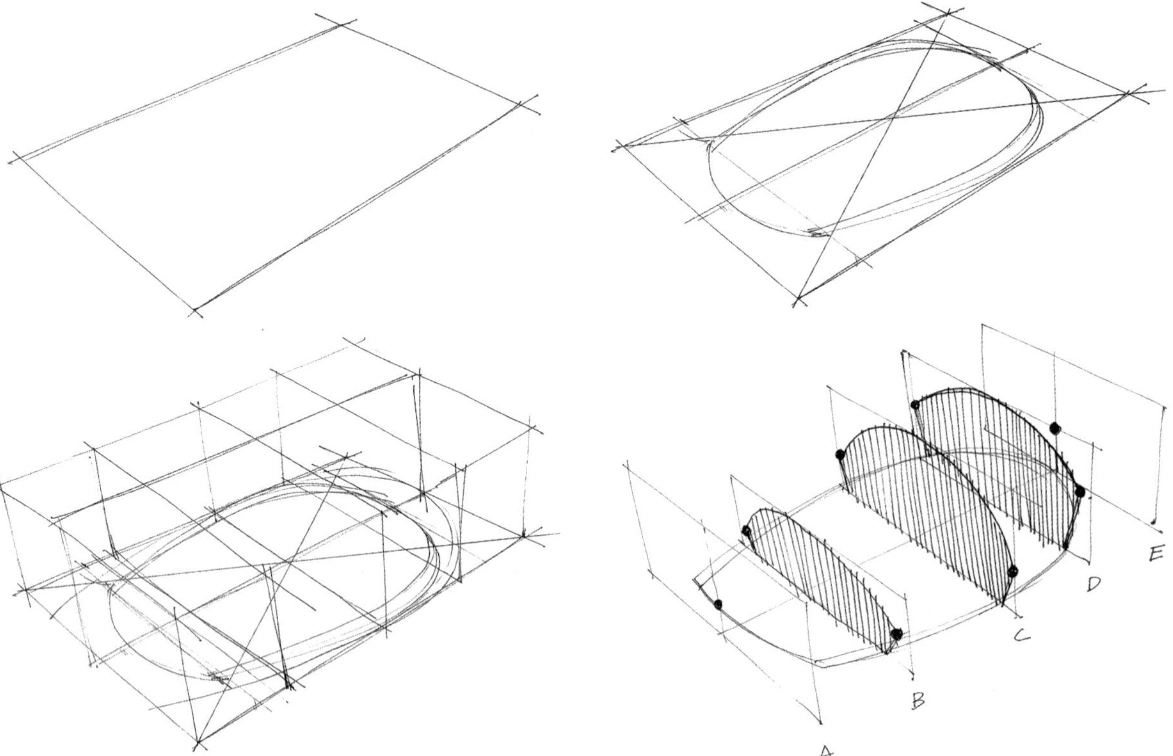

5. Additionally, you can take slices from any point along the mouse to add information to the 3D view as needed. For example, a detail deviates from the overall contours and flow of the mouse's form, construct a plane to incorporate that detail in the three-dimensional view.

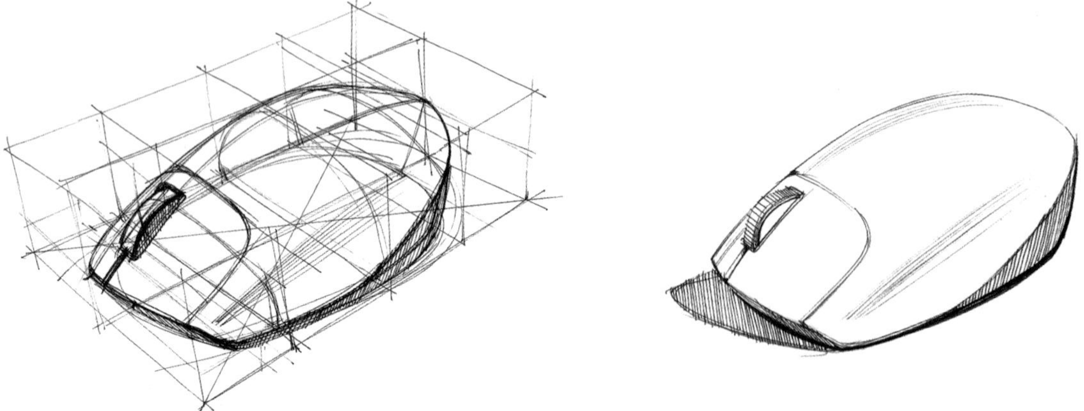

6. Once you've sketched the main planes of the form along with secondary interstitial planes, draw a line tangent to the outside of each sketched profile on each plane. You can sketch these lines in a rough and loose manner before completing the final sketch.

For this demo, let's stop here: You have constructed an outline and placed the details in a rough fashion, breaking the overall form of the mouse into functional shapes. In Chapter 13, "Tighten Up," we will discuss strategies for cleaning up a sketch like this and refining your work so it's more suitable for presentation.

Drawing with Planes Demonstration: Shoe

Much like a mouse, a shoe is made up of more complex geometry. Using slices (mmm bread) to understand a shoe can be a helpful way to sketch an accurate representation of the shoe. Let's take a look at how this technique may be applied to a shoe sketch.

1. As with the mouse example, starting with a three-view setup of a shoe is a helpful way of understanding and drawing the shoe in three dimensions. While this may lead to a more structured sketch, the practice here is invaluable in building your understanding of the three-dimensional geometry of the shoe.

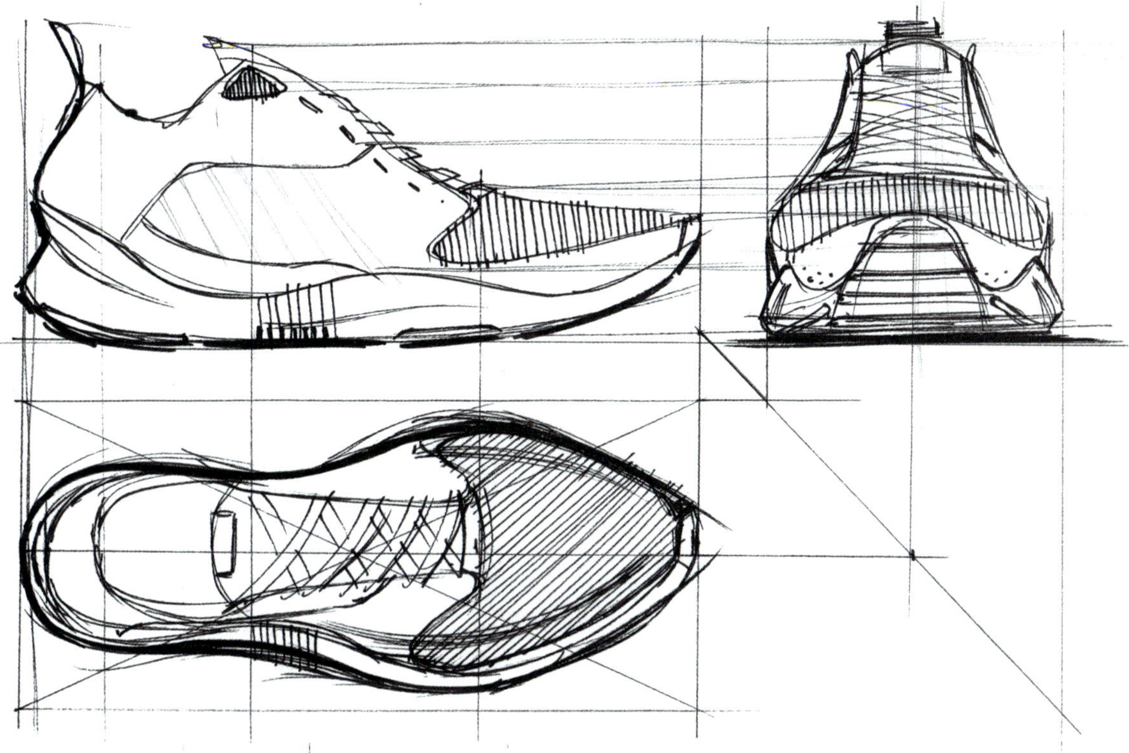

2. With the general dimensions of the shoe established in the three views to the set-up, roughly sketch out planes to describe the changes and angles of the base of the shoe. We will use these planes to draw additional cross-sectional planes that describe the geometry of the shoe.

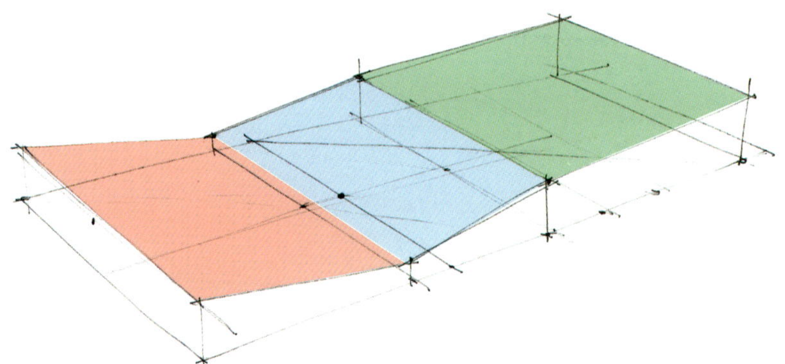

3. Sketch a plane orthogonal to the base surface plane at the midpoint. On this new plane, sketch as best you can the profile of the shoe in perspective. If needed, use the grid method mentioned in this chapter to transfer your two-dimensional sketch into three dimensions.

4. In this step I use the profile of the shoe in a quasi-three-dimensional way. Notice the slight deviation from the profile of the shoe to create the appearance of the throat (opening) of the shoe.

5. Notice the planes being referenced here are interpretations of the two-dimensional sketch set up. I removed the construction lines of the shoe to more clearly point out what these planes or slices look like. Additionally, the top surfaces of the shoe are shown as well to indicate the three dimensionality of these planes and how I see and interpret the geometry of the shoe as a whole. Consider these as guides.

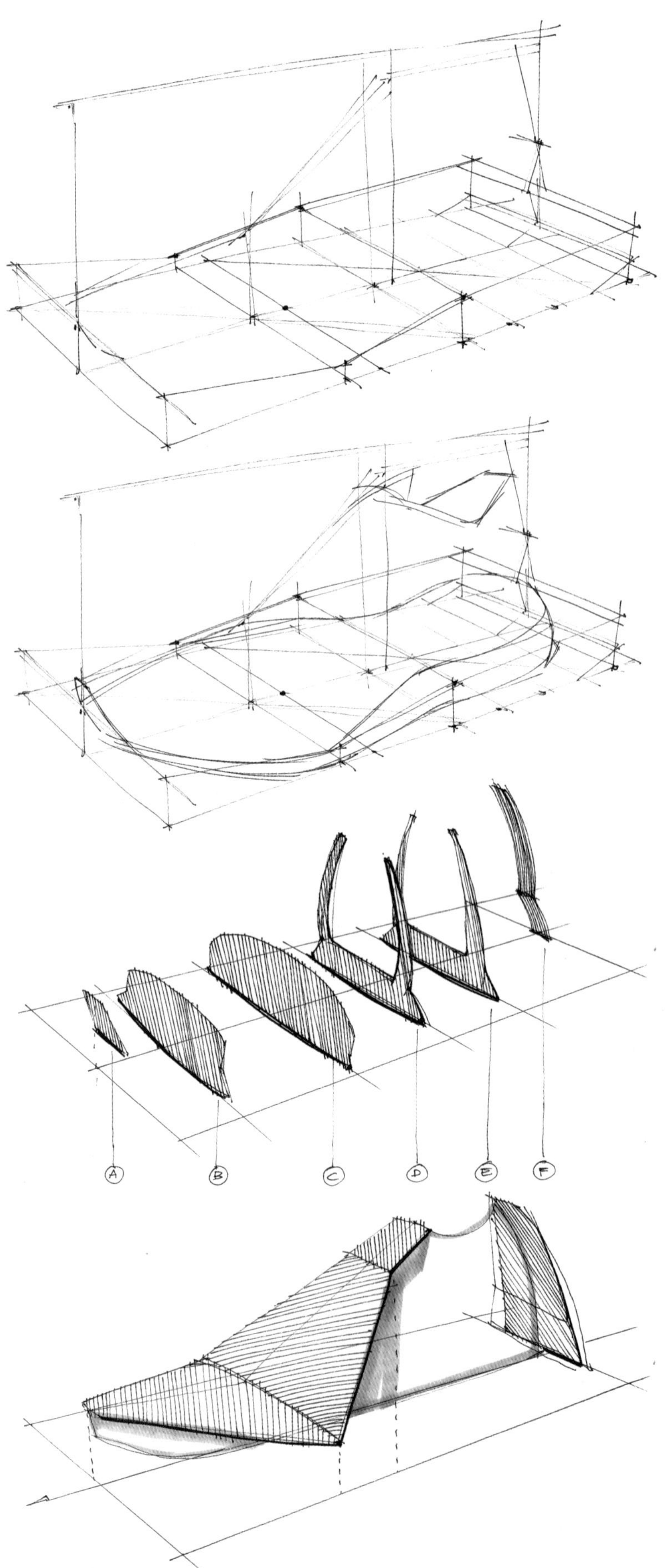

6. Now that the shoe has been roughed out, a bit of definition is added with lines that follow the surface geometry we established. Sketch the outline of the shoe by drawing tangentially to the planes sketched, much like the mouse example previously showed. Additionally, divide portions of the shoe into laces, overlays, and any other details related to the shoe.

7. Finally, if desired, you can overlay the sketch to create a tighter version of the shoe itself. For more information on how to do this check out Chapter 11, "Roughing It Out."

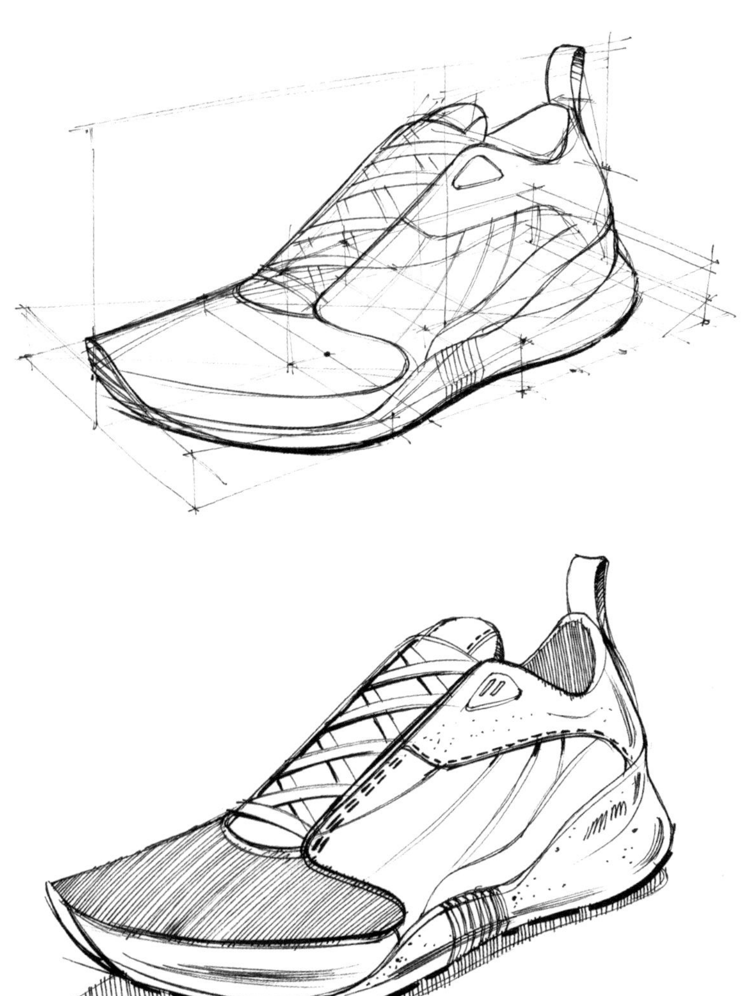

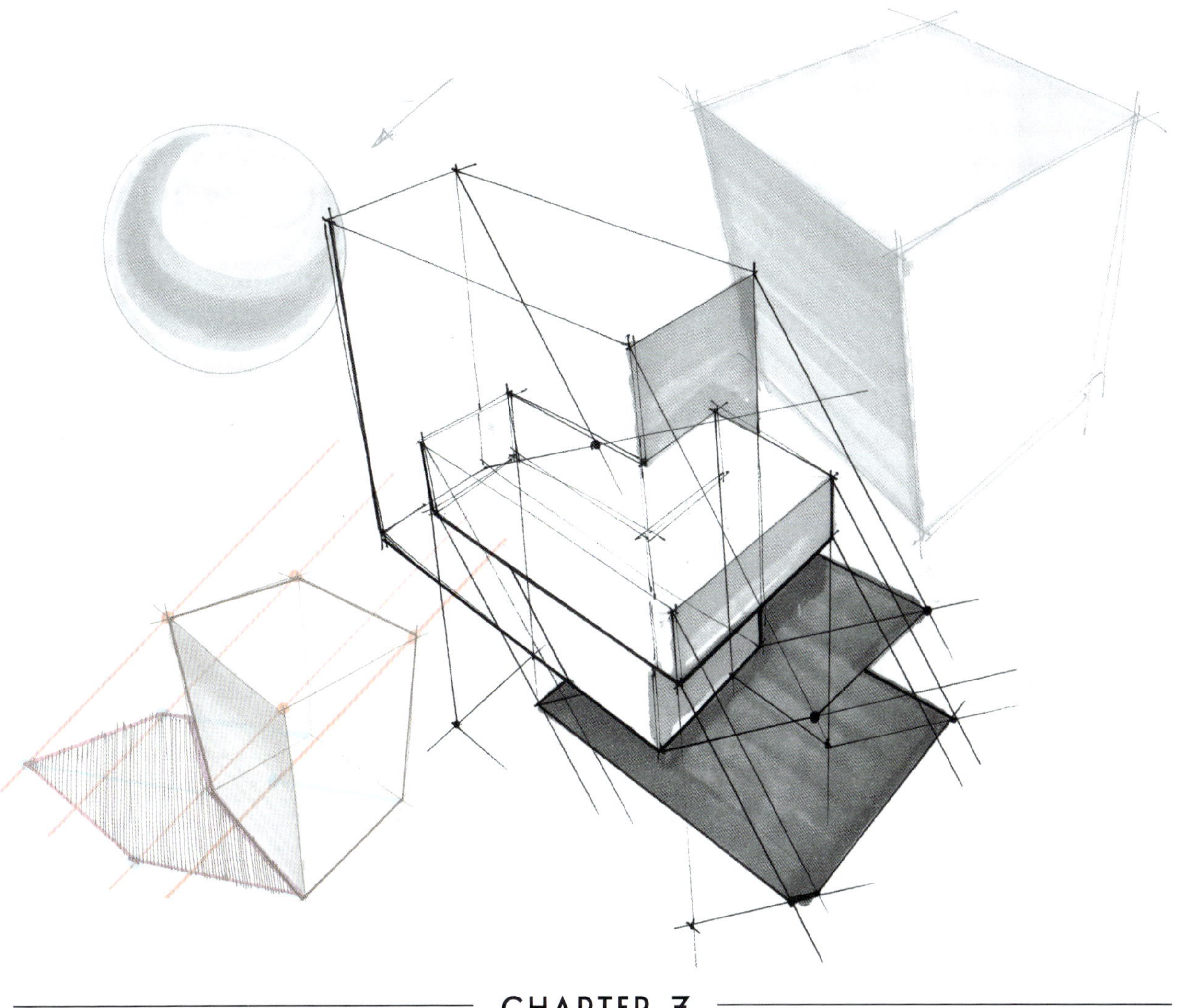

CHAPTER 7

LIGHT AND SHADOW

Lighting plays a key role in bringing your drawings to life. When combined with good quality, expressive, and confident line work, lighting adds a level of depth and presence to your perspective drawings of objects. All of what you observe in real life is the result of light interacting with the surfaces of objects. To handle lighting correctly in your drawings, you need to understand to some degree what happens when rays of light interact with objects.

For purposes of this book, consider light as traveling in very high-speed waves that are high energy and high frequency. In simple terms, you can think of light as imaginary or invisible lines that are emitted from a light source. These light rays, or lines, are emitted from a single source and interact with a surface of an object or the environment and reflect toward us. Our eyes then detect light rays and interpret what we observe with the help of our brains.

If a light source has higher energy, the resultant rays that reflect toward us are more intense and appear bright and concentrated. Conversely, if a light source is dim or low energy, the rays that reflect toward us also appear dim. If an object has a rough texture or finish, light rays still reflect toward us, but these rays may be slightly dispersed at different and inconsistent angles, thus conveying a more dull matte appearance. (You'll learn more about texture in Chapter 10, "Texture: Ink & Color")

The source of light can vary depending on the type of context or environment in which an object is located.

Direct Lighting

Direct lighting is the light emitted from a point light or natural light source (although even the Sun itself may be considered to be a point light source). Direct lighting may be primary, secondary, or tertiary in source and intensity to create a more interesting scene. More often than not, I choose a simpler lighting setup with a direct light source and ambient or reflected lighting as a secondary light source.

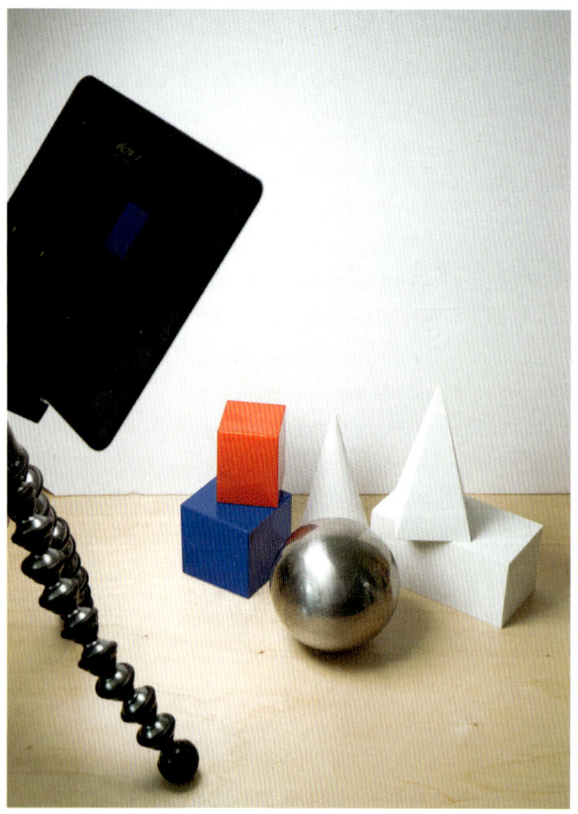

Artificial light shadows cast by primitive objects.

Ambient and Reflected Lighting

Ambient light is the general, or global, light resulting from reflected light in an environment. Reflected light cast on the observed or imagined object you're drawing may come from light bouncing off surfaces and other objects in the proximate environment. Reflected ground light comes from the surface an object rests on and is particularly noticeable on objects that are spherical and smooth and resting on a flat surface.

Because light reflects and influences other objects, lighting is most often uneven when interacting with a surface of an object. Take a minute to look around you at objects in your environment. Notice the interplay of color and light that may be cast by other objects in proximity to the main object you are observing. Consider your walls, too. Although painted a certain color, they also take on the reflected color of other objects in the environment, as well as cast reflected light onto other surfaces in the room.

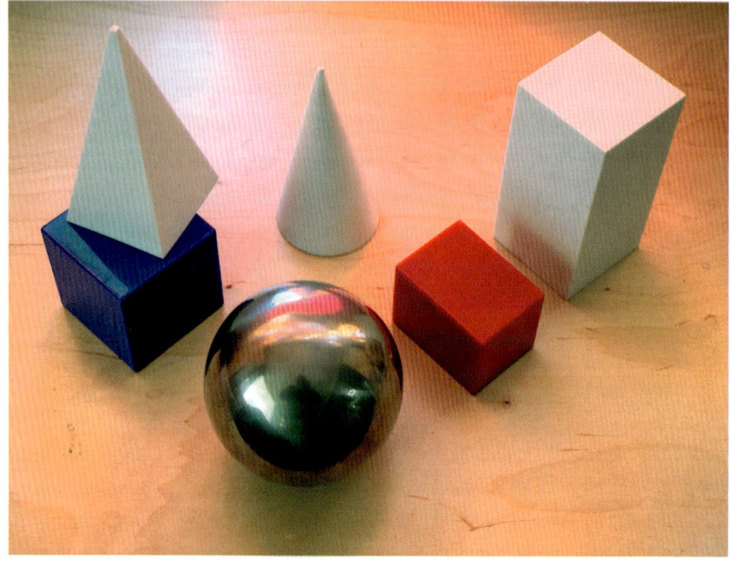

Light will reflect and color other objects in a scene.

Contrast Is Key

Much of what we see is the result of contrast in how objects are lighted. When a surface with the same color changes direction relative to a light source or is juxtaposed with a surface in contact that is incongruent, the contrast value changes on the surface. This contrast happens whether the surface is planar, curved, or organic in nature. With planar surfaces, there is a generally even, though somewhat varied, value in how the surface appears. When the surface is curved, shadow cores and reflected light help define the nature of the surface through contrast.

Consider, for example, these two planar faces orthogonal to each other.

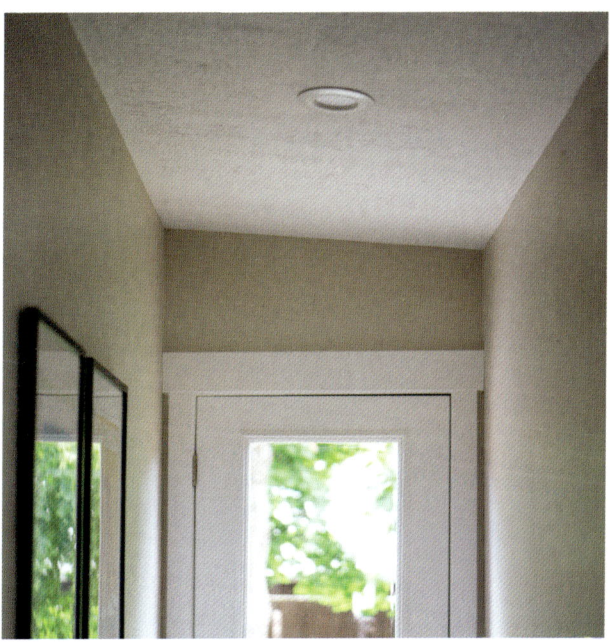

Contrast in value on the walls creates a sense of depth. Bonus, one point perspective!

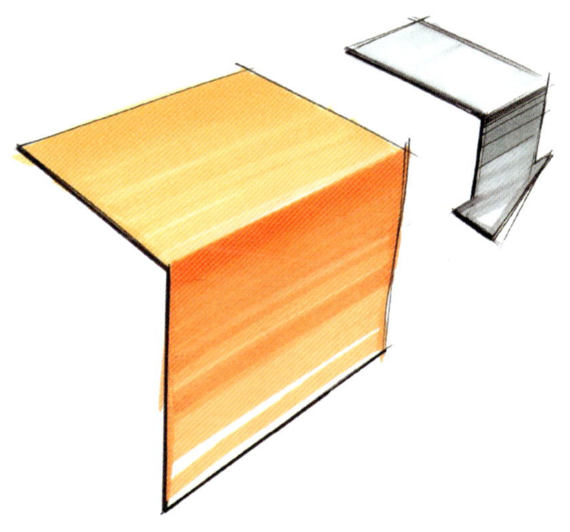

The surface that diverges away from the light source appears darker to the viewer compared to the surface that is facing towards the light source. These simple observations make it much easier to draw from imagination and work more quickly while sketching objects to capture ideas, as well as to add depth and a level of realism to your work.

Shadows on Surfaces

As mentioned, the surface on an object that diverts away from the light source will appear darker to the viewer compared to the surface that is facing towards the light source. In effect, the surface receives less light and is shadowed. Shadows on flat surfaces are fairly simple to understand and apply. To add shadow to a surface, simply darken the tone and value of the color, shading, or texture on the planar surface. For curved surfaces, shadows (and reflections) become a bit more complicated.

To understand shadows, you need to know a bit about how light bounces off a surface. Whenever light interacts with a surface, there is an angle of incidence, an angle of reflection, and a surface normal at each point light hits the surface. Consider, for example simple planar surface. The light ray has a trajectory and hits the surface at a point. At that point is a *surface normal*, a vertical line that is perpendicular to a tangent line at the point of contact. The same would be true for a curved surface (more on this in a bit).

At the point of incidence, the light ray then reflects away from the surface, and if you are looking at the surface, your eyes detect those light rays and others that are reflecting toward you that also may have been incident to the surface. This angle of reflection is always equal to the angle of incidence. This idea makes it a bit easier to understand shadows on curved surfaces as well as reflections.

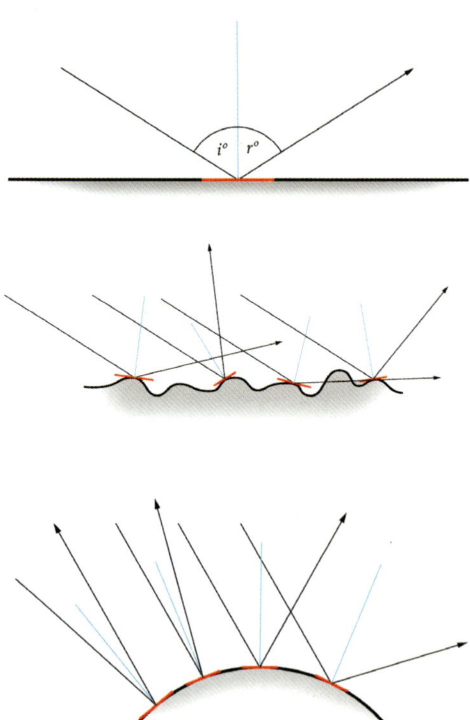

Shading and Shadow Demonstration: Cube with Markers

Let's practice drawing and shading a cube.

1. Start by drawing a cube of any size. For details on how to do this, refer back to Chapter 6, "Drawing with Depth in 3D." When working with markers, I go light until I get it right. For this demo, I used a 30%, 50%, and 70% gray marker selection. If using color, choose colors that work together and have a 20% to 30% value spread. (For more advice on markers, see Chapter 9, "Color.") Rotate the paper to draw at the best angle for you.

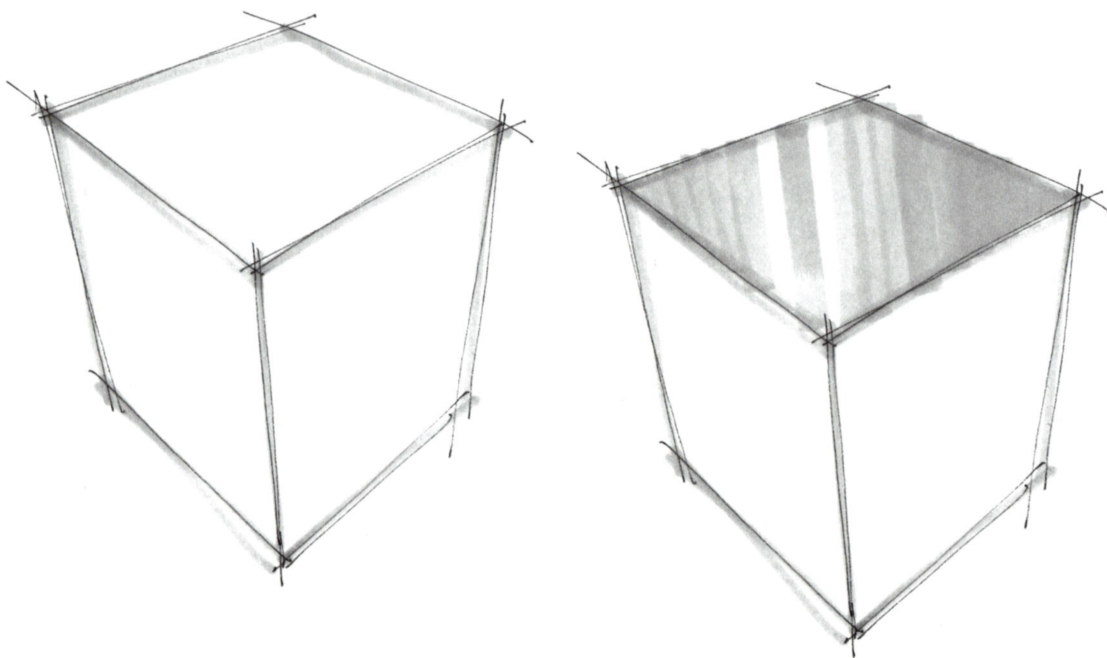

2. Outline the cube with your lightest marker. Next, work on the shading for the lightest surface. This will be the top of the cube, assuming the light is located above and to either the left or right of the cube. As you shade, create a gradient with the marker from the back of the top to the front.

3. Shade in either the darkest side or midtone side of the cube, being mindful to evenly apply the marker. Once the marker is dried, apply another few strokes close to the edge to add additional contrast at the edges of the cube.

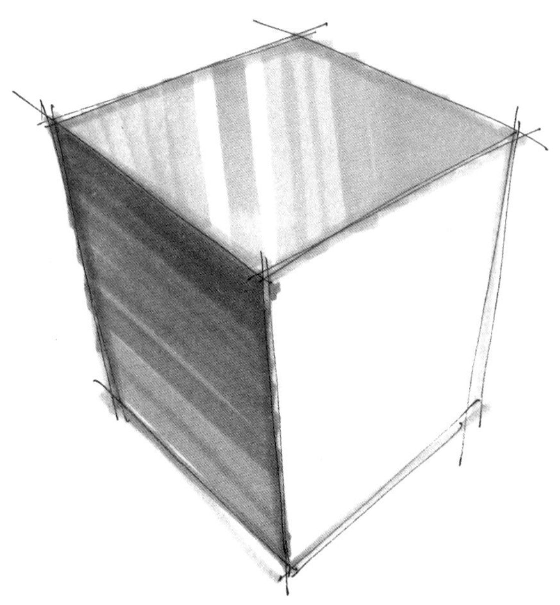

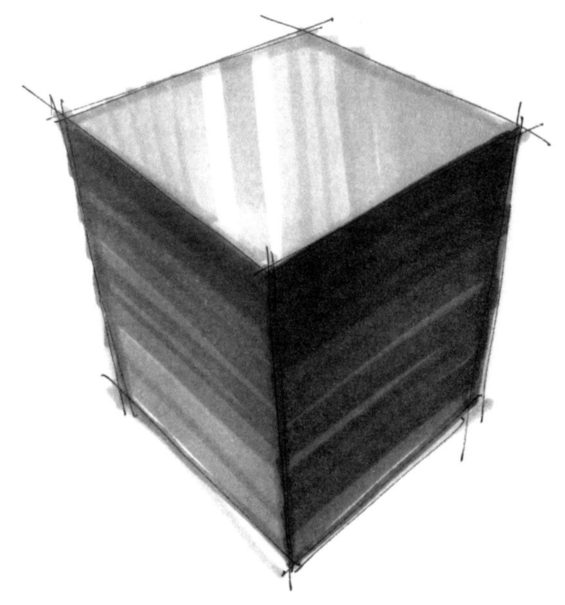

4. Finish shading in the surfaces with gradated marker strokes. The gradient is important as it adds a bit of realism to your drawing as light will hit the surface the object is on and create an uneven shade on the planar surface of the cube. This technique should work for most planar forms.

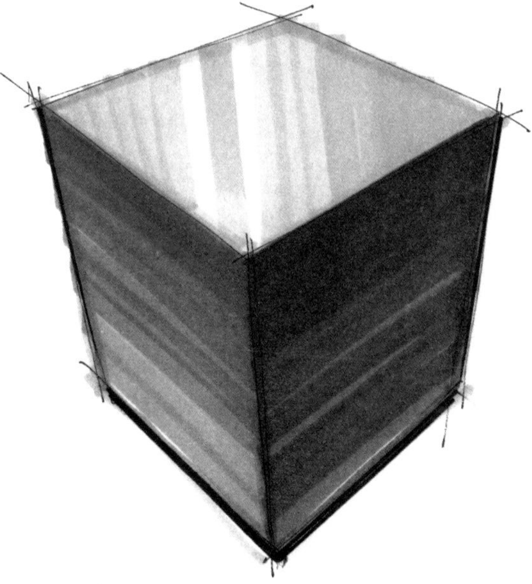

Shadow Core

Because a curved surface is always chang-ing direction relative to the light source, lighting on that surface will be uneven and varied.

A *shadow core* is a concentration of shadow along a surface that represents the areas at which light passes the surface as the surface changes direction away from the light source. In this illustration, the surface normals and angles of incidence and angles of reflection change as the surface changes and diverts light away from you, the viewer. Additionally, as light passes the perceptual edge of the object, the rear of the object is in shadow.

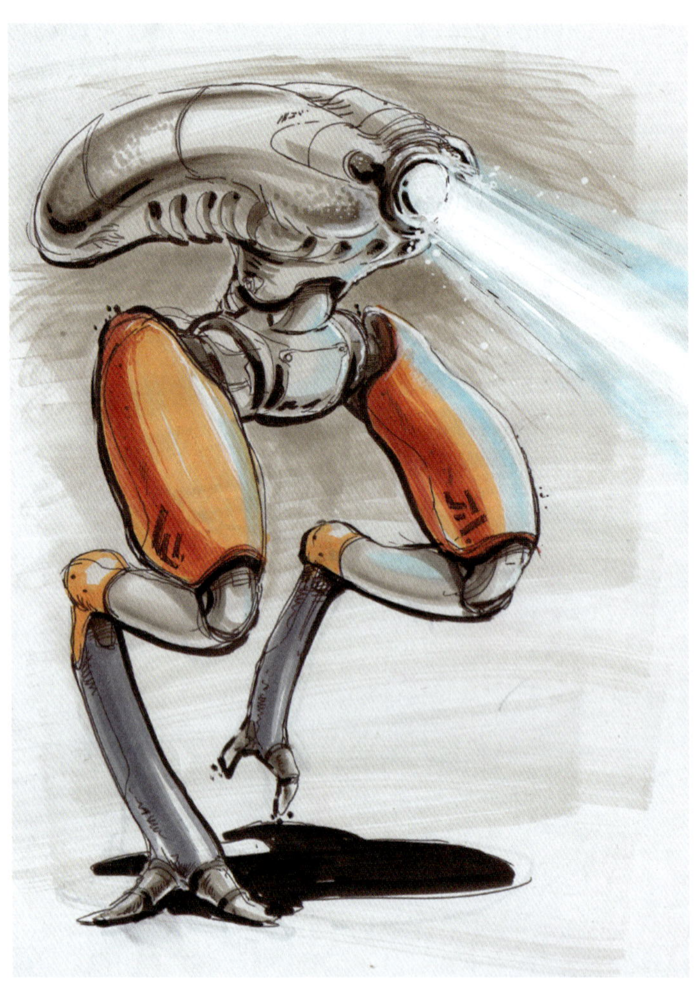

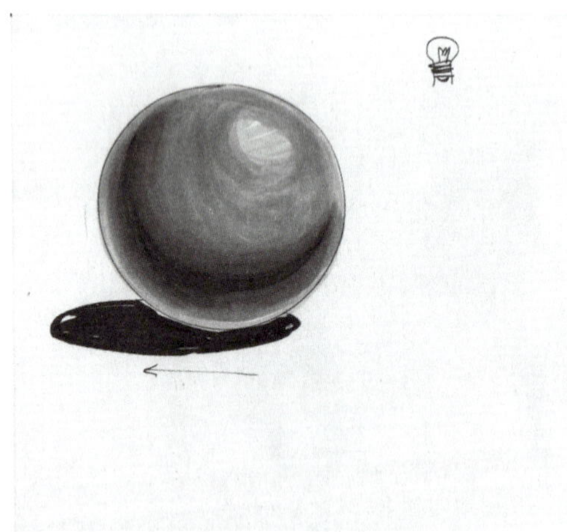

Without any kind of ambient lighting, the rear half of the object would appear flat and dark. When ambient or reflected light is present in the environment of the object or form, a core shadow forms along with rim light and highlights. (We'll discuss reflections, highlights, and how they affect shading in Chapter 8, "Reflections.")

Because curved surfaces are not flat, midtones appear between the shadows and the bright spots. To portray the depth of objects, it's important to master blending tones to shade and communicate a range of values. For example, look at the shading of this cylinder, sphere, and cone. Each object features a highlight, shadow core, and midtones. Because the light source is off to the right and slightly elevated, the high-light appears to the right of the objects, as that side of each object is closest to the light source.

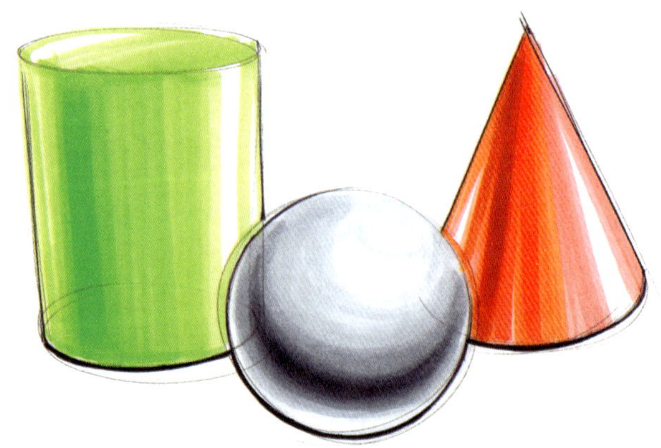

Shadow Core and Blending Demonstration: Cylinder with Markers

Cylinders are a useful building block for complex form. Let's shade one to understand a bit more about how light communicates its form.

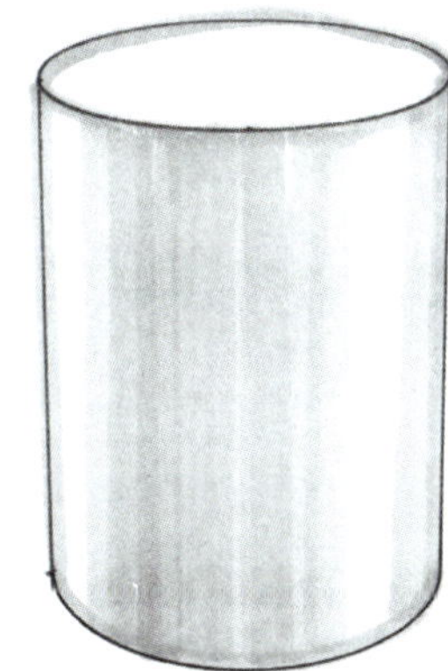

1. Start by drawing a cylinder of any size. For details on how to do this, refer back to Chapter 6, "Drawing with Depth in 3D." As with the cube, I used a 30%, 50%, and 70% gray marker selection, but if you're using colors make sure they work together and have a 20% to 30% value spread. Rotate the paper to draw at a comfortable angle.

2. Outline the cylinder with your lightest marker. Start with the vertical surface of the cylinder and shade in a shadow core and midtones. Depending on the surface finish of the cylinder, leave a vertical band blank for a highlight.

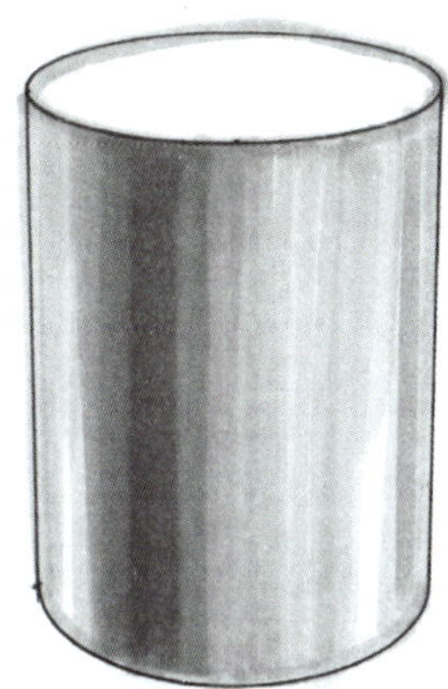

3. Next, use your midtone marker to shade in and deepen the shadow core and blend with the lightest tone as you move from the shadow core to the highlight. How wide or narrow do you make the shadow core and highlight? That depends on your cylinder's surface finish. The darker, narrower, and crisper the shadow core is, the shinier the surface will appear. The more evenly blended, the more matte it will appear.

4. Add more contrast to the shadow core with your darkest marker and blend into the midtone shade using your lightest and midtone markers to complete the blend.

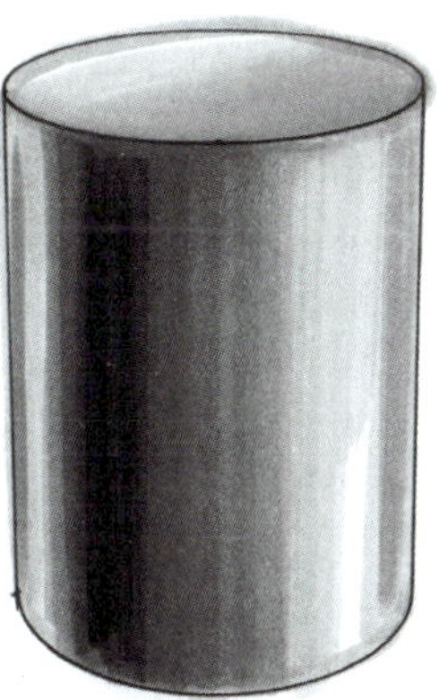

Because the top of the cylinder is facing the light source, use your lightest marker to shade in a way that contrasts the vertical surface of the cylinder. This is a great technique for any form with a cylindrical base.

Shadow Core and Blending Demonstration: Sphere

Spheres are also a useful building block for complex form. Let's shade one to understand a bit more about how light communicates its form.

1. Start by drawing a sphere of any size. Any circle will do as a sphere is a circle anywhere in perspective. Once again, I went light until my shading was right, used a 30%, 50%, and 70% gray marker selection, and recommend colors that work together and have a 20% to 30% value spread.

2. With your paper angled comfortably, outline the sphere with your lightest marker. Align the chisel tip of the marker with the outline of the sphere, and shade in the sphere so that the path of the marker follows its curvature. Leave an oval-shaped spot for a highlight.

3. Locate the position of your shadow core based on the widest point at a cross section of the sphere.

4. Next, use your midtone marker to shade in and deepen the shadow core, as well as to blend with the lightest tone as you move from the shadow core to the highlight. It's up to you, based on surface finish, how wide or narrow to make the shadow core and highlight. The darker, narrower, and crisper the shadow core is, the shinier the surface will appear, and the more evenly blended, the more matte the surface will appear.

5. Try not to shade all the way to the edge of the sphere with the darker markers. A blend is necessary to capture the effect of reflected light.

6. Add more contrast to the shadow core with your darkest marker and blend into the midtone shade using your lightest and midtone markers to complete the blend.

7. Finish up with a light marker to soften the blend as necessary and ease the transition into your highlight spot.

This technique also works well for organic forms with no rational or rectilinear characteristics.

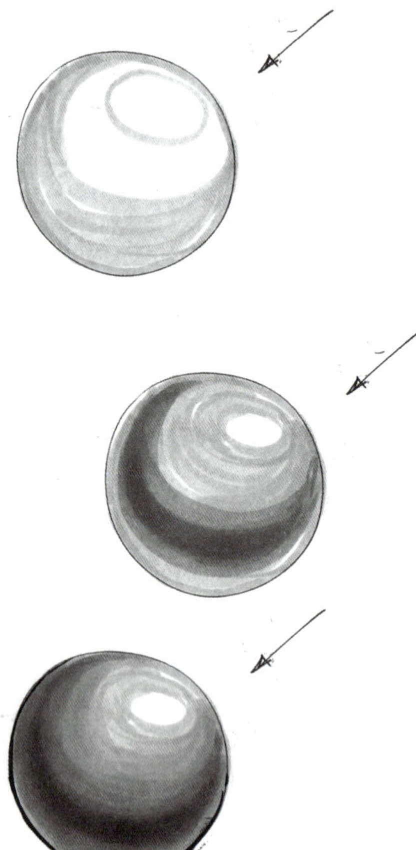

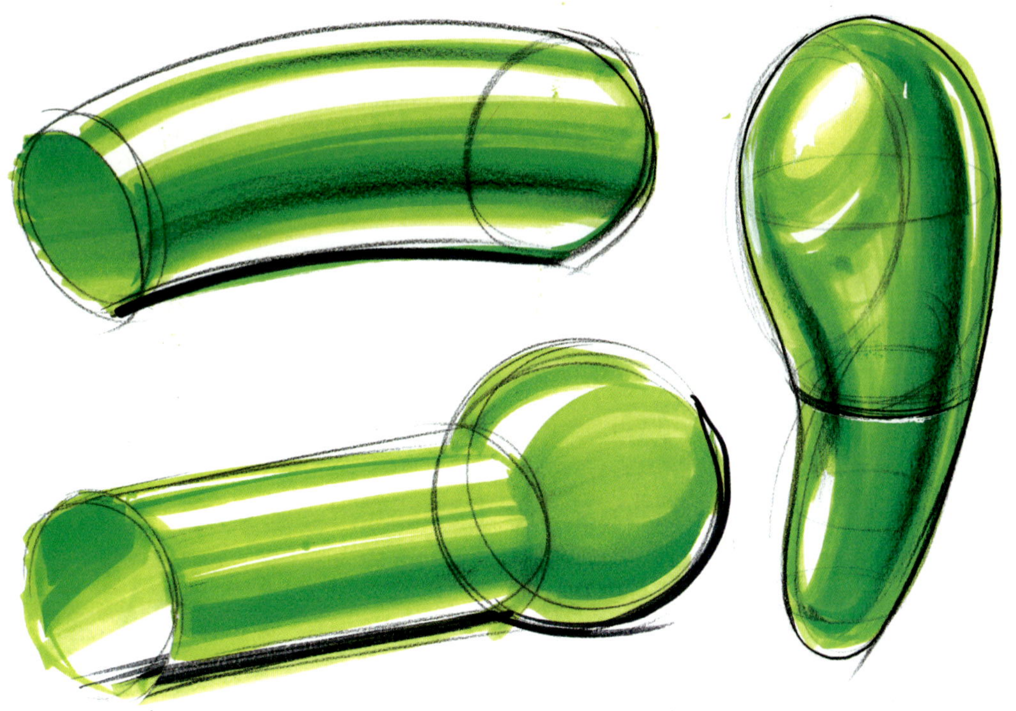

Cast Shadows

An object may not only be in shadow, but also can cast a shadow onto surfaces and other objects in its environment. Cast shadows stretch away from an object based on the direction, angle, and intensity of the light reaching the object. Think of a summer's day. At noon when the sun is directly above you, your shadow is relatively short. As the sun lowers toward the horizon, your shadow lengthens behind you. You can mimic this behavior in your drawings to enhance the illusion of depth and perspective.

Cast shadow outlines may have soft edges or hard edges. This is dependent on the light source and whether it is diffused, making the propagation of the light multidirectional. Generally, in my sketching, I don't worry too much about the softness of the shadow. Instead, I focus on the value of the shadow being cast on the object or by the object onto the surface where it rests.

Shadows that are cast follow the rules and norms of measured and estimated perspective. However the way that shadows are drawn differs based on the nature of the lighting source. When drawing, I divide light sources for shadows into two categories: natural light (sunlight) shadows and artificial light shadows.

Natural or Sunlight Shadows

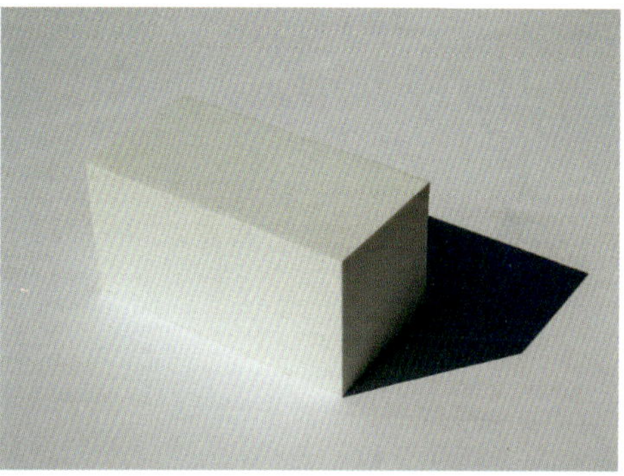

Natural light shadows are created when the Sun is the primary light source in a scene. Although the term *natural light* is used as a distinction, the Sun in effect is also a point light source. With any point light source, light rays can be assumed to be divergent in nature. However, because of the relative distance of the Sun from to the Earth (and anything you want to draw with a shadow), it's safe to assume that with natural light shadows light rays do not diverge and are effectively parallel. This important detail makes calculating natural light shadows much easier to understand and draw.

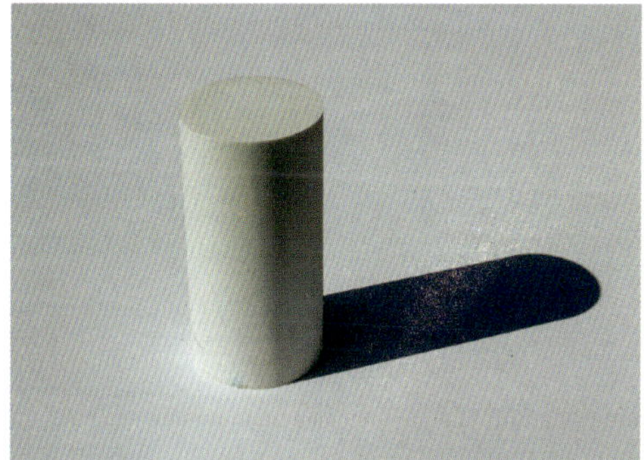

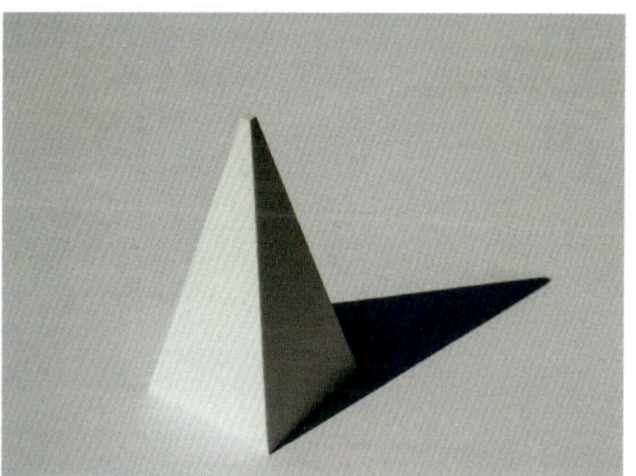

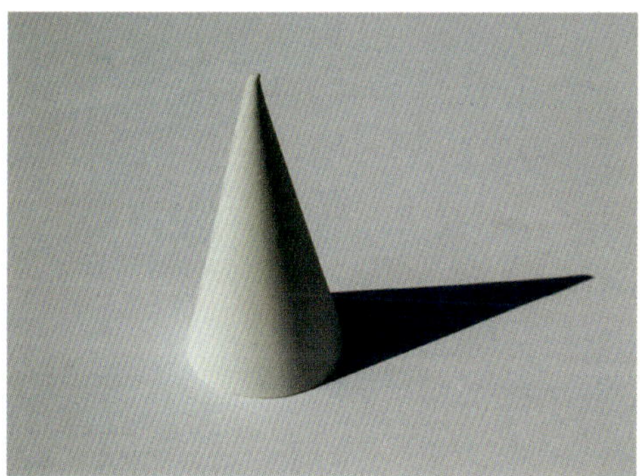

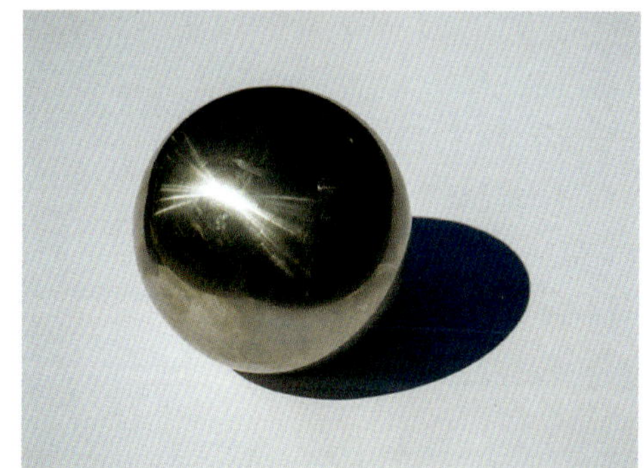

Natural Light Shadows Demonstration: Cubes

Let's cast a shadow from a simple cube to begin. To draw a natural light shadow, pick a relative position for the sunlight in relation to your cube. This position is based on the angle relative to the cube, which is determined by the position of the sun (time of day) as well as the relative rotational position to the cube on an axis centered at the middle of the cube. It is not important how large the diameter of the ellipse is when considering relative position of the sunlight source to the object.

Draw a simple cube and be sure to draw through to show the rear corners and edges of the cube in your drawing. You will need to use these edges and points for your learning.

Next, mark a point where the general direction of your sun resides in your scene relative to the central axis of the cube. From this point, project your first line through the top corner of the cube.

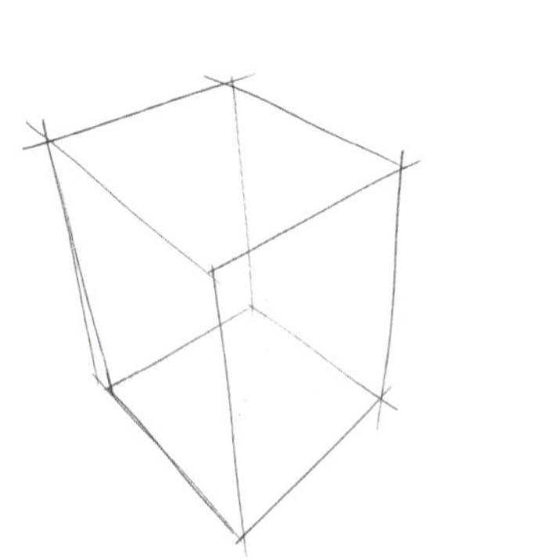

Draw another line parallel to your first line, but not converging to the point marking the location of the sun. Instead maintain the parallel relationship between these lines and subsequent lines through each corner of the top of the cube.

From the general direction of the sun point on the virtual ground plane, project lines that are parallel through each of the bottom corners of the cube to intersect with the lines projected from the sunlight source direction.

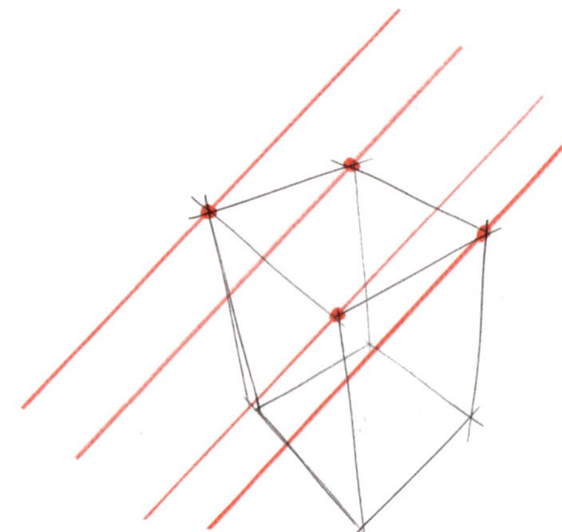

You should have four points, one of which may be located internally to the cube. This is to be expected in the calculation of the shape of the shadow. What you may notice is that the shadow is merely a projection of the top surface of the cube on the ground plane on which the cube rests.

Notice also the shape of the shadow and how the lines of the shadow seem to converge to a vanishing point to the left and right in your scene.

Cubes are simple objects, because of the four easily identifiable corners of their top surface. The resultant shadow, while simple, shows how the lines behave relative to vanishing points and the light source.

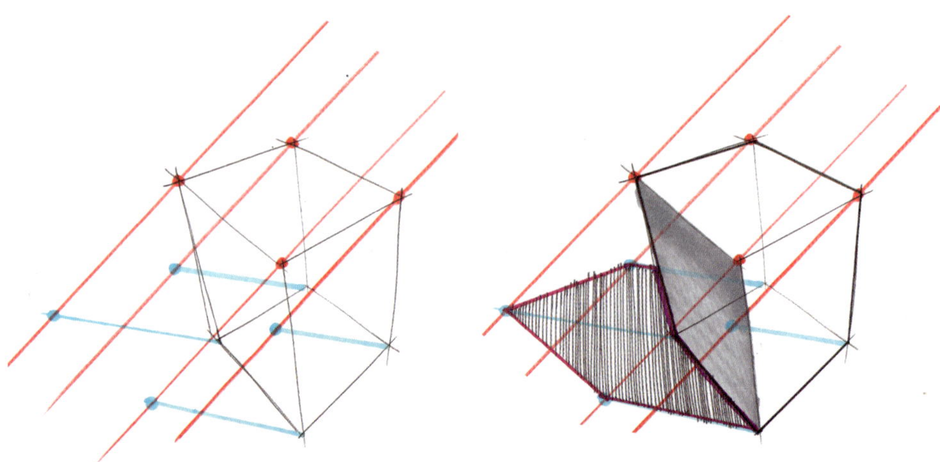

Natural Light Shadows Demonstration: Cylinders, Spheres, and Cones

A cylinder is a bit more complicated to cast a shadow on the ground plane. You can, however, use the methodology of casting a cylinder's shadow to determine the shape of the shadow of other curvilinear objects that may cast a shadow onto a ground plane surface.

To cast a shadow, start by drawing a simple cylinder. Draw two ellipses connected by vertical lines to create the volume of the cylinder. Like the cube example, draw through to the backside to show the structure of the cylinder. You can draw this cylinder in two- or three-point perspective.

Pick any number of points along the top of the cylinder. I tend to divide the top of the cylinder into eight parts by drawing four lines that intersect at the center of the top surface.

Project lines down to the base of the ellipse from each of these points that you selected to find the corresponding points at the base of the cylinder. You should now have eight points on top and eight points on the bottom of the cylinder to calculate your shadow.

Much like for the cube, project lines along the ground plane and project lines down from your chosen light source direction to intersect your lines along the ground plane. These eight intersecting points are the points you need to form the shadow. Complete the shape by drawing lines tangent to the new ellipse on the ground plane. Much like the cube, depending on your light location, you may have points on the inside of the silhouette of your cylinder. Focus on the overall shape of the cast shadow that was plotted.

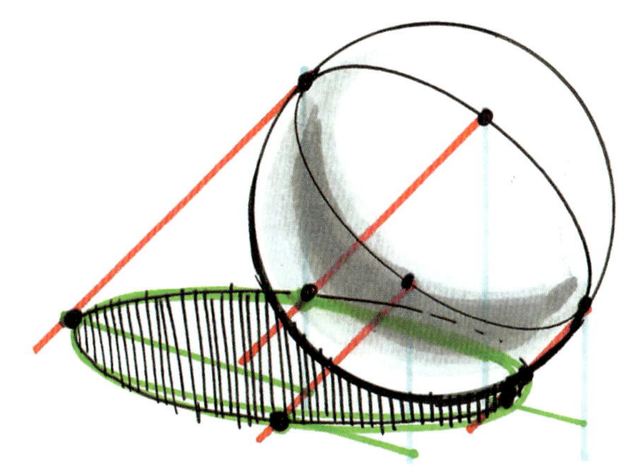

A cone follows essentially the same process, save for the fact that the top of the cone is a single point, rather than a circle.

A sphere requires a bit of understanding of what the cross section of the sphere looks like. Spoiler: It's a circle, no matter how you slice the sphere. In perspective, circles are ellipses and thus, calculating the shape of the shadow is as simple as projecting an ellipse onto the ground plane.

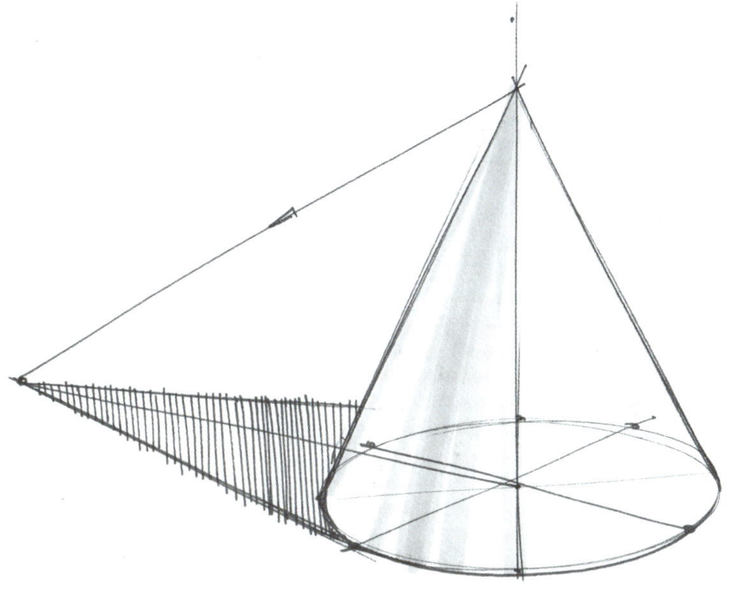

Determine the relative location of your sun to the sphere and mark its location. At the widest point of the sphere, where light would then cast a shadow, mark an ellipse.

Divide the ellipse into any number of points and project lines downward from these points to intersect with the ground plane where the sphere would be touching the ground. Draw an ellipse. This can be approximate, or if you prefer, construct a plane and place the ellipse within it.

Next, being mindful of your chosen sun location, project lines representing the light rays from the light source through the points along the widest part of the sphere. This point is shown by the elliptical cross section that was sketched in at the widest part of the sphere. Choose any direction that is indicative of the relative position of the sun to your spherical shape, and project lines from the base elliptical shape to intersect the projection of lines from the widest point of the sphere.

Project lines from the elliptical shape on the ground plane to intersect with the lines that represent the light rays. Find an equivalent number of intersections to the number of points chosen along the widest part of the sphere.

You should have an elliptical profile cast on the ground plane that represents the area of shadow that would be cast by the sphere.

You can construct cast shadows from organic or non-rectilinear shapes in a similar way as for a sphere. Rather than an elliptical profile, the shadow of an organic shape necessitates figuring out what the cross section of the organic shape looks like and projecting lines representing light rays from the profile of the cross section on the ground plane with corresponding intersection points.

Try it a few times and see how it feels!

Artificial Light Shadows

Artificial light shadows are similar to natural light shadows with one key difference: The light rays that create them diverge from the originating source that emits them rather than remaining parallel with each other. Because of this light behavior, the shape of the cast shadow is divergent and distorted relative to the shape of the object casting the shadow.

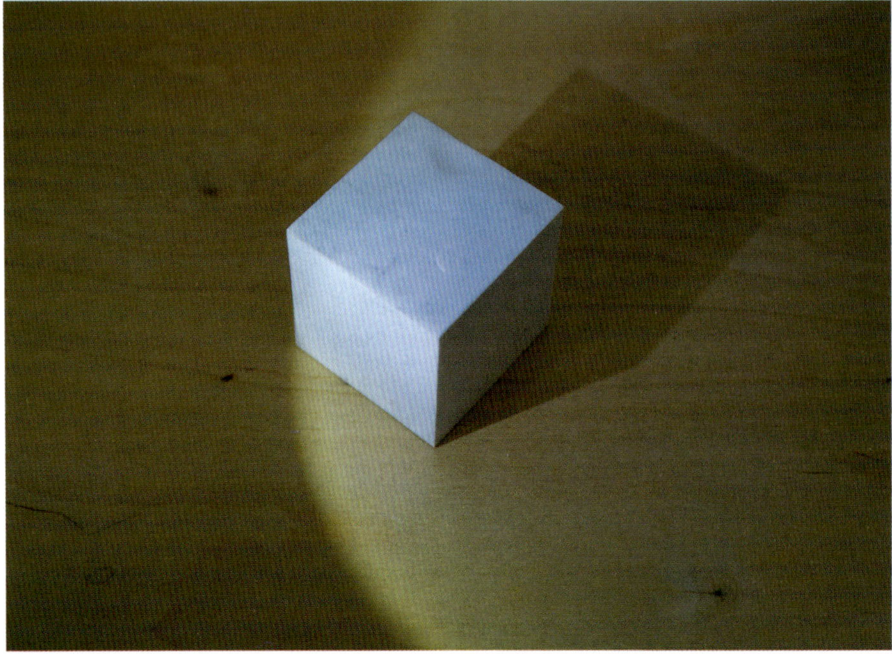

Notice the shadow appears larger than the cube itself.

Artificial Light Shadows Demonstration: Cubes

To cast an artificial light shadow, start by drawing a primitive of your choosing. I used a cube in this example; it's easy to understand, and the principle can be applied to other shapes.

Similar to the example with natural light, choose a point to place your light source. This time, draw a line vertically upward toward it from a corresponding point on the ground plane. This line (and therefore, your light source's position) can be as high as you like. The closer to the ground plane, however, the longer the shadow will appear.

With the light source positioned, draw lines from the top-most point of the light source and project the lines through the corners of the top surface of the cube toward the ground plane. Make sure the lines extend far enough to intersect with the next set of lines that will be projected from the base of the light source line.

Project lines from the base of the vertical light source you drew. Draw through each corner of the base of the cube to intersect with the lines projected from the top-most point of the light source line. (You can do this process in either order: from the top or from the bottom as the first step.)

With the intersection points, you should have an outline of a cast shadow. The divergent lines are emitted from a special vanishing point at the base of the light source, giving the cast shadow its distorted appearance. Some of the shadow lines should converge at the regular vanishing points in the scene.

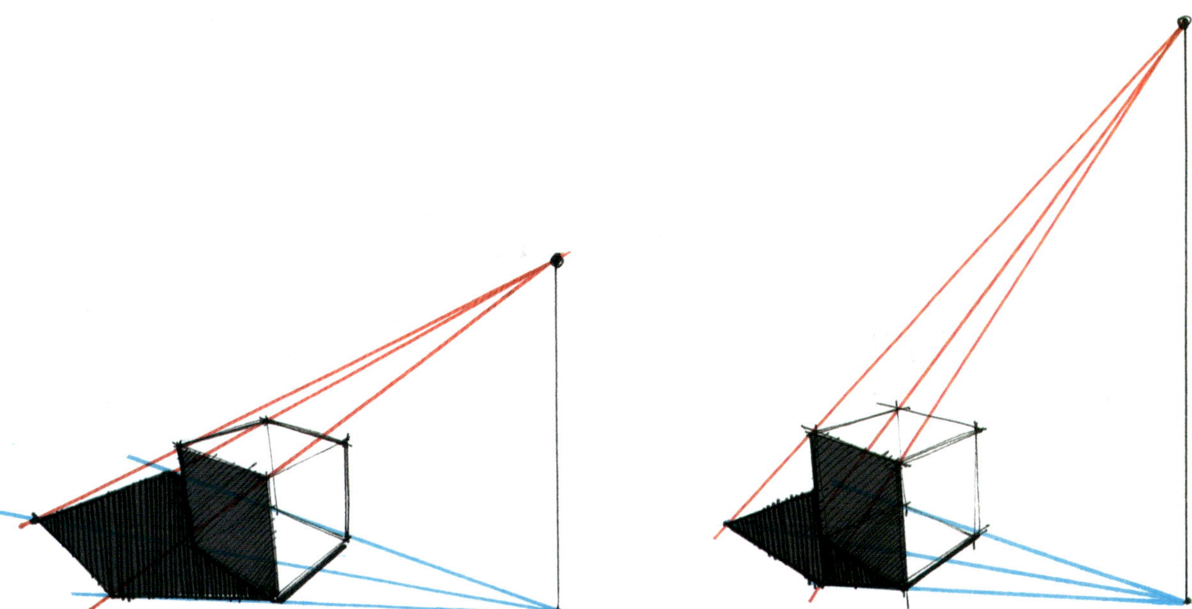

Be mindful that the closer in proximity to the cube you place the base of the light source, the more divergent and distorted the shadow will appear. The further out the base of the light source, the less distorted the cast shadow will appear.

Simplified Shadowing and Drop Shadows

Many times when you draw, you may place a simplified shadow on the ground plane. If you have been following along, you may have noticed that a shadow is a projected cross section of the object you're drawing. Sometimes you can estimate and project a shadow in a way that conveys the general cross section of the object without precise calculation, thus saving time. Taking things a step further, when quickly sketching an object, I often project an elliptical shape onto the ground plane as a simplified version of the profile of the cast shadow.

Alternatively, rather than creating a scene with a light source that is angled somewhat relative to the object on view, you can add a drop shadow as a simple way to provide some depth in the scene.

For drop shadows, try a setup where the light source is emitting parallel or near parallel rays of light from above the object toward the ground plane. The object can be resting on the surface or slightly raised.

Consider this organic form. By placing it on the ground plane or above the ground plane, you could cast a simple drop shadow by projecting parallel lines through points along the cross section of object at its widest point.

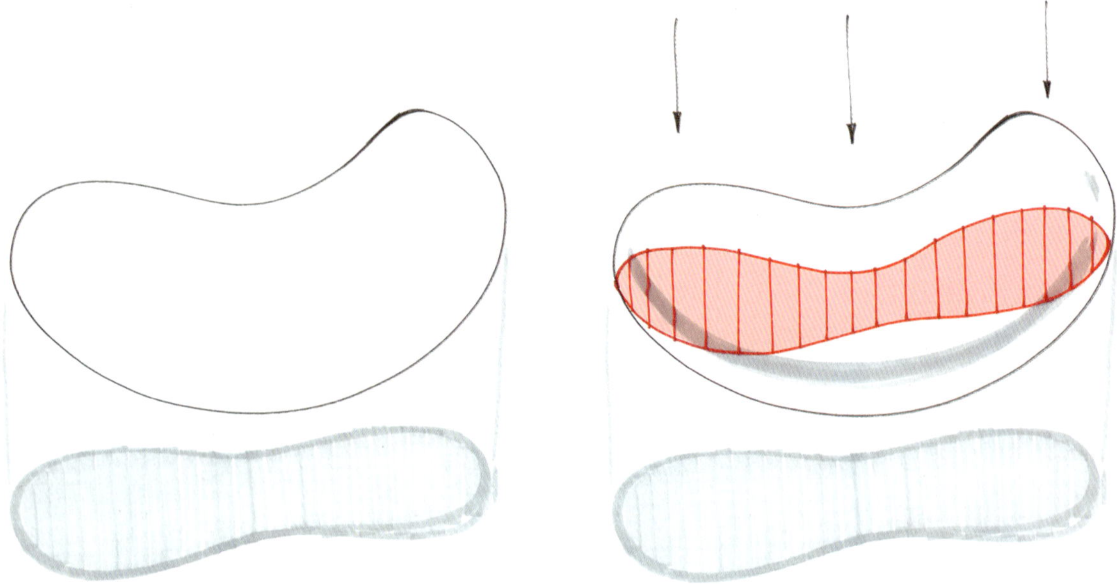

Figuring out how far away from the object to place the cast drop shadow is simply a matter of estimating optical difference. There is no wrong answer given the fact that you are in control of how to present the object. Because the shadow is being cast by an overhead light source, the relative distance from the object to the shadow is a means of communicating depth or distance from the ground plane. The further away the object is from the ground plane, the lighter the shadow may appear because of diffusion and ambient light in the environment illuminating the surface below the object at a distance. Still, for effect, you can simply pick a value, shade the shadow, and not worry too much about this factor, although it's worth observing from real-life experience.

Shadows Cast by Complex Forms

To draw shadows for a more complex form, break the form down. Much like drawing complex objects, you can calculate shadows for complex using a breakdown of the simple elements that compose the object. Project lines in a similar fashion to calculating a natural or artificial light shadow in the previous demonstrations, and then find the overlap in the lines.

It takes a bit of time and patience to figure out where to find the intersections. After a few times through and some practice, however, you can create a simplified shadow instead, one informed by what you know about constructing shadows.

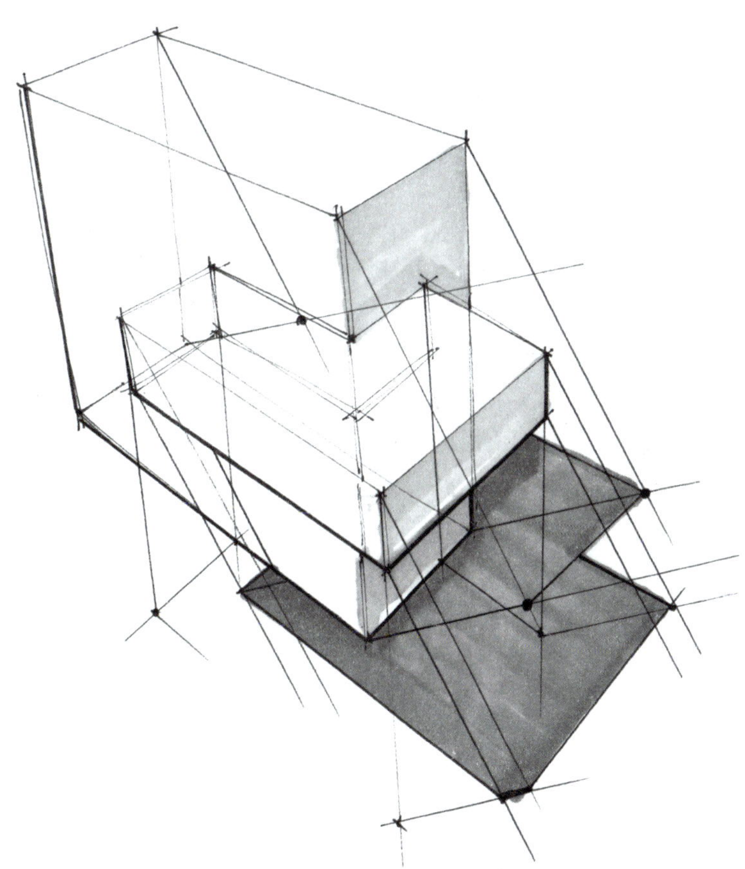

With enough practice, much of the *how* and the *why* becomes intuitive and you will be able to draw in your shadows much more confidently and quickly. Remember, contrast is your friend, and shadows will further add to the "pop" in your drawings of objects and their environments.

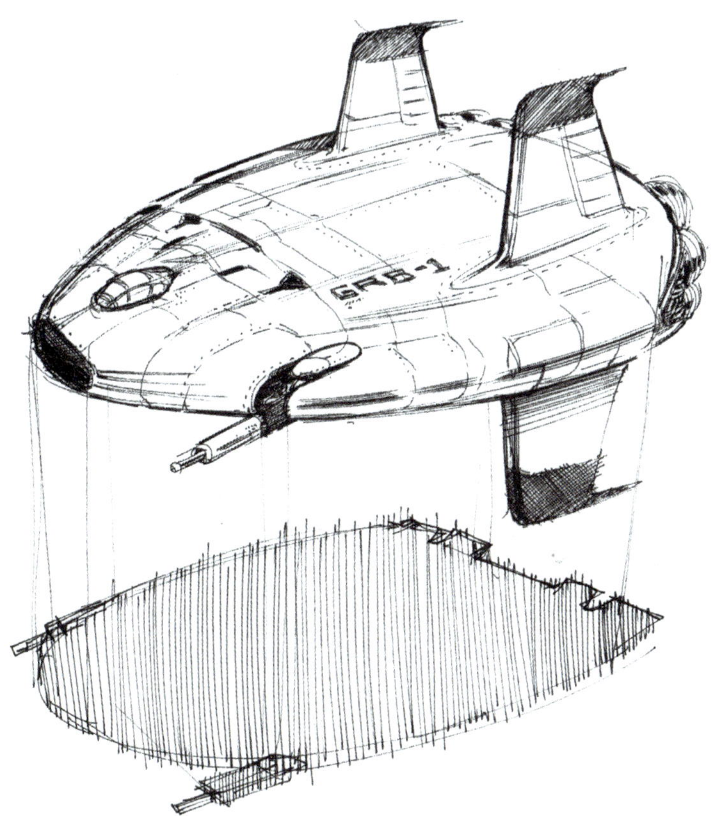

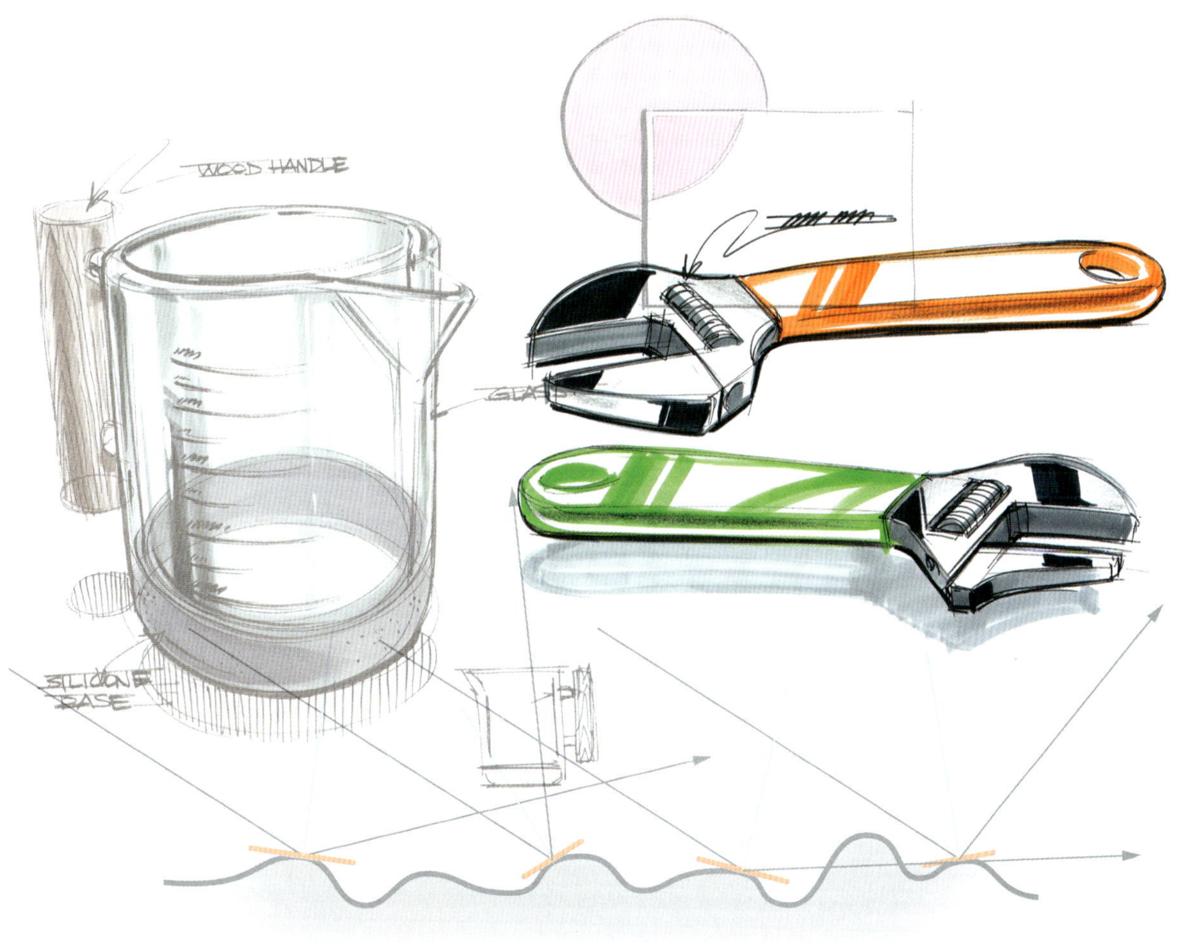

— CHAPTER 8 —

REFLECTIONS

In the last chapter, we discussed light, how it creates shadows, and how shadows add depth and realism to your sketches and drawings. Light also creates reflected images on some surfaces when we observe the object. Reflected light is fundamental to how we see everything in the real world—every object's color, tone, shade, and texture. Reflections are caused by light being incident to a surface and the viewer observing the reflected light. To produce clear reflections, a surface must have a few characteristics that allow light to bounce to our eyes.

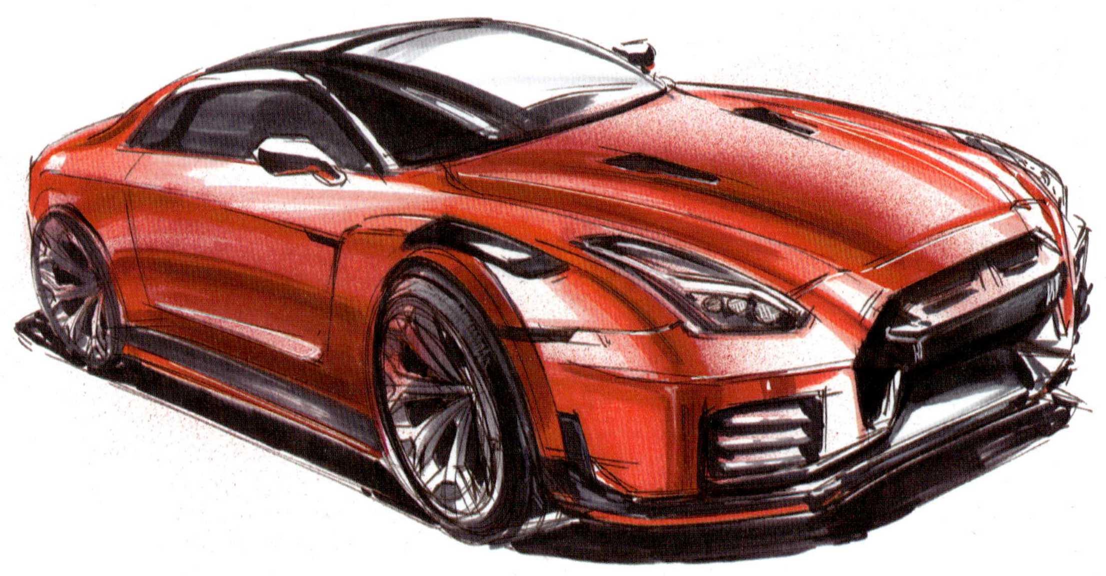

Smooth vs. Rough Surfaces

As you know from real-world observations, reflections from smooth, flat surfaces look different than those from uneven surfaces. The reason why relates to how the trajectory of light interacts with the surface and how that affects what you, the observer, see of the object and the reflected image.

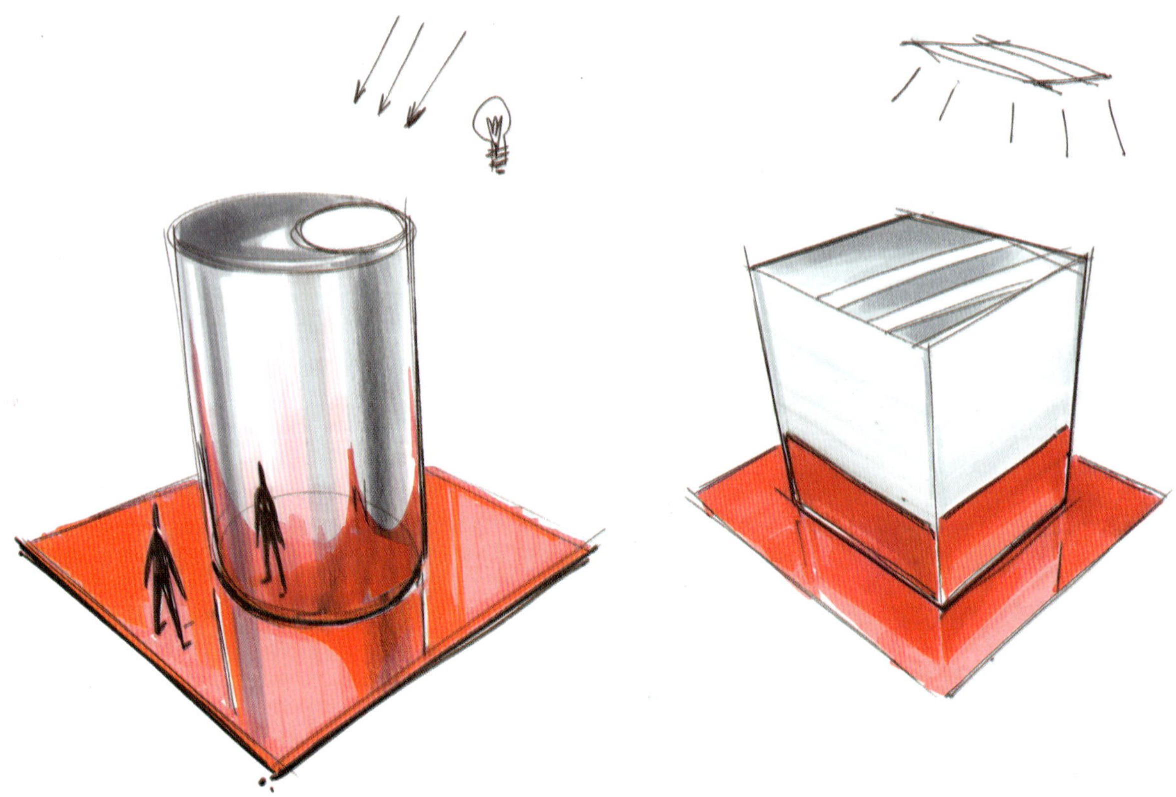

Imagine a mirror (or other highly polished, flat, smooth surface) with a light source and objects nearby. Rays emanate from the light source and hit the mirror's surface at a point of contact; the angle at which the light hits the surface is called the angle of incidence. In math terms, the angle of incidence is the angle between the surface normal (vertical line that is perpendicular to a line tangent to the point of contact) at the point of tangency located at the point of incidence (the contact point) and the trajectory of the ray of light from the light source that hits that point. The path of light that is reflected from the surface is at the same angle at which the light was incident to the surface. This second angle is called the angle of reflection. This is true for flat surfaces as well as curved surfaces.

The less polished a surface is, the less refined the reflection will be, and the more polished the reflective surface is, the clearer the reflected object will appear. Additionally, the color of the reflective surface may affect whether the reflection is clear like a mirror or more fuzzy. Adding color to a reflection can also enhance the visual realism of the drawing.

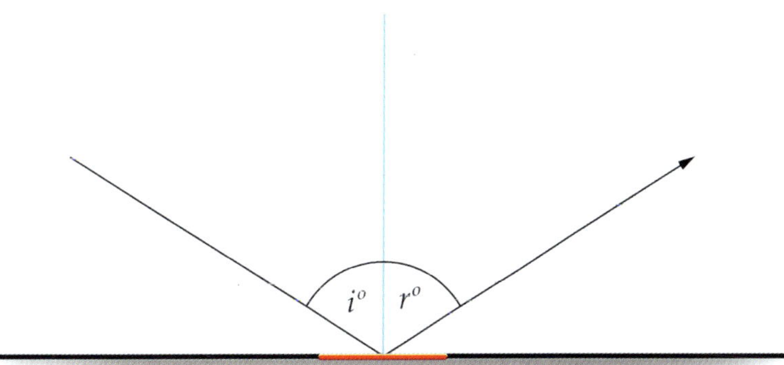

With a curved surface, each ray of light that is incident will have a different surface normal and angle of reflection. This is in part why shadow cores work the way they do on curved surfaces and value is varied on a curved surface.

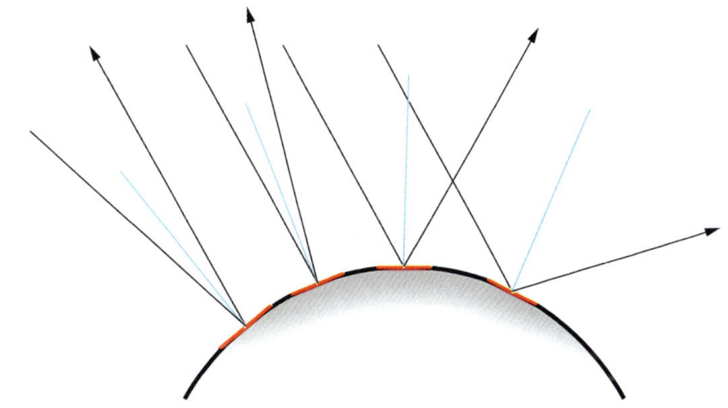

The rays of light that are incident to the curved surface may be reflected in a divergent or convergent pattern, thus intensifying the reflected light or spreading it out. This spreading or converging of reflected light rays causes a value change in surface appearance as well as distortions in reflections. Study a shiny, curved object nearby, and compare its reflections to that of a smooth, flat surface. (We'll revisit this concept a bit later in this chapter.)

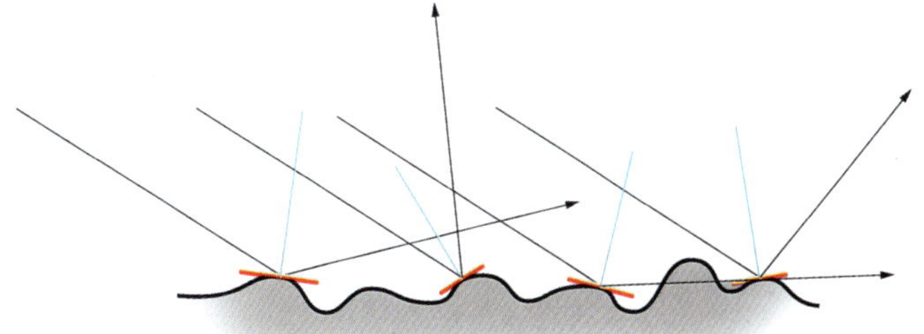

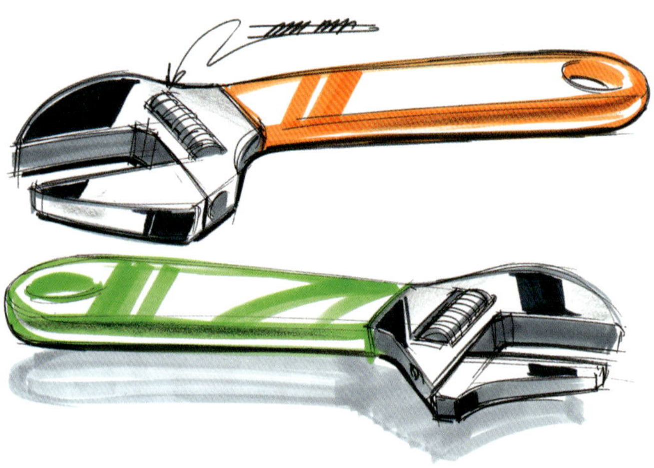

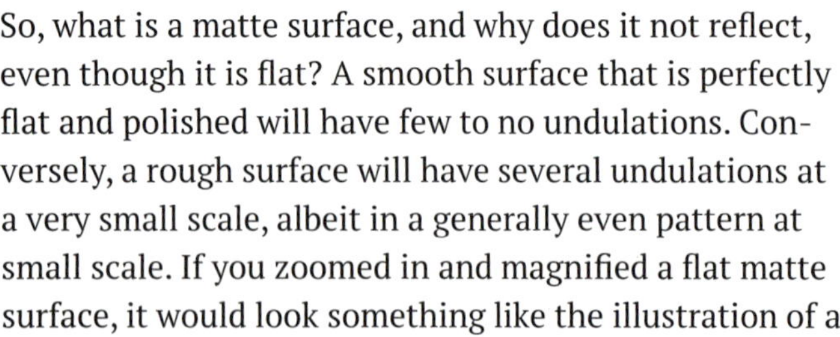

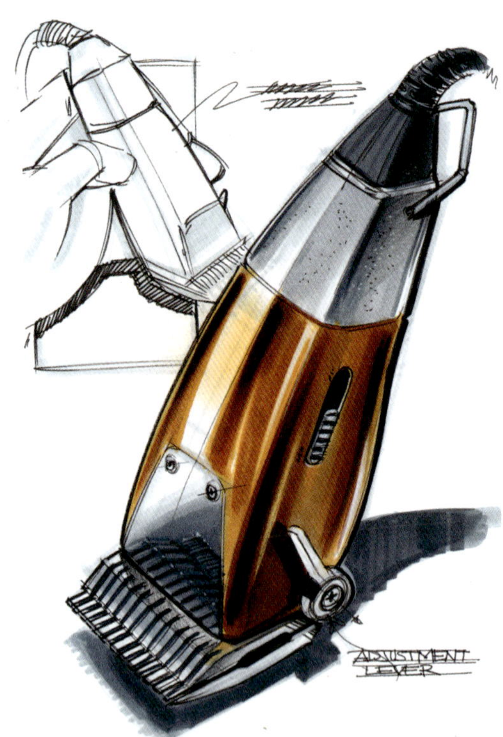

So, what is a matte surface, and why does it not reflect, even though it is flat? A smooth surface that is perfectly flat and polished will have few to no undulations. Conversely, a rough surface will have several undulations at a very small scale, albeit in a generally even pattern at small scale. If you zoomed in and magnified a flat matte surface, it would look something like the illustration of a flat surface up close with undulations on page 93. Each undulation on the surface is a small deviation in the flat surface, so small you cannot see it without magnification. Because of these changes in the surface topography, the light that it reflects is diffused as it bounces from the surface. Why? With each undulation, the angle of incidence and, therefore, angle of reflection change with each successive ray of light that is incident to the surface. These differences in angles of incidence mean that each light ray is reflecting toward the viewer at a distinctly different angle. This varied reflection of light causes the diffused matte appearance in surface finish.

Simple Reflections

With reflections, the light the viewer sees is secondary light, reflecting off an object before being seen by the viewer.

Look at the diagram for a simple reflection example. The viewer can see into the mirror from their perspective and notices that the subject is inverted. Why? The light the viewer is observing is the light reflected from the surface of the mirror. (In the diagram, the dotted line represents the image of the trajectory of the reflected light traced "into" the mirror.)

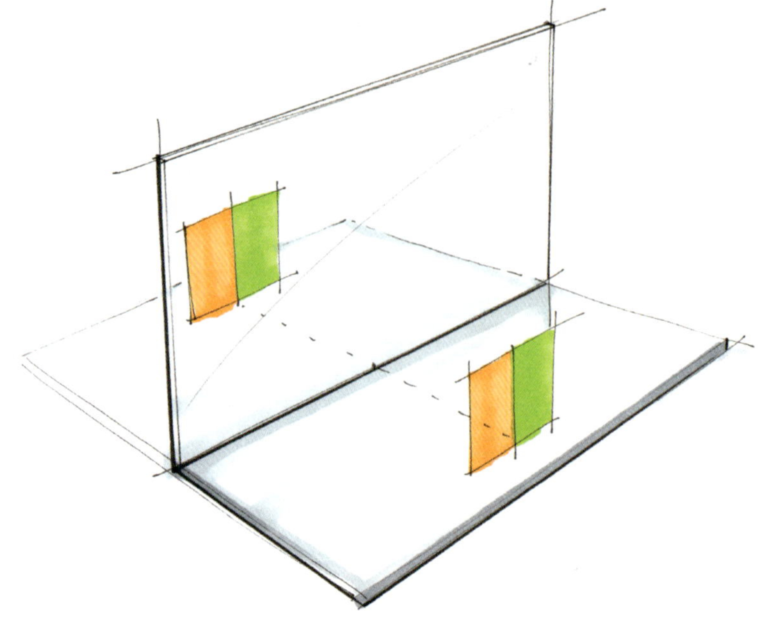

Remember, the angle of incidence is equal to the angle of reflection, which explains why the image the viewer sees is inverted. In this case, the inversion is top to bottom because the subject is resting on the mirror. If the subject was in front of the mirror and the subject was also the viewer, the image in the mirror would be flipped as the light being observed would be the light that is reflected from the subject to the viewer.

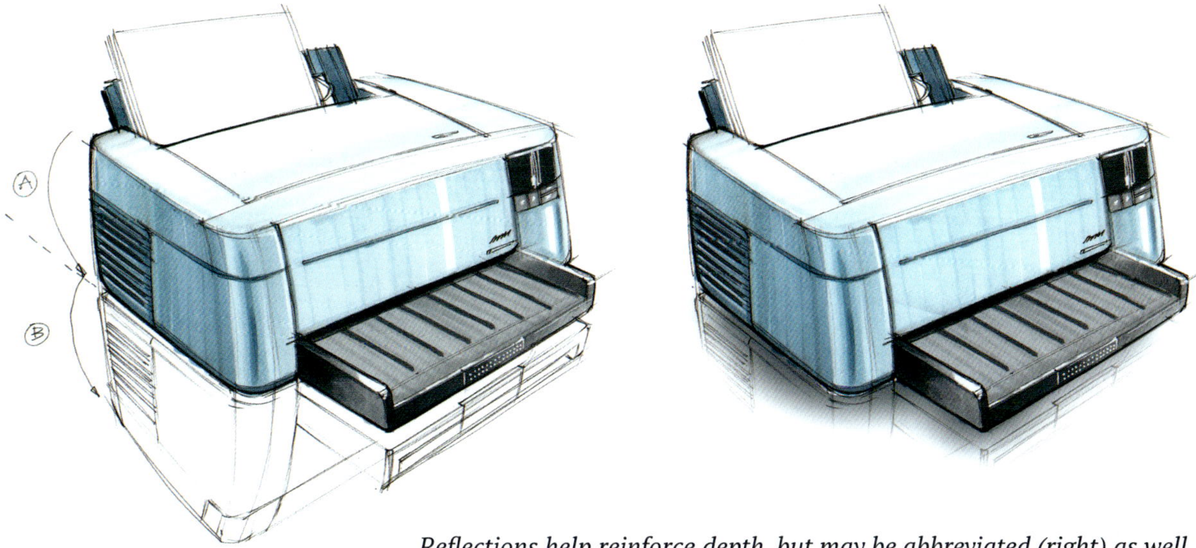

Reflections help reinforce depth, but may be abbreviated (right) as well

This may seem confusing at first but try replicating the example shown with a few simple objects to get the hang of it.

Try drawing a similar setup and tracing lines to calculate where an image would be produced relative to the object in this two-dimensional scene.

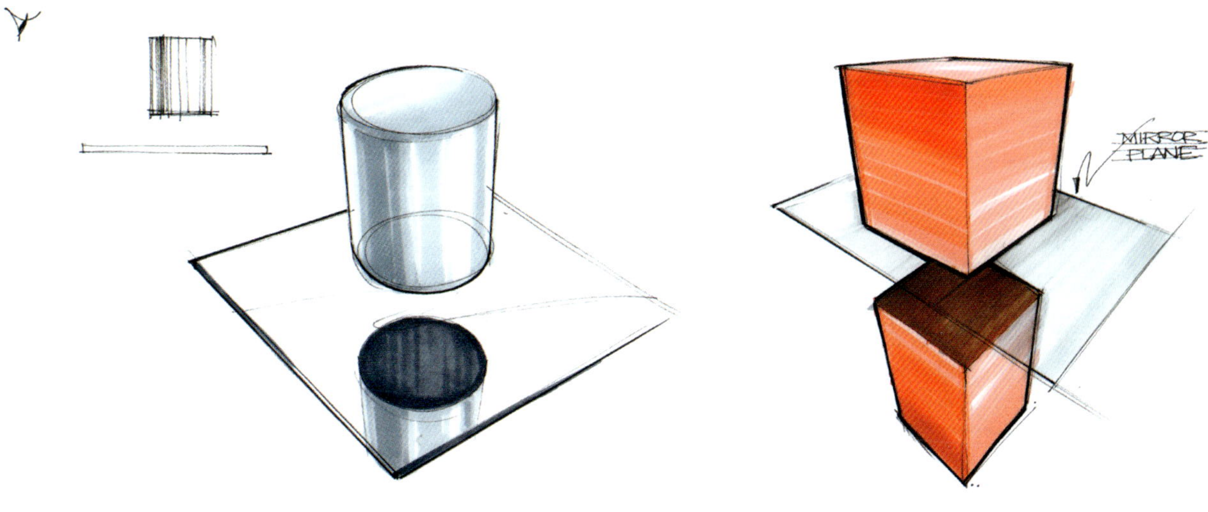

In perspective or three-dimensional drawing, reflections work much the same as shown in the previous two-dimensional example. Remember, the reflection in view is the result of light reflecting from the object to the viewer at the same angle.

In the two-dimensional example, when distance is placed between the object and the mirror, the distance is also reflected in the mirror. Simply put, the distance of an object to the mirror is equal to the distance of the image of the object in the reflection. Remembering this relationship simplifies drawing reflections in planar faces when drawing in perspective.

There are multiple ways to estimate the distance of an object from a mirror in perspective drawing, similar to working with square faces and boxes in perspective when calculating double or triple distances. One simple and useful method is to draw a rectangle, find the center, and extend the rectangular shape into the mirror.

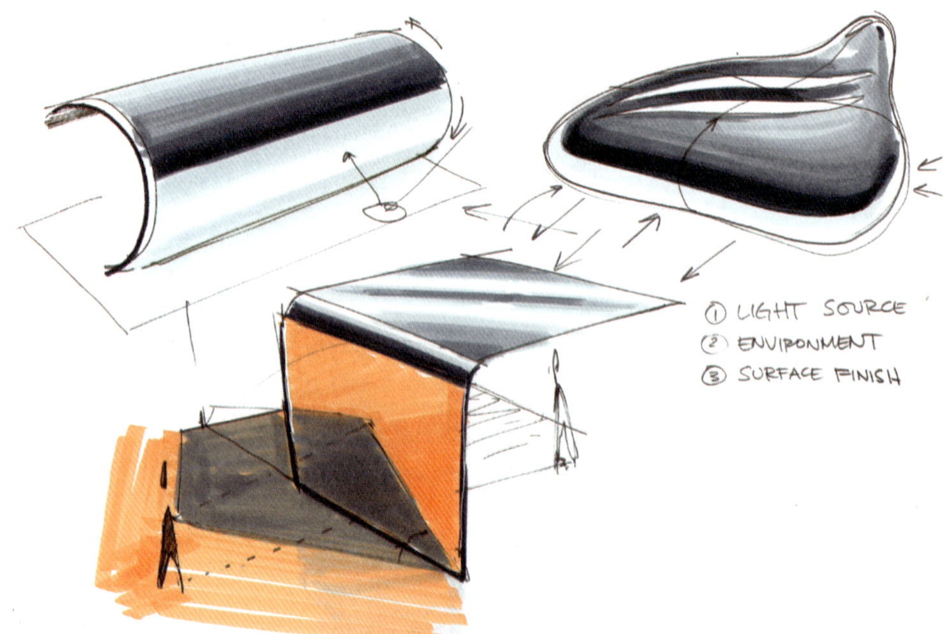

Estimating Reflection Distance in Two Dimensions Demonstration

1. Draw a rectangle and extend the base of the rectangular line. You'll use this extended line to find the length of the new rectangle. This method will work with any rectangular shape or a square.

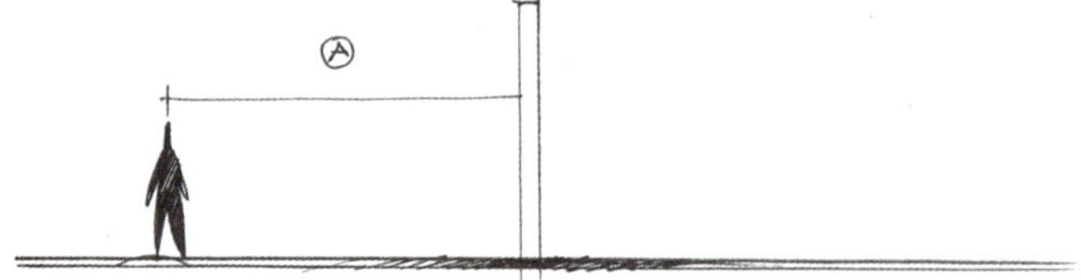

2. Draw lines from corner to corner of the rectangular shape and find the center of the rectangle. It is important to use this method as it translates well in perspective drawing.

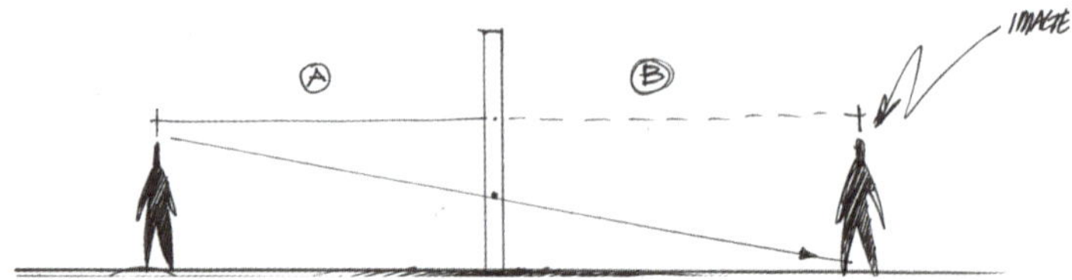

3. With the center located, draw a line horizontal from the center of the rectangle to intersect with one of the vertical sides.

4. Draw a line from the opposite topmost side of the rectangle through the new point on the vertical side of the rectangle.

5. Extend this line to intersect with the base line that was extended. The length between this new point and the rectangular shape should be equal.

Estimating Reflection Distance in Perspective Demonstration

Applying the same technique in perspective, you can figure out the optical distance of the reflection from the surface of the mirror. Because distances are shortened in perspective drawings, it's important to be mindful of placing the image that is the reflection in a way that represents this shortened distance.

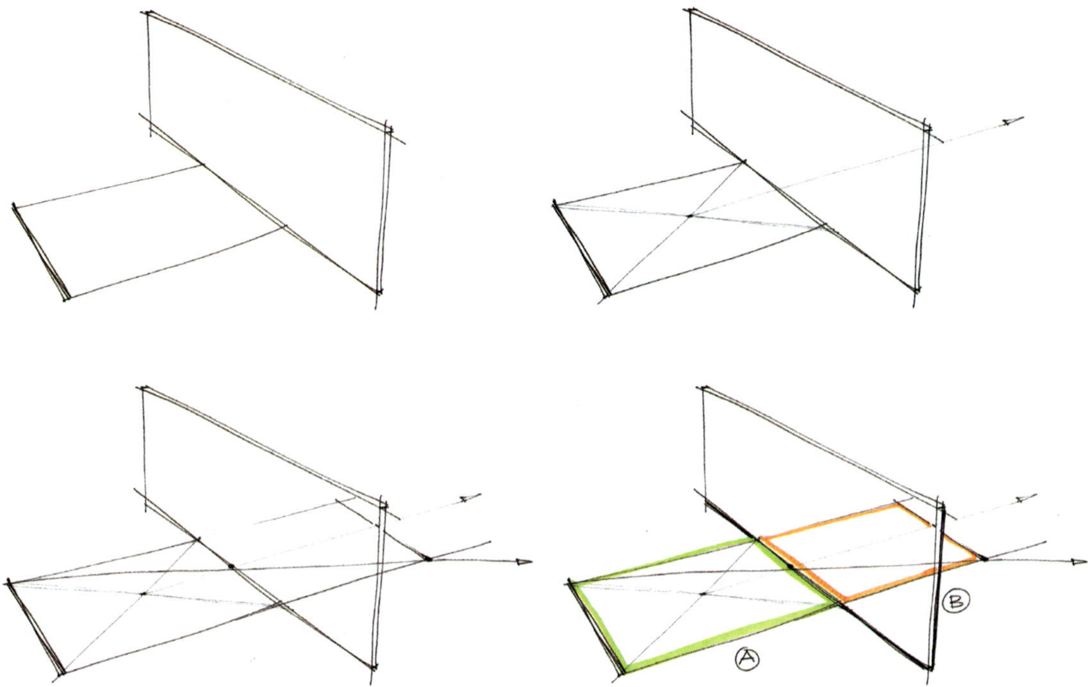

1. Draw a rectangle using perspective lines that converge at the vanishing points to create a rectangle that touches the mirror surface. Centering the rectangle on the object isn't critical.

2. Extend one side of the rectangle in perspective through the reflective surface of the mirror. Much like in the two-dimensional example, this line will be used to find the equivalent distance in perspective.

3. Find the center of the rectangle by drawing two lines from corner to corner and extend a line from the center of the rectangle to intersect the mirror surface. This is the midpoint of the rectangle's short side.

4. Draw from the opposite far corner, much like the two-dimensional example, and extend a line to intersect with the extended side of the rectangle.

5. Complete the rectangle. You should now have the estimated distance from the object to the mirror and from the mirror to the reflection of the object in the mirror.

You can use this technique to find distances in a precise way when drawing in perspective. In most cases, however, a simple visual estimate of the distance (keeping perspective in mind) should be enough to visually place the reflection on a reflective surface. Practice estimating perspective, and measuring will feel much more natural.

Curved Surfaces and Reflections

Curved mirrors and surfaces can be complex to understand. Curved surfaces and mirrors can be convex or concave and also have such additional properties as a focal point for a concentration of light rays that reflect and interact with the surface. Curved surfaces and mirrors will distort the image of a subject produced when reflected as seen by the observer of the image in the mirror. This image distortion may be compressed, elongated, or expanded based on the relative position of the subject to the mirror. These reflections are sometimes referred to as *artifacts*, as the image is not as clear as you would see in a planar mirror.

Without delving deep into the mechanics of a curved mirror, you can learn much by observing real objects. The Cloud Gate sculpture in Chicago is a great example of curved mirrors and the type of reflections they produce. As always, observation is often the best teacher; pay close attention to the reflections in this photo.

Another good way to observe curved reflections is by studying reflections in chrome pipes and mufflers, as well as the surface paint on automobiles. Notice the way colors shift, as well, based on the color of the reflective surface.

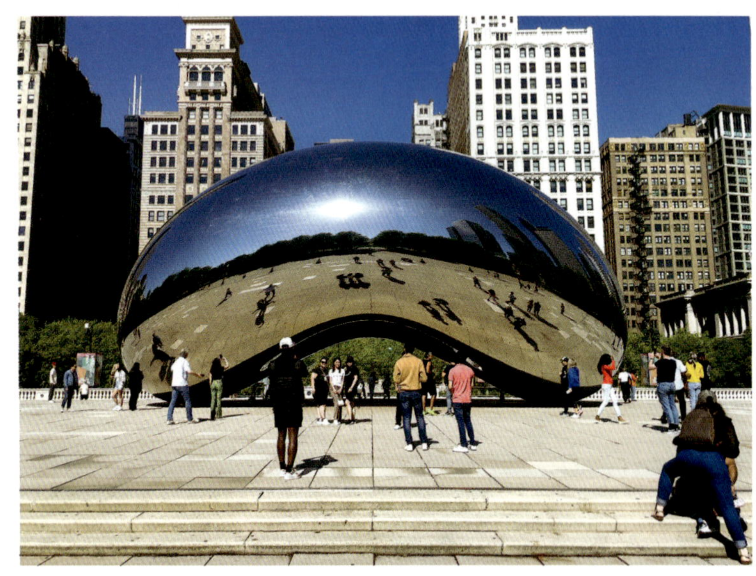

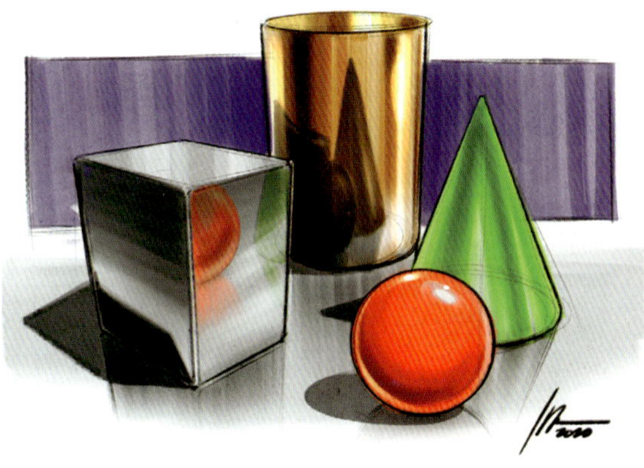

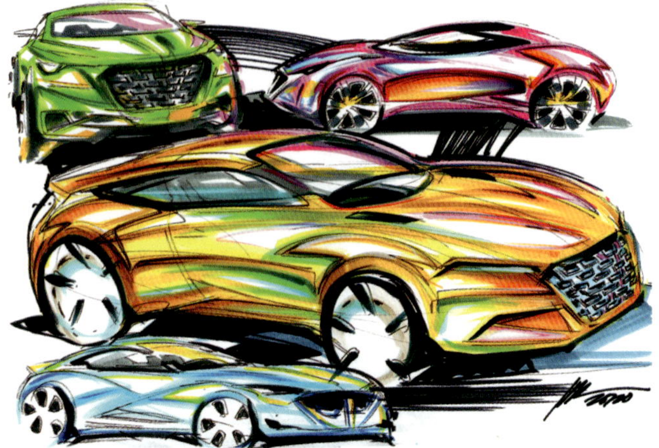

Ground Plane Reflection

Ground plane reflections, along with shadows, are a great way to add depth to your drawing. With your subject on the ground plane, adding a reflection is fairly simple as the ground plane is flat. Imagine the plane being a polished mirror much like the examples shown earlier. Finding the reflection is a matter of measuring downward and sketching the inverted image into the ground plane at equal proportions as the object viewed resting on the ground plane.

Because the subject is the main component in the composed scene, be mindful to not let the reflection overshadow the main subject. To ensure it doesn't, I sketch the reflection with lighter tones and lines to show that the ground plane itself is not a perfectly smooth surface.

Cube Reflection in Ground Plane Demonstration

Let's practice sketching a vertical reflection with a simple cube resting on a reflective mirror-like surface.

1. Sketch a cube in the perspective of your choice.

2. Shade the cube as you would like. I have used markers in this example.

3. Estimate or measure in perspective the vertical distance of the cube's height and draw this distance downward as the image in the mirror.

4. One way to do this is by finding the midpoint of a horizontal base edge of the cube. Draw diagonally through the midpoint from a top corner of the cube to intersect with the extension of a vertical edge.

5. This new point will be the height of the cube as reflected. This technique is especially important if using three-point perspective.

6. With the height of the cube reflected into the ground plane, project lines to the vanishing points or in the same direction as receding lines converging to the left and right and find intersecting points.

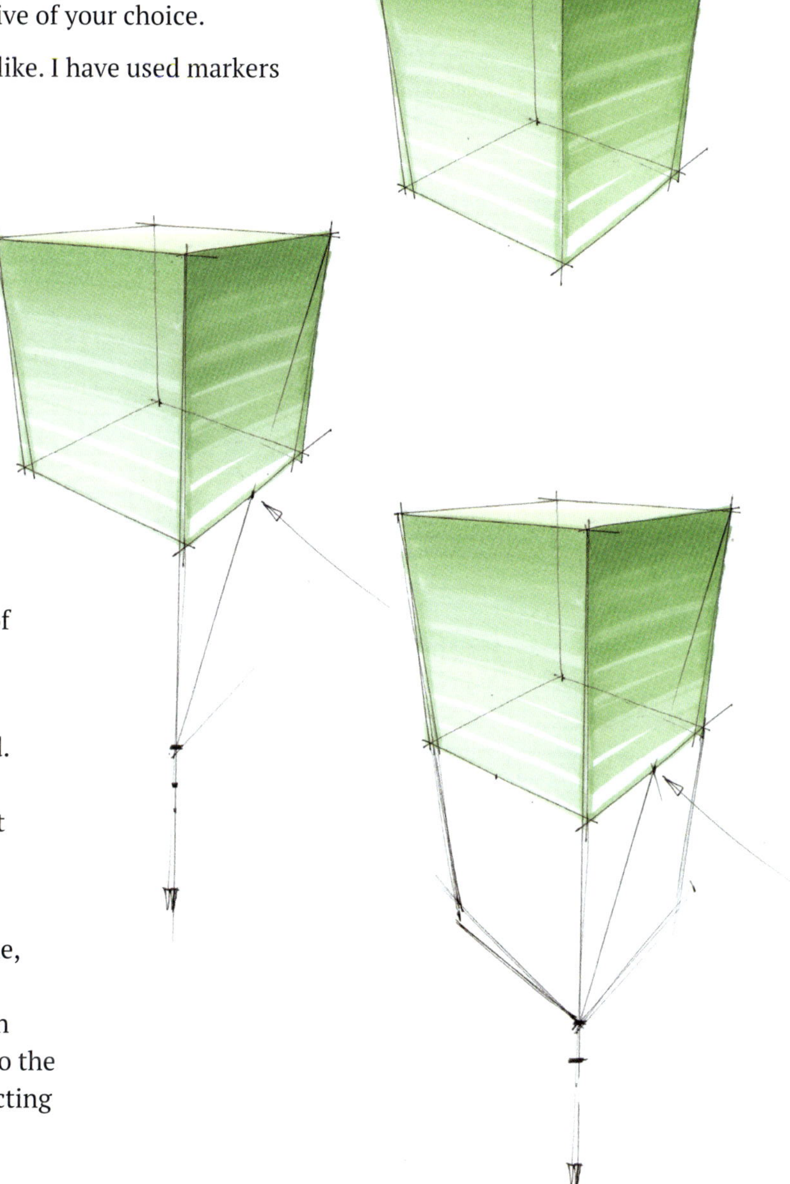

7. Complete the outline of the cube and shade, if desired.

Reflecting other objects is simply a matter of applying these steps to the broken-down components of a more complex form.

Abbreviated Reflections

For ground reflections, rather than creating a full reconstruction of the object that is inverted into the ground surface as an image, you can add an abbreviated reflection to convey the same visual symbol of having a reflection. An abbreviated reflection may include a small portion of the reflected image closest to the object as it rests on the ground plane.

It is up to you to decide how much of the image to show. If the object is fairly complex, adding an abbreviated reflection saves time and effort rather than constructing a perfect image for the reflection.

Glass and Transparent Objects

Sometimes you'll need to draw a transparent object, and understanding how light interacts with such an object is important when drawing in perspective. Internal reflection and refraction are also characteristic of some transparent objects. The space light travels through is called a *medium*. Air is a medium for light to travel through, as is water or glass. As light travels through an object that is one medium and enters another, the light bends and is refracted on its path. This bending of light creates distortions when viewing the medium; a pencil that is partially submerged in water is a good example of this effect.

When light enters another medium and is refracted, it may also be reflected internally on the surfaces of the medium, based on the angle of incidence to the

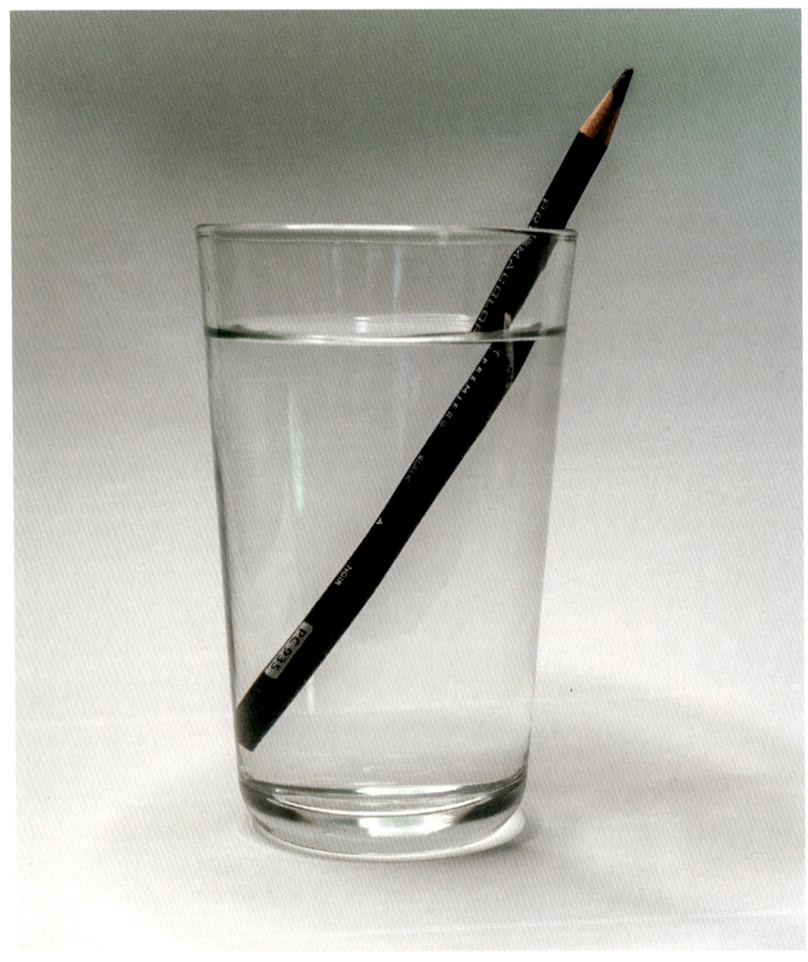

internal surface and subsequent angles and trajectories of the reflected light rays.

Refraction of light coupled with internal reflections creates artifacts in different mediums as light travels from one medium to another. You can observe these artifacts in the edges of a glass where it thickens or at the base of a glass. Add water to a glass and add an object so that it is partially submerged to observe this effect in action.

With observation, you can learn much about refraction, reflection, and artifacts in transparent and translucent media. Practice simplifying artifacts to build your visual vocabulary. Many times, a symbolic representation of the real phenomena is enough to convey a sense of depth and realism.

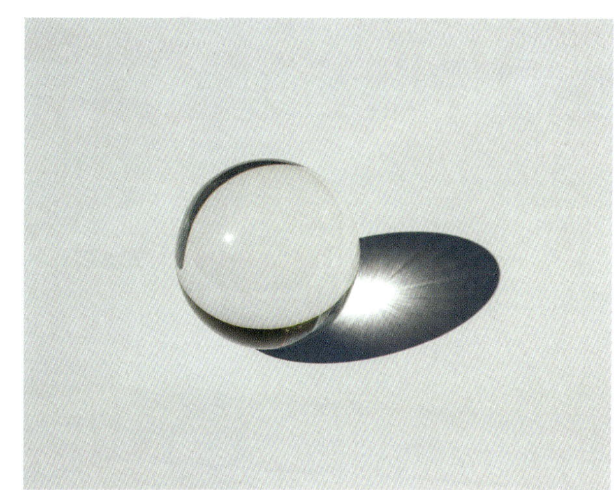

Overlapping Transparency

When a transparent object is placed in front of another object, be mindful of how light affects the object. Even in a simple two-dimensional drawing, the shift in optics of an object interacting with a translucent or transparent object can be a powerful way of showing depth and overlap with two objects.

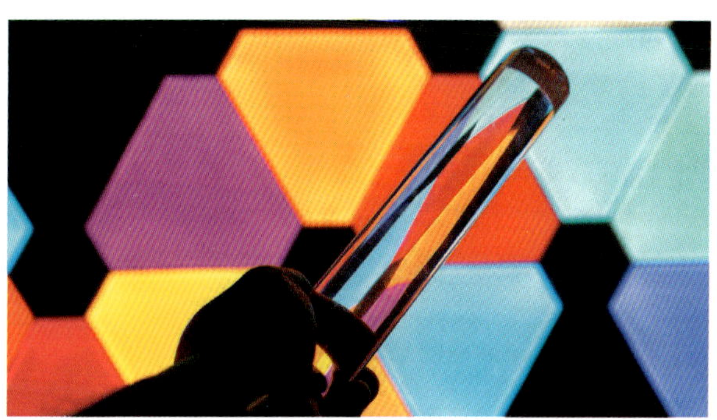

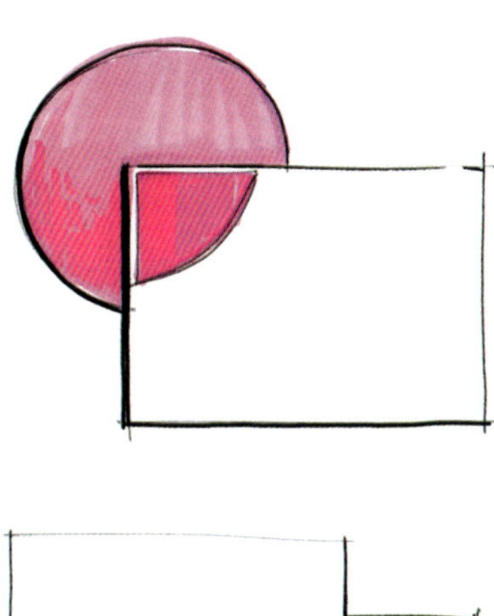

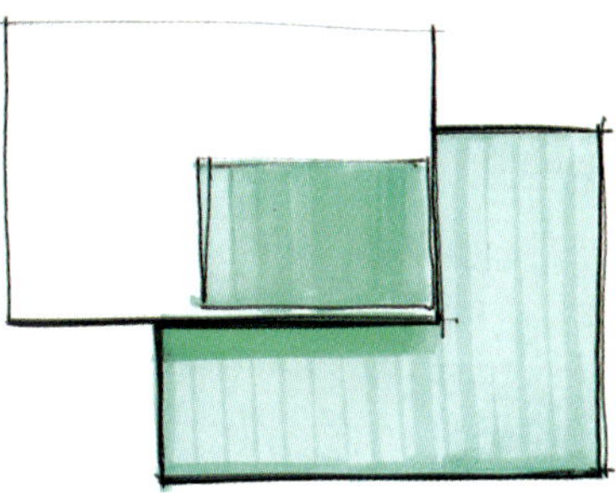

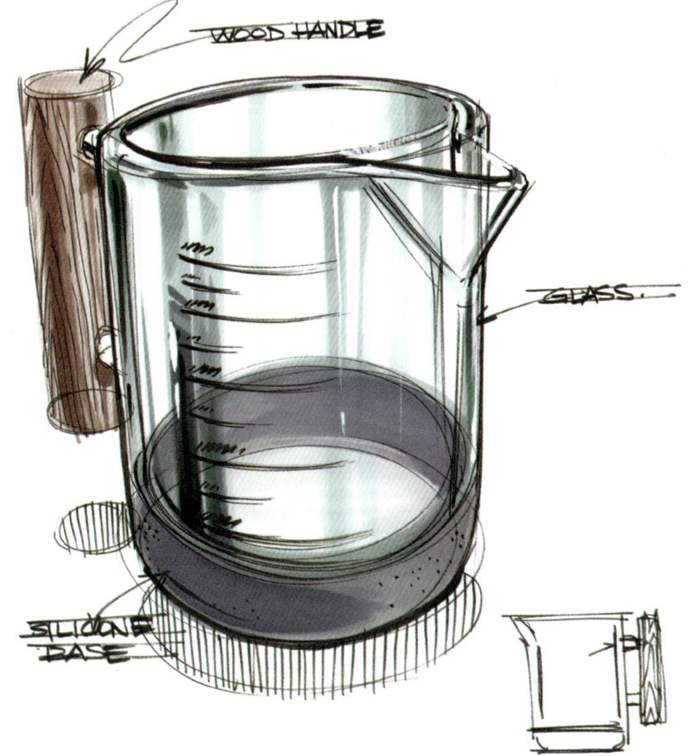

With three-dimensional objects the optical shift also can be a way to simulate the refractive and reflective quality of translucent or transparent objects that happen to overlap another object such as a simple background or another element in a scene.

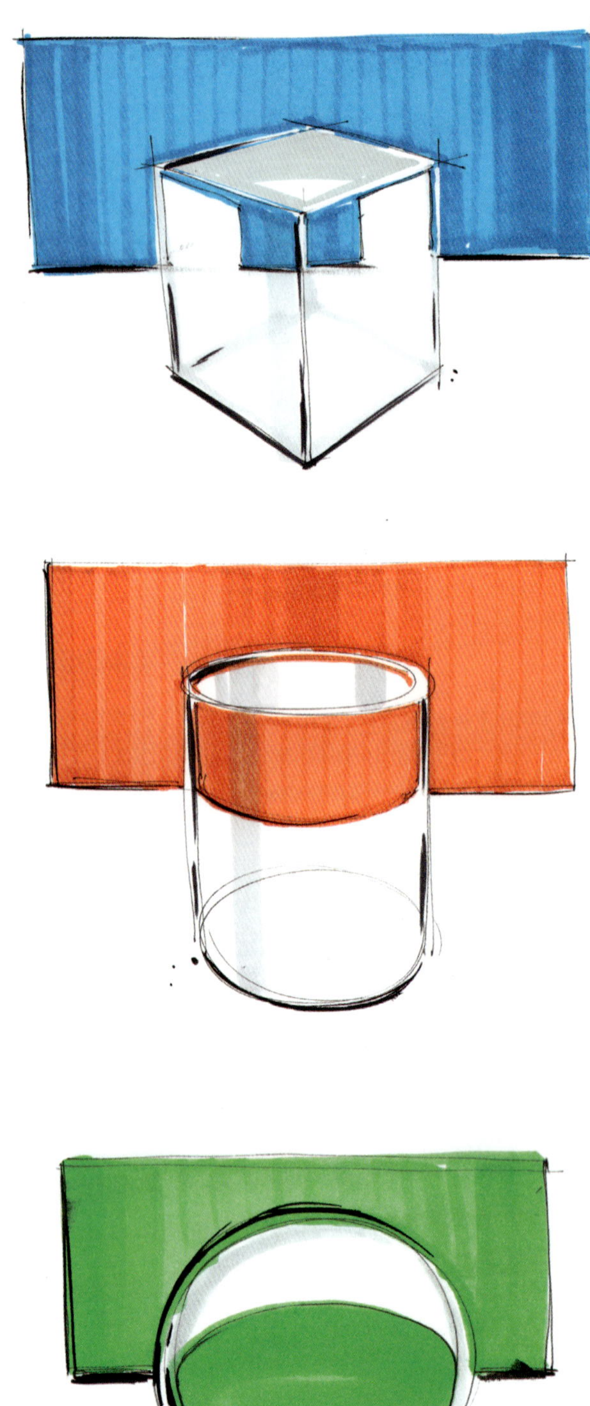

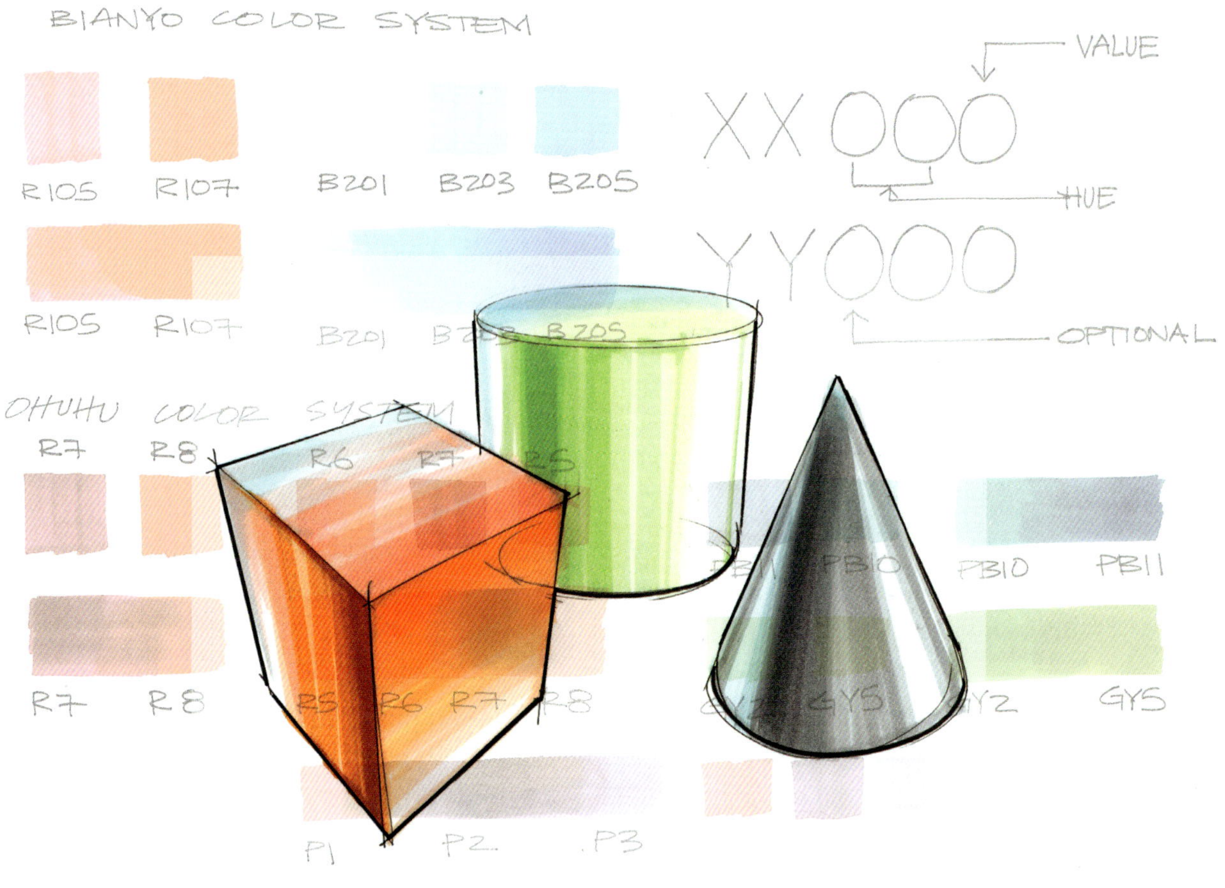

CHAPTER 9
COLOR

Color is a fantastic way to further add life to your drawings. Much of what we encounter and see in real life has color, and thus, using color in your sketches and drawings can bring a level of believability and realism to them. When used the right ways, color can help a material or texture feel even more believable, as well.

Color Properties

Visible light is the result of the mixing of red, green, and blue hues to produce variations of color. However, when painting or working on a computer project intended for print media, colors are based on the CMYK system, which mixes four colors — cyan, magenta, yellow, and black — to produce a variety of colors (with some limitations). When working with colors, particularly with markers, I find it easiest to refer to color as having the properties of hue, saturation, and brightness.

Hue is the appearance of the color within the visible light spectrum. An example of a hue is red, which refers to a range of color viewed in the rainbow of visible light. Colors that have names are simply referring to a hue within this spectrum of visible light.

Saturation refers to the amount of pigment present in a color hue as viewed in the spectrum of visible light. If you were to remove the saturation of pigment in a given color, the result would be black and white or a shade of gray rather than visible color. The black and white for grayscale shading is controlled or defined by brightness.

Brightness is the amount of light or dark in a color that has hue and saturation. A color without hue or saturation is simply a grayscale tone. The difference between dark red and a light red is simply brightness. The difference between light green and a dark green is both hue and brightness.

Often, I apply color to drawings with markers or pencil, and occasionally, I use paint. With markers, I find it easy to select colors and understand the color system as compared to other media because of the association with hue, saturation, and brightness. Depending on the brand of marker, this connection is a bit simpler and easier to understand.

Color Matching

Color matching can be done visually. I always recommend that if you are drawing and working with color, "check yourself before you wreck yourself." In other words, test the colors you plan to work with along with the mixes or varieties you plan to work with before committing.

Colors can be visually opposite or harmonious in appearance. Without getting into the weeds on color theory, you can learn much when testing colors on the medium you plan to work with.

A *color wheel* is a great way to study color theory at a high level. Colors that are complementary are found on opposite sides of the wheel. Analogous, split complementary, secondary, and primary colors may all be found on the color wheel.

For much of my work, the process is intuitive and much like learning to see in three dimensions. The process of working with color is enhanced by observing how color interacts with objects in a physical environment.

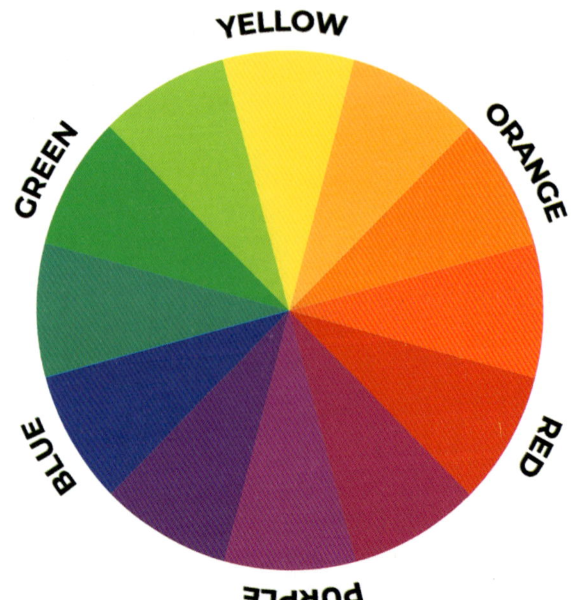

Colors, much like light, are rarely observed evenly on a physical object. Because objects exist in 3D space along with other objects also impacted by direct light, ambient light, and reflected light, color is often varied and more than just the solid hue, saturation and value of the color observed on an object. If care is taken in applying color while blending, realistic effects may be achieved while applying color. The still life image with the shoe, bottle, apple, and cup is an example of a painting where reflected light and colors influence other objects in the scene.

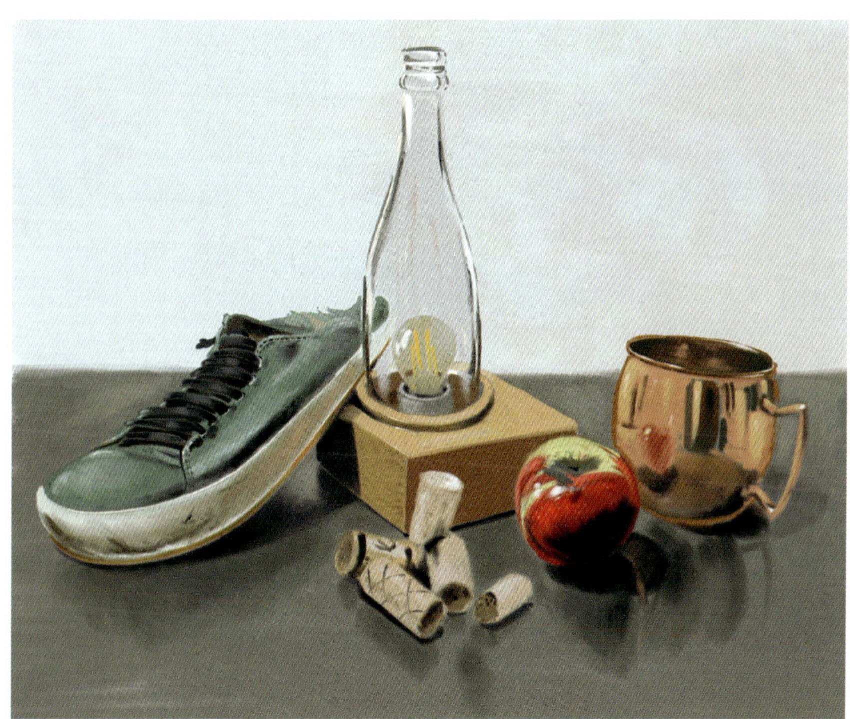

In this marker sketch, color can also be used to create a very vibrant and moving piece with depth and interplay of light.

When of drawing quickly, rather than blending disparate colors, I often focus on varying the amount of light and intensity of color on a surface by creating gradients and blends on the surface. If you are working with markers that apply color evenly, you can add variation to the color with airbrushing (accessories may be available for your brand of markers) or by using some additional pencil shading to vary the appearance of the color, particularly where reflected light impacts the object.

Markers

Markers are a convenient way to apply color, and they travel well for sketching on the go. Markers often are sold in sets of multiple colors that are bright and pop well. You may need to spend some time finding values and hues that fit nicely between other included values and hues in a set. The same is true for color pencils that you find in pre-packaged sets.

Much like the value shading you can do with gray markers, coloring with markers requires values that are complementary and in between whatever main colors you choose. Ideally, a color family will be of the same hue and have a 20% to 30% spread in value or brightness. This value spread allows for ideal blending and contrast, because of the way you can build up saturation when working with markers on paper. If you prefer, however, you can use a more complete set of markers with a wider range of colors and shades for even more subtle blends.

Whether water-, alcohol-, or xylene-based, marker ink is translucent. Because of this, you can build up the saturation or intensity of color your markers produce with subsequent strokes when working with paper. My advice, therefore, is always to work light until you get it right; build your color in slowly in layers. There is a limit to how saturated or intense the

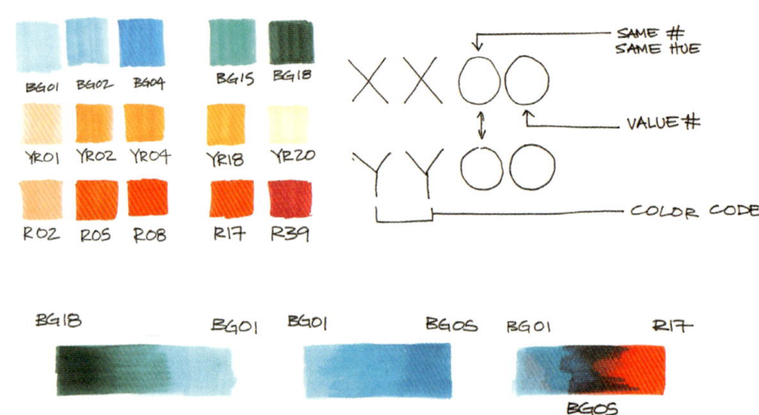

marker will appear, however. Test each marker to determine how much you can build up each color. Also, be sure to test how your markers react with ink and pencil work if you plan to combine mediums (see Chapter 3, "Getting Started," for more detail.)

Tread carefully when blending colors from different marker brands in a drawing—especially an important one. As you can see here, color codes can vary widely between brands of markers. Take some time to experiment, and note how the color codes show up in real life, especially if trying a brand of marker you may not have much experience with. Test how marker brands combine and react to each other before combining them in your final drawing. Testing is never a waste of time; ruining a drawing because you were unfamiliar with your tools is however a waste of time and effort.

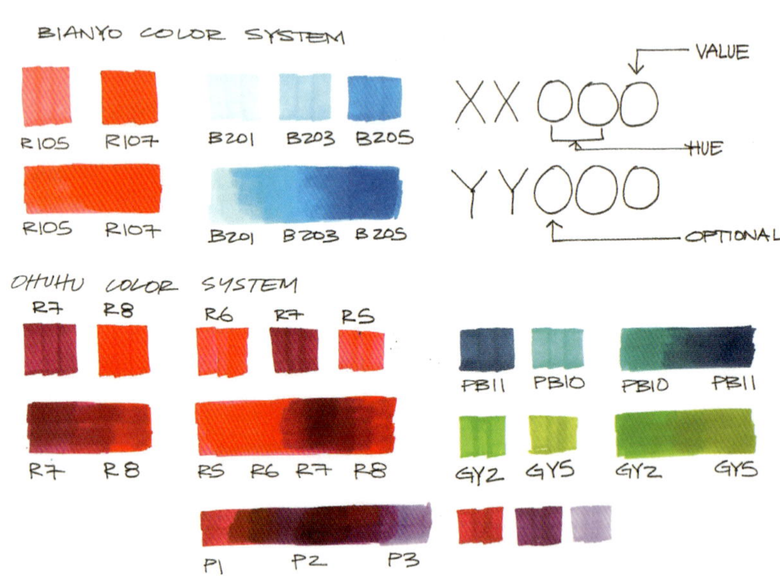

Blending

Blending your markers may seem tricky or even impossible at first, but with a little bit of technique, you can figure out how to create visually subtle and interesting color blends, even if the colors are not close in hue, saturation, or brightness. Most importantly, if you plan to blend your marker colors, ensure your color families play well with each other. Understanding how to blend your markers not only can help you come up with interesting drawings, but also give you the skills to work flexibly in other media (even digital) or on the fly with a more limited toolset.

Remember to pay attention to the hue, saturation, and value of the colors that you're using.

Colors from a similar hue will play nicely together, however colors from different hues will be more challenging to blend. Likewise, as we discussed, you'll have more success blending within the same marker brand than blending across brands.

When blending disparate colors, consider trying a varied stroke or borrowing a bit from pointillism or stippling to create a textured blend. A textured blend provides a decent visual transition between colors that have very incompatible hues (non-analogous or harmonious). For example, this marker sketch contains colors that would ordinarily be difficult to blend but stippling and texture ease the transition between the two vastly dissimilar colors. A smooth gradient would be much harder to achieve without

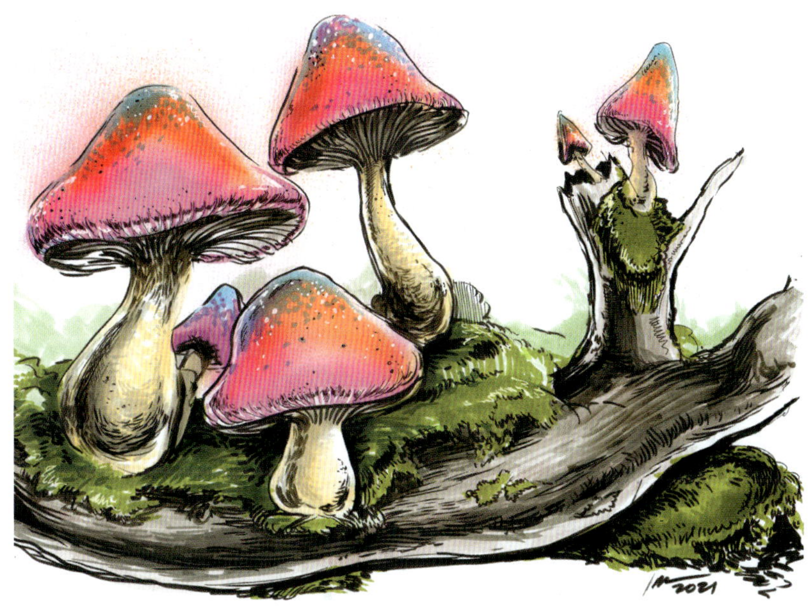

applying a textured effect. Still, you usually can achieve a smooth blend when working with markers, provided there is enough room in the drawing to apply marker ink and have the inks bleed into each other.

Sometimes introducing a third color into a difficult color blend can create a smoother transition, as well. Play around to see what works for your drawing and remember each marker brand will be different. There is no hard and fast rule to the number of colors you may use in a blend or in a drawing. For time and cost savings, however, I tend to stick to three to five colors in each color family when working with markers.

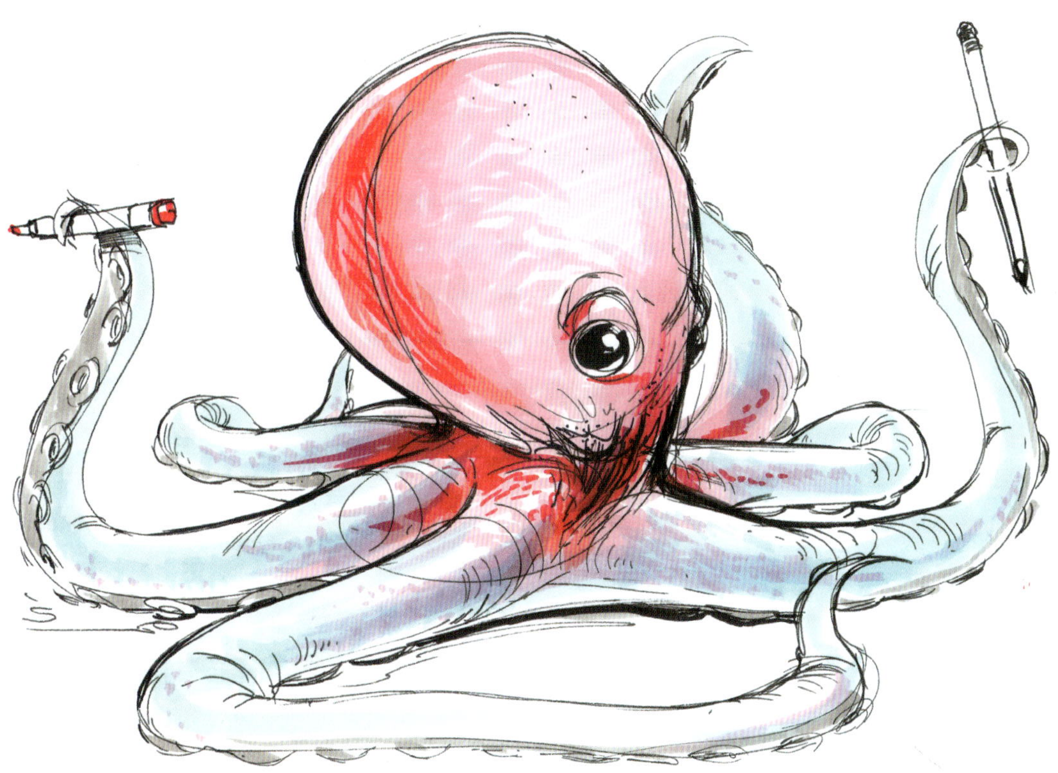

Nah... You Don't Need a Full Set

Because marker ink is translucent, you can build up the color appearance by simply waiting for the marker to dry and reapplying the stroke. For example, a 20% gray marker repeatedly applied to a piece of quality marker paper will yield a range of values.

Here's an example of all 10 markers in a series of Copic brand Cool Gray markers. Suppose you start with C02 or Cool Gray 20%. You can simply pick a marker, skip over a value to the next marker, say Cool Gray 40% (C04), and blend in between. This means that you don't need to buy a full set of gray markers, unless you plan on creating professional illustrations for clients and need a bit of additional flexibility and variety in your marker color selections.

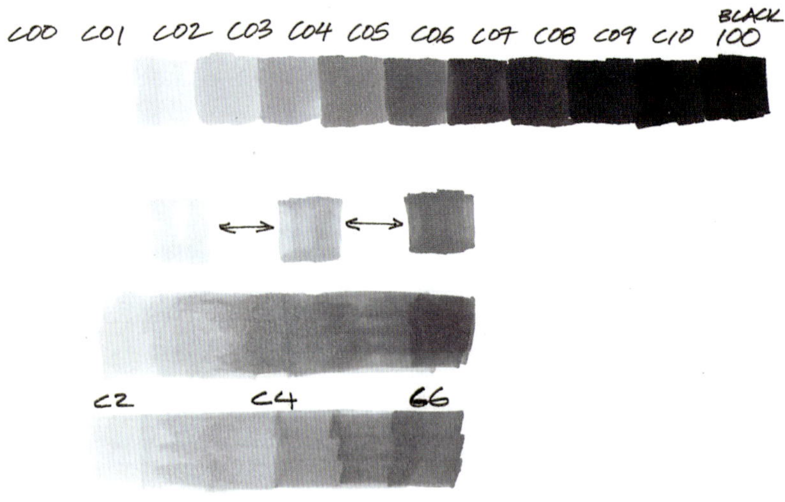

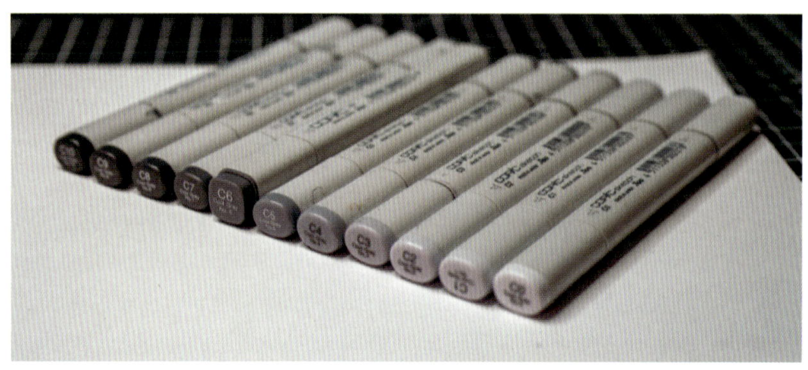

In the example image, I used three markers to create a blend that you could also achieve with several more markers. If you pick markers that aren't too far apart in value, you can create your own blends and save money.

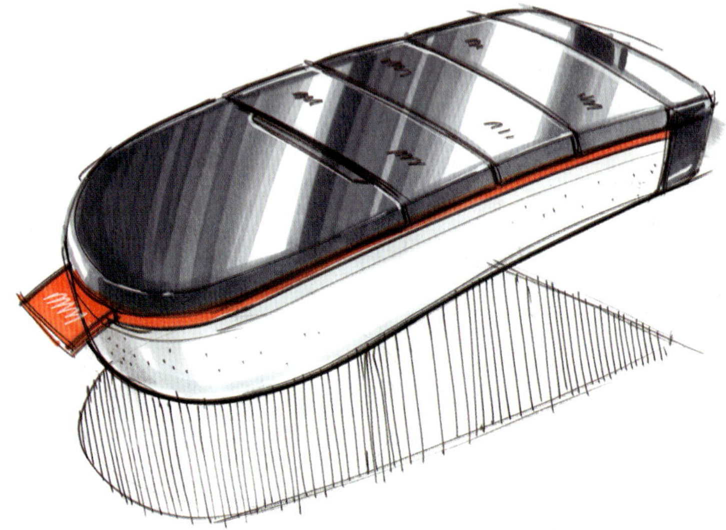

Or, Maybe You Do

Sometimes, however, having gaps in your marker value spread can work against you. When I'm creating more detailed illustrations, for example, I sometimes need to split the difference between a value or having additional color hits here and there. That's why I have hundreds of markers. You may need to be able to represent colors more accurately in more complex sketches and illustrations.

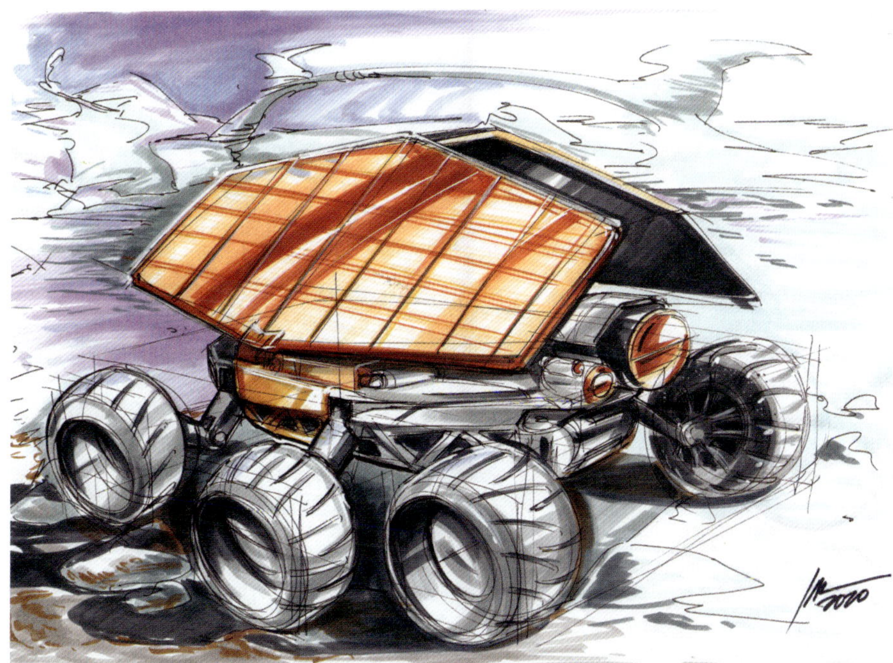

If you find that you really love working with markers or plan on doing so professionally, a full set of markers is definitely worth the investment; at the very least, you'll want additional colors and shades of colors that blend well. At this point, you might consider how long you're going to have the markers, how often you use them, and whether you'll use them out and about. Your answers will tell you if you need to go with a premium, refillable brand like Copic or something more affordable and disposable. Prismacolor markers are a great alternative to the more expensive Copic brand, but you'll give up such features as refillable ink and replaceable nibs on both ends of the markers. Because I use my markers so frequently, I opted for Copic.

Storage

To make my blending decisions easier, I keep my markers organized by brand, as well as by color groups. For longevity, I store them in airtight containers.

Ah, yes, but what about the great debate, you ask: Do I store vertically or horizontally? In my experience, the physical orientation of markers does not make much difference in their longevity. What *has* proven most important is to keep the markers in an airtight container, one that doesn't allow the ink of the marker to evaporate and dry out. Additionally, be sure to properly cap your markers after using them. Many brands have

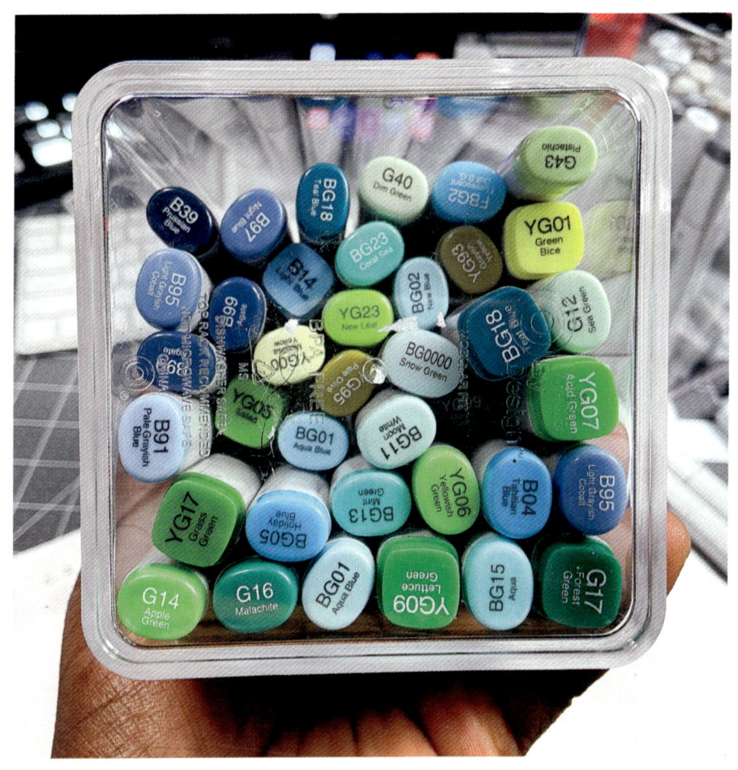

caps that click on tight; listen for that sound when you replace a cap. The airtight container is a double measure against the ink of the marker evaporating. I still have and use markers from my college years that are about 20 years old!

Marker Control, Stroke, and Technique

Many alcohol-based markers have a chisel tip on one end and another tip on the other. With the chisel tip, you can achieve a variety of strokes and effects when drawing. To create crisp highlights or shaded areas, for example, angle the marker so that the full width of the chisel tip is in contact with the paper. The flat, wide stroke this produces is useful when covering large areas, as well. You can achieve a medium-width stroke by slightly lifting the chisel's tip from the paper while drawing. Depending on the angle and pressure, the width of your line may be narrower or wider. Try a few strokes to find a pressure, angle, and width that works for your drawing, and continue to practice until it feels natural. You can also rotate the marker to draw with the short, narrow width of the chisel tip; controlling your stroke can be a bit challenging when holing the marker in this fashion, however.

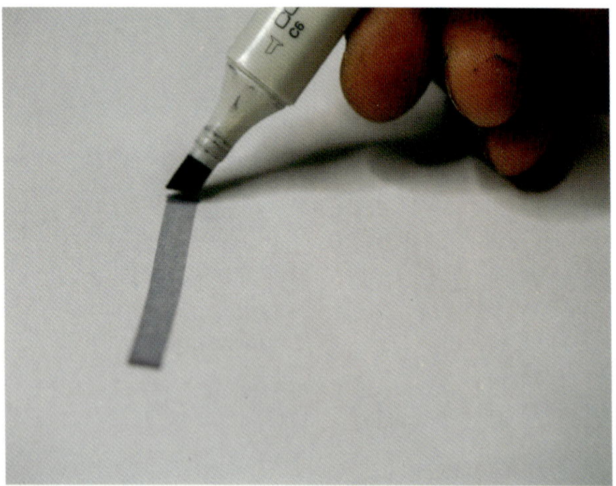
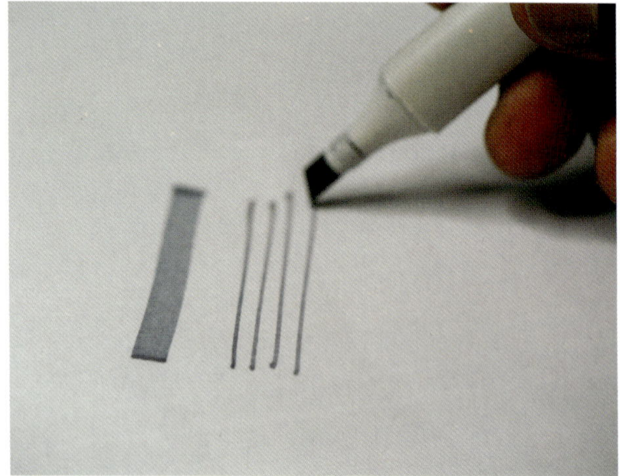

Some markers also have a brush tip that you can use for a variety of expressive strokes. The Copic Sketch markers, for example, have both chisel and brush tips, plus the high-quality tips are replaceable. Applying just the right amount of pressure with brush-tip markers will require a bit of practice, but they are a fun way to get a bit more expression in a sketch.

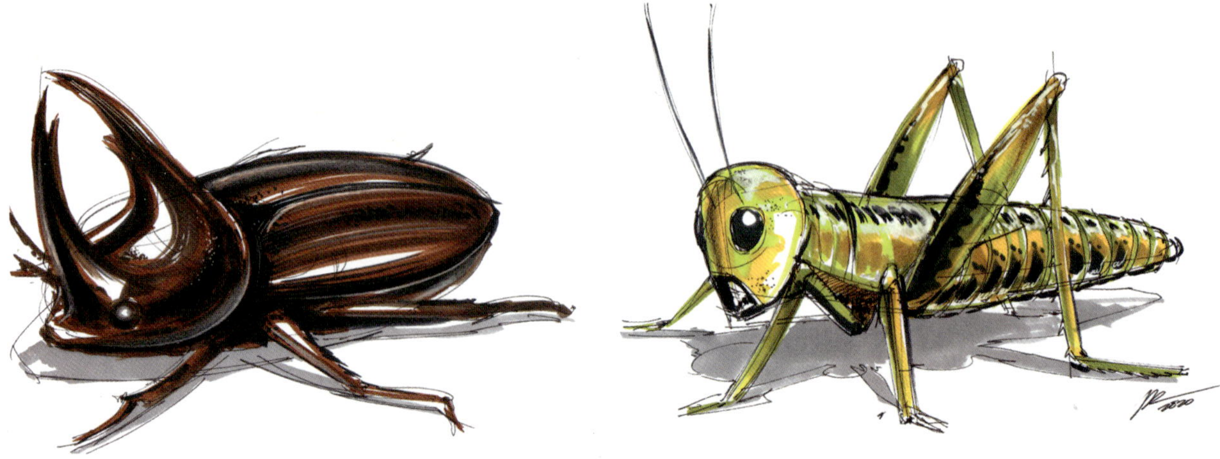

Take the time to play with your markers and understand how the tip, brand, paper, and your approach affect your drawing. Experiment with stroke direction, consistency, and contrast to create different looks and feels, as well. By varying your strokes, you can achieve different surface finishes and effects for your sketch elements. Some common marker strokes I use are the parallel stroke, fast dash, and a scrub or mixed direction stroke.

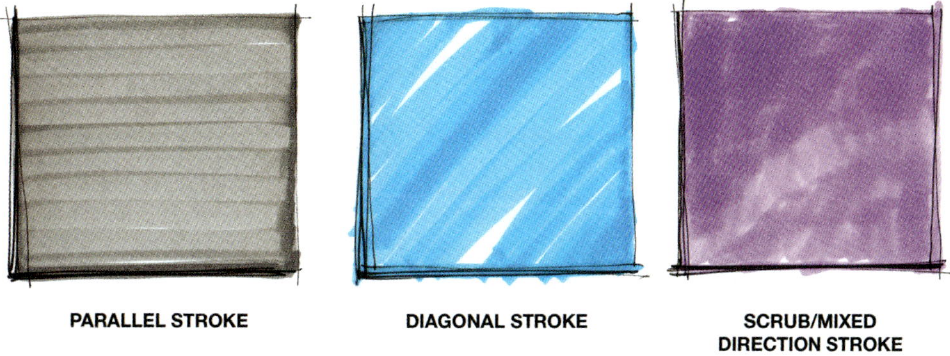

Parallel Stroke

To shade color in a way that appears mostly even, fill an area with parallel strokes. In other words, fill in the area by drawing in parallel lines with as little overlap as possible. How far you move the marker for the next line depends on the width of your marker chisel tip. Practice filling in squares and other shapes with a parallel stroke. To clean up coloring, I usually start by outlining the area with a thin marker line or finish up by applying that outline to the area. Be mindful and use a pen that will not bleed with the marker ink when applied.

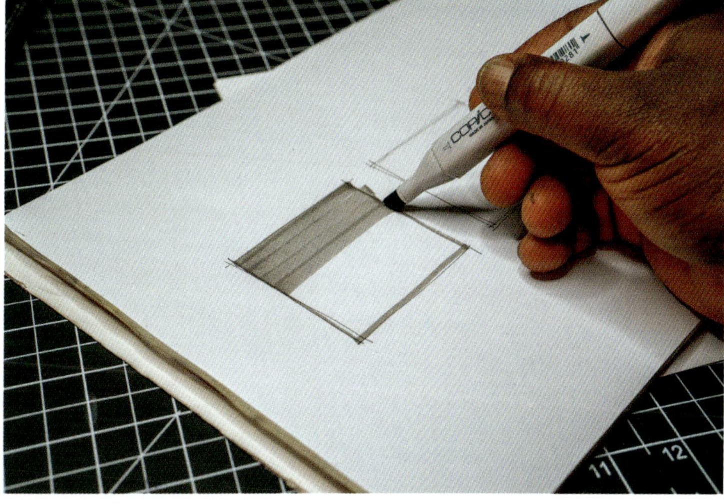

Diagonal/Dash

A diagonal or dashed stroke is a way to create a more dynamic fill. I find it particularly useful when working with reflective surfaces or trying to create a sketchier look. The gaps in the fill are achieved by strategically skipping areas as you shade in an area. Think about reflections, shadows, and artifacts while shading, even if working with a two-dimensional sketch.

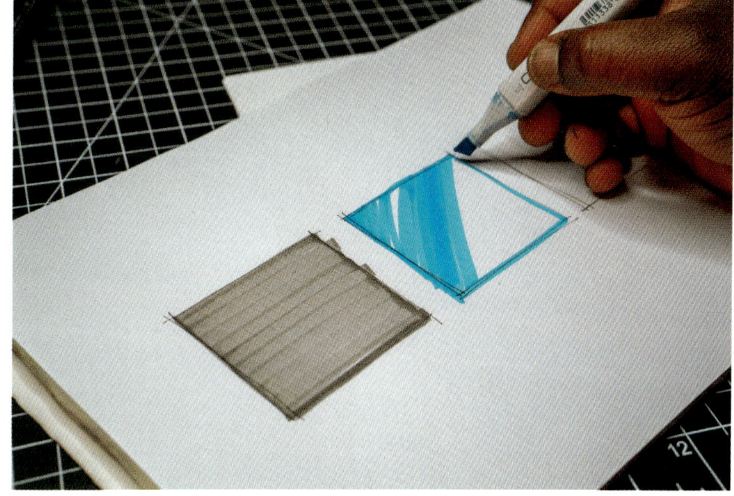

Scrub/Mixed Direction

A scrub or mixed-direction stroke is a good way to create fuzzy or matte surface shading with a marker. Because of the all over approach, the color that results will mimic the feeling of a matte surface. Depending on the material you wish to convey, a scrub stroke may be the best option to capture it. For example, using a scrub stroke is the basis of creating such textures as cement or fabric and can help with the visual appearance of the texture or material.

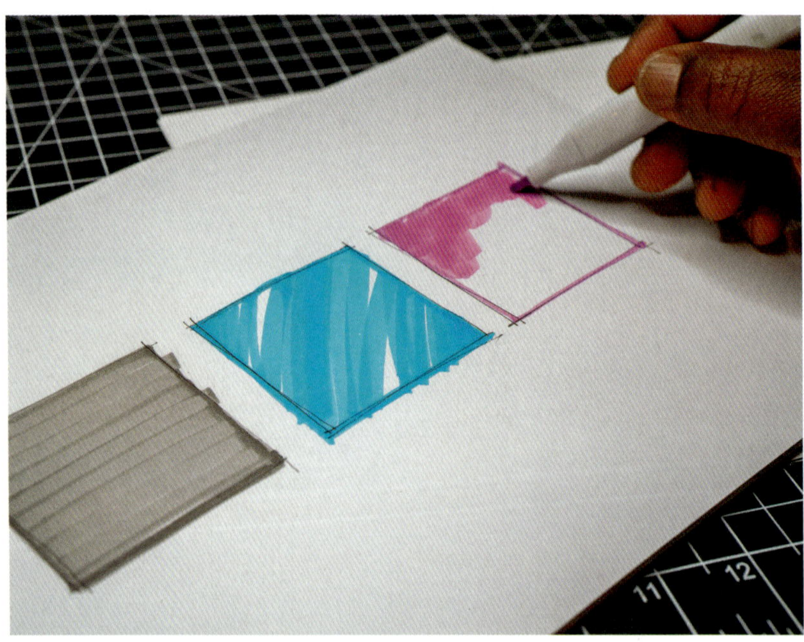

Exercise

Fill a sheet of paper with squares about 2 to 4 inches (50 to 100 mm) in size. Practice different marker stroke types and fill in the boxes. Experiment with each and even try angles to come up with your own technique.

Surface Finishes with Markers

When considering how shiny or dull to make a surface's finish, think about what in the environment might be influencing that surface. Is there a couch reflecting on something, or is the light from a window reflecting off to the side? As you remember from Chapter 8, "Reflections," a simple flat or curved surface will pick up reflections and distortions. While your calculation of these reflections need not be precisely accurate, the symbolism you add to your drawing should be representative of reflections you observe in real objects.

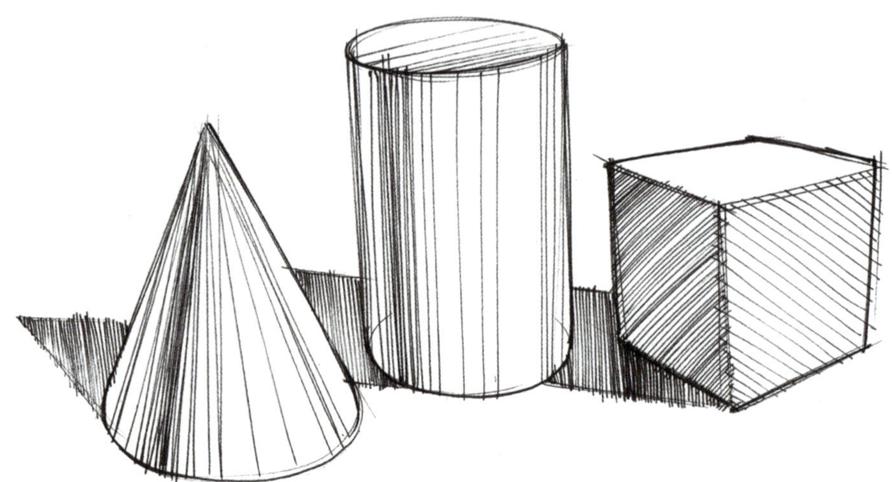

These pen and ink examples are simple, but the more confident you are, the more complex your reflections can be.

When shading with markers, it's a little bit different because with markers there are a variety of values and colors you can use to shade. Consider, for example, a shiny cylinder that may be reflecting dark spots in the environment or a bright light off to the right side. These reflections lessen with a rougher surface or one that is dull or matte. The top of the shiny cylinder may be picking up reflections of things at the top of the room, as well as a bit of shadow. It may seem counterintuitive but try to imagine your surroundings wrapped onto the shape itself and what that might look like on a shiny surface.

Even though the second cylinder isn't completely polished, try to pick up and express reflections in the top surface as well. Use the different marker strokes you have practiced, seeing what kind of reflective surface affects you can achieve with markers on paper.

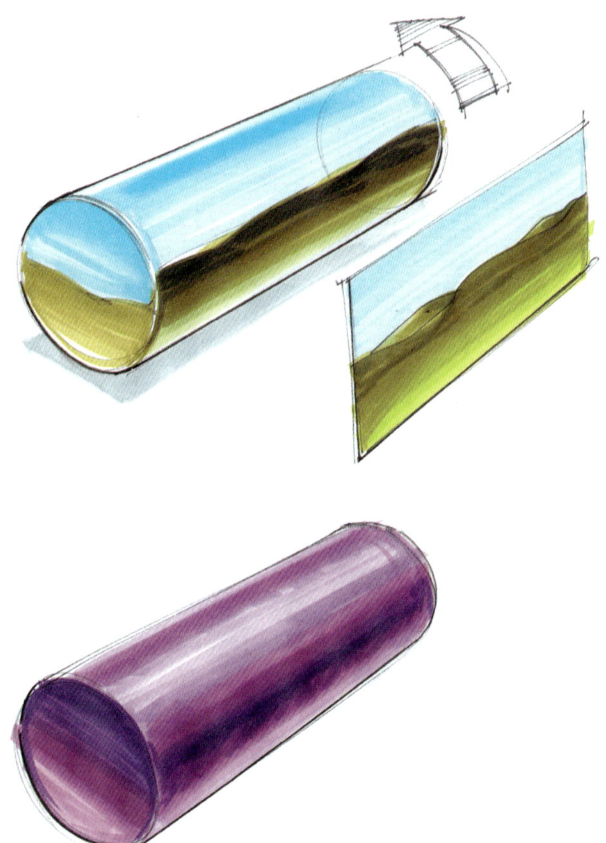

Color and Depth

Another way to reinforce depth in perspective drawing is by using color to communicate how far or close something is to the viewer. Atmospheric perspective, as you remember, is the tendency for colors to appear less saturated the further away they are in relation to the viewer of a scene. Typically, atmospheric perspective is apparent with objects far off in the distance because of refraction and diffusion caused by the atmosphere.

Colors also appear warmer when an object is closer to the viewer. Even at a small scale, the interplay between warm colors (reds to some greens and purples) and cool colors (purples to bluish greens to blues) can really make your drawings pop. Thus, it is possible to reinforce the appearance of depth in your sketch or drawing by using this principle.

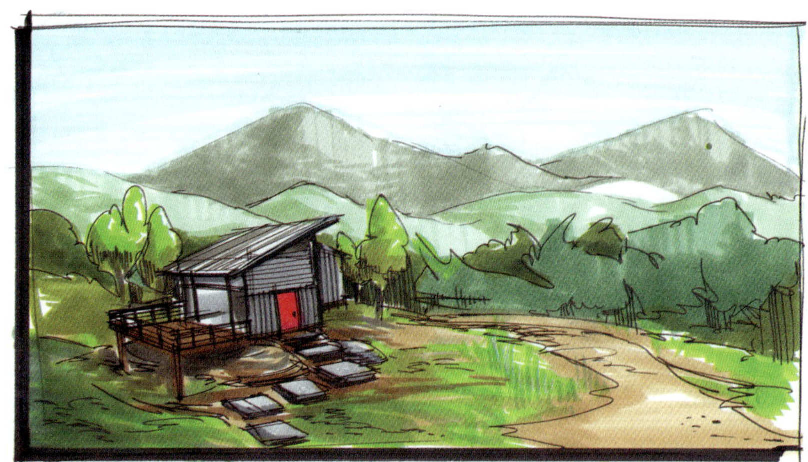

With warm and cool color applied to a sketch, the object takes on a rich dynamic appearance that communicates depth. Try working with warm and cool colors on simple objects and work your way up to more complex objects. Using warm and cool grays is a good way to practice the interplay of color temperatures that can affect depth perception and volume when drawing three-dimensionally in a 2D medium. You can also experiment with blending on surfaces with varying degree to create interplay between them.

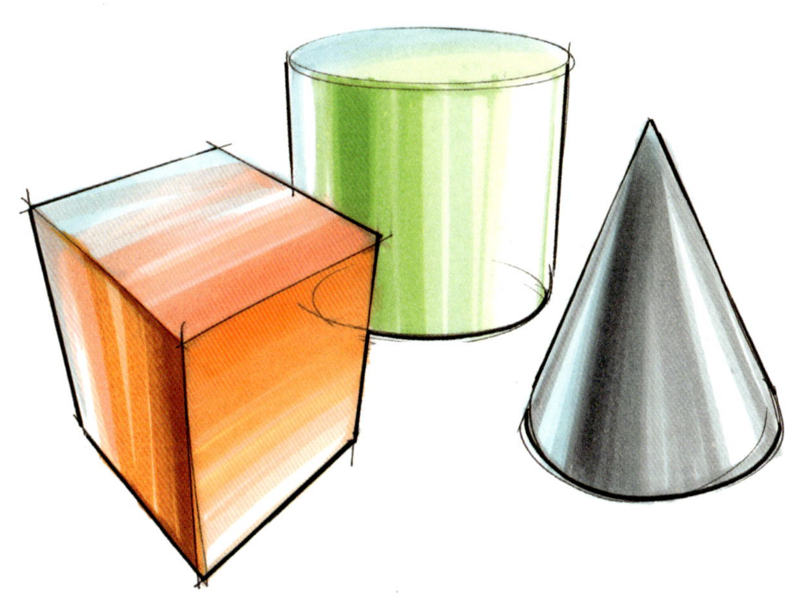

Color Demonstration: Car Sketch Rendering

To illustrate my process of applying color to show surface finishes, reflections, and general shape, let me walk you through how I would use markers to color this sketch of a car.

1. For this drawing, I decided to use a series of orange and brown Copic markers, as well as some blue marker for highlights. As you can see, the drawing is a cleaned-up version of a rough sketch. (Refer to Chapter 13, "Tighten Up," for more information on this technique.) Rather than tracing my previous try, I opted to re-draw from scratch, focusing on clarity while maintaining expression in my lines. Roughing out the sketch was a great way to figure out the perspective taper and scaling before committing to the final design of the car. Because of perspective, drawing the car in three dimensions involved scaling and tapering lines consistent with the type of perspective I used. The ellipses were critical. They established the placement and "attitude" of the vehicle and helped me proportionally measure and place elements of the car in a three-dimensional space.

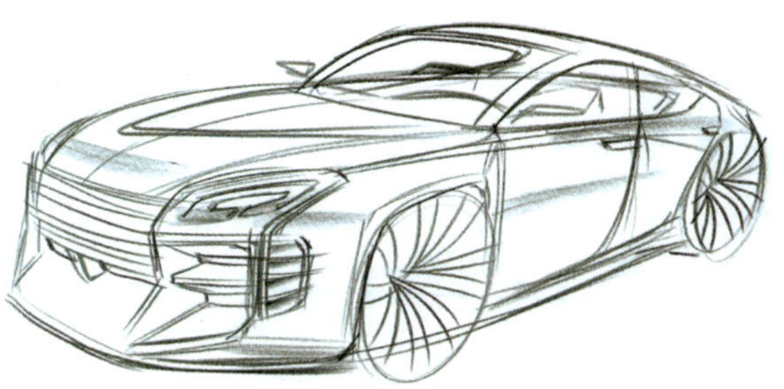
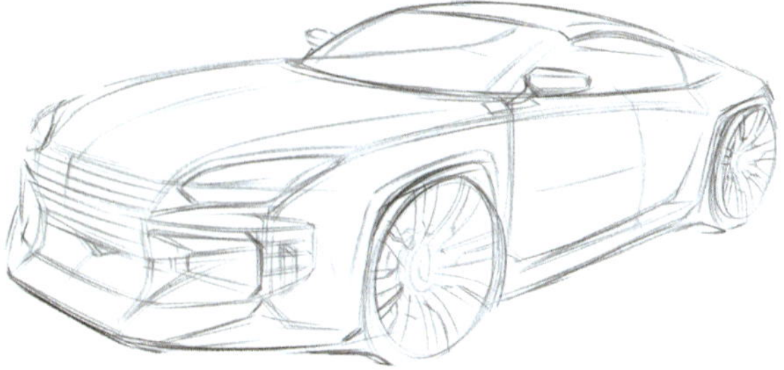

2. To apply color, I begin with my lightest marker: A Copic YR02 marker. By laying down my initial tones around the perimeter and any key areas that I may use to find the surface, I allow myself to find some regions in which I can apply color. Always use your lightest marker color for the initial outline; remember, work light until you get it right! I find that this helps me not be stressed when coloring, as any overdrawn marker strokes usually connect with the outline. The outline also provides a visual guide as to where to start and stop shading.

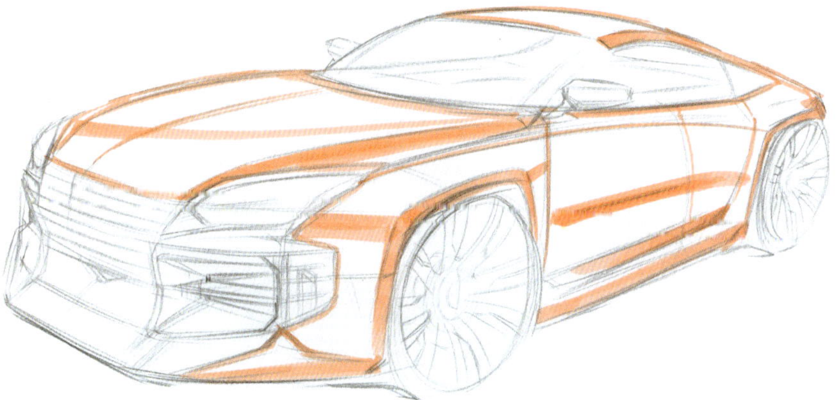

3. Next, I focus on what I think of as reflections coming from the environment. As the illustrator, you're in control of what's happening in your scene, so try to imagine where your object may be located in a scene, the light source for the scene, and other objects that may be reflected into your main subject. This requires a little bit of imagination, but you should also pull from observation of objects around you. For this example, I paid close attention to how the shape of a car influences the shapes of objects reflected in it. Watch for your own reflection when next looking at a car and how your reflection changes with the surfaces of the vehicle. While working, I leave some areas white for highlights, because marker ink, while transparent, is difficult to correct. Likewise, take care to be aware of any reflective spots that you identified and leave blank.

   Once my initial tones are in place, I squint and try to eliminate some of the detail in the line drawing. Squinting causes you to focus on the overall contrast and the appearance of color rather than the detail in the drawing. Post-squint, I switch to a YR07 marker to introduce some contrast on the wheel wells and body side of the vehicle. Remember, when a surface changes direction, contrast in value will communicate three-dimensionality along with the lines you choose to use.

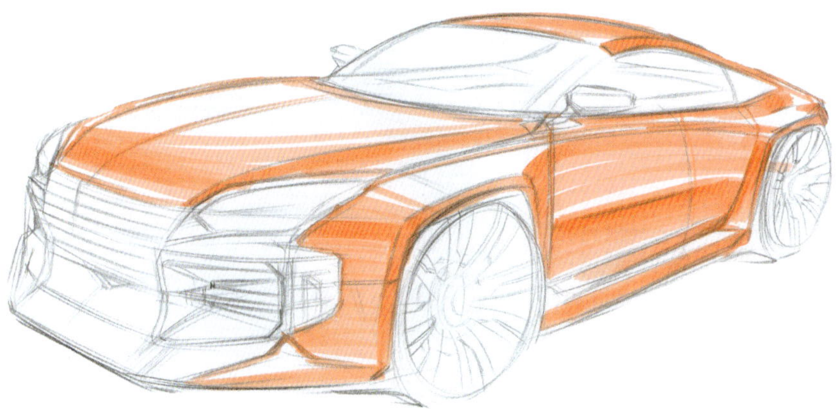

4. Next, I squint and work to improve the contrast in value in the sketch. For these, I use Copic YR07 and YR09 markers along with Copic E08 and E09 markers for my shadows. Remember to watch for areas to leave white for highlights.

5. Another round of squinting reveals additional areas where I can continue to improve the contrast in value in the sketch. I also add blue using a Copic B32 marker to hint at the environment in which the vehicle might be. Because the sky is blue and there is blue on the car, the inference is that the car is outdoors. The blue colors also serve as a way to introduce some atmospheric perspective through the use of color.

6. Next, I fill and block in the wheels with some darker values, reflections, and highlights to communicate the reflectivity of each material. In a marker rendering, I sometimes use tools such as an ellipse guide, circle templates, and French curves to tighten up the sketch; however, I don't this time, because I want to keep this drawing loose and sketchy.

7. To finish up, I block in the interior details around the car's cabin or "greenhouse," and enhance the contrast and fidelity of lines. This step will help your sketch tighten up a bit and feel more consistent and cohesive overall.

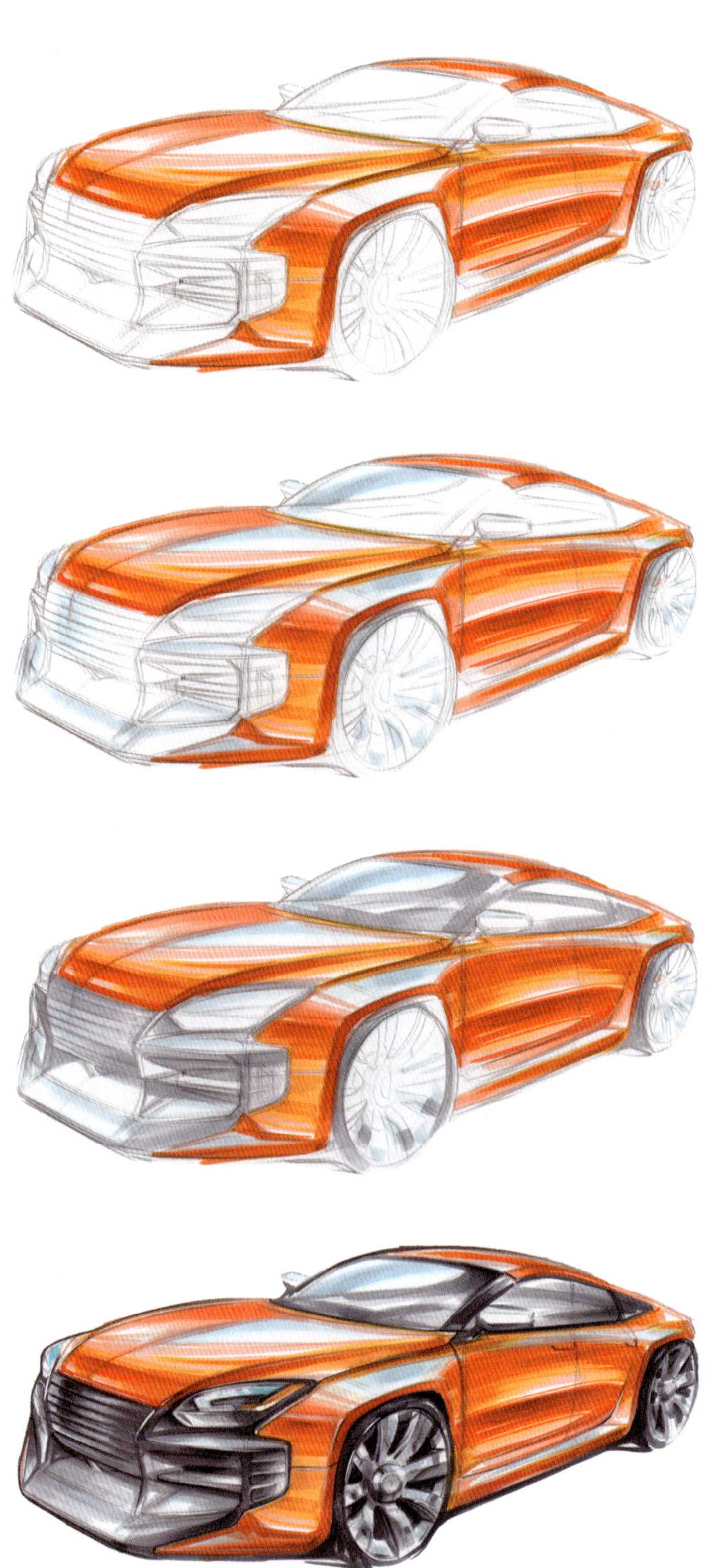

Because I consider myself more of a line artist, I typically start with the original line drawing, and touch up lines toward the end of my marker sketch. This way, I create the right balance of crispness and expressiveness so that the drawing isn't too static.

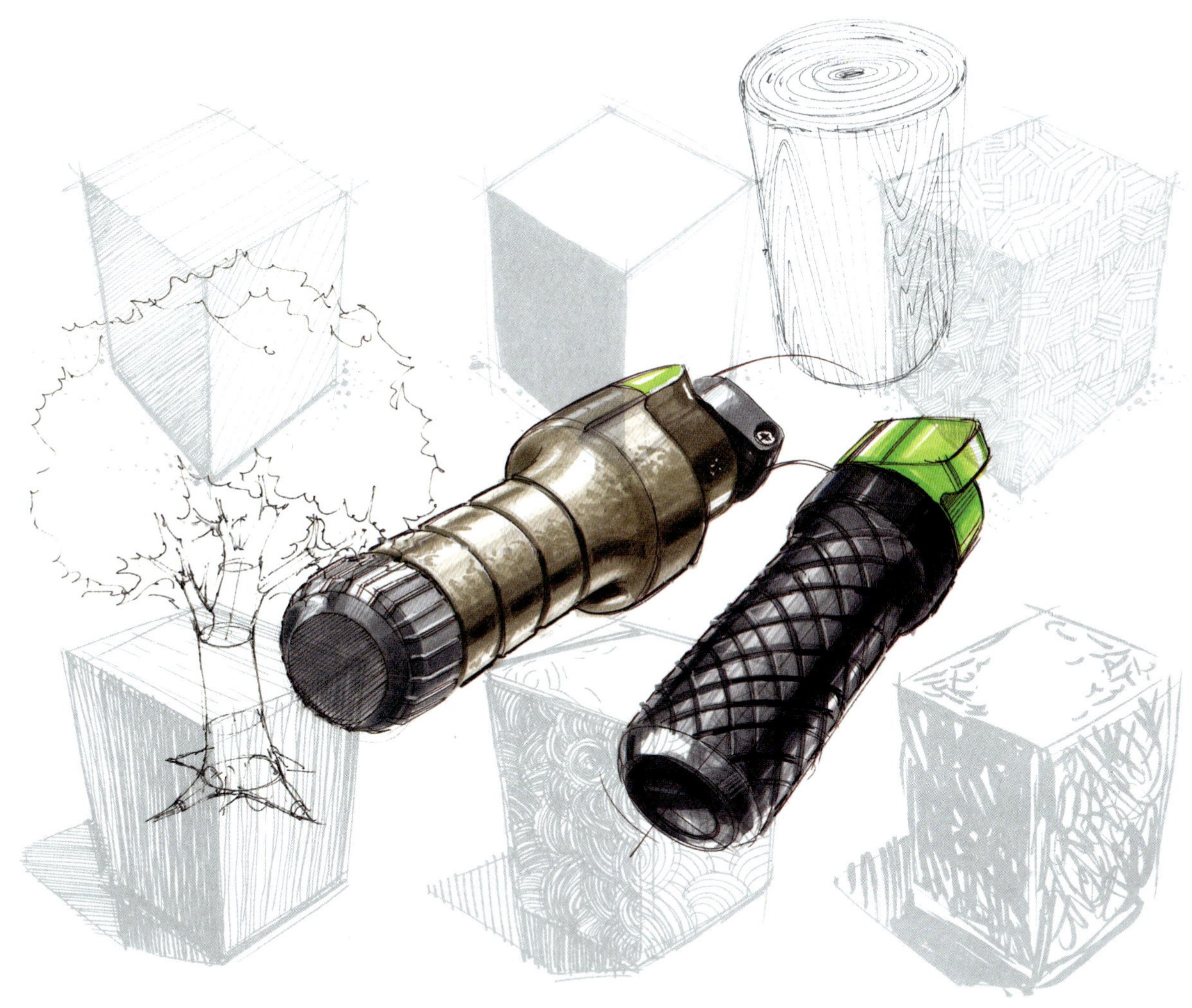

CHAPTER 10

TEXTURE: INK & COLOR

Texture is the three-dimensional topographical change within the bounds of a surface. Some surface textures have deep and high spots and others are more subtle. Textures are found on many objects to varying degrees and often can contextualize an object and its use. You can even use texture to imply the nature of an object. For example, an object or product that is rugged may have a particular texture in key parts as opposed to one that is geared toward everyday use.

In nature, textures inform us as to how dangerous or docile something might be. Textures give us a sense of depth within an object, but also contextualize an object in a broader sense. Step into a forest and you are transported into a completely different world with a variety of textures that you may not encounter in an urban setting. Each setting has its own textures that are indicative of the context.

While color, contrast, and value are key components of three-dimensional drawing, texture is another important element that we can use in communicating objects in their context. Textures are driven by light, and its interaction with the surface itself. Remember textures are three-dimensional at a very small scale, but sometimes at a larger scale. As such, light will interact with these textures in a way that reinforces the three-dimensionality of an object and the scene at large.

Texture, Light, and Value

Textures in drawings and sketches are made up of a variety of strokes or ink marks in a variety of directions. You can use these to communicate light and dark values and topographical changes in the surface and overall shape. Textures add a distinct richness to your drawings that will help them be more visually inviting and engaging.

You can express a texture in different ways with different pens. Each pen you use may have a different look and feel depending on how you use it. The direction and nature of your strokes may communicate different looks and feels for your textures. You can achieve a variety of values while drawing with pens as long as you choose the right strategy. On a cube, for example, values may be expressed by a series of parallel lines drawn close together or far apart. The variation in distance creates the appearance of a lighter or darker value. The more spread out the lines are, the lighter in value the appearance of that area becomes, and vice versa. By placing contrasting values expressed in lines next to each other, you can create the illusion of depth with just a pen.

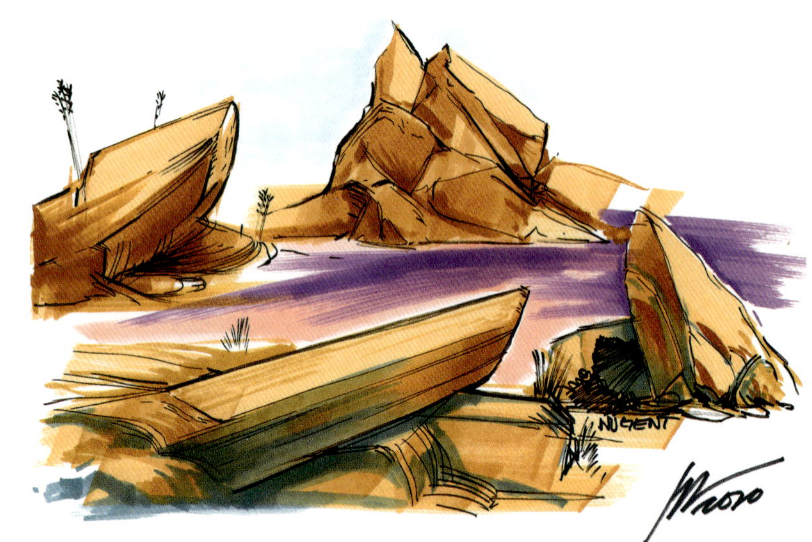

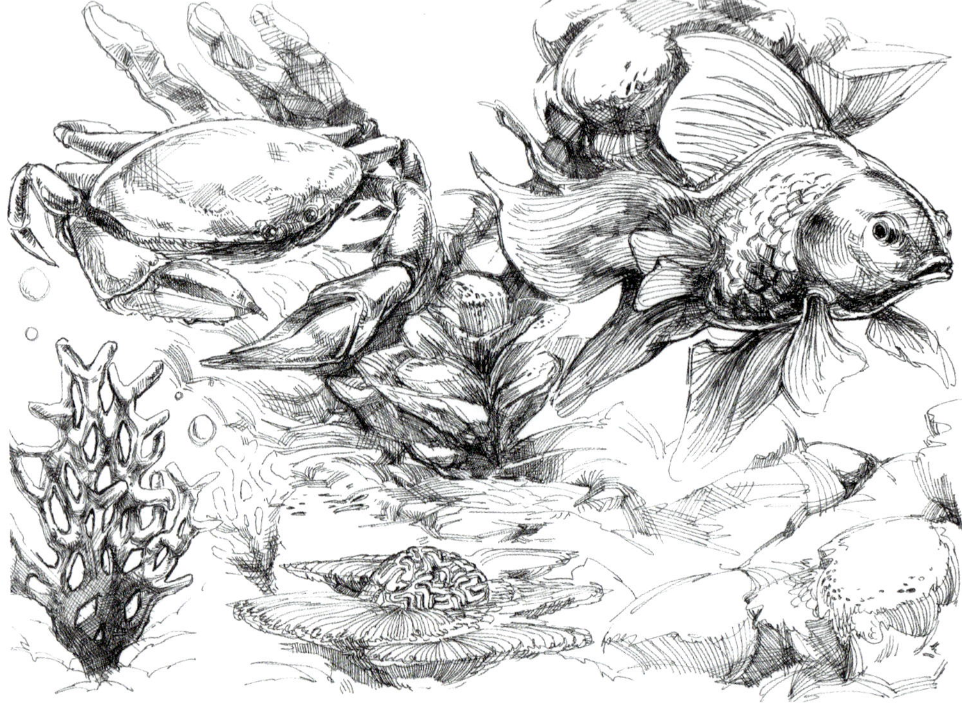

Additionally, creative use of varied strokes enables you to create textures of different values and a variety of tones in similar effect. Whatever technique you choose, just be sure to place contrasting faces or elements next to each other.

While pencils provide some flexibility in creating textures when drawing, much of the process is the same or similar to shading with a pen: You can create a texture by using lines and repetitive patterns. Changing your pencil pressure is another good way to vary the texture and include some in-between values in your drawing.

You can also use pencils to pick up existing texture from materials, if you're drawing with thin enough paper, such as tracing paper. Place a material beneath the paper, then shade on the paper to transfer the material's texture to your drawing. This technique is particularly useful if you have access to real texture swatches. When drawing footwear or apparel, for example, texture swatches can bring a level of realism to the texture in the drawing with a fraction of the work of recreating the texture. This method works best with drawings that have significant flat, two-dimensional areas. Making

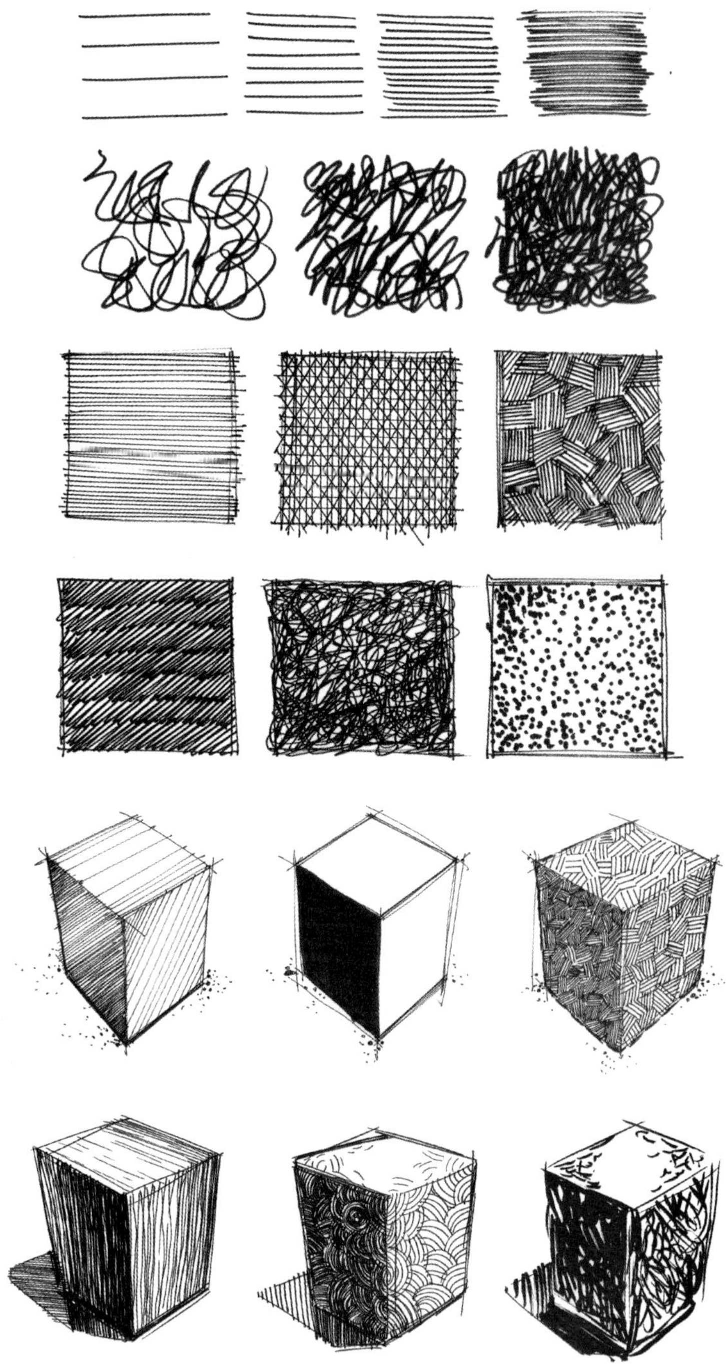

the texture wrap on an organic or curved form might take a bit of adjustment while shading and transferring the underlying texture; however, adding a shadow core to the curved portion of the sketch can help create the illusion of depth. I'll take a look at this specific technique in the demo section of this chapter. (Camera with Grip Demonstration: Pencil)

As I mentioned before, light and shadow are essential in drawing an object or scene in three dimensions. You can use a variety of stroke types to show the intensity or absence of light on a surface, or if you are using a blocking technique, the presence of a reflection in a surface. For the value shading, you can use pencils or markers along with other media, and shade or fill a flat surface with a series of parallel lines. Remember, because light typically does not hit an object evenly, it is important to be mindful while shading surfaces to show light variation by varying pen, marker, or pencil strokes. You can represent this scattering of light by varying the distance between strokes (more distance for lighter, less for darker) to create a gradated effect. Following is a comparison of shading with a pencil, felt tip pen, and ballpoint pen to show varied lighting on a two-dimensional surface.

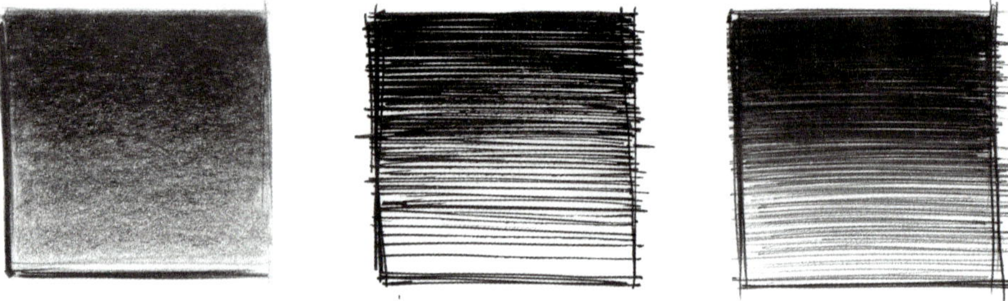

When shading a 3D object on paper, the same ideas apply. Here are a few examples of a progressive shading of cylinders.

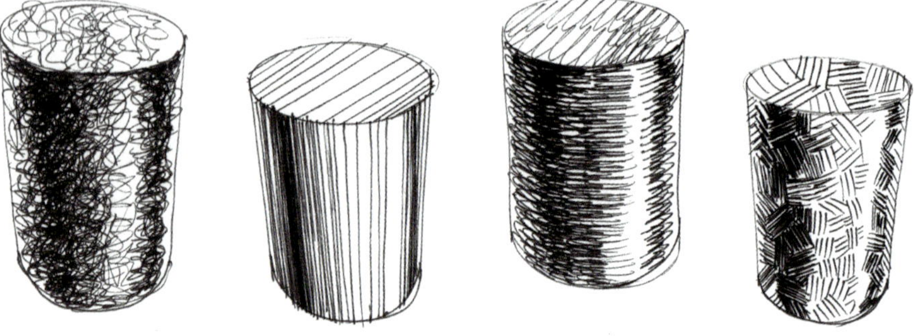

When sketching some complex or organic surfaces a simple line shade that crosses the body of the form will not do enough to show depth on an object. For example, shading across a sphere would be challenging and somewhat distracting unless executed expertly well. For design sketching and quick illustration, I prefer to outline the region I intend to shade in and then follow through with hatching in the area. For a more traditional illustration, I lean toward a randomized pattern with a pen or a more subtle shading with pencils. Paint is also a good option for a good visual tonal blend.

Stroke Types

You can use several types of pen strokes to express value while drawing, including parallel hatching, cross-hatching, multi-hatching, squiggles, and stippling. Take a look at a few samples of each stroke type and how they form two-dimensional textures.

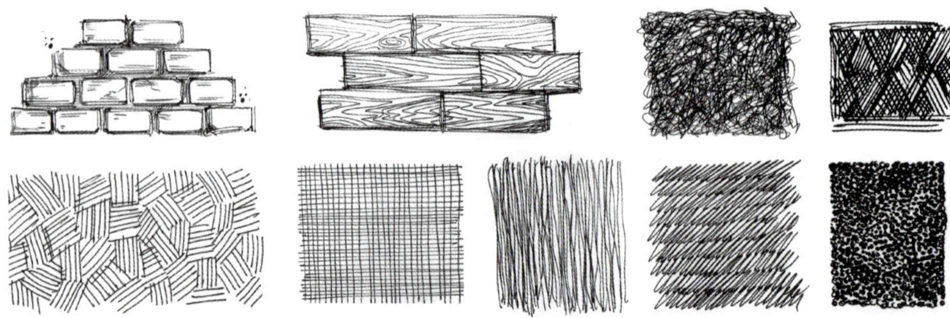

Shading objects with varied directional pen strokes will take some thinking in three-dimensional terms because some textures may work better for a sketch of a particular object than others. For rational geometric forms, I prefer to use hatching or a *motor stroke* (a parallel series of hatching strokes) to show values for the sides of objects. Organic forms and objects may require a more organic and randomized stroke pattern.

Varying the spacing, the stroke direction, the pen angle, and the pen pressure can create a different feeling for each shading pattern that you create. Take some time to experiment and explore your tools, paper, strokes, and pen grip to see what interesting patterns you can come up with to express different textures. Additionally, consider a variety of objects with texturing opportunities that you could practice drawing.

Here are a few examples of rational geometry shading.

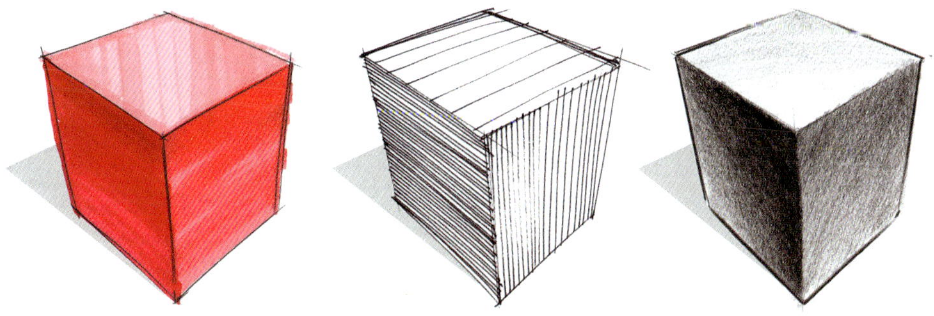

With pen drawing, notice how the lines describing the forms tend to follow the overall geometry of the form itself. Pencil shading and marker coloring to create texture can be done this way, as well.

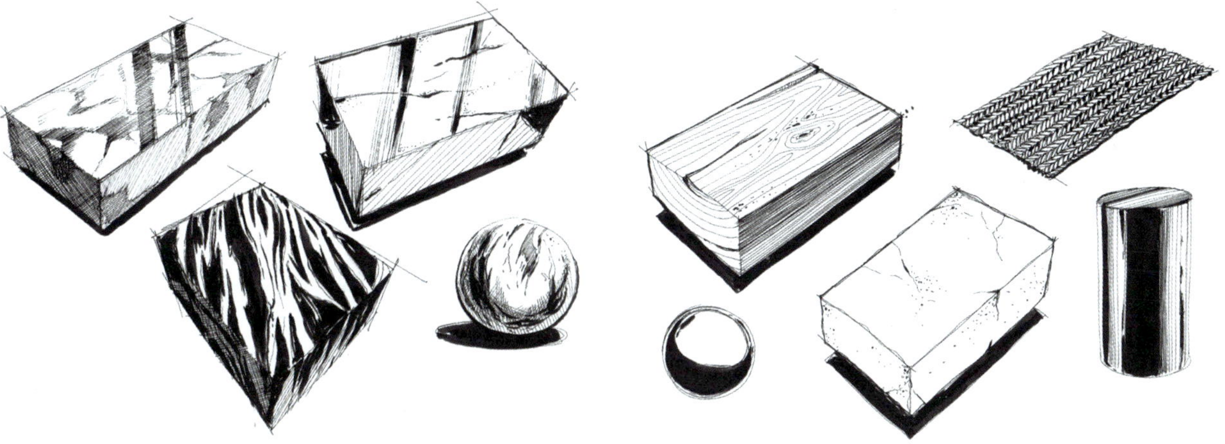

When applying texture, your drawn lines should follow the geometry of the form for the most part. Try to mimic the shape and flow of a form. This will lead to a more realistic, even if sketchy drawing. When shading a sphere this approach tends to be cleaner in appearance, and much easier to execute, than hatching.

To create a texture, think about stroke direction, proximity, consistency or variation, and repetition of your lines. Lines placed close together can give an effect of wood or fabric, depending on how each of these elements is used.

You can also stipple in a texture by creating a repeated pattern of short or dotted marks or points. The denser the points, the darker the texture, and the less dense the points, the lighter in value the texture will appear.

Be sure to focus on the texture pattern by paying attention to the flow and the rhythm you create through the way your lines are drawn. A complex texture may seem intimidating to draw but breaking it down into a patterned stroke that is executable in repeated fashion can make it much easier to create. Analyze what material the texture is communicating. Simplify what you see, and you'll be able to come up with your own strategies for drawing whatever texture you want while being creative with the use of tools and your analysis of the texture itself.

3D Textures

Three-dimensional textures, much like their two-dimensional counterparts, are a combination of strokes executed in a manner that is indicative of a certain materiality in three dimensions. Remember, when you apply a texture to a 3D object in a sketch, perspective, point of view, line weight, and value are all very important. Take a look at a few example textures.

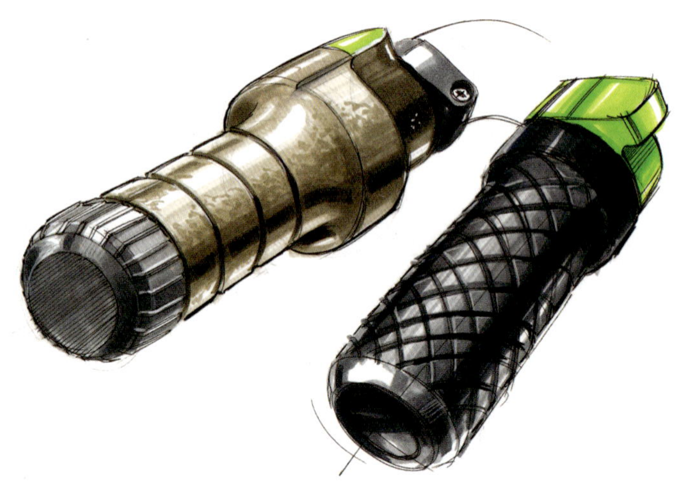

Each is a plane or surface with a texture or finish applied to it. At times, the texture may wrap across the edge of these objects, and so you must give attention to the three-dimensionality of the drawing. The appearance of continuity in theme and pattern by pen stroke will help reinforce the three-dimensional appearance of the object you are drawing. With pencil or marker, the same care and attention to stroke makes for better texture appearance on a three-dimensional object.

Natural Textures

You can also use texture and stroke to bring to life elements from nature, such as trees, rocks, clouds, and so on. Different tools may also work better for one texture or another. For example, drawing clouds may be easier with a wet brush and ink than it would be with a pen or even a pencil. A marker may be better for hard surface finishes than a pencil.

Still, it is a matter of technique when creating a texture while drawing with different materials. As you practice, you may find yourself coming up with your own textures and means of communicating light and shadow appropriate for the subject of your drawings.

Tree Demonstration - Pen & Markers

Drawing a tree requires a bit of simplification but leaves plenty of latitude for creative texture work. Creatively combining markers and pens can create a nice result. Let's take a look!

1. Start by analyzing the shape and form of the tree. Many have a somewhat cylindrical profile. Try constructing your tree with segments of cylindrical forms that are connected and vary in shape—just a quick, basic cylinder should do for each segment.

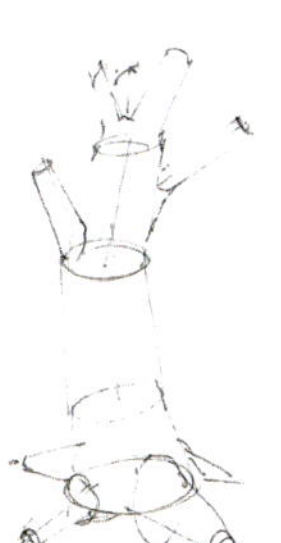

2. Sketch in cylinders and estimate where you'd like branches to go on the tree. Once you're happy with the rough placement, sketch and overlay the construction with lines to rough in the tree. Add your leaves. For the example, I used a combination of loosely applied color and loose organic and randomized strokes to capture the feeling of leaves.

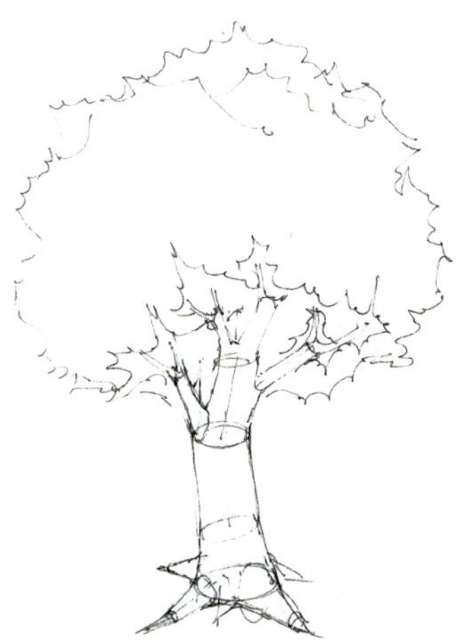

3. Now that you have a silhouette, you can work on the color, texture, and foliage.

4. Add color as desired.

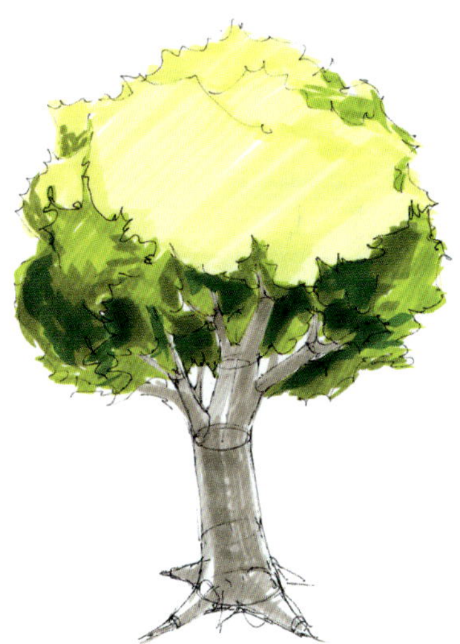

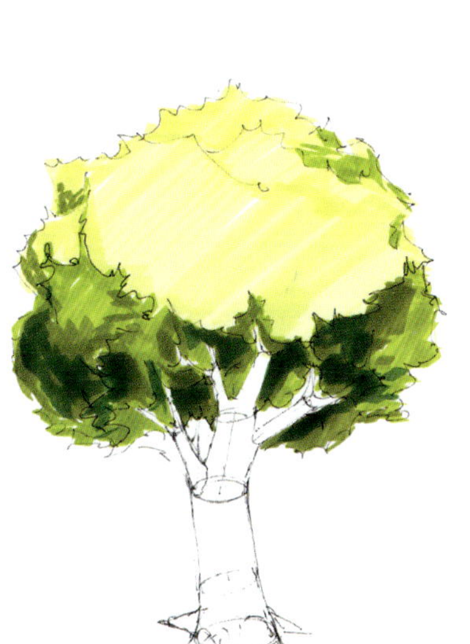

5. To help you draw the texture of the bark, study some real bark, looking for a pattern or flow to the textures. You can create the appearance of tree bark as precisely or abstractly as you like.

6. For this demo, I overlaid my texture on top of the marker.

7. Be mindful of the shape and curvature of the tree trunk. This will guide you as to where to place more detail on the texture or less to convey that curvature. Be sure to consider the lighting of the scene with the tree, as that will impact the texture sketch process as well.

8. Continue to build and contour the form of the tree with texture and loosely define the outline of the tree with pen.

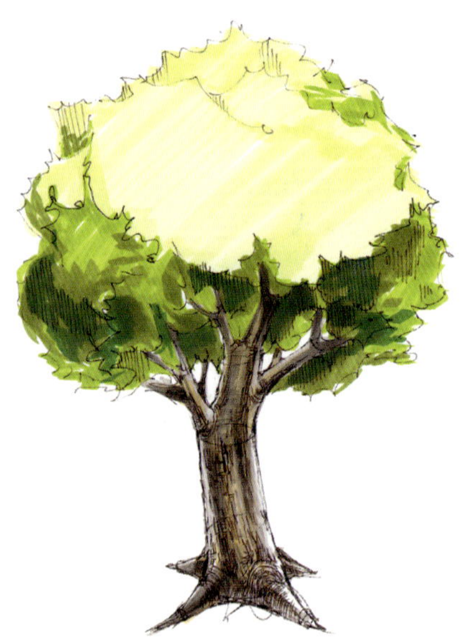

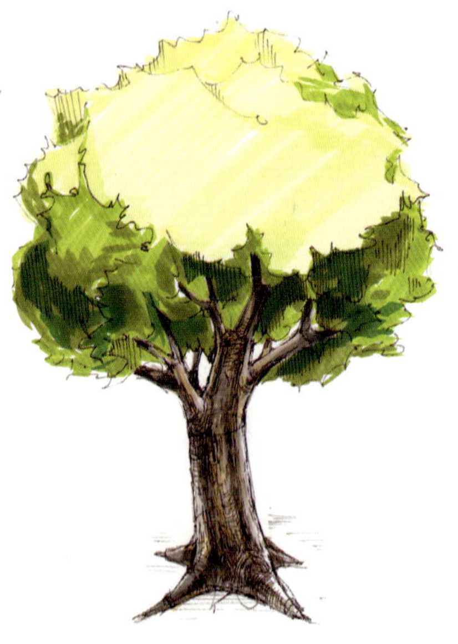

Cement/Stone Texture Demonstration: Marker

Let's create a cement or stone texture that can be used in a variety of areas in your drawings. For help with marker stroke types refer to Chapter 9, "Color."

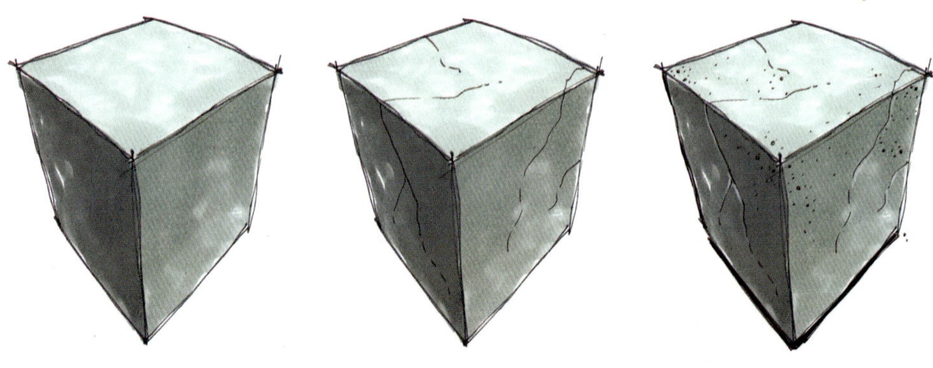

1. Start with a sketch of a cube. In this case, sketch the cube lightly as you will need to make adjustments to the edge of the cube later.

2. Shade each side of the cube by scrubbing the paper with a marker. Always start with your lightest marker and tone. Shade each side accordingly.

3. Much like for the cube examples discussed earlier, pay attention to the lighting of the scene and use enough contrast to show highlight, mid-tone and shadow.

4. While shading, use an erratic and varied pattern to create the graininess inherent to concrete.

5. Add a few cracks with light and dark marks to create the appearance of a natural concrete material.

6. If desired, add stippling to further enhance the texture of the concrete appearance.

Wood Demonstration: Pen or Pencil

When drawing in nature, wood may be a common texture that you encounter. At a glance, woodgrain can be complex and intimidating to draw, but understanding visually what's happening makes it a bit easier to approach. Let's take a look at drawing a simple wood log with a pen.

1. Start by drawing a vertical or horizontal cylinder and if desired, add any branches or deformations you would like to the log.

2. In this example my log is bark-free. Re-create the grain pattern using offset lines representing the cathedrals found in plain, sawn lumber. For a look at drawing a log with bark, check out the previous demo on how to draw a tree.

3. On the top or cut side of the log, make patterns that mirror the concentric rings of a log.

4. Pay attention to the value of each side of the block. You can create differences in value by varying the spacing between grain lines on the block of wood. Notice where the lines are closer together on the log, the value creates a shadow core. This will help communicate the three-dimensionality of the log.

5. Add stippling for additional texture or a knot to the wood to make the texture seem more natural. This project is less about precision and more about capturing the essence of the real texture. Get creative! Try a few different shapes for logs and see what you can come up with.

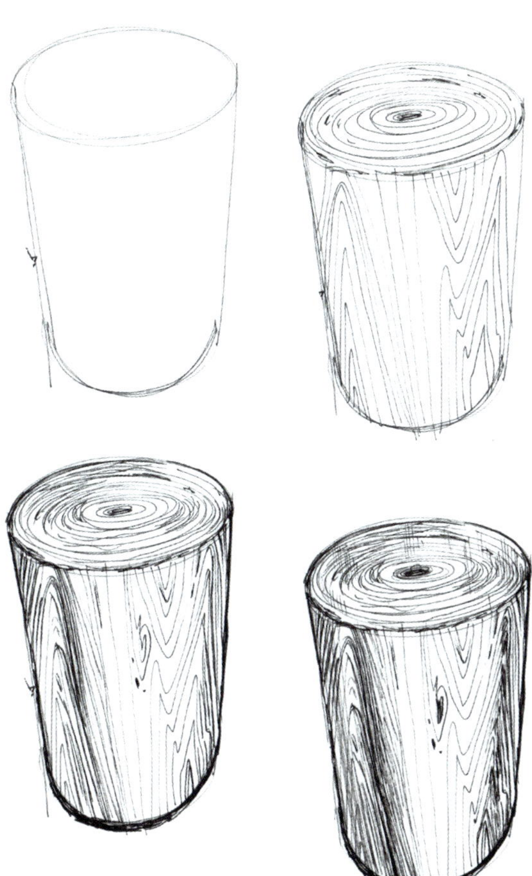

Other Textures

Sometimes you may want to include a texture not found in nature in your drawing. In this case, a more direct approach like a repetitive stroke or capturing an existing textile texture by shading with a pencil may be a better strategy for dealing with textures found on real objects. By carefully observing the repetition, direction, and relief of a texture you want to capture, you can develop strategies for tackling the texture. For example, in this next demonstration, a simple texture for a mesh pocket can be achieved with a repetitive pen stroke.

Backpack Texture Demonstration: Pens

1. Loosely sketch the outline of a backpack, either in perspective or two-dimensionally. I chose sketching in perspective.

2. Draw rough shapes that represent the volume of the backpack. Depending on your design, an ellipsoid or cuboid may be most appropriate.

3. Block in additional form elements by dividing the backpack into functional components, such as a main compartment, pockets, or accessories.

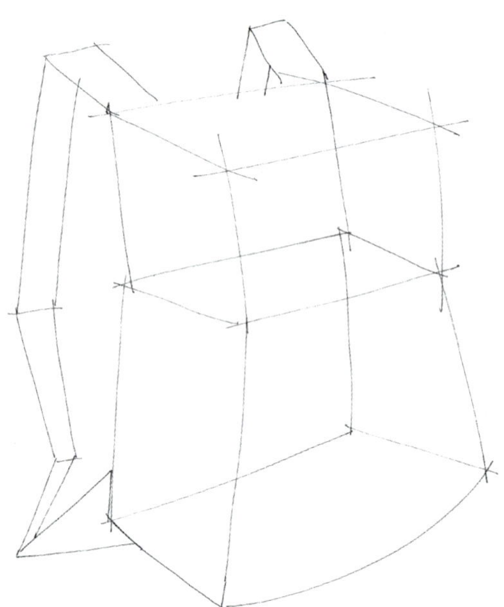

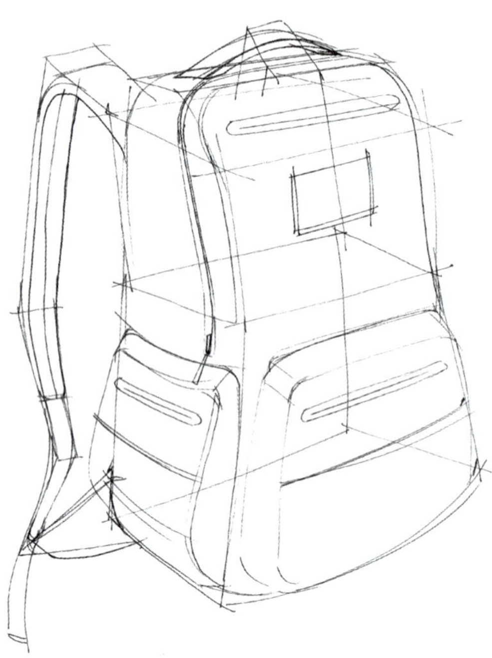

4. Further divide the backpack by adding functional shape breaks within the form.

5. Clean up your line work by adding crisper lines with enhanced line weight.

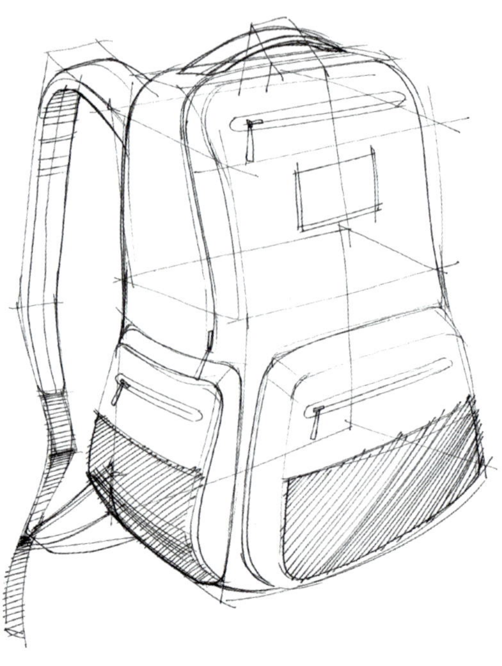

6. Add texture by sketching in patterns with repeated line strokes to communicate the types of textures desired. If a texture is visually complex, you can simplify how much complexity you see in the texture and try to mimic it by effect. Be strategic about where and how you place strokes.

7. Be mindful of the three-dimensional nature of the form as you apply texture.

8. Finish up by adding effects, such as stippling to reinforce the fabric or other textures you may be communicating in the sketch.

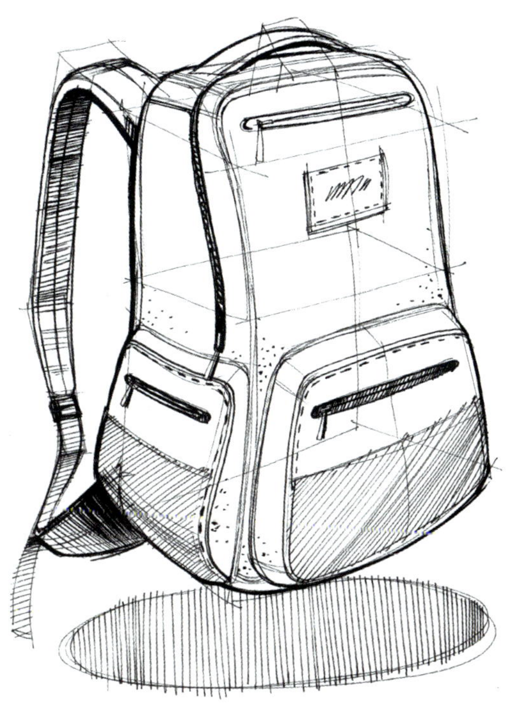

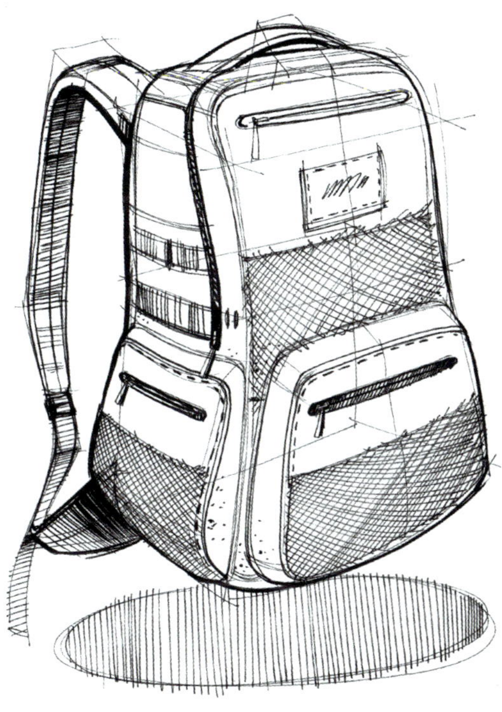

Camera with Grip Demonstration: Pencil

As I mentioned, one quick way to include textures in sketches is to shade in a texture by using a pencil overlaying a real textile or material. Let's give it a try. If you don't have a piece of fabric or material with texture, check out your local hardware store or fabric or hobby store to see what you can find!

1. Start by blocking in the rough form of the camera. Try using cuboids and a cylinder to compose the camera's form.

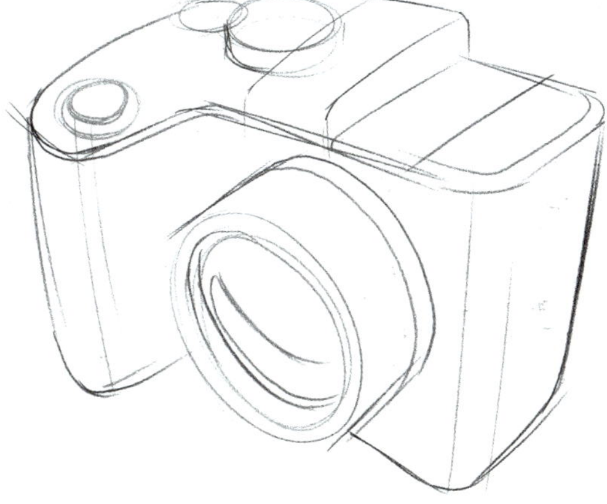

2. Add modifications to the form and shape as needed. For instance, you could add fillets or rounded elements to the basic form combination as transitional areas.

3. Continue to break up the form into functional elements and add substance to the camera drawing.

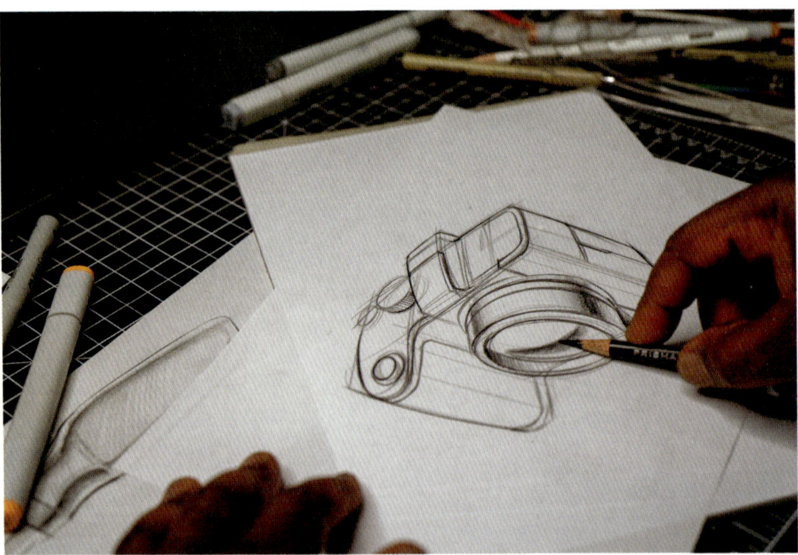

4. I found these two material samples at my local fabric store. They were cheap "sample cuts."

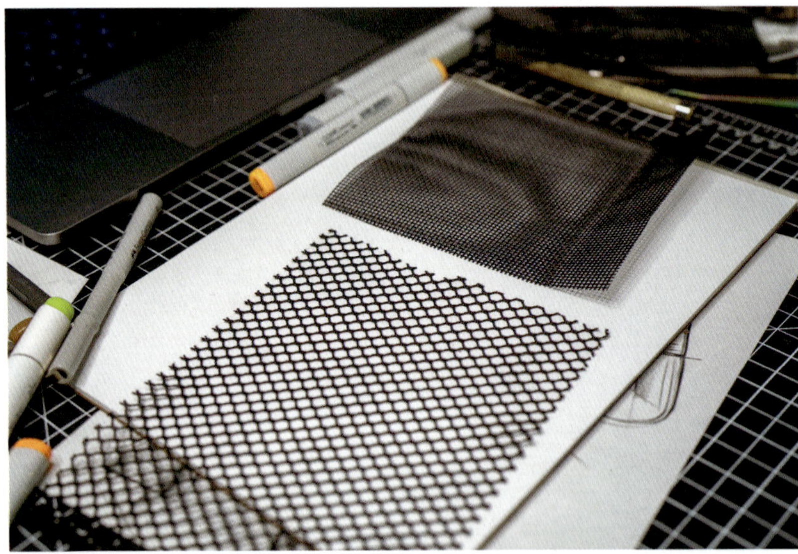

5. For the camera grip, either create your own texture by sketching in with a variety of strokes or find a texture that you can transfer to the drawing by shading with a pencil. In this example, I'm using the textile samples I found at my local store.

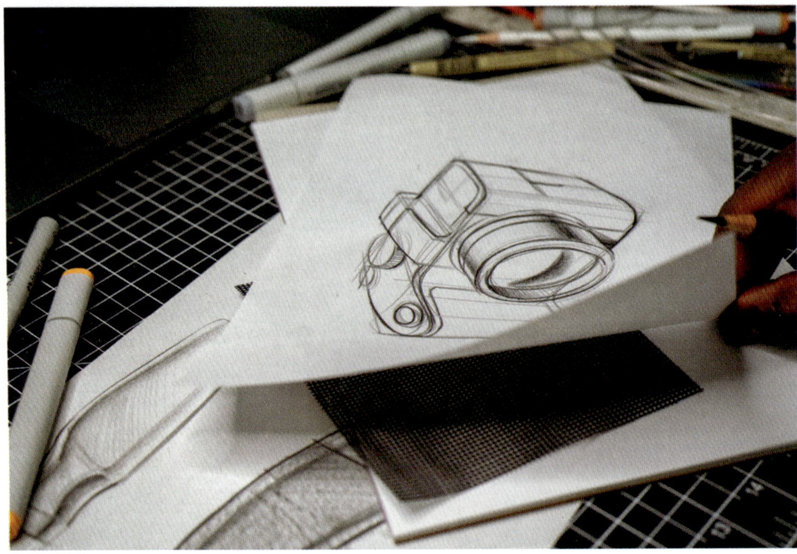

6. Hold your pencil at a low angle as shown, and shade along the shadow core of rounded areas of your camera. Increase the intensity of value shading do you add to the three dimensionality of the camera grip or other rounded areas. Shading in this way will pick up the texture of the source material.

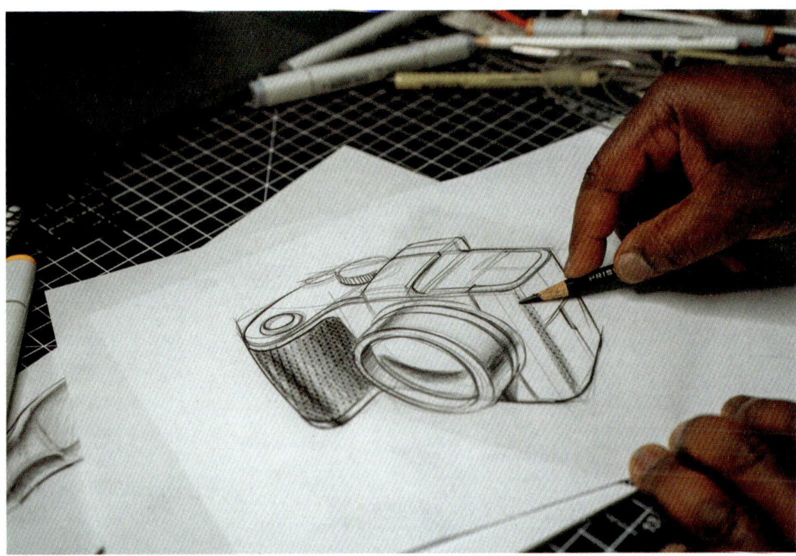

7. With shading complete, tighten up the rest of your drawing and clean up for presentation.

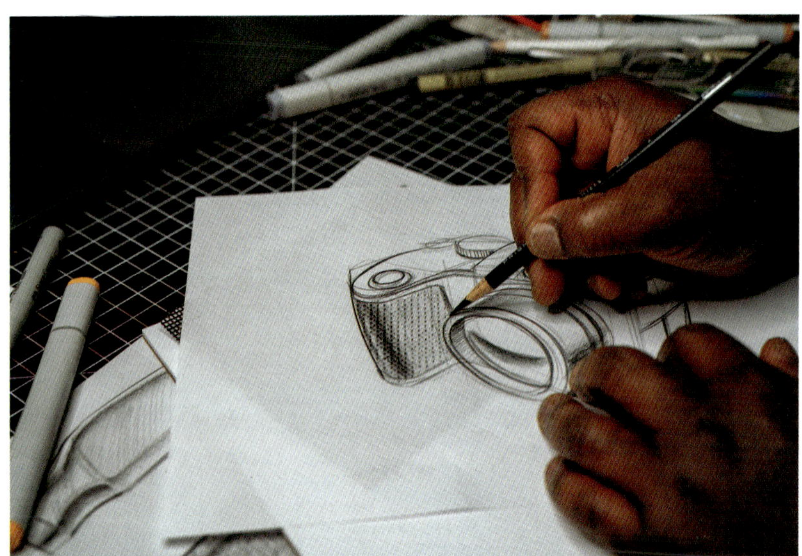

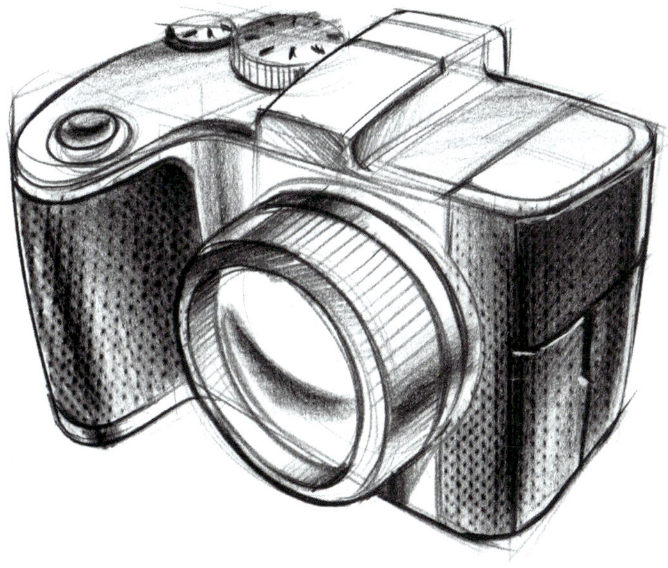

Chrome Thermos Demonstration: Marker and Pen

Many objects in real life will have a variety of finishes. Chrome is a common material found at home, on transportation, and in architecture. Let's take a look at drawing chrome using markers and pens.

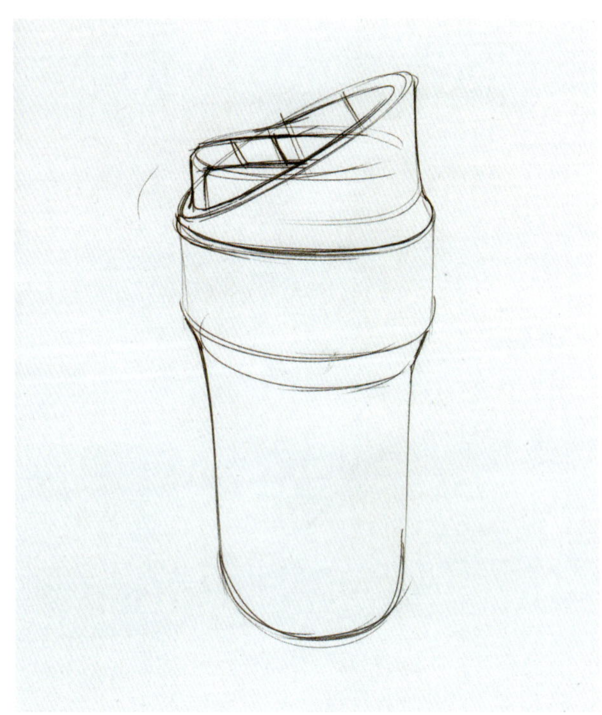

1. Start by drawing a simple cylinder or tube, either as a two-dimensional drawing or a three-dimensional sketch.

2. Plan your reflections. A good way to think of the reflection image on the cylinder is to think about the environment the cylinder is in. Wrapping the environment onto the cylinder is what creates the shiny chrome look. I chose an outside environment, which will work with markers, pen, pencil, or any other medium.

3. Shade in the upper portion of the thermos using a scrub technique to create a look of matte rubber. Remember to be mindful of shadow cores and highlights.

4. Since the cylinder is vertical, the vertical reflection of environmental elements are in the center of the cylinder. This will create the effect of a shadow core or reflection on the mug.

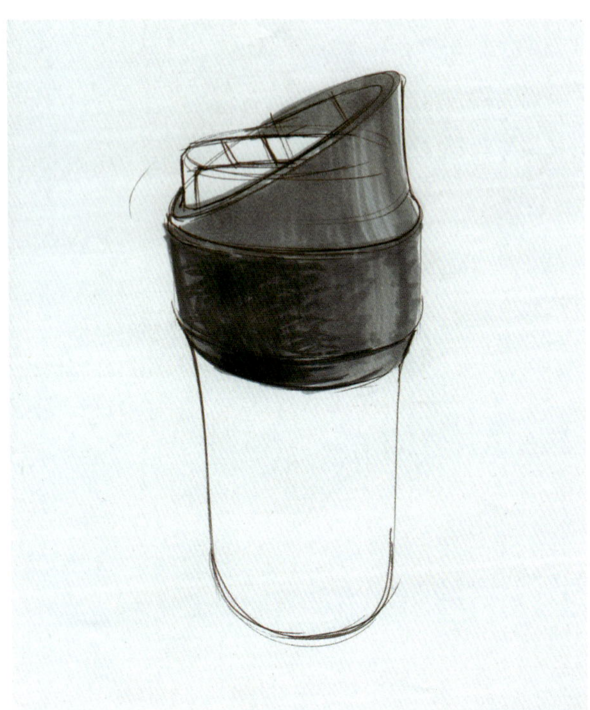

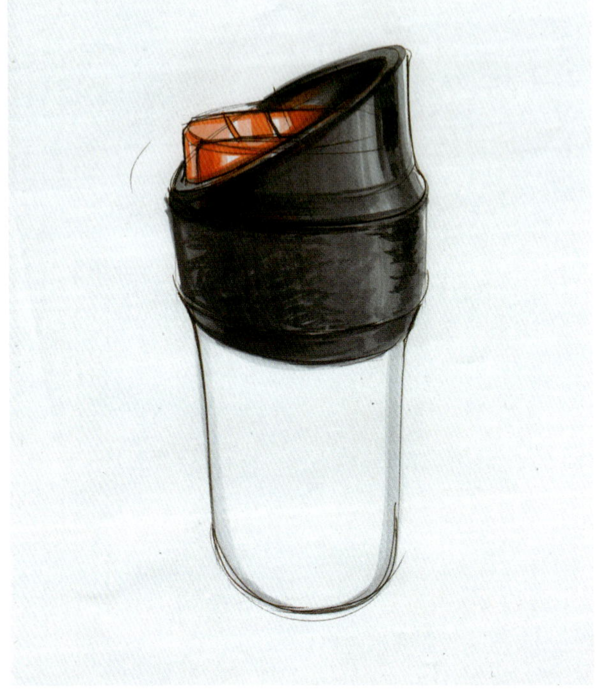

5. To the left and right of the compressed artifact, leave a lighter area by shading with your lightest marker and adding a few thin lines to communicate additional artifacts that may be present in the side of the thermos.

6. Add lights, subtle colors that may suggest other objects in the vicinity that may be reflecting into the cylinder. If using just pen, thin lines maybe used to communicate with similar field. In this example I'm using light value markers in conjunction with pen lines to show environmental lighting.

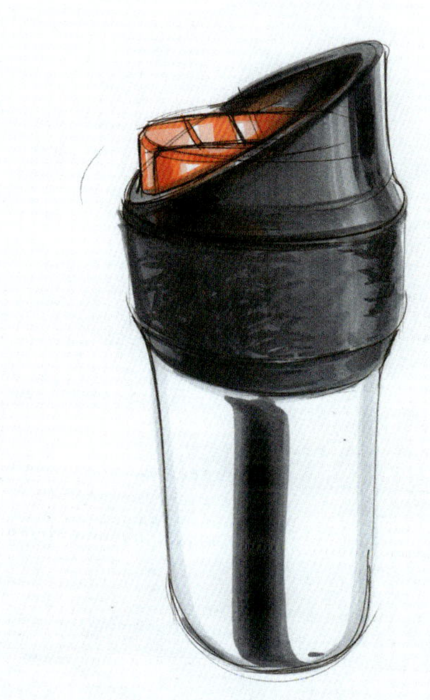

7. Again, think about what might be reflected into the cylinder. If using a monochromatic tool to sketch the cylinder, consider ways to abstract and represent what might be reflected into the cylinder. Refer Chapter 7, "Light and Shadow," and Chapter 8, "Reflections," if necessary.

8. Clean up your final drawing by adding a thicker outline, shadows, or a background if you choose.

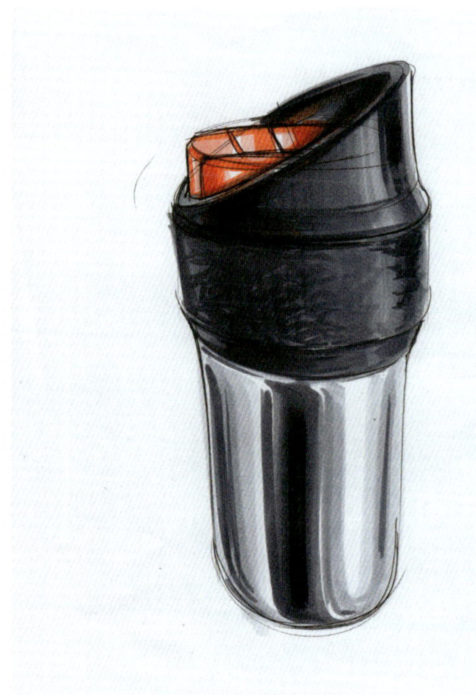

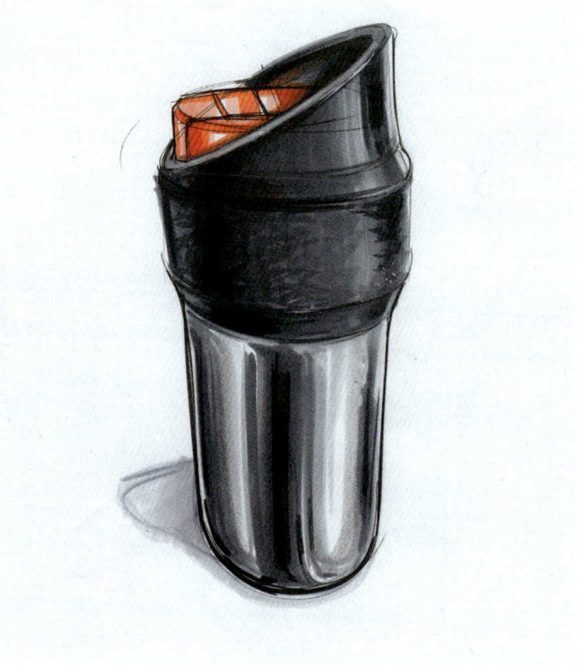

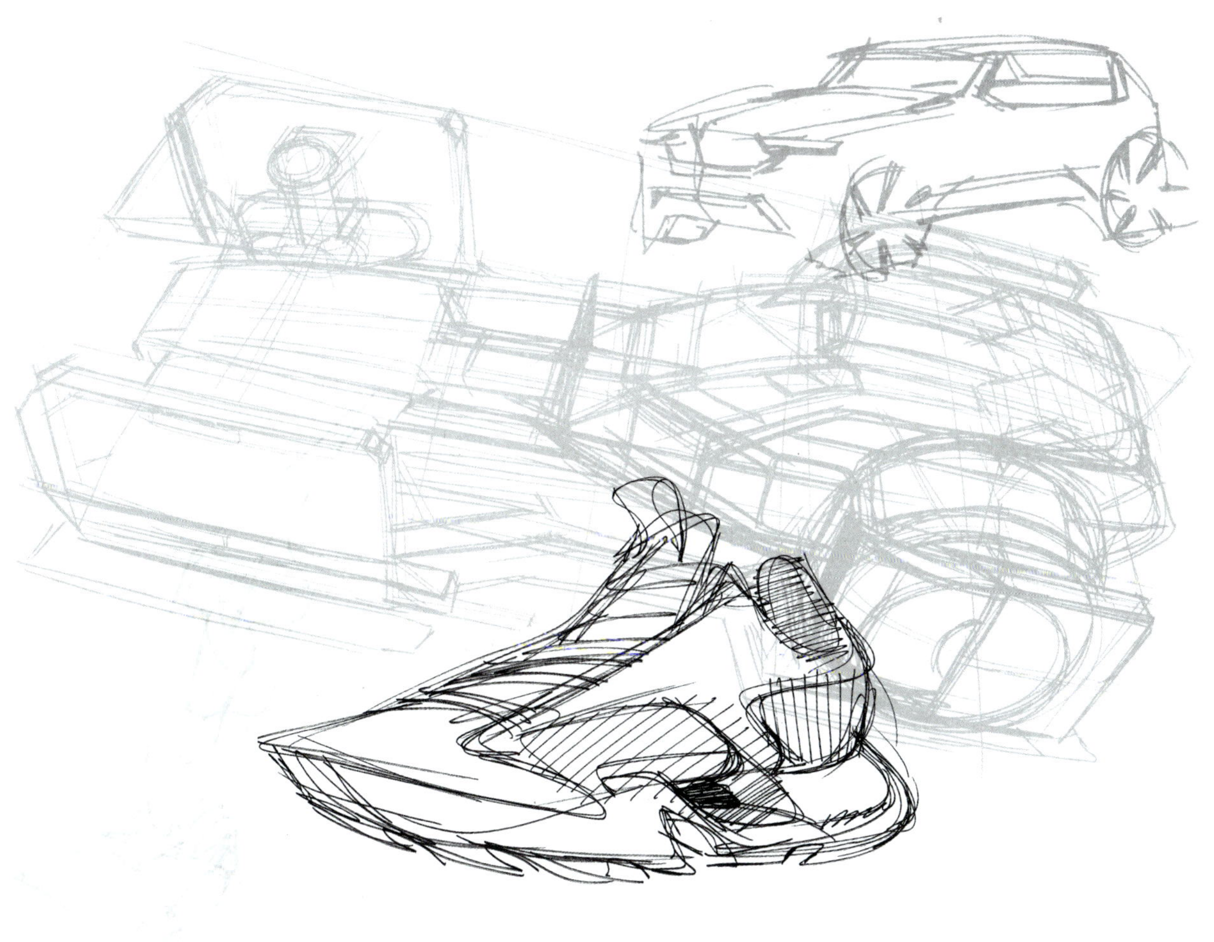

CHAPTER 11

ROUGHING IT OUT

Visualization is the process of imagining an outcome and executing toward that outcome on paper. The process of visualization happens in three phases. Imagining an object and seeing the idea in your head is the first step. Next, you execute the idea on paper or other medium. This means taking action and trying the first line or shape to begin describing the object. The final but critical step is to evaluate or be aware of what you're drawing. A simple comparison of what you drew with what you feel or imagine the catalyst of your drawing to be in your head is an important step in making sure that your idea is brought to life the way you envision it.

Having this level of mindfulness in your sketching is important. Sketching isn't just about throwing lines or shapes at the paper and having it make sense, but rather a conscious process of strategy and logic related to drawing lines, shapes, forms, and objects.

Ideas for me tend to be fuzzy and somewhat nondescript, because I have a form of aphantasia, which is the inability to clearly visualize in my head. Because of this, I've learned to use paper as a thinking medium when conceptualizing ideas and drawing objects. Quite literally, I am processing the idea on paper as I go, because I rarely see a very clear image in my head. Because ideas tend to be fleeting or fuzzy, I have found thumbnails are a fantastic way to quickly document ideas in abstract or to quickly capture as many as possible, then I can return to them later.

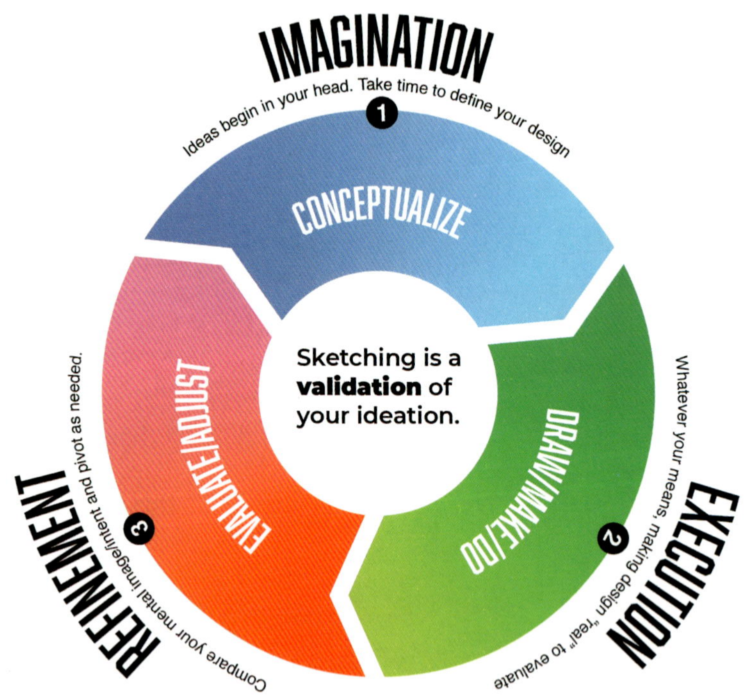

A *thumbnail* is a small-scale sketch that captures the essence of your intended final sketch. A thumbnail can range in focus from a single object to an entire scene. There is no specific size to a thumbnail, but I try to work with thumbnails that are 2 to 3 inches overall, so I can rough out a concept and move quickly to the next. Think of a thumbnail as a snapshot taken at a distance of the concept or object you're trying to draw. When creating thumbnails, work quickly and use gestural lines to represent the final concept. Focus on loose, confident, and flowing lines that capture the essence of the object or idea.

Thumbnails are also useful way to compose a drawing or sketch page. You can experiment with compositional elements in thumbnails before committing to a final drawing that is much more complex or detailed. If you're drawing a product idea or concept that requires a bit of context or storytelling, for example, a thumbnail is a great way to quickly rough out the composition before spending a significantly greater amount of time and effort creating a tight final drawing. You can then review the idea or concept with a team or on your own before spending additional time.

Additionally, a complex idea with many parts or details may seem daunting at the onset. Thumbnails help lower the temperature, so to speak, by simplifying the process. A thumbnail sketch can help you focus on what matters before you decide what you want to communicate. In other words, a thumbnail sketch is a bit like the 10,000-foot view of your idea, and a subsequent sketch the up-close view of the idea you're visualizing.

Composition

Composition in drawing, much like in music, deals with the arrangement of elements within a drawing setup. Balance, symmetry, flow, and tension are just a few qualities of composition that have visual inferences when used in certain ways. For example, a sketch page or a drawing that is symmetric may feel balanced but lack variety in the placement and scale of elements on the page. A balanced drawing may feel simple and easy to understand, but you would lose interest fairly quickly when looking at it. *Asymmetry*, or creating imbalance with purpose, makes for more interesting compositions in terms of scale and placement of elements on the page.

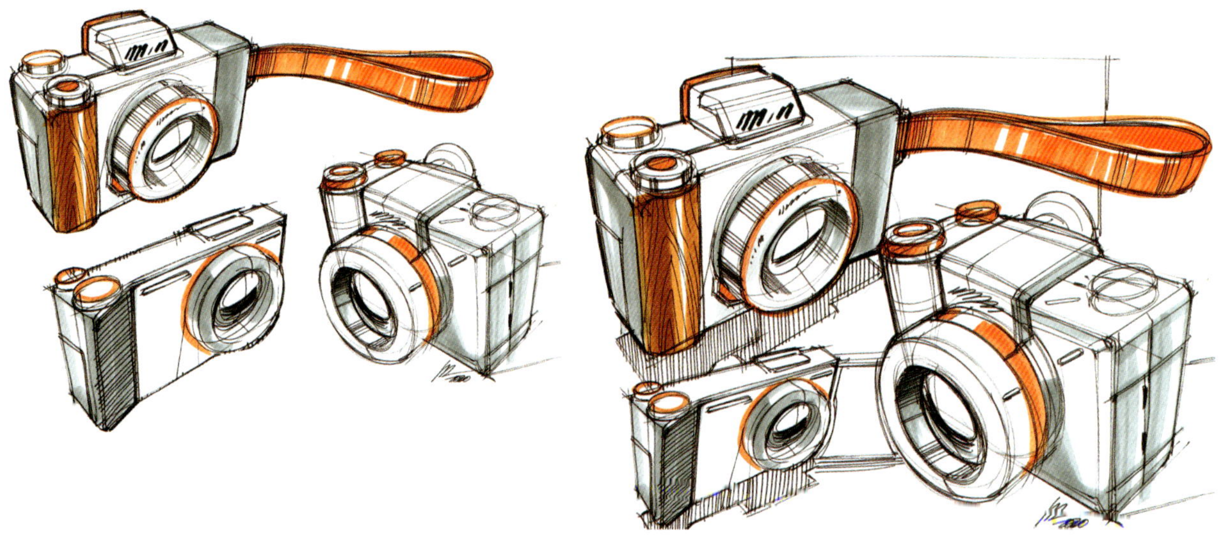

Composition also deals with the elements and hierarchy that are inherent to the approach you take when drawing. Color, for example, is often an attention-grabber in a composition. Something that is textured, even with just a pen, will garner more attention than a simple line drawing of an object. You can quite literally control the flow and presentation of your drawing by mastering composition and considering how and where you want the viewer to focus and interact with your piece.

As mentioned in Chapter 1, "All About Lines," a hierarchy of line weights also impacts composition flow and emphasis in a drawing. The conscious application of line weights to create emphasis is a powerful means of reinforcing depth in a composition, particularly when you are using lines as a foundational element in your drawing.

These concepts of composition also apply in two-dimensional drawing. The relative placement of one object next to another with a different scale, color, texture, or line weights, can affect depth perception even in the simple setup of drawing in two dimensions.

Thumbnail to Sketch Demonstration

Here's an example of how you can use thumbnails as a precursor to sketching a more complex object. Cars are notoriously difficult to draw and take years to master. However, sketching a car at small scale, as in a thumbnail, can be easier than attempting to draw a car at large scale.

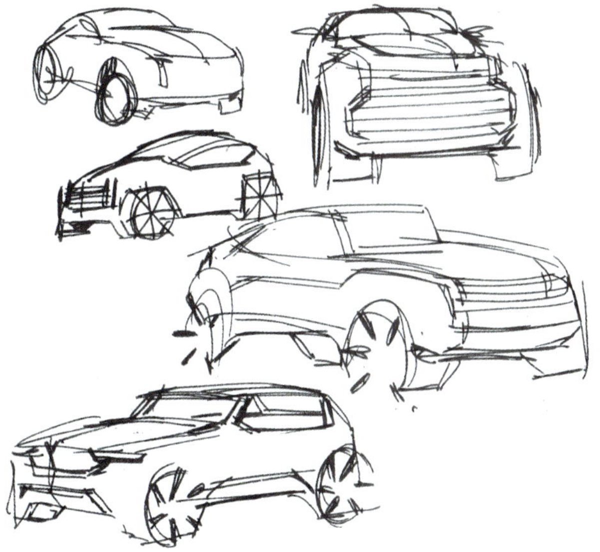

1. Start with a small thumbnail that is gestural that captures the design intention of the car you want to draw. For the example, I drew an SUV with gestural strokes that capture the flow and feeling of the vehicle. I recommend doing several of these thumbnails until you find one or two that work within the parameters of what you want your vehicle to look like.

2. Take a photo, scan, or photocopy of your chosen design, and enlarge it enough to compositionally feel like the appropriate size for the paper you're working with. At this point you may notice that some things are out of alignment in perspective, and details may appear fuzzy and unrefined. This is okay, because now you have the raw energy and presentation of your thumbnail at a scale appropriate for a more complete drawing presentation.

3. If desired, lighten the enlarged thumbnail to serve as an underlay or light sketch that you can further refine. Here you can see with some work and careful consideration, perspective corrections and details are introduced to create a more final drawing.

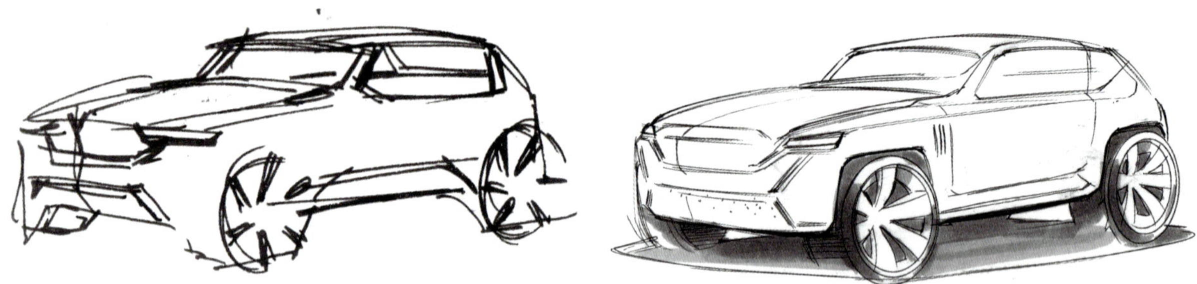

This approach to working with thumbnails not only works well for drawing objects, but also for drawing things like landscapes or a city scene. In the following examples you can see the progression from thumbnail to a more detailed landscape or scenic urban view.

"When in Doubt, Rough It Out"

Paul Skaggs, one of my college professors would often tell us, "When in doubt, rough it out." To this day, I find the technique a great way to reduce the pressure to create a perfect drawing, so instead I can lean into producing content representative of the idea or object. Your rough sketch does not need to be perfectly executed; don't fall prey to feeling uncomfortable drawing lines that don't have "good line quality"—like I used to. Despite Paul's advice, I used to spend many hours trying

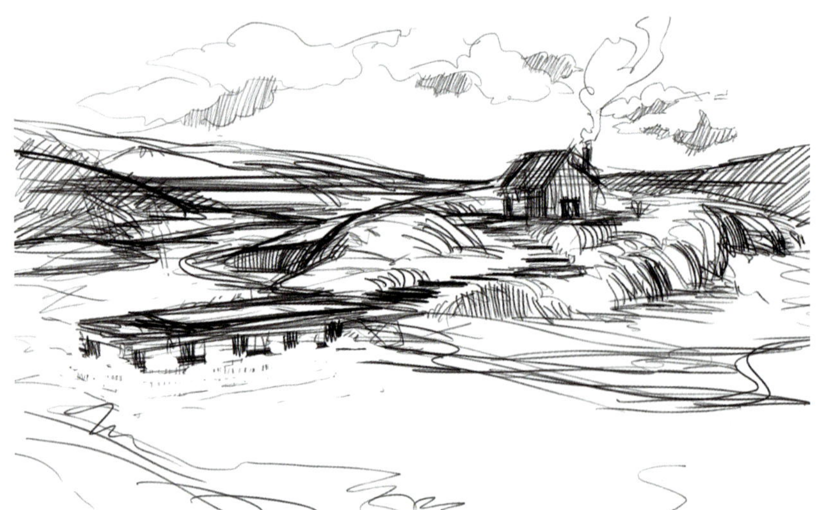

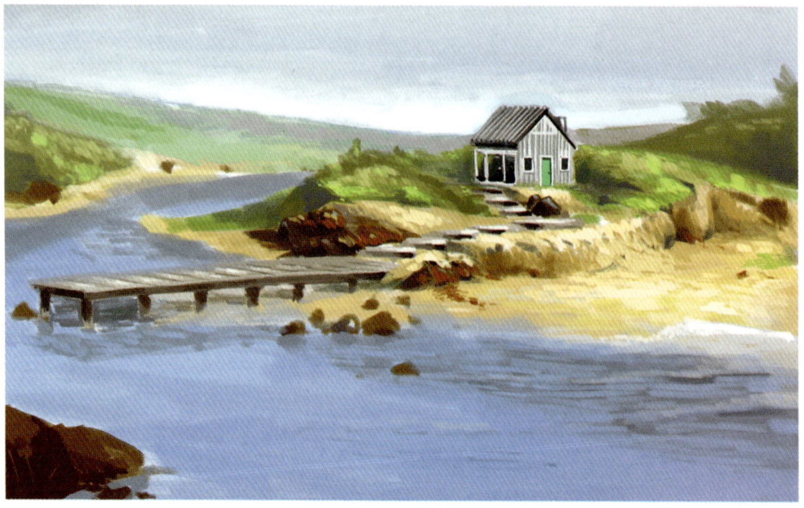

to perfect my initial sketches and often would skip over techniques that would have made ideation a smoother and much easier process.

Sketching in a rough way simply means paying less attention to the fidelity of your lines and more attention to the essence of the idea or object you have in mind. Regardless of the drawing tool, a rough sketch is a springboard to additional thought and consideration where you are able to remove the pressure of perfection and focus on content at the right point in the process.

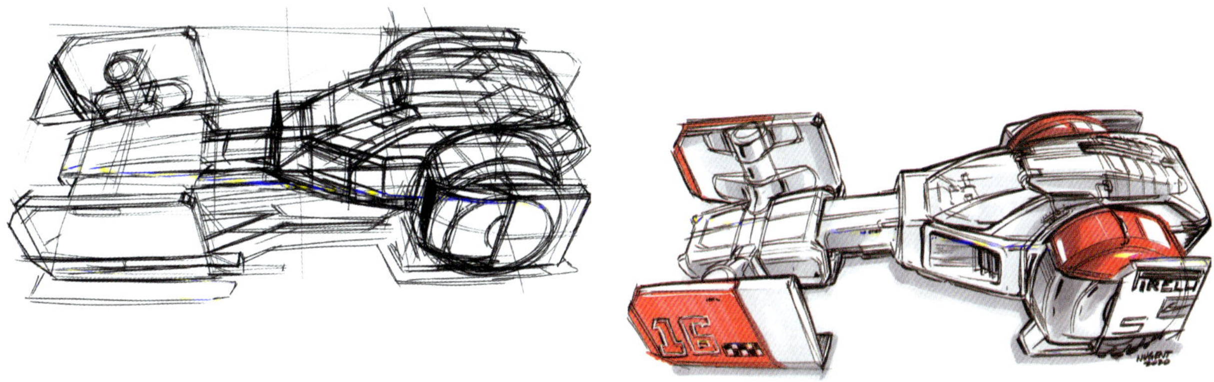

Because perspective drawing can be difficult and take years to master, creating a rough sketch with the right perspective or point of view can minimize the mental effort it takes to produce a perfect or near perfect final drawing. With less care, roughing in the lines and framework used to establish a progression of scale, convergence, and even less detail, are ways to figure out perspective and plan ahead for final drawing.

This technique of roughing out ideas works best if you use paper that is translucent enough to see the rough sketch beneath. Tracing paper, marker paper, vellum, and thin printer paper all work well for creating overlays as they tend to be translucent. Take care in deciding which paper to use, however, because the various types will work differently with your chosen drawing medium. I prefer to use marker paper, for example, because I usually use markers to quickly sketch a roughed-out concept from which I can create an overlay.

I usually use a three-step progression for this technique. I start with a rough sketched impression of the object, such as this shoe, and forego the precision shown in the final sketch. The outline of the shoe is made up of "hairy" imprecise lines that at a glance may seem lacking in confidence and clarity. I quickly address details with rough strokes of my pen as I draw other elements of the shoe. Hints of what may come are represented by fleeting quick strokes of the pen.

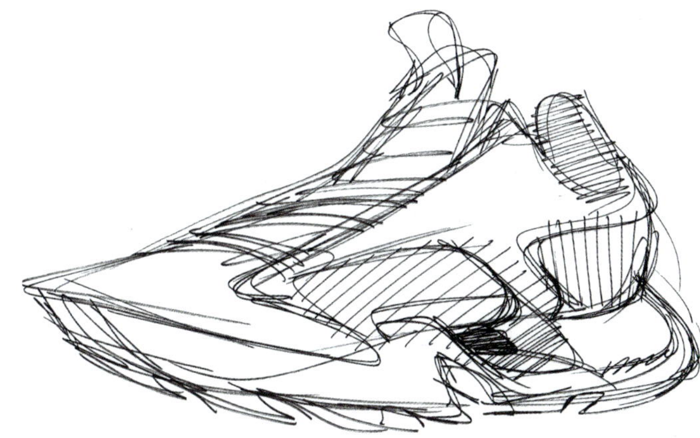

I use an intermediate sketch to clarify any details that may be pertinent to my idea, such as the laces on the shoe. Laces can be a complex element to sketch somewhat accurately in perspective. For example, the center line of the shoe isn't exactly visually centered on the tongue of the shoe, but rather would appear to be further back in distance because of perspective and the progression of scale. By working on the laces at the right time, I can focus my energy on just that element and work on the precision and placing the laces somewhat accurately in perspective. Additionally, I can give focus to a few other elements related to my shoe design.

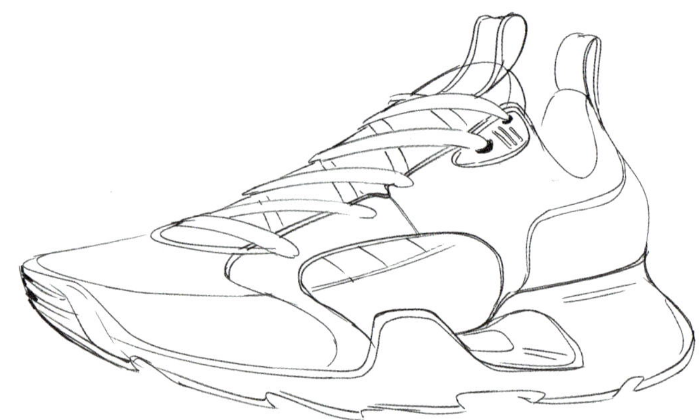

Finally, I create an overlay by placing a sheet of fresh paper over the intermediate or initial rough sketch and tightening up the line work while using the sketch below as a reference. Be sure to choose paper that is somewhat translucent so that you can see the rough sketch underneath while working. You may find it helpful to tape the underlay sketch down so that the overlay paper does not shift while you're sketching. This is entirely a matter of personal preference.

While this may feel like tracing your initial rough sketch, the goal is to re-sketch what you initially drew in the rough sketch. Think of it a bit like using "light training wheels" for your drawing. Use your initial under-sketch as reference but try to not methodically or precisely recreate the drawing on your new sheet of paper. Drawing without tracing means you can put new energy into each line as you sketch. Tracing your under-sketch will make the final drawing feel rigid and low energy as opposed to visually engaging and dynamic. Remember lines have a visual quality to them as you sketch, and having loose yet confident lines will make for a much more interesting final drawing.

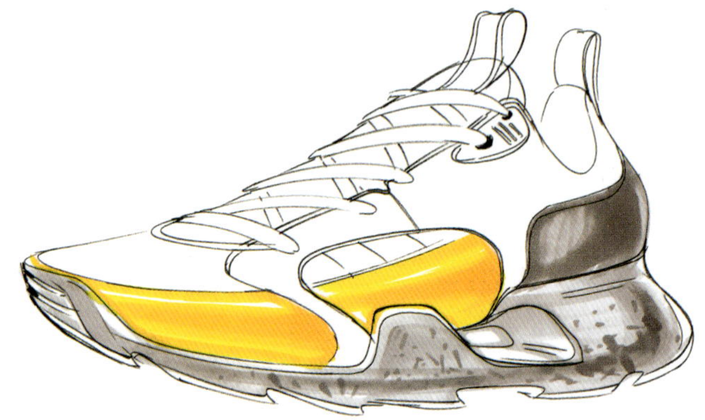

Remember to draw with your shoulder and a loose yet confident grip to get the best line quality and expression in your drawing. Drawing with your shoulder will reduce the odds of having small aberrations and errors with each of your lines. Practice each day to build confidence and fluidity.

With the overlay now completed, I can add colors, shadows, textures, backgrounds, or labels, along with appropriate line weight, to further enhance depth and richness of the shoe for presentation as needed. Notice how the line weight, color, and texture enhance the appearance of the shoe. You can add some stylistic elements at this point in the form of notes, stippling, or hatching. I've been known to even add a circle over the sketch with an arrow to make the object more interesting. Have fun with it! Much like creating the overlay, some measure your attitude and energy will carry through your lines in your final drawing presentation.

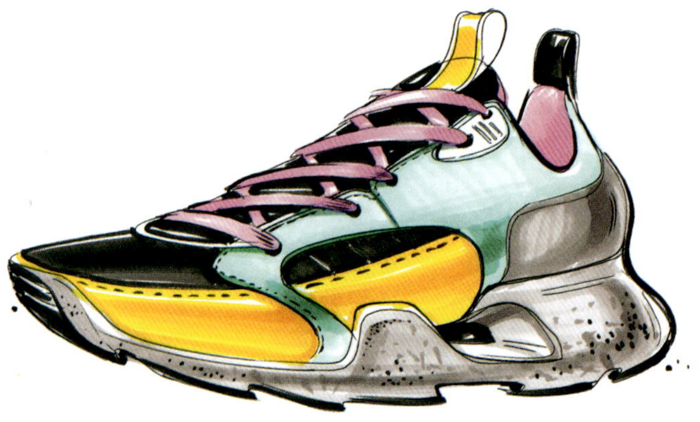

Light Until You Get It Right

Another winning strategy for lowering the temperature and pressure when drawing complex objects is to work light until you get it right. Working light until you get it right simply means drawing in a loose, light fashion that can fade into the background of your drawing as you introduce more contrast and detail.

Tools

To work lightly, use tools that enable you to draw nearly unnoticeable lines. A very light marker, a pencil, or even a ballpoint pen works great for sketching and light construction lines prior to committing to a final drawing of your object or scene. You can also combine the techniques of working lightly and roughing it out. Your light sketch need not be perfect, because drawing lightly gives you a chance to work out the perspective, placement, and composition prior to committing to the final presentation of your drawing.

Working Light Demonstration: Vacuum Cleaner

For this example, start with a rough, but light sketch of a vacuum cleaner by placing the fundamental form elements in combination. (If you use pencil, you can erase the construction lines later.) I used gray marker and cheap printer paper for my sketch, but the choice is yours. One of the benefits of working lightly you don't have to use transparent or semi-transparent paper for the final sketch, as with the overlay method. You can, instead, start with something thicker that will hold up well to paint or an ink wash.

1. Once you are satisfied with the form and perspective of the vacuum cleaner, sketch in loose and confident lines that define the shape and silhouette of the form.

2. Complete the drawing to a level that includes functional details, part separations, and some texture. I focus on breaking the vacuum cleaner into functional bits essential to its nature first, adding lights, buttons, dust compartments, and filters, all of which could be derived from the main form.

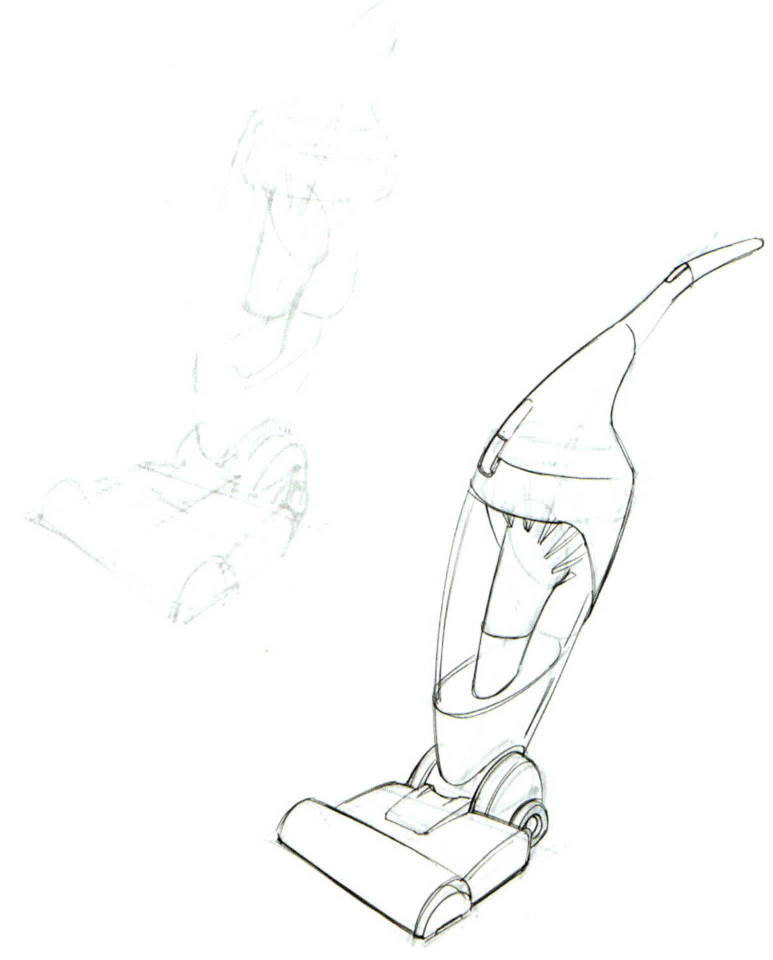

3. Before you add color, decide on the lighting in your scene and where the primary light source is located relative to the vacuum cleaner. My tendency is to pick a light source to the left, and elevated relative to the subject, thus placing shadows to the left side of the object.

4. With your lightest marker (or whatever medium you chose), outline each area you intend to color. Next, continue to build up form with contrast as well as being mindful of where reflections might be, based on the materials you choose.

5. Finish up by adding shadows to the sketch where there are overlaps in the compound form of the vacuum cleaner, as well as a shadow being cast on the ground plan that the vacuum cleaner sits on. This way the vacuum cleaner feels a bit more grounded with a three-dimensional presence. Additionally, you can add a background to further create a perception of depth. A background in this case is just a simple rectangle with a complementary or somewhat contrasting color to help make the sketch pop. Additionally, a slight contrast difference where the background meets the

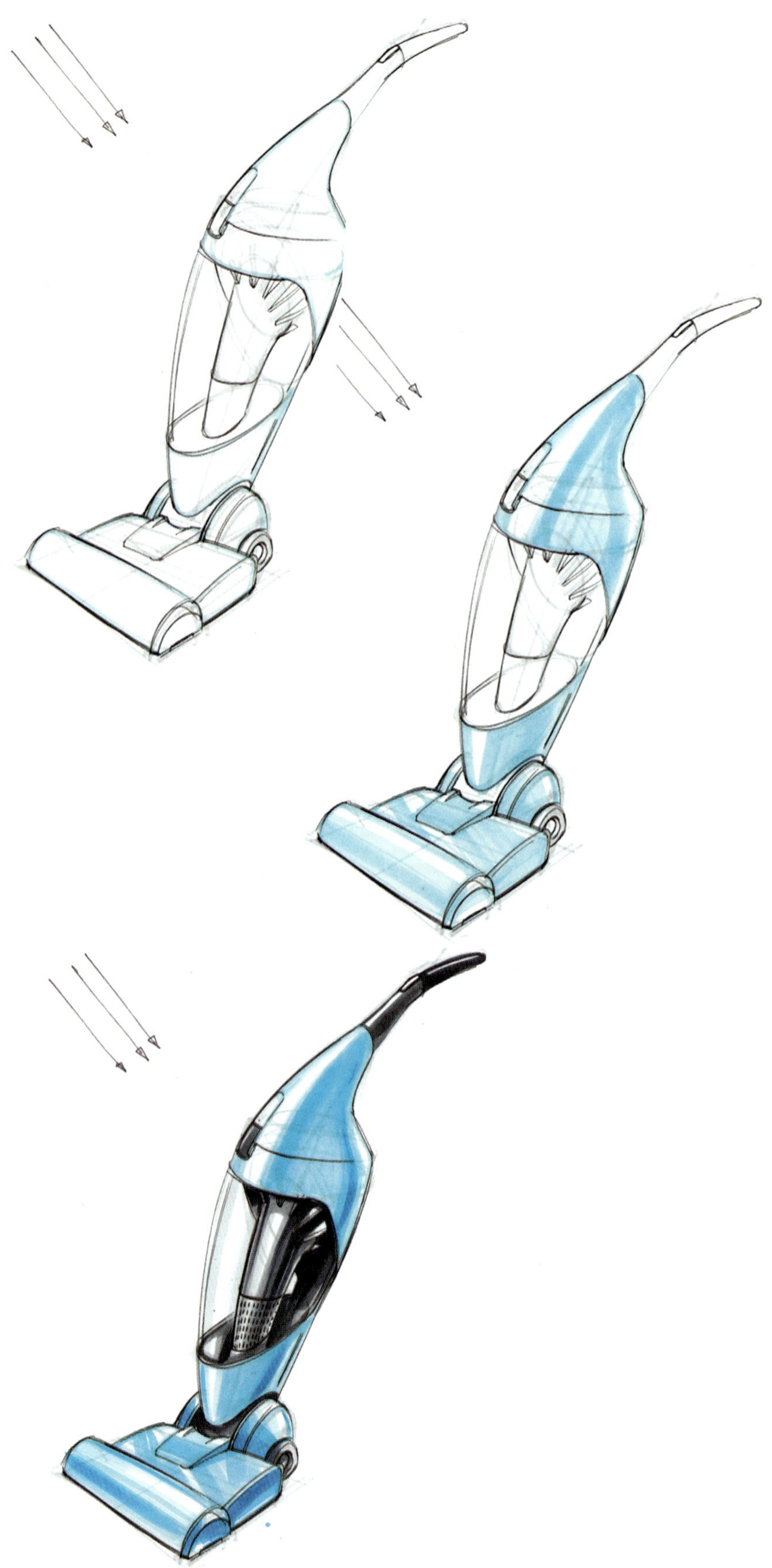

vacuum cleaner can help reinforce the depth and relative placement of the vacuum cleaner.

6. To further leverage light in a way that conveys three-dimensionality, consider placing a thin white line around the perimeter of the object. While not something directly observed in reality, a white line or lighter area around the object can be suggestive of reflective lights in the environment or scene.

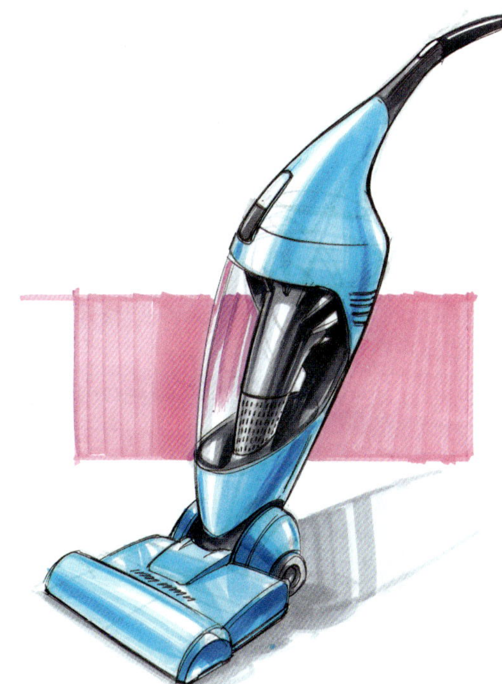

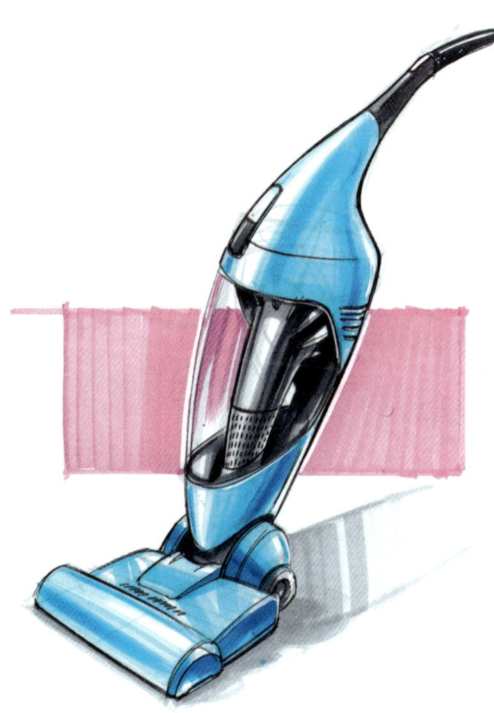

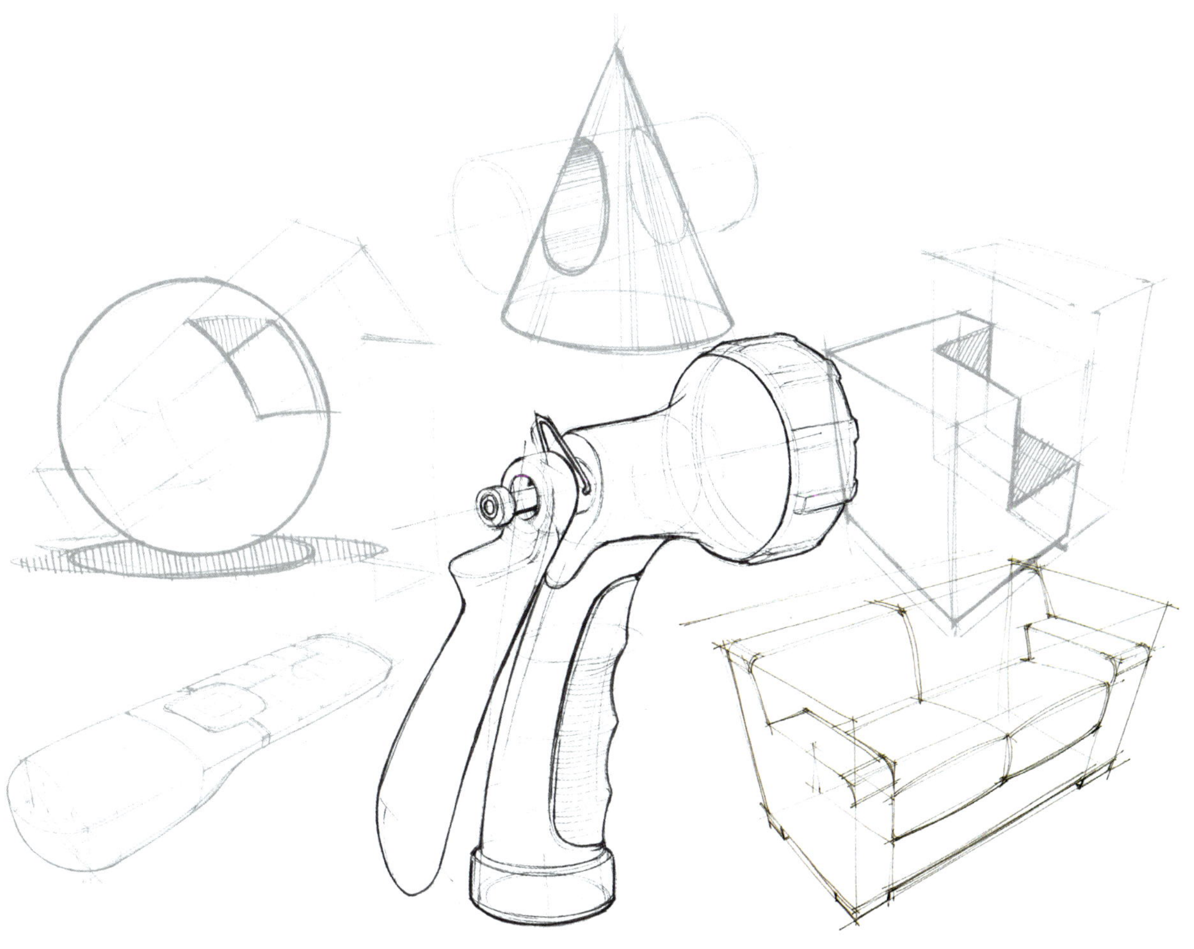

CHAPTER 12

TACKLING COMPLEX OBJECTS

I was traveling with my children, Oliver and Leo, after a visit from Grandma's house one Sunday. Leo, seated in the back of the vehicle exclaimed "It's all shapes!" I asked him what he meant. He was referring to the buildings, vehicles, signs and trees. He could see that everything around him was indeed "just shapes."

Certainly, much of what you draw will not be as simple as a plain box, a cylinder, a sphere or a cone. However, much of what exists as objects in real life can be described as being made up of these fundamental and simple forms in some combination or another.

Anatomy of Form - Line Shape Form Object

As previously mentioned, lines do not exist in reality, but these lines are the foundation to being able to draw complex objects. There are different expressions of lines and different types of lines. Lines may be straight, curved, jagged, hatched, scratchy, or clean. Lines can be short, long, thick, or thin. With lines that are repeated, texture can be expressed and depth visualized. Additionally, lines can be used in a combination to form shapes.

Shapes in turn are the fundamental building blocks for form when drawing a three-dimensional scene in a two-dimensional medium. A drawing of a box is a combination of shapes presented in a way that evokes a dimensional representation of the object itself. Each face of the box that you see as it is presented in a perspective view is a shape, and those shapes are placed and arranged to communicate the overall form of the box. The combination of these shapes is what makes up the essence of forms.

Shapes are also what are called "surfaces" within forms. These surfaces may be two-dimensional and flat, but can also be three-dimensional with twists and curves, convex or concave geometry, or a combination of directional changes within the bounds of the face or surface. Understanding surfaces is key to being able to build more complex forms and draw reflections, shadows and textures along surfaces that feel realistic. A combination of good understanding and drawing technique will really bring your drawings to life.

With an understanding of lines and how they fundamentally build shapes, and how shapes are the foundation of form, we then have the ability to further combine and modify these forms to create drawings of real objects. Understanding the combination of forms and modifications to forms is vital to drawing real objects.

Find Winning Strategies

Finding winning strategies for drawing complex objects is vital to being a quick, efficient visualizer. There is no objectively singular path that is "winning." Winning simply means finding what works best for you to get a drawing done.

As a prior math and computer science major in college, transitioning into the visual arts required me to think differently about how I saw objects around me. In hindsight,

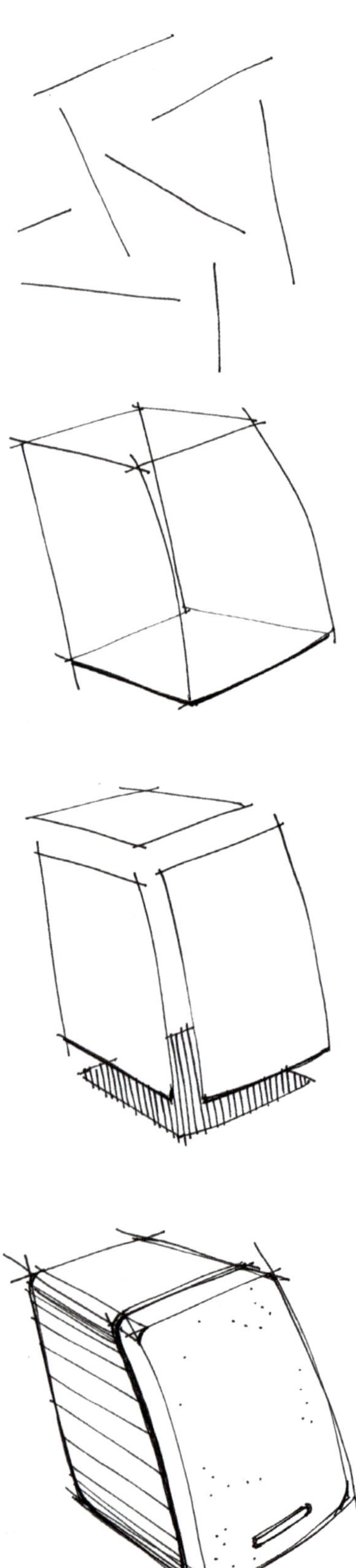

I would often make visual notes for math problems that were difficult to process. Still, the lack of understanding about visual structure and processes was a hindrance to truly being competent at visual communication.

In my transition into visual communication, my winning strategy was to simply understand what I was looking at and why it looked the way it looked. This process involved breaking down objects into simpler bits that were easier to process visually. Also critical was recognizing what processes a simpler form or forms would have to undergo to become the more complex form as an object.

Complex to Simple - Breaking it Down

Forms may be combined in a variety of ways to express a more complex and full view of an object. An object, thus, is a combination of lines, shapes, and forms of varying sizes and placement. These form combinations naturally vary object to object, thus expressing each object's own unique character and nature.

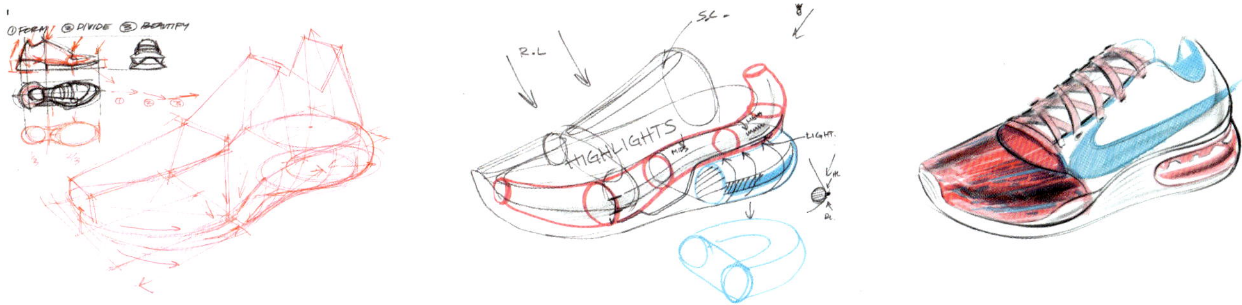

Breakdown of a shoe as simple geometry.

Generally, when drawing an object, I look for certain fundamental shapes, then break those shapes up into functional bits as needed. For example, a flashlight could be described as a cylinder with a cone-shaped aperture at one end. This general cone form is where the light would be emitted. This cone also gives the object directionality and tells someone where to hold the flashlight.

Consider a simple camera with a lens. The camera may be defined generally as a rectilinear form body with a small ergonomic extension as a grip, and a barrel or cylinder for a lens. Additional details make up the camera, such as function wheels, knobs, buttons, and toggles. Each of these elements may also in part or whole, be made up of primitive form bodies at varying scale and placement within the overall presentation of the camera itself.

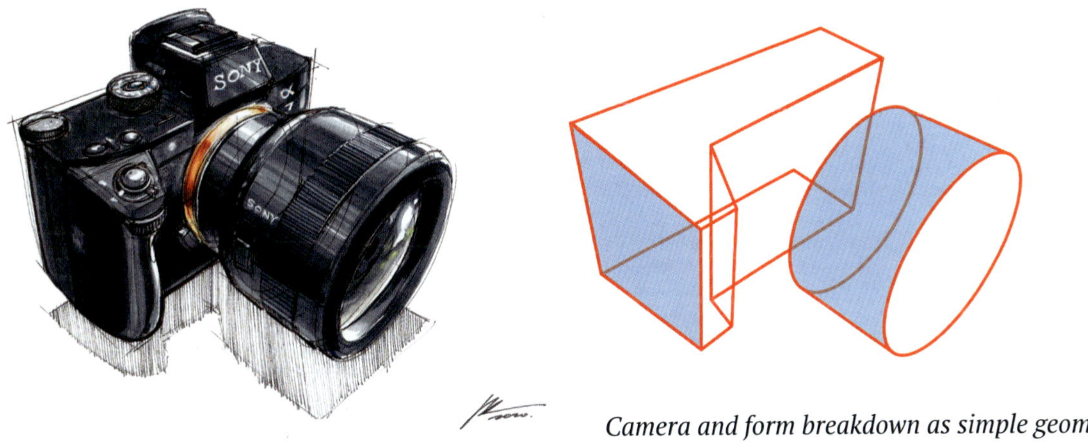

Camera and form breakdown as simple geometry.

Taking this approach to seeing the fundamental in the complex makes for a much easier drawing process when tackling complex objects.

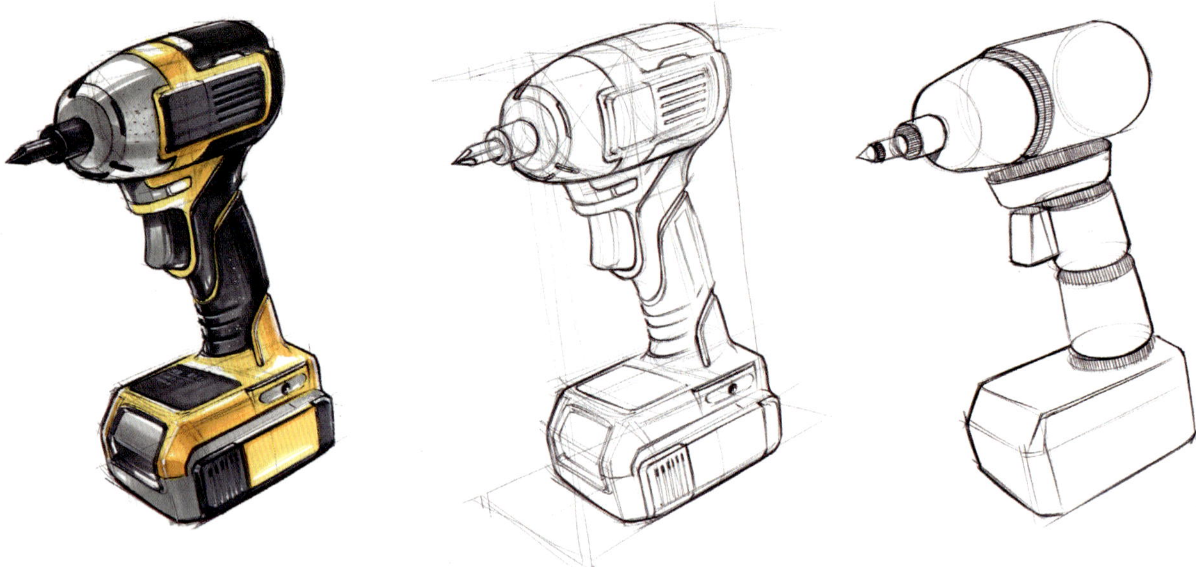

Break down complex forms into elementary primitives to understand how to draw them.

Common form combinations can be found in most objects, even the most complex objects that we encounter day-to-day. Drawing more complex objects is simply a matter of "learning to see in 3D" as well as learning to see the parts that make up the whole. Even something as complex as an automobile can be distilled to its essential fundamental forms as a starting place for perspective drawing. Of course, the drawing would be much more detailed and include softening and transitional surfaces when refining the design of the automobile.

Without delving into foundational two-dimensional compositional principles, I tend to think of the process of creating forms much like composing music. A musical composition with receptive beats, equal, and consistent pacing, amplitude, pitch, and key tends to be palatable but largely uninteresting. Of course, one's taste and circumstance may impact the perception of the musical piece.

Meanwhile, a more varied and diverse compositional arrangement, albeit structured, does create a more pleasant and fulfilling listening experience. Take a moment to think about your favorite music and what makes it so. Often, I find myself coming back to that one spot in a song that stands out. Perhaps it's a section of the song that feels "off" or "out-of-place," or off-tempo but it just works!

Form creation in visual communication is much like the compositional process in creating interesting music. Keep in mind variety, symmetry, placement, and proportion when using any combination of these operations on forms.

When combining forms, there are a few common combinations that may be applied to create more interesting forms:

Addition

Addition simply means combining two more forms into a more complex form. The resultant combination is viewed in totality as a single object. Rather than show the intersecting overlap, the silhouette of the combination becomes the new form. This process is not limited to combining two forms and may include many primitive shapes.

Think of objects around you that might be the result of one combination or another. This exercise will help you see in real life how objects are composed and give you insight into how to draw your own when you can simplify and see the secret to the sauce.

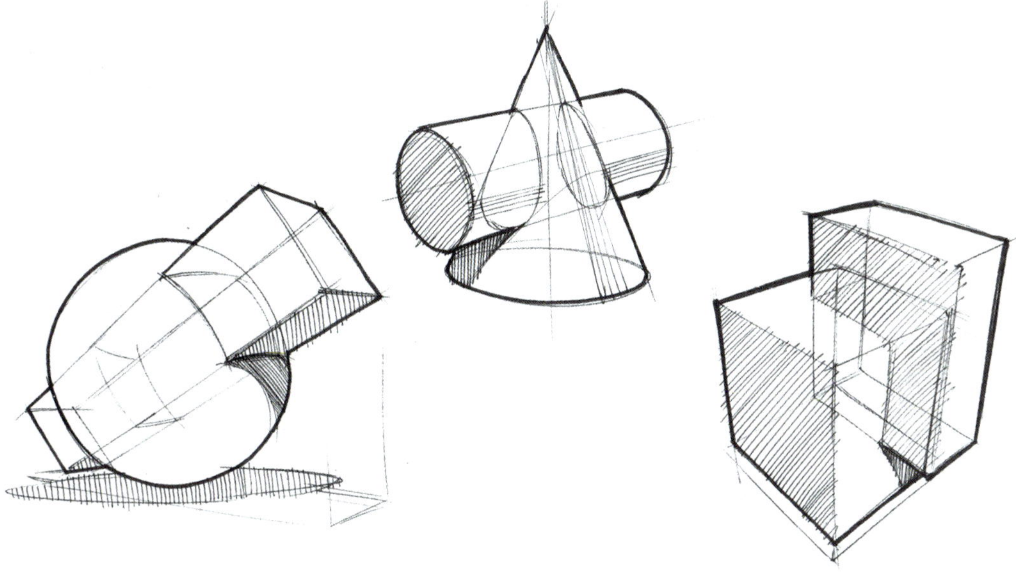

Subtraction

Subtraction means removing a portion of a primary form by intersecting or overlapping a secondary form. These forms need not be the same type or size. Additionally, many forms are comprised of several subtractions that go beyond one or two subtractions.

Think of objects around you that might be the result of subtractions between a primary and secondary or even tertiary form. This exercise will also help you see in real life how objects are composed and give you insight into how to draw your own forms based on subtraction.

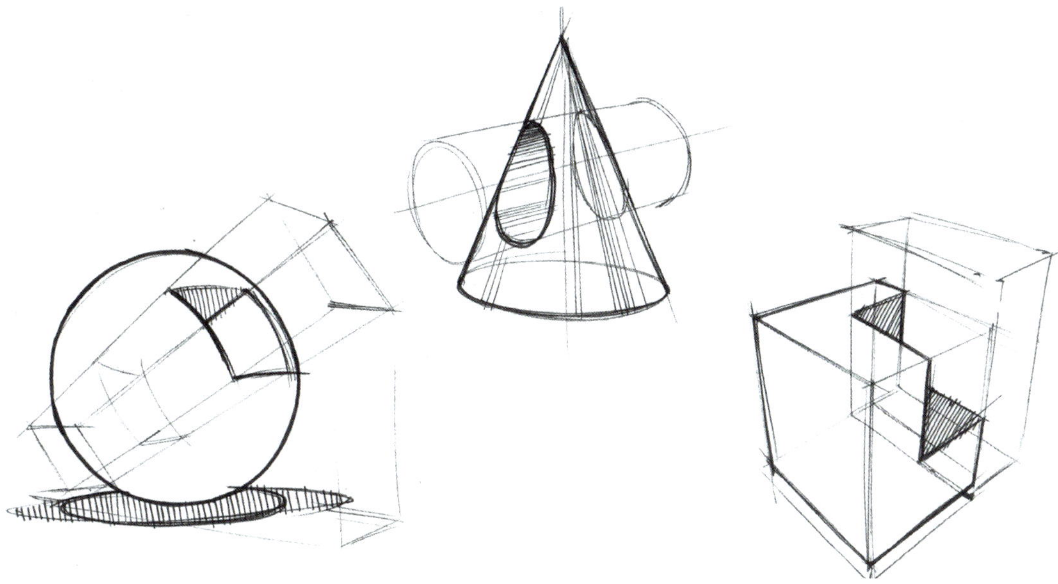

Intersection

Intersection means finding the overlapping area that is common with two or more forms. As with form additions and subtractions, these forms need not be the same type or size. Similarly, intersections may be the foundation of objects around you.

Take a minute to look around and see what intersecting forms may be the basis for objects you see in your environment or throughout the day. Remember, much of learning how to draw comes from taking a minute to observe the world around you and connect what you see with what you imagine so that you can build your visual vocabulary.

These form combinations may be applied symmetrically or asymmetrically for varying results when creating forms.

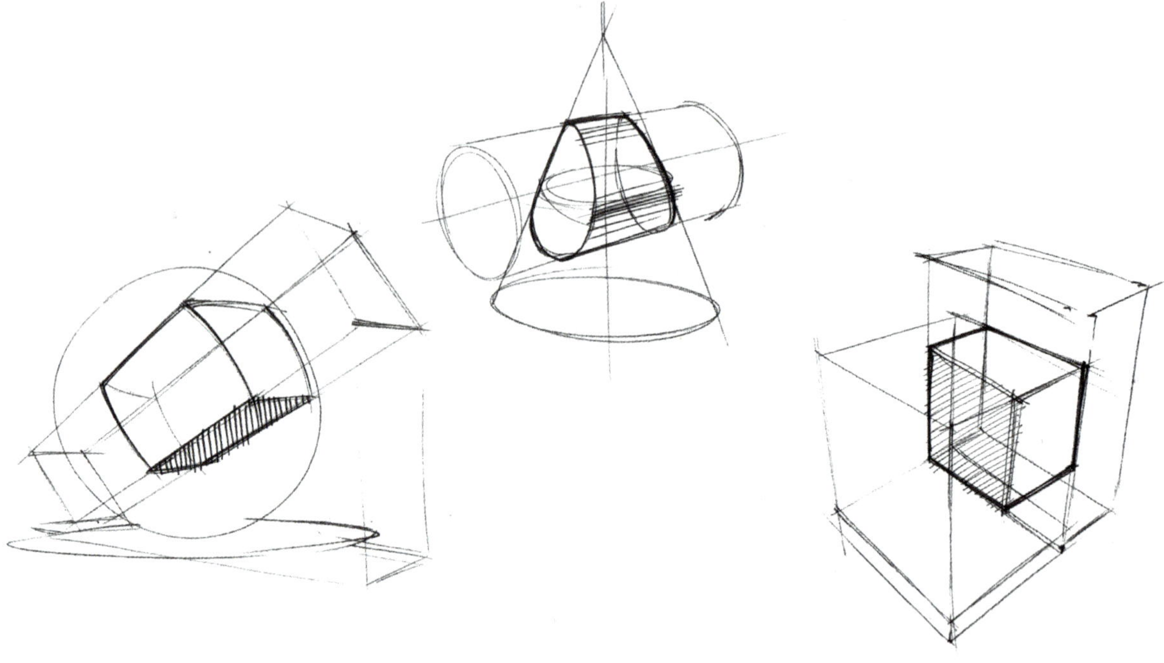

Loft

A loft is an interpolated connection between two disparate shapes or surfaces. The resultant connection is a three-dimensional form. Lofts vary in how they are formed depending on the shapes of each surface or shape as well as whether there is a secondary operation affecting the interpolated form. For example, a loft may be straight, curved or twisted along a virtual path.

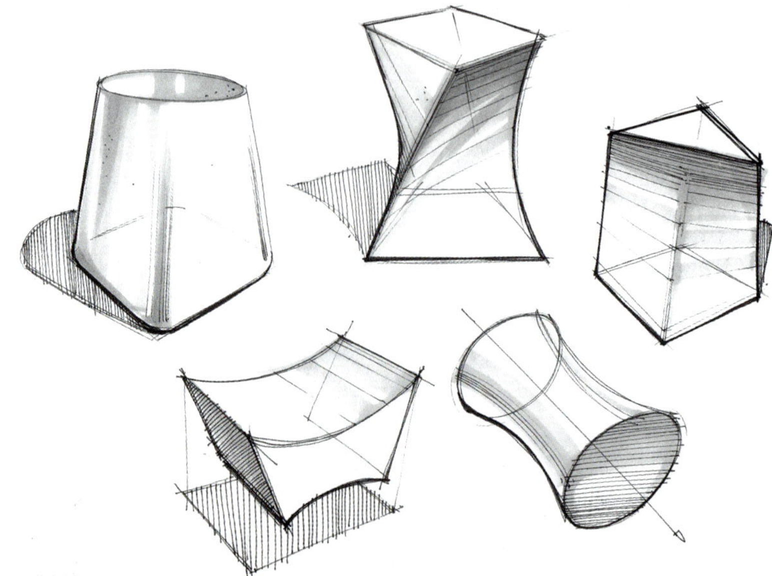

Sweep

A sweep is the form-based representation of a shape traveling through three-dimensional space along a chosen path. For example, a triangle moving through space along an "S" curve produces and interesting form.

Revolve

Much like a sweep, a revolved form is a resultant shape-based form that has traveled along a given path. The path in this instance is a circle in part or whole. For example, a torus may be described as a circle revolved through three-dimensional space.

Transformations

Modifications are visual and perceptual operations that involve changing base primitive forms. For example, a cube can be stretched, slanted, or squeezed to change it into another type of form expression. This is somewhat of a mental exercise, but I find it useful to use something like clay, or if you have the skillset, a simple exercise in 3D software can be used to illustrate how each operation changes the nature of the primitive being worked on.

Modifications to primitive forms make more interesting shapes. A cube can become a cuboid by being squeezed in one or more dimensions and a sphere becomes a spheroid or ellipsoid by being squished in one or more dimensions.

Bending a cylinder enough to complete a rotation makes it into a torus. Another way to think of a cone is as a cylinder where the top circular face has been reduced in size enough to be a single point while maintaining the dimension of the base face.

I find it useful to understand these operations as, because knowing what operations are possible makes it much easier to describe and draw each of these forms. This is particularly useful when working with lighting, shading, reflections, and textures.

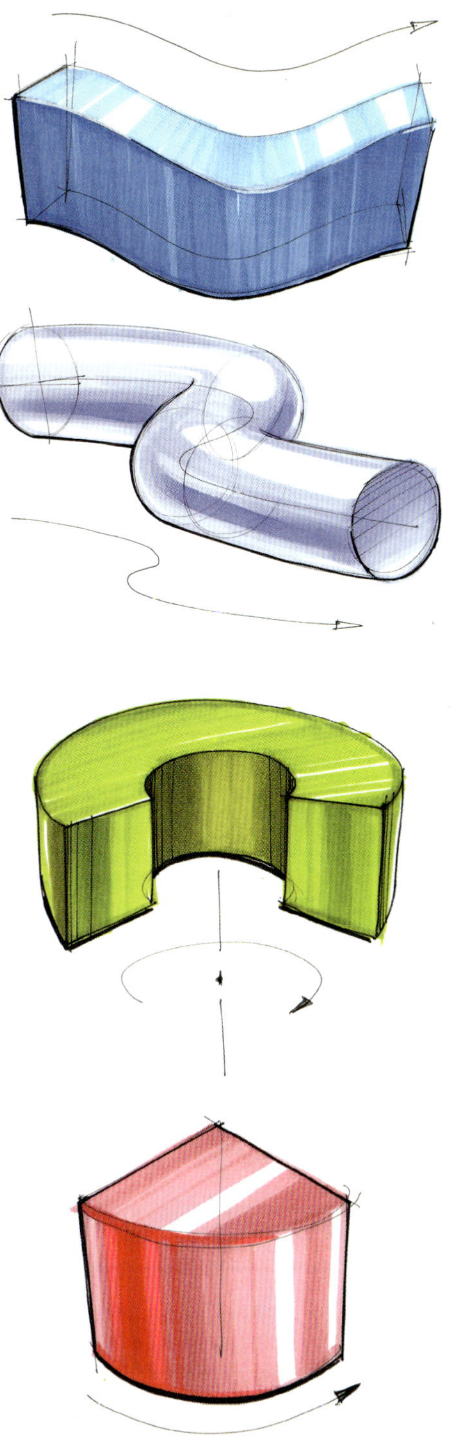

These forms can then undergo further operations such as addition, subtraction, or intersection to create more complex and interesting resultant forms.

Stretch

Stretching a form involves extending an object in one dimension or another to distort and elongate the object in that direction. By stretching a cube, the resultant form is a cuboid. The very building you are in now may be comprised of a cuboid or several cuboids of varying shape and proportion. Your phone may be described as a cube that has been flattened and stretched with rounded corners.

Stretching is a useful technique when creating forms either in whole or in part.

Slant

Slanting a form means sliding one part of a form, usually in a planar direction parallel to another plane, thus shifting and adding a slanting gesture to the resultant form. For example, a cube with one face shifted in one direction can result in a rhomboid—a form made up of six parallelograms.

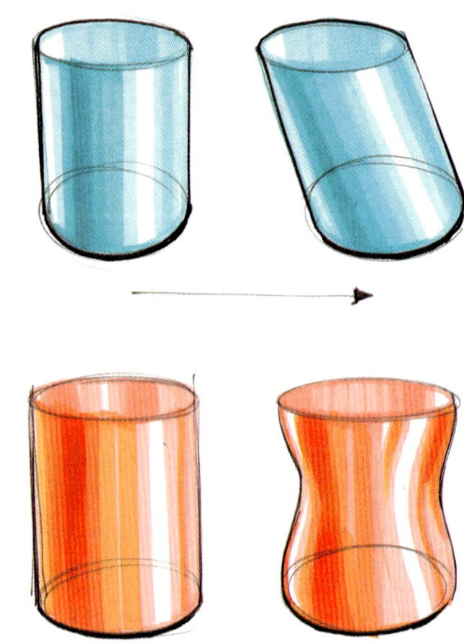

Squeeze

Squeezing a form means compressing the form in one or more directions uniformly or asymmetrically across one or more dimensions. Squeezing is similar to stretching in that it distorts a base primitive shape.

Twist/Bend

Twisting a form means rotating the opposite ends of the form clockwise and counterclockwise on opposite ends of the form to create a spiral effect in the resultant form. Much like other operations, twisting can be done to varying degrees and combined with other operations to create new forms.

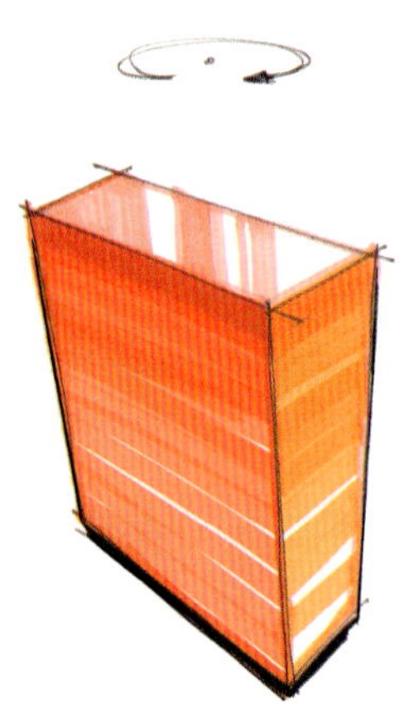
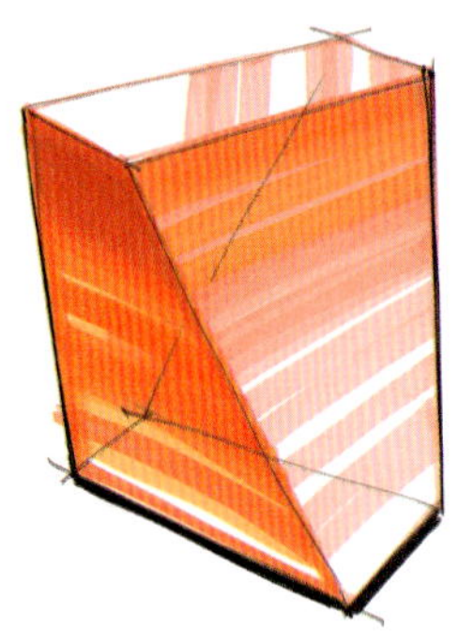
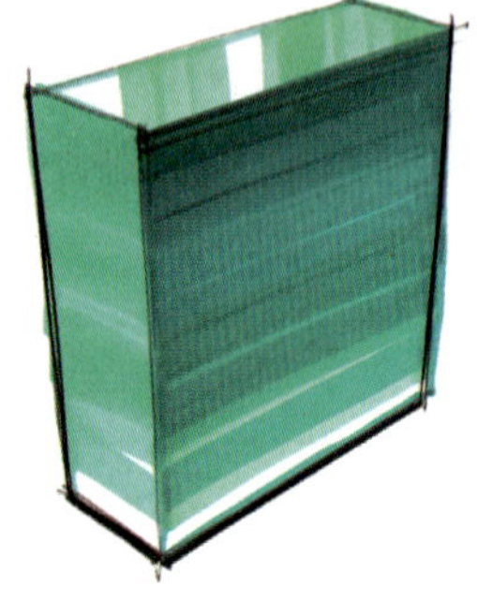
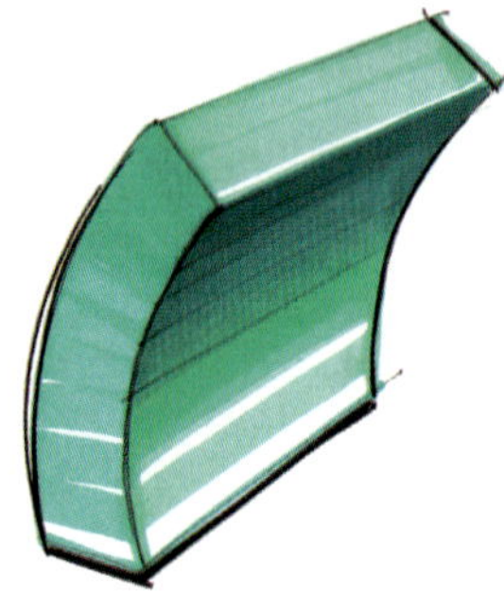

Transitions Between Surfaces

Transitions help further with the combination of forms to create more unified complex objects when drawing. Transitions are features added to an object that make them feel more unified and complete as a whole. A few common transitions you may have seen on objects include lofts, blends, fillets, and chamfers.

A fillet is a rounded transitional surface between two incongruent surfaces. One way to think of a fillet is as the part or section of another form like a cylinder or torus. In some instances, a fillet has a consistent circular profile and other times, the fillet may be asymmetric and/or varied along the length of the transitional surface.

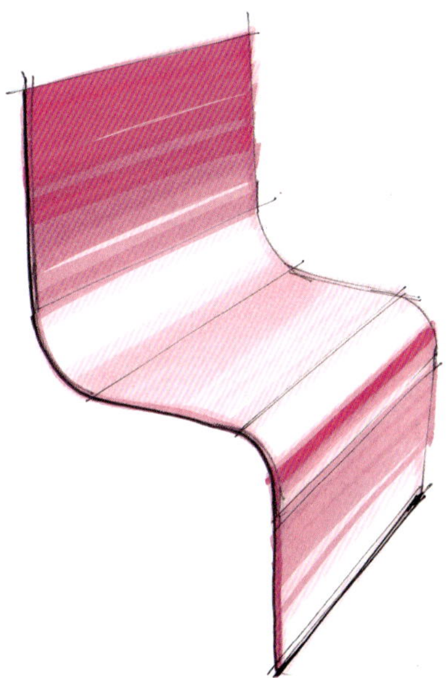

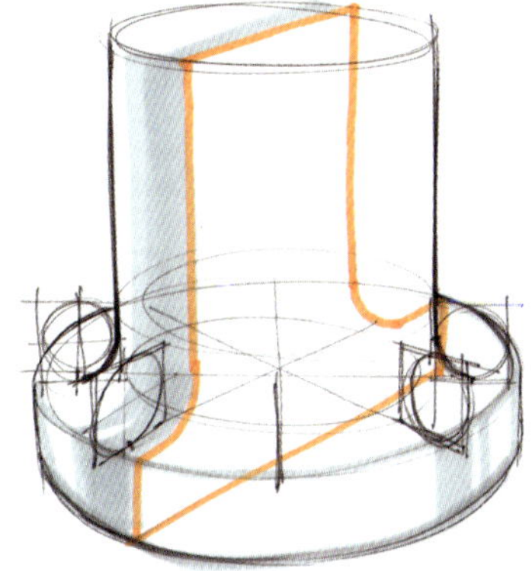

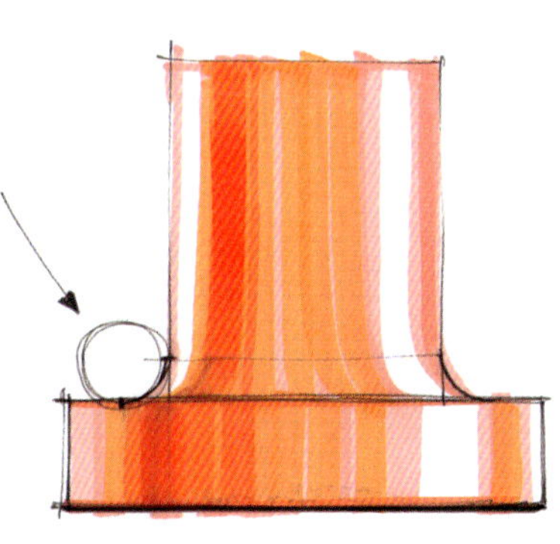

A fillet can also be shown in three-dimensions by tracing the revolved path of a circle in perspective.

A chamfer is another type of transitional surface that is commonly found on many objects. A chamfer is a straight, planar lofted surface between two edges or primary surfaces on a combination of two or more forms that make up a larger more complex object. A chamfer can sometimes have some curve or crown to the profile, but the important bit is that the connecting area on a chamfer is not tangential and merely positionally in contact with the primary and secondary surfaces that it connects to.

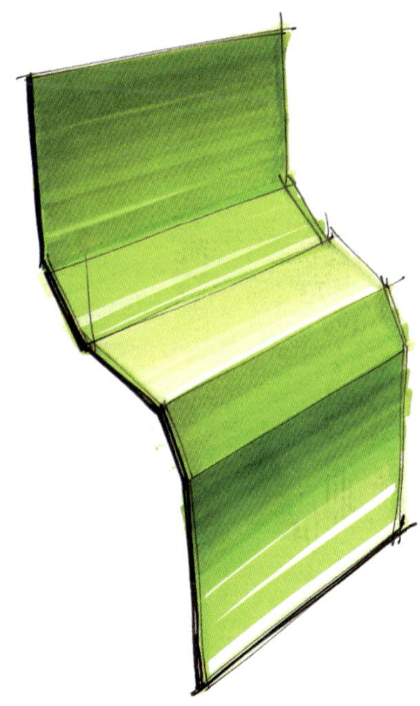

Fillets and chamfers are not the only ways to transition between surfaces. Again, using these strategies in drawing is a matter of trial and error and picking what is "winning" for you as a visual communicator. While not comprehensive, the preceding list of topics and approaches may be combined in your drawing practice to produce interesting results when coming up with complex forms.

Silhouette, Shape, Substance

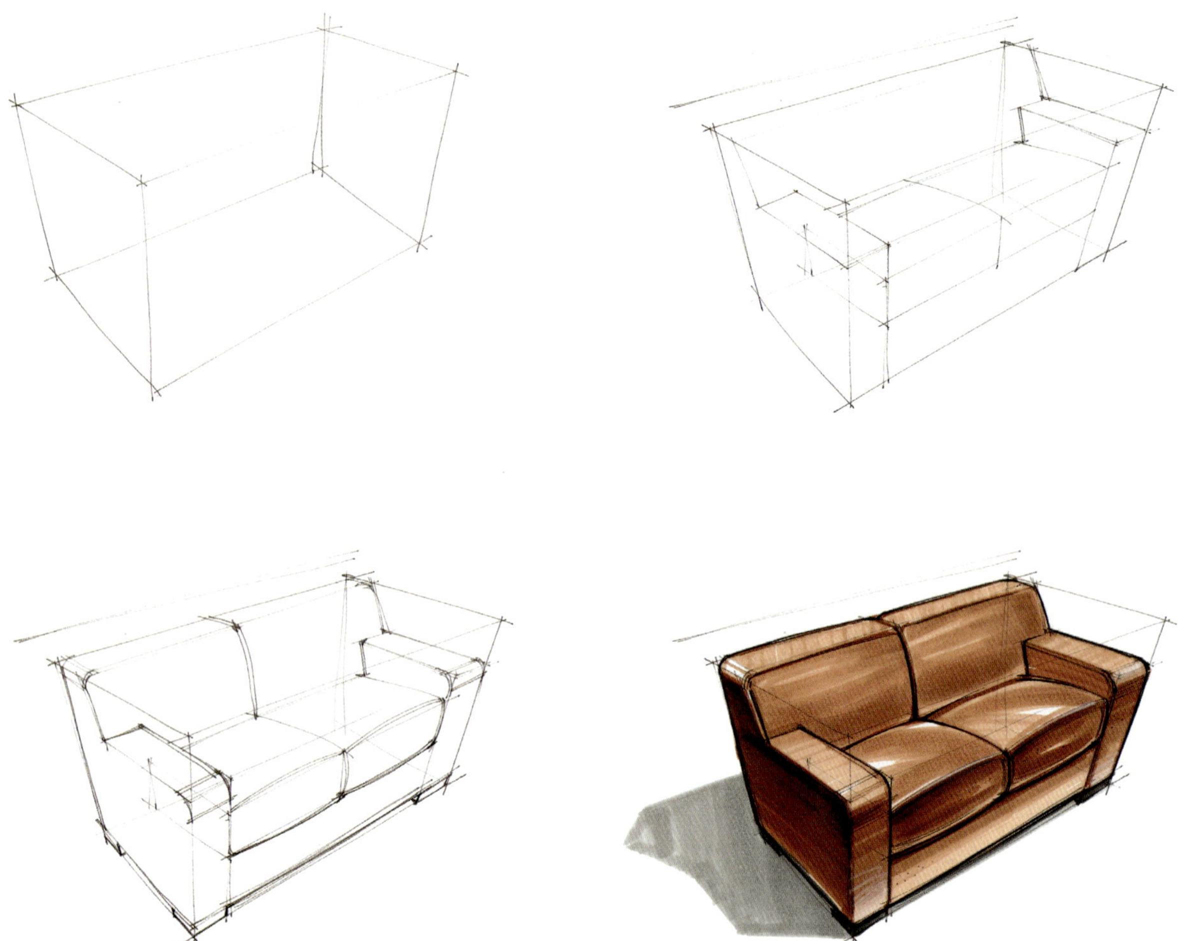

When drawing complex objects, I divide my tasks to complete the object into groupings of activities. Starting with the silhouette or overall form of the object and its component parts is a good way to ensure that the whole picture in reality or imagination is being considered. At this point, work is done to make sure that the proper perspective is constructed or represented in the drawing. By not focusing on the details, there is room to get a sense of overall proportion, placement, and perspective, without having to worry about the small details at the onset of drawing.

Next, work to define shapes based on divisions within the form. Depending on the type of object, these divisions may be cosmetic or functionally based. Remember, shapes are formed with lines that create boundaries areas in a drawing. By focusing on shapes at this phase, work can be done within the set parameter or the perspective of the overall object. It is also much easier to accurately draw lines on the surfaces of your object that travel along the surface in any given direction given that consideration is taken to understand the nature of the forms that make up the object you wish to draw.

Finally, substance refers to the detail, the color, and the texture that may be a part of the object you are drawing. Details help bring a level of realism, abstract or precise, to any drawing you may be working on. They also inform the viewer about the nature of the object you are drawing and its intended function or purpose. With my background in product design, I also make an effort to include meaningful functional details when drawing an object.

Deciding on Detail—What to Draw and When

Even though an object may be visually complex. It's important to be mindful when drawing or sketching about what to draw and when to draw it. Depending on the scale of the drawing medium, more or less detail may be appropriate when drawing an object. Additionally, the tools you are using may impact the nature of the drawing that you create and the level of detail you are able to communicate. Fine lines and details necessitate the use of finer-tipped pens. If the drawing is more expressive or gestural, a larger drawing medium may be necessary to achieve the right amount of detail without overburdening the object while using a more expressive tool like a brush pen with varying line weights.

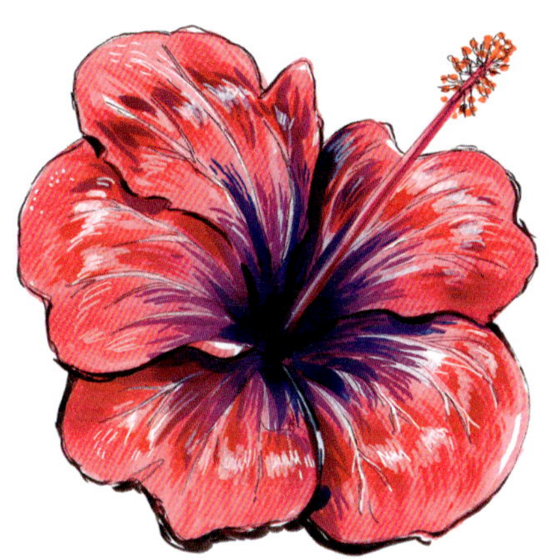
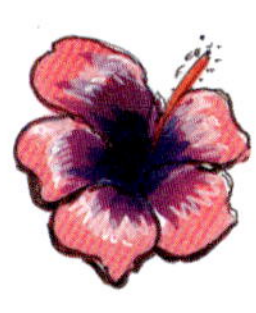

Take this sketch comparison, for example. Attempting to include all details at a small scale will make a drawing visually heavy. With a small drawing, balance in detail, color, and texture is key. Sometimes, the shapes we draw can also overwhelm the drawing.

Communication is paramount when sketching or drawing, and for this reason, clarity and intention is very important. Much like speaking, we use clarity and intention in language to make sure that what we intend to communicate is clear and understood.

Often if a subject object is complex, I will consciously reduce the overall complexity and detail. To do this, think about what is essential to communicate the nature and presentation of the object in a way that would still allow it to be understood.

For example, in this series of sketches, detail is progressively added. These space-ship drawings, completed at the same scale, each have essentially the same message, however with more detail, the image gets a bit more complex. Finding the right balance has somewhat to do with the purpose of the sketch or drawing itself. More complexity and precision may be needed in a functional presentation, while less detail may be needed for a quick sketch or drawing meant to capture an idea's essence. You're the artist and you're in control!

Let's take a look at two demonstrations that show ways to tackle building complex (compound) objects.

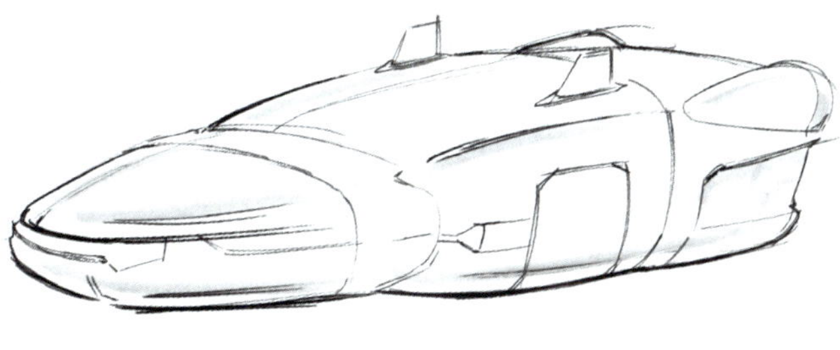

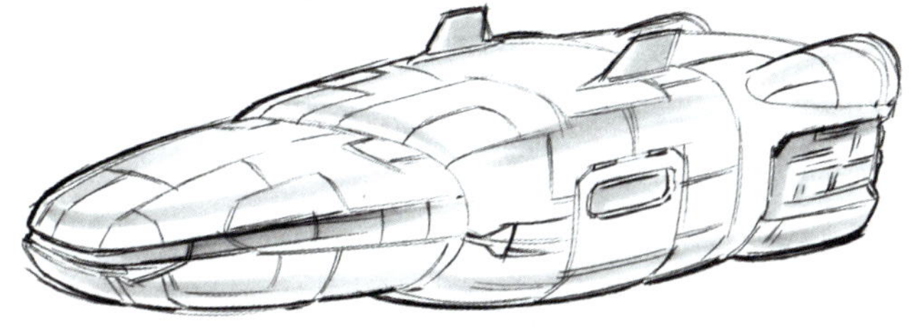

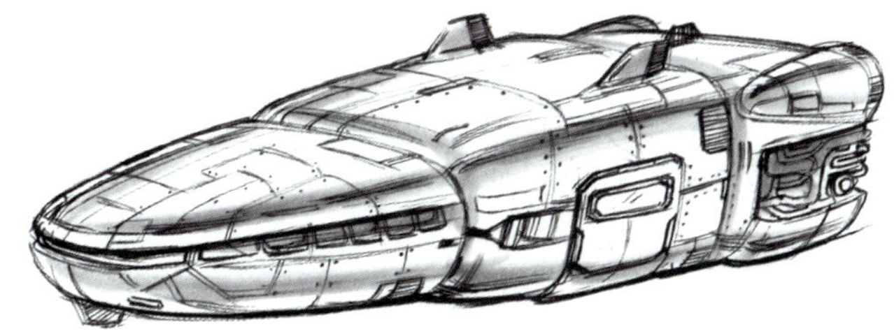

Building Form Demonstration: Remote Control

For the first example, we'll draw a remote control. It's important to make sure that you understand perspective and select the perspective that will best showcase the three-dimensional object.

The remote control can be described as two cuboid shapes combined. One cuboid forms the portion of the remote where the batteries would be, and the other cuboid forms the portion located where the control buttons are placed.

1. Start with a simple perspective sketch with a very thin pen or light strokes to establish a framework for the rest of your drawing.

2. Next, think about transitions on the corners or between the main segments of the remote. In this example I've drawn ellipses to show fillets at the corners of the remote as well as crowning or slightly curving the top surface of the remote where the buttons will be located.

3. At this point I've rounded out the bottom of the remote and begun to divide the remote into shapes representing buttons or functional divisions in the construction of the remote.

4. Enhancing line weight at this point creates a bit of definition for the remote.

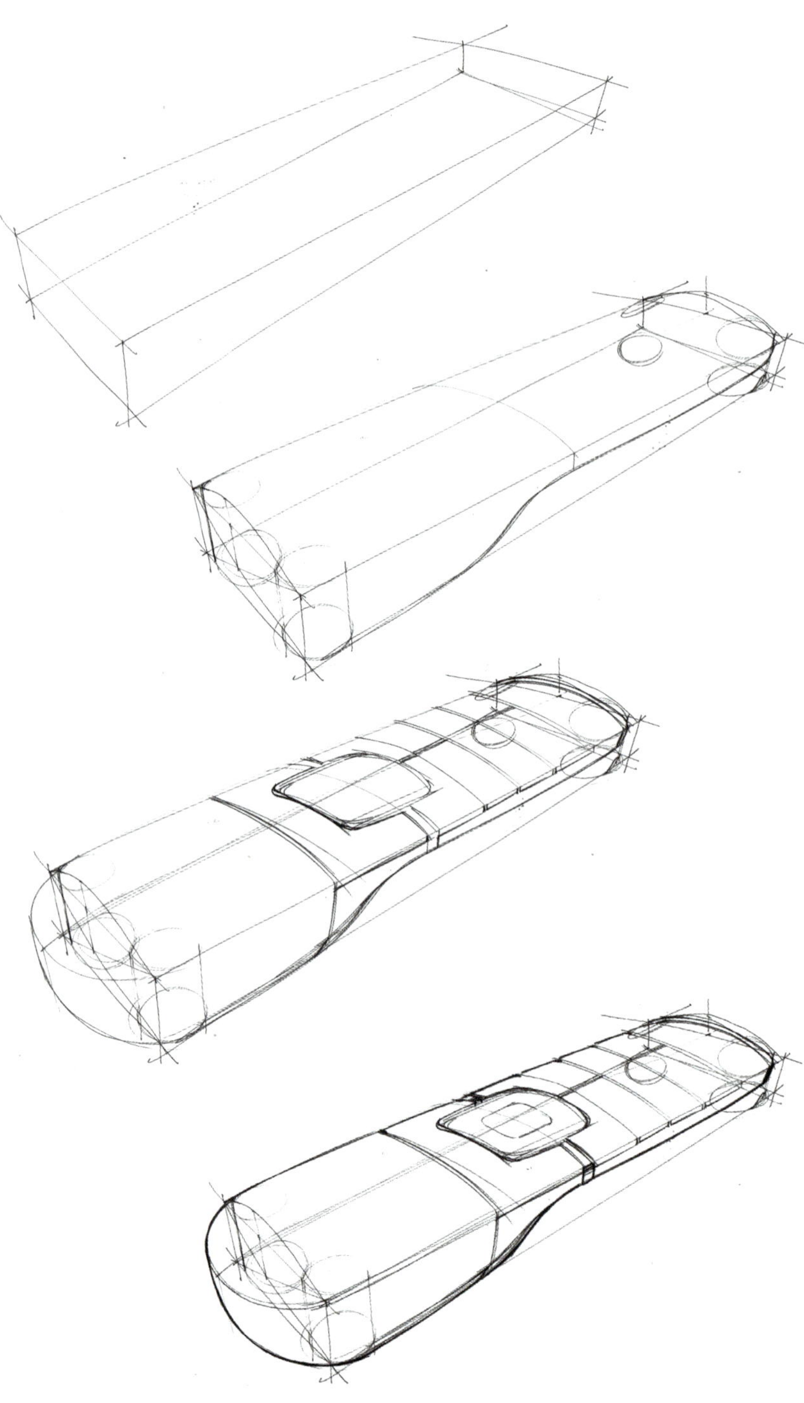

5. Continue to define the drawing by sharpening your lines with a few repeated strokes. For more information on tightening up a sketch, check out Chapter 13, "Tighten Up."

6. If desired, round out your sketch with some light shading with marker, pencil, or other media of your choice. I've added a shadow to further communicate depth and placement of the object in a three-dimensional space.

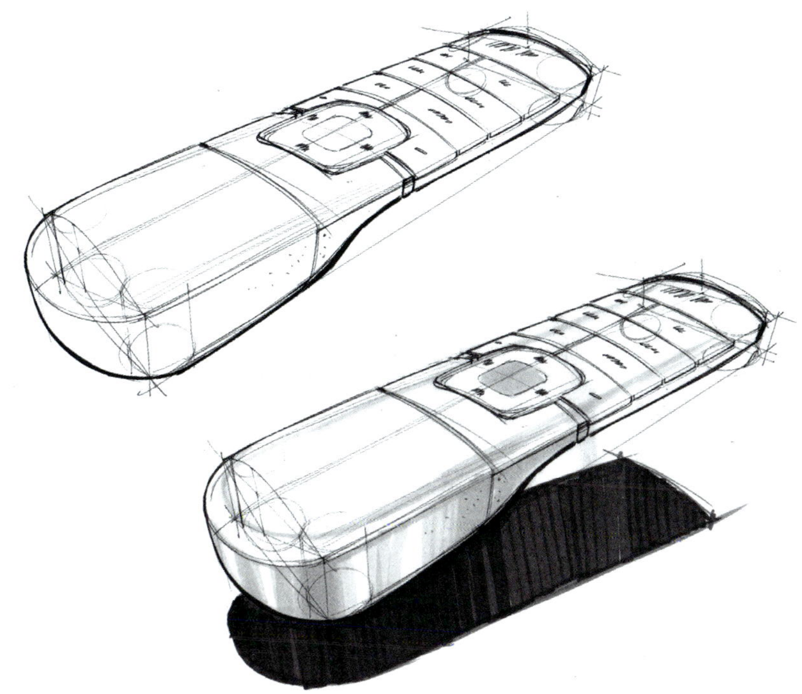

Complex Form Demonstration: Garden Hose Sprayer

In this example we will look at a common object many people may be familiar with — a garden hose sprayer. A garden hose sprayer is complex because it is made up of a variety of forms, and includes details geared towards ergonomics and functionality. We will also be using a little bit of color to communicate material change and help the drawing pop.

1. I first start by thinking about the position of the cylinders that are going to form the main body of the hose sprayer. A key component of the cylinders is determining the direction-ality of the cylinders. They're not 90° to each other, so sketching two lines at an angle representative of the handle and barrel of the sprayer helps me orient my cylinders.

2. Draw a series of ellipses along each line to define segments of the sprayer nozzle as well as the handle. Be mindful to align the minor axis of each ellipse to the lines you sketched as guides.

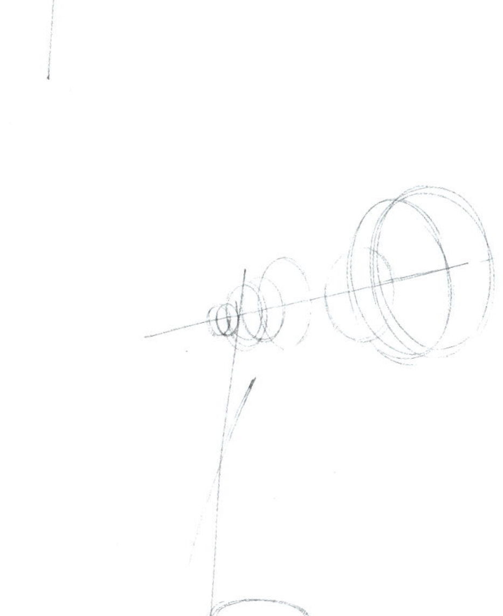

3. Connect each ellipse tangentially using lines or curves as needed to define the outline of the garden hose sprayer and handle. Add any details like adjustment knobs or parting lines as you draw.

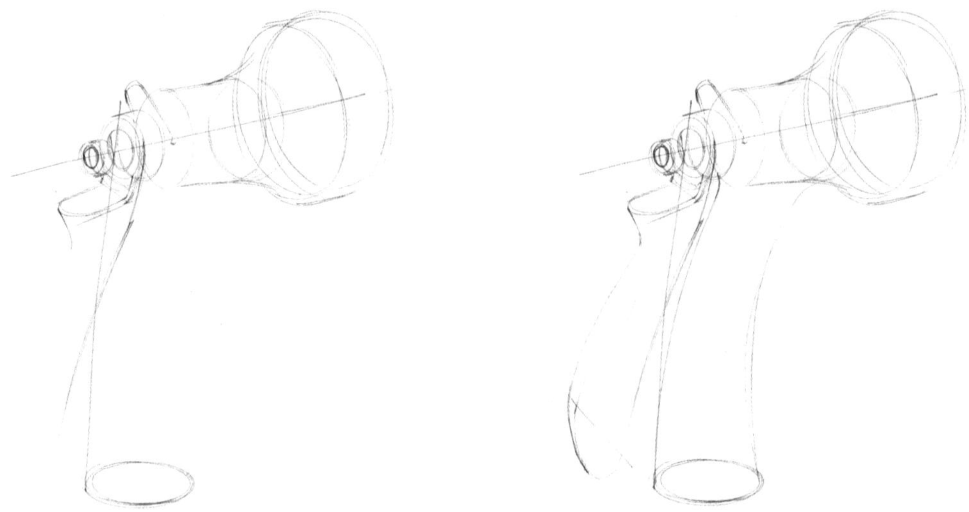

4. Next, I draw a series of ellipses along the shaft of the handle. These will be used to create affordances (grip spots) along the handle. Try to keep these in line with the overall curvature or shape of the handle for your design. If working from reference, eyeball the position and placement of each feature you intend to include. With your construction lines in place, finish the silhouette of the sprayer by drawing an outline. This can be a light line or heavier if you are confident and happy with the drawing at this point.

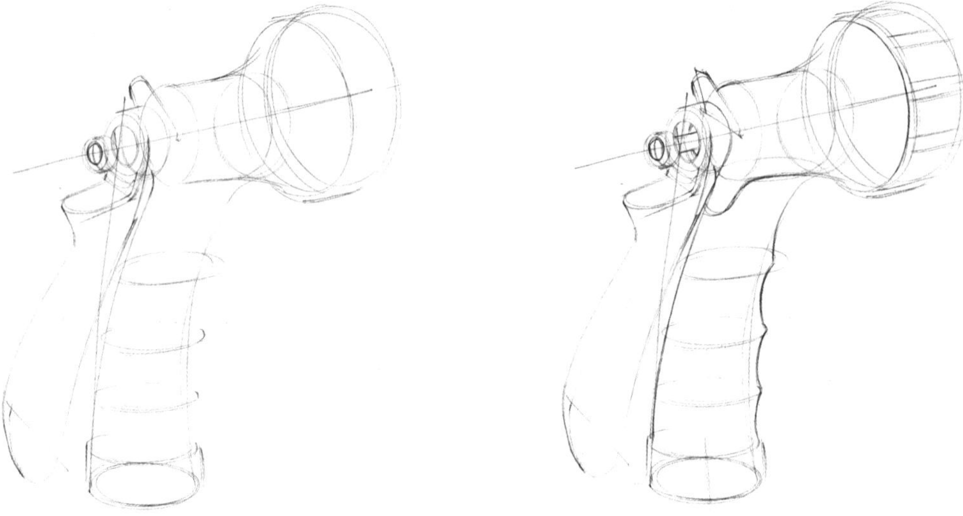

5. Draw lines within the silhouette of your sprayer and add line weight to define functional breaks like a grip, adjustment nozzle, and pivot points. Light shading may also be used to help communicate the three dimensionality of the sprayer as discussed in Chapter 10, "Texture: Ink & Color."

6. I've chosen to add some color to my sprayer drawing. Pay attention to the shape and nature of surfaces of the sprayer, as that will dictate where to place highlights and shadow cores, and to concentrate texture to communicate the three-dimensionality of the sprayer. You can also add texture to enhance the color after coloring certain areas. For more information check out chapters 7–9, covering color, lighting and shadow and reflections.

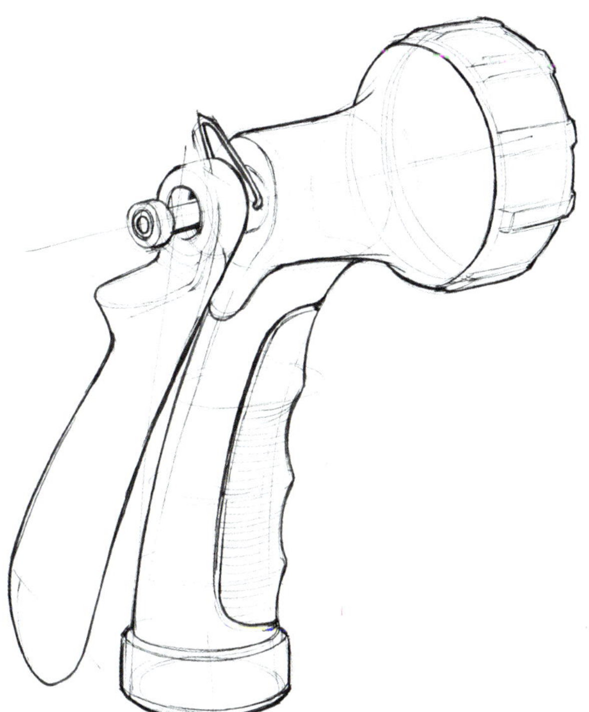

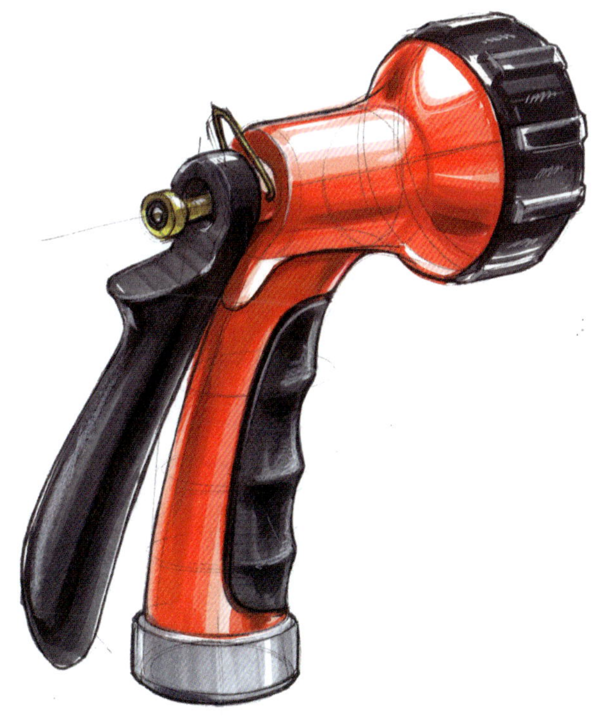

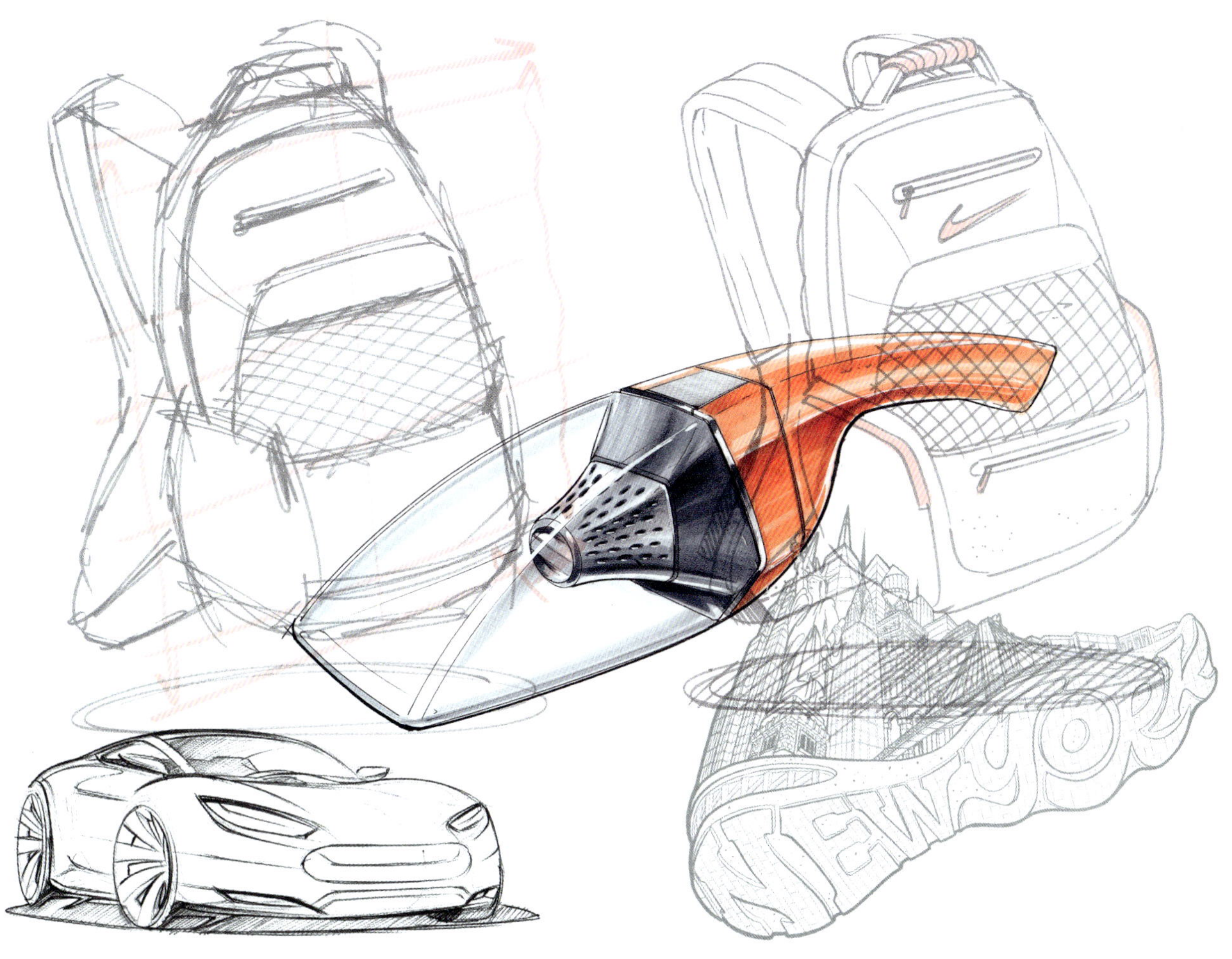

CHAPTER 13

TIGHTEN UP

Although I tend to sketch more loosely and freely when drawing in perspective, at times I need to add a higher degree of precision to a sketch. For quick ideas and concepts sketches in perspective, I tend to leave my line work loosely constructed, as the nature of my work requires balancing speed and efficiency and capturing concepts. For more considered and thought-out drawings, however, tools may be necessary to help increase clarity in a sketch, especially when you need to present a concept to a client or plan to sell or display the artwork. On these occasions, templates, tools, and strategies may be useful for creating tighter sketches and drawings of objects in perspective.

Overlays: Loose but Tight

For a long time in my drawing education, I resisted the idea of overlays. *Overlays* are simply a way of building on prior work to create an object drawing in accurate perspective. There's nothing wrong or bad about using overlays when drawing. Just remember that you are building on the work that you created before.

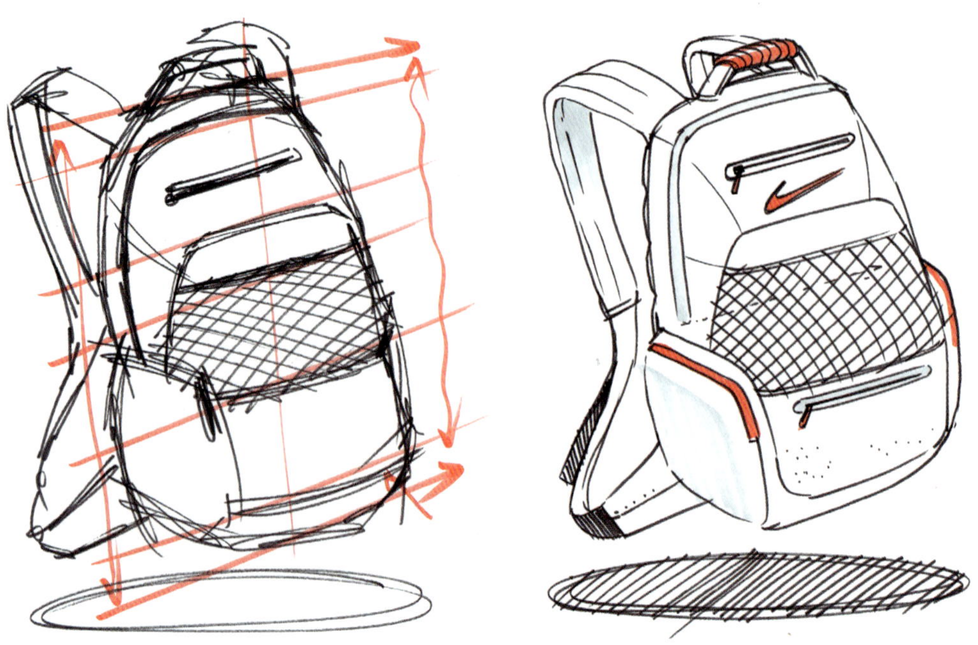

When creating overlays and tightening up drawings, remember to carry through the energy that is inherent to the under-sketch. If you place too much care and concern on the fidelity of the overlay, you may end up with a static and more boring presentation of the object or scene. Be sure to draw with your shoulder and use loose yet expressive and energetic lines when creating the final drawing. Remember, "loose" does not necessarily mean sloppy, imprecise, or thoughtless. Rather, it communicates a level of confidence in your own ability to draw your lines.

Overlays work best when using a paper that is slightly translucent, but having access to translucent paper may not be an option for the final drawing. For example, tracing paper and vellum are cheap papers that are often thin and not always archival. I have drawings from over a decade ago where the inks and pigments in the drawings completed on vellum and tracing paper have bled into the paper and spread over time. It is painful looking back at the time and effort put into those pieces knowing that I could had something much more enduring. While I'm not entirely certain as to the reason for the spread in this case, I do know that certain papers, inks, and media may react adversely with each other. For this reason, having a light table can be a useful tool when creating overlays.

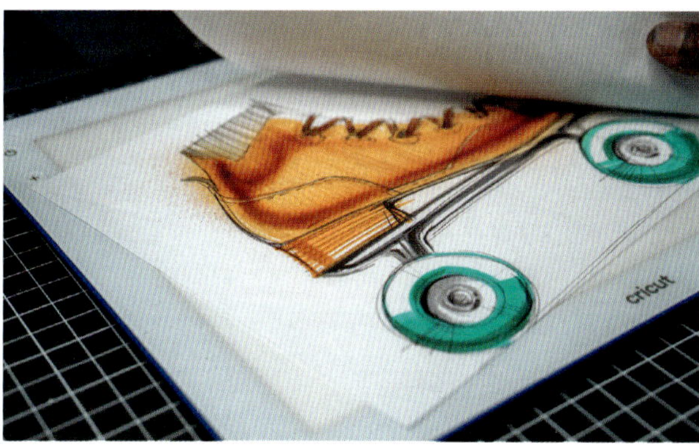

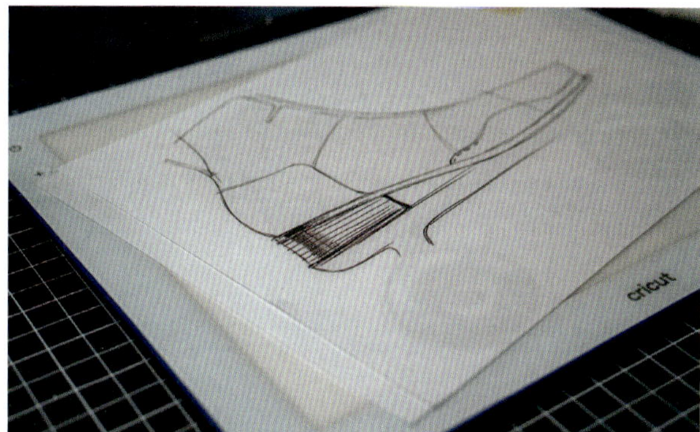

In this example I'm using a light table to reference a previously completed sketch to create a new sketch with differing details. Not only does this allow you to work quickly but it can also help you achieve a higher level of detail than you normally would be able to achieve. You can even use a photo as reference in your overlay process.

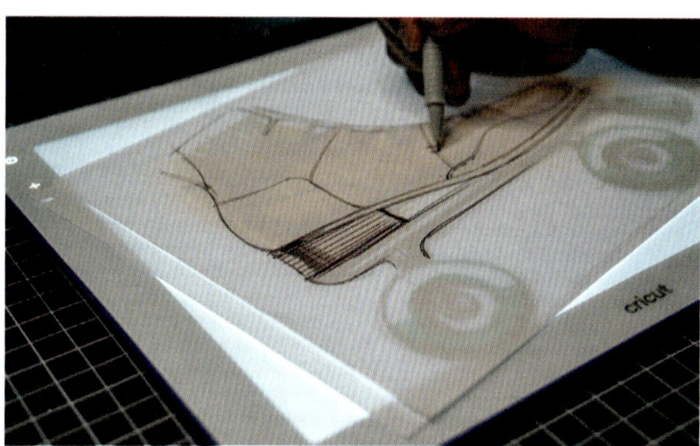

Repetitive Strokes

Repetitive strokes are one way to add a level of fidelity to a sketch. *Repetitive strokes* are executed along the same path in the same fashion as the previous stroke to bolster or refine the resultant line. Repeating a stroke does come with some risk; if your precision and execution are off, it can result in less precise line work that is rough or fuzzy.

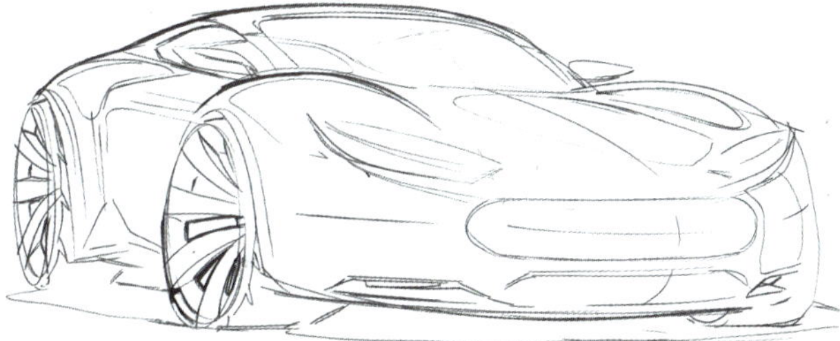

Many years ago, I learned an important lesson from a coworker who consistently created tight yet expressive drawings. When I asked what their secret was, they said that they committed to limiting the number of strokes they would use to express a part of the sketch. By counting off one, two, three mentally, they were able to commit to limiting how rough or hairy the resulting lines would be.

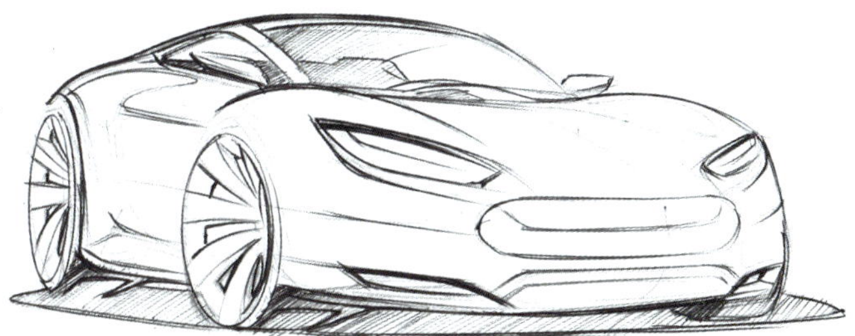

So, while my sketches tend to be loose, I try to stick to limiting the number of attempts at communicating a line when drawing. Being able to sketch loosely is a direct outcome of your daily warm-up and sketch practice exercises. The more mileage you log while sketching, the more confident and consistent your sketching will be.

Whole Lines

A slower and more considered drawing can be an effective way to present a final concept, as well. Even though my tendency is to want to preserve the looseness and energetic presentation of objects, you may want to draw more slowly and in a more considered manner, depending on your objective. These slower, more considered drawings tend to be comprised of mostly whole lines that are consistent and well-paced while drawing. The times I find myself using whole lines in a slower fashion tend to be while storyboarding or explaining an experience with multiple panels of illustrations that show interaction and flow with an object.

Whole lines are also well suited for drawing objects for presentation. When presenting an object with whole lines, be aware the drawing may lack some energy and dynamism inherent to sketches constructed more quickly and intuitively. Still, this technique is useful in creating a drawing that feels more deliberate and considered. In this example, I created a conceptual sketch related to shoe culture and the city of New York. Because of the complexity of the drawing, sketching slower than I normally would allowed me to achieve a higher level of detail and crispness in the sketch.

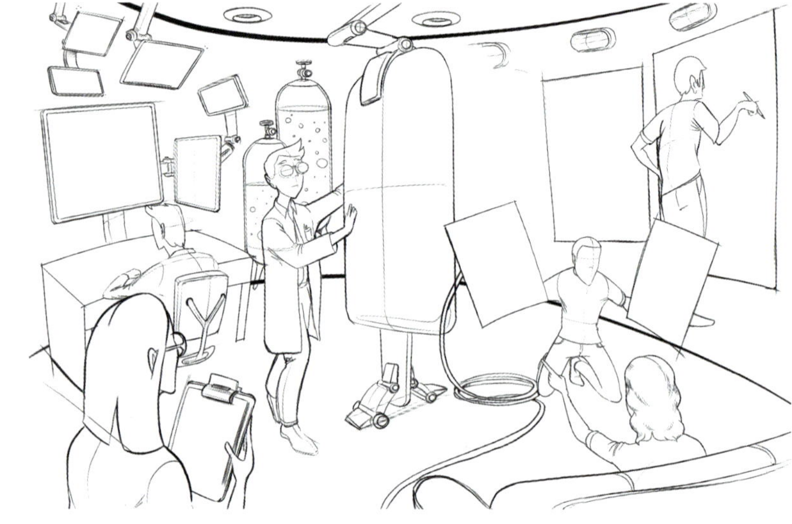

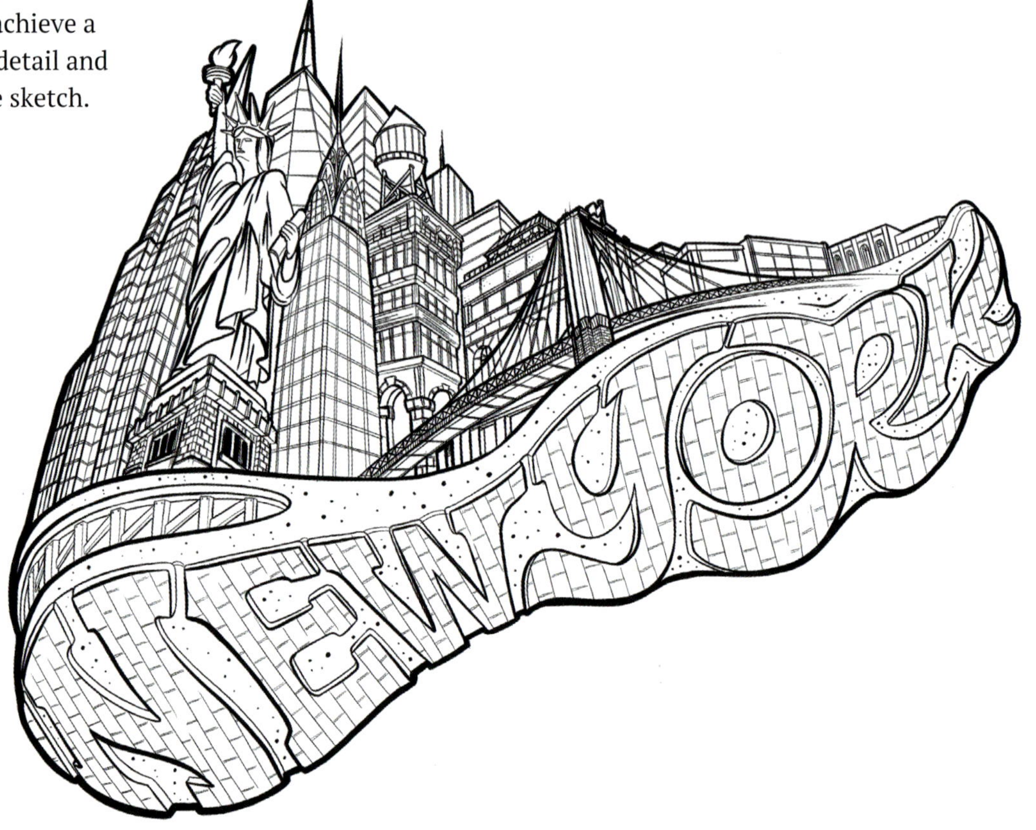

Templates

Adding a few hard, crisp lines and visual elements can help tighten up an overall drawing—especially those destined for presentation or display. As skilled as you might be, there will always be imperfections in drawings when relying on your own motor skills without use of templates. Using an ellipse guide, circle template, French curve, or ruler to create quick, crisp ellipses, curves, or straight lines can really make a noticeable difference in fidelity of the final sketch or drawing. (If templates are cost prohibitive for you, consider using other methods for refining lines, shapes, and color in sketches.)

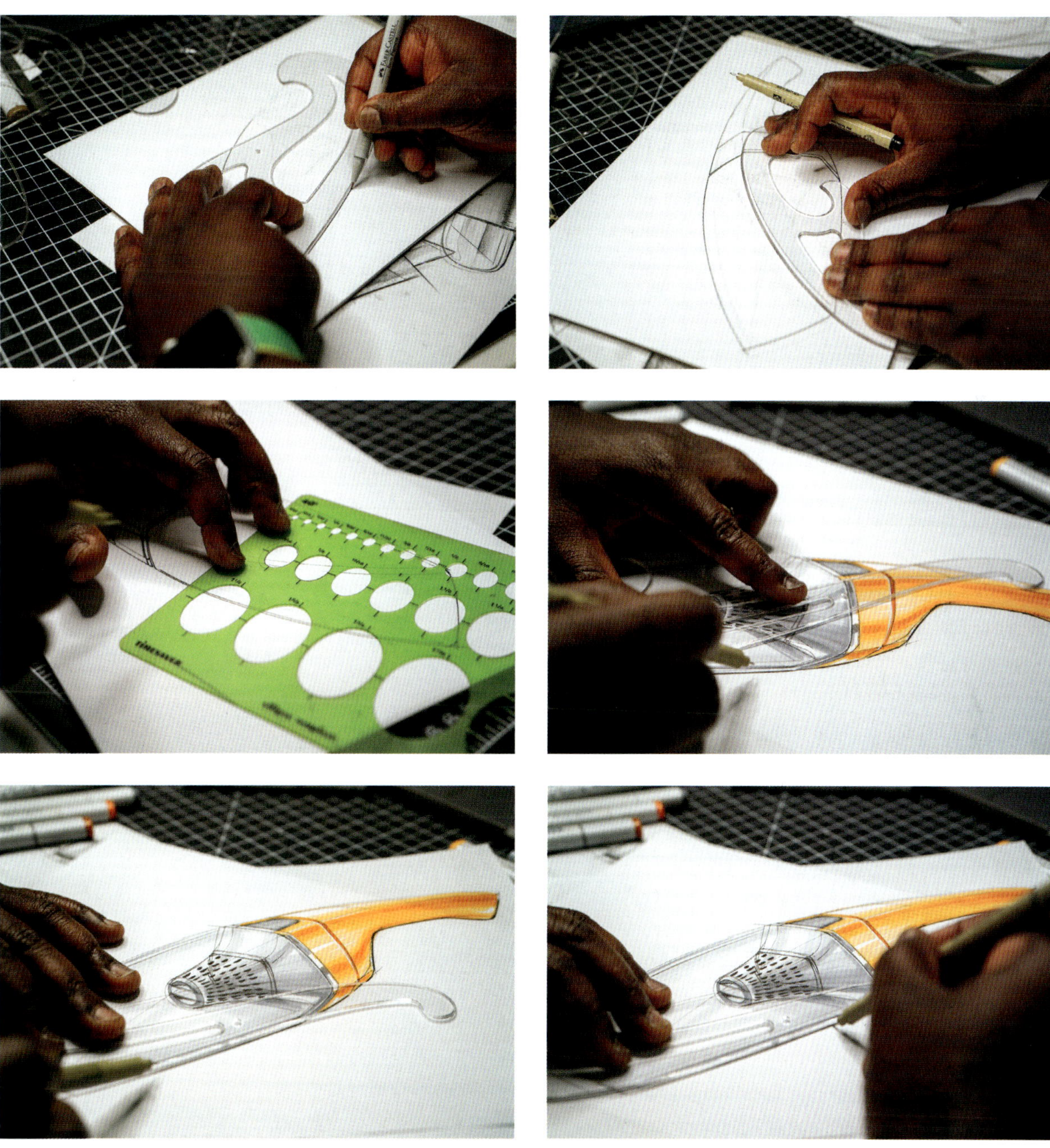

Compare these two sketches. I did not give the left sketch a tightening pass with a template. For the top sketch, I added a few lines with the help of templates to help refine the presentation.

Peripheral Elements

You can also tighten up a sketch by complementing the sketch itself with more defined elements, such as a background, arrows, text, or other objects that have more precision to them. Adding a background is one of the common ways in which I tighten up a loosely sketched concept for presentation.

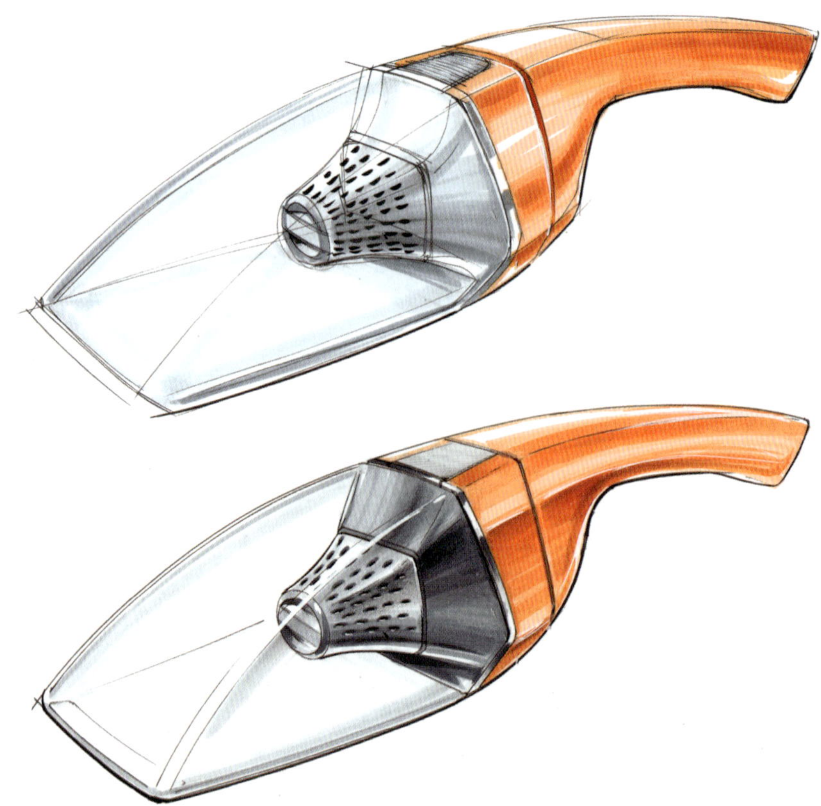

Top sketch completed freehand without tools, bottom sketch completed with tools by overlaying rough sketch.

Strategies

When creating a sketch for presentation or a more refined drawing, having a winning strategy that will result in a cleaner drawing is another way to tighten things up. Working with a light pencil sketch or overlay is a common means of planning ahead for a final sketch. Try working rough or lightly before committing to the final sketch. These beginning pencil lines can serve as a guide in creating a tighter sketch as a final drawing. Simply erase your pencil-sketched guides after replacing them with clean line work. This way, the ink line work will show through more than the pencil lines would have. Because the underlying sketch was done in pencil, erasing means that only the ink lines will show through. This method is similar to working with a light gray marker; with marker, however, you lose the ability to erase.

Digital Correction

While digital sketching and drawing are not covered in this book, scanning, or digitizing your work and modifying in the digital environment can help you fix issues with perspective, line quality, and execution. I caution against relying on digital correction, however, as much as I caution against using tools and templates in your regular drawing process. Relying on digital tools can create dependencies that hinder your ability to master drawing with your hand. Given enough experience and understanding, on the other hand, digital tools can help speed up your workflow and level up the fidelity of your drawings.

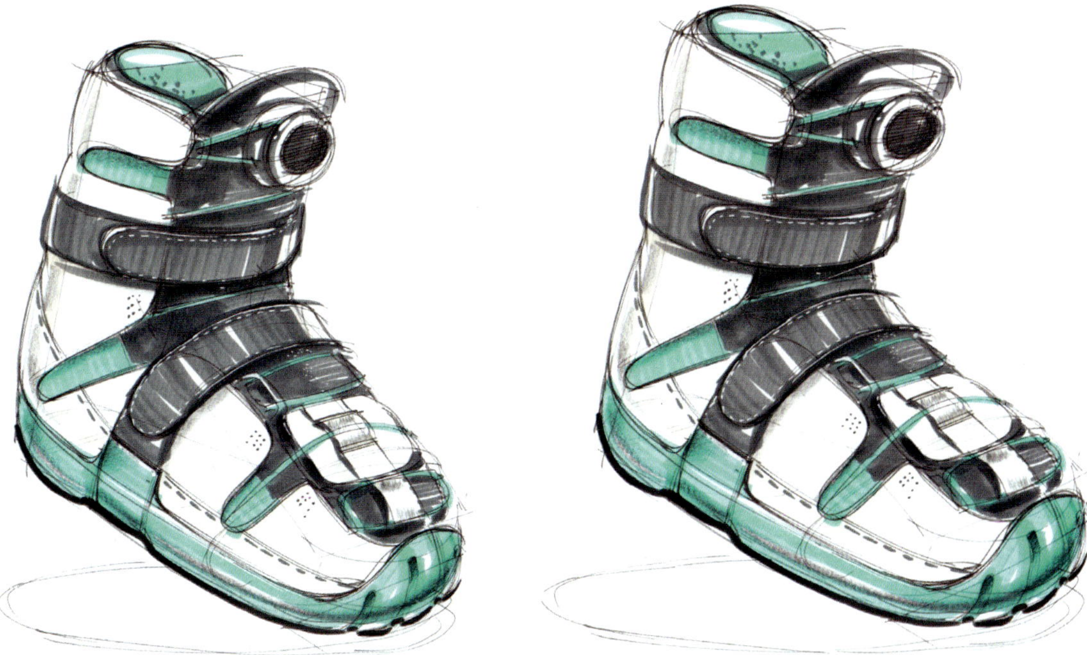

Right: Original sketch. Left: Digitally corrected sketch.

Ultimately the purpose of drawing is always communication—whether that communication is emotive, functional, or explanatory. Deciding whether to increase the fidelity of a drawing depends on the purpose of the drawing in the context of how it will be reviewed and understood. It is up to you as the illustrator, designer, or artist to determine what level of fidelity is necessary when presenting sketches and drawings of objects in perspective.

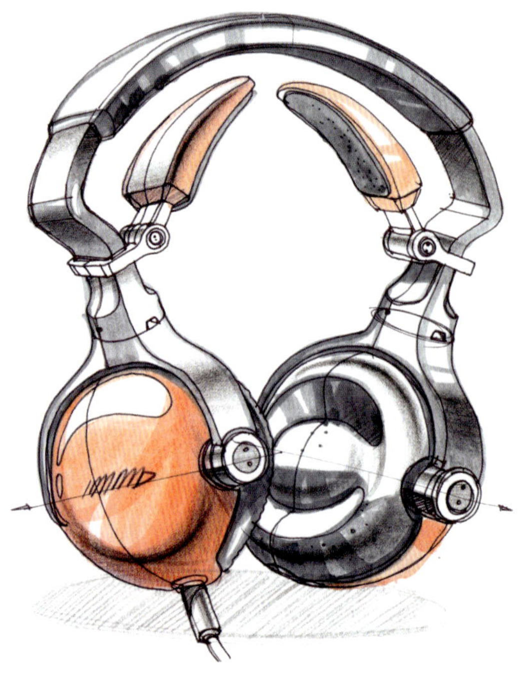

CONCLUSION

You did it! You made it this far. You're now at the end of this "chapter" of your drawing experience, but really this is just the beginning of your journey. Every journey, no matter how long or short, begins with taking the first step.

I'm not what I would consider to be naturally talented at drawing. Even though quite often people compliment me on my drawing skills and my ability to capture ideas and concepts quickly, it's taken a lot of work and effort to get to this point.

It turns out that the arts and sciences are not too dissimilar. To be a successful scientist, or in my case wanting to be a mathematician, understanding the concepts, rules and formulas is key. The other key to success comes from learning how and when to use those tools and formulas through practice and problem solving. It takes work and effort!

My hope is that in reading this text you have acquired new tools, new skills, and new appreciation and awareness for three-dimensional objects, spaces, and principles that can help you create compelling visuals by hand.

Now that you have the tools and skills to continue your journey, it really comes down to practice. Commit to yourself to doing a little bit every day and the results will come. For me, I find it useful to commit to three small things every day I want to accomplish. One of those things is usually the completion of some drawing or adjacent activity. There's an old saying that goes, "If you don't use it, you'll lose it." This is true for drawing skills as well. If you don't actively use your drawing skills and apply what you've learned, you won't ever see improvement in your ability to draw the way you want to draw. I've even seen this in my own practice, when if I am not as consistent as I should be, my skills dip a little.

Draw from observation every opportunity you can, so that you can confidently draw from your imagination. Take visual mental notes of your surroundings and of real objects in real places so that you can create things from your imagination on paper.

But if you are not as skilled as you would like to be, keep pushing and you will eventually be able to draw the way you want to draw. You can be a great visual communicator and command excellent skills.

So, what's next? Stay hungry, and keep sketching, and don't give up. In short order, you'll see results too. If you learn something from this experience, be sure to take some time to sit with someone else who may be struggling to understand these concepts. Ultimately, teaching will help you get better at understanding why, how, and what you're doing when drawing in perspective.

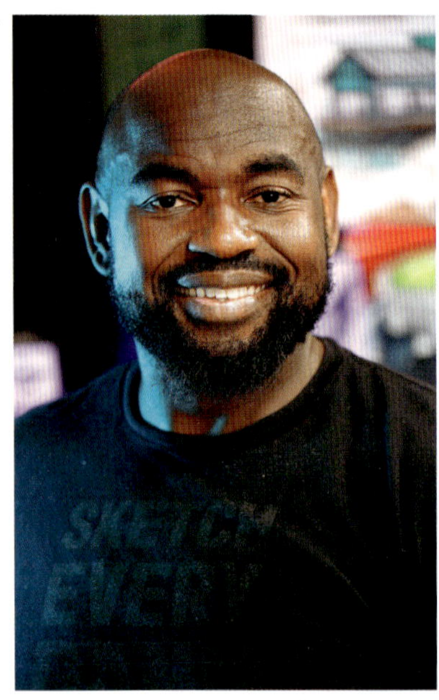

ABOUT THE AUTHOR

Spencer Nugent is a Jamaican-born creator and educator currently based in Salt Lake City, Utah. He is the founder of Sketch-A-Day.com and has been providing free, high-quality online design sketching tutorial content and on-site sketch workshops since 2008. He has created an extensive online network and following within the Industrial Design community and continues to connect with students and design professionals via his online properties. With his live YouTube streams, he continues to share his passion for creating and drawing on "Sketch-A-Day LIVE" as well as the Sketch-a-Day Instagram and TikTok accounts.

Spencer's professional experience includes working at General Motors in Michigan, San Francisco-based design firm Astro Studios, heading up his own design consultancy, Studio Tminus, where he worked with several clients primarily in the consumer electronics and apparel industries. Spencer has worked with brands such as Microsoft, Intel, Hewlett Packard, BodyGlove, Adidas, Verifone, Kyocera Altec Lansing, Hasbro, Dell, Tupperware, Motorola, and Vivint Smart Home. Spencer has led workshops and presentations for many higher educational institutions and corporate clients including designers at Adidas HQ, Herzogenaurach Germany, Apple Retail, LG, Adobe MAX, and frequently presents on Adobe Live on Behance.net.

In 2020, Spencer was awarded the Industrial Design Society of America's individual achievement award for his consistent work and passion related to industrial design education related to producing online educational content. Most recently, Spencer has been running his creative design lab, 5050.design, where half his time is dedicated to personal projects and the other to client work.